The American Foreign Policy Library
Edwin O. Reischauer, Editor

John King Fairbank

The United States and China

Fourth Edition

Harvard University Press
Cambridge, Massachusetts
and London, England
1979

Copyright © 1948, 1958, 1971, 1972, 1979 by the President and Fellows of Harvard College

All rights reserved

Printed in the United States of America

Library of Congress Cataloging in Publication Data

Fairbank, John King, 1907-
    The United States and China.

    (The American foreign policy library)
    Bibliography: p.
    Includes index.
    1. China—History.   2. United States—Foreign
relations—China.   3. China—Foreign relations—United
States.   I. Title.   II. Series.
    DS735.F3 1979   327.51'073   78-13667
    ISBN 0-674-92435-5
    ISBN 0-674-92436-3 pbk.

For Lorena King Fairbank
1874-

Foreword to the
Fourth Edition
Edwin O. Reischauer

When the first edition of John King Fairbank's *The United States and China* appeared in 1948, it was greeted with acclaim and soon came to be regarded as a classic. The term "classic" suggests something fixed in time, but that is not the case with this book. Through successive revised editions, it has grown and developed. A second edition in 1958 added the Communnist victory and the experiences of the first decade of the People's Republic. A third edition in 1971, taking the analysis forward another decade, proved even more popular than the first edition and reaffirmed the evaluation of this book, not just as a classic, but as a continually up-to-date classic. The same, no doubt, will be true of this fourth edition, coming still another decade later.

Revised editions suggest the addition of new material to bring a book up to date and the revision of interpretations as time brings past events into clearer perspective. The author has done both of these, but more significantly he has added a great amount of new information and insights produced by fresh scholarship, not just on recent events, but also on earlier phases of Chinese history, stretching all the way back to the palaeolithic age. John Fairbank is in a good position to do this, for he, more than anyone else, is responsible for the vigorous development of Chinese studies in the United States and an astonishingly large percentage of the authorities he cites were once his own students, whose research activities he encouraged, supervised, and often saw through to publication. As a result, in this fourth edition, he has not just updated his earlier work but has rewritten considerable sections of it on the basis of recent scholarly findings.

Sumner Welles, in the opening sentence of his Introduction to the first edition of this book, wrote, "The Harvard University Press can offer the readers of its Foreign Policy Library no more timely or important book than John King Fairbank's *The United States and China.*" The same can be said today, exactly thirty years later, of this fourth edition. The Chinese people constitute a fifth or more of all mankind; the American people control about a quarter of the world's wealth. The relations between these two great nations, their understanding or misconceptions about each other, their cooperation or friction, will play a large part in determining the future of humanity.

No one has written more clearly or perceptively about China during the past three decades than John Fairbank, and no one has contributed more to American understanding of that country, its traditions, its tumultuous recent history, and its enigmatic present conditions. The portions of this book carried over from earlier editions still sparkle with insights, expanded and refined by the results of recent scholarship. Anyone interested in China will read or reread these with pleasure and enlightenment. The extensive new sections on recent events, the present conditions in China, and the prospects for Chinese-American relations constitute, in my judgment, the clearest and most judicious brief

Foreword

presentations of these extraordinarily complex and obscure subjects that I have yet seen. John Fairbank has a knack for combining broad perceptions and deep analysis with clarity of expression. That is why this book has been and will long continue to be a classic.

Preface to the Fourth Edition

Any author who publishes a fourth edition of a thirty-year-old book has some explaining to do. Like any sincere professor, I aimed in writing this book to explain China to Americans so they could live in peace and friendship. After the first edition appeared in 1948 we fought China for three years in Korea (1950-53). After the second edition appeared in 1958 we fought for eight years on China's southern border in Vietnam (1965-73). After the third edition of 1971 we began to normalize our relations with the People's Republic, following President Nixon's visit to Peking in February 1972. But only in 1979 did we begin to liquidate our cold-war military alliance with Taiwan. While recognizing Peking yet still selling arms to Taipei, we hoped they could end their confrontation. But China's past does not die away so easily.

This book has found readers, I think, because it tries to sum up what we know about China. This is of course impossible, but hundreds have tried it ever since Marco Polo, simply because China fascinates the foreigner—just as it indeed fascinates the Chinese people themselves.

When I first put this book together, I could profit by two experiences—first of all, an experience of living in the old

China, four years as a graduate student in Peking, 1932-35, with a good deal of traveling about, and two years as an official under the American Embassy, first in Chungking, 1942-43, and then in Nanking, 1945-46, during the onset of the Chinese Communist rise to power. My second experience had come from inaugurating the Regional Studies program on China at Harvard after 1946: this area-study approach brought each of the social science disciplines to bear and gave a more analytic structure to the Chinese history that I had taught there after 1936.

Two things have contributed further to this fourth edition: first, visual on-the-spot impressions of the People's Republic in the manner familiar to so many travelers today. Through his entourage I had met Chou En-lai first in 1943 in Chungking and again in 1945. In May-July 1972 at his invitation my wife, Wilma, and I spent six weeks visiting places familiar to us from the 1930s and 1940s. We found a new land and a new people.

The second and larger contribution to this edition has come from the hundreds of important monographs, symposia, articles, and reports recently put out by scholars and journalists of many countries. They are represented in the Suggested Reading, which indicates my debt to others.

Rewriting a book is chastening. Lean insights of years ago may have swollen into enormous platitudes today. History moves with the times, issues fade and other concerns arise. I have eliminated some empty talk and some bits of nonsense, when I could spot them. But I am tremendously impressed by the flood of new scholarship and have tried, sometimes unavailingly, to bring it to bear on the story here recounted. At the same time, since the subject matter has grown so greatly, I have tried to make

Preface

the text shorter, in the belief that anything worth saying can usually be said better more briefly.

December 1978   J.K.F.

Contents

Contents

Figures

Introduction

Man as part of nature. Sung landscape: "Buddhist temple amid clearing mountain peaks," ca. 1000 A.D.

Chapter 1

The Chinese Scene

The Chinese people's basic problem of livelihood used to be readily visible from the air: the brown eroded hills, the flood plains of muddy rivers, the patchwork of green fields and hives of simple huts that formed the villages, the intricate silver network of terraces and waterways that testified to the back-breaking labor of countless generations—all the overcrowding of too many people upon too little land, and the attendant exhaustion of the land resources and of human ingenuity and fortitude in the effort to maintain life.

Today in the People's Republic the fragmented strips of cultivation have been efficiently consolidated into bigger fields, millions of trees have been planted along new roads and on the mountains, and electric pumps fill the new ponds and irrigation ditches. The face of China has been transformed. But the population has doubled: it is now roughly a billion people.

The Contrast of North and South

To any traveler who has flown through the vast gray cloud banks, mists, and sunshine of continental China, two pictures will stand out as typical, one of North China and one of the South. On the dry North China plain to the south of Peking where Chinese civilization had its first flowering, one sees in summer an endless expanse of green fields over which are scattered clusters of darker green, the trees of earth-walled villages. It is very like the view of our Middle West, where farmsteads and their clumps of trees are dispersed at rough half-mile intervals. But where our corn belt has a farm, on the North China plain there is an entire village. Where one American farmer's family lives with its barns and sheds among its fields in Iowa or Illinois at a half-mile interval from its neighbors roundabout, in China an entire community of several hundred persons lives in its tree-studded village, at a half-mile interval from neighbor villages. The American people in spite of their farming background have no appreciation of the population density which subtly conditions every act and thought of a Chinese farmer.

In South China the typical picture is quite different, and like nothing to which we are accustomed. There during much of the year the rice fields are flooded and present a water surface to the airborne observer. The green terrain is hilly and the crescent-shaped rice terraces march up each hill almost to the top and on the other side descend again from near the crest, terrace upon terrace in endless succession, each embankment conforming to the lay of the land like the contour lines of a geographer's chart. In fact the curving pattern of the rice terraces seen from above is a visual index to the slope of the valleys in which they are built—narrow concave strips of paddy field touch the hilltops, and lower terraces grow broader and longer and bulge out as they descend to the valley floor. Gray stone footpaths are built on many of the embankments and the latter form intricate patterns like the product of some giant's doodling. When the sun is out one sees it from the air reflected brilliantly in the water of the rice fields. The sun seems in fact to be shining up through the fields from below, so that the whole ornate network of the embankments and paths and hilltops appears to rush beneath one as though on a great rolling screen, a black lacework moving across the bright silver of shining water.

No one can fly over the rugged green hills of the South without wondering where the billion or so people of China live and what they eat—such vast reaches of mountain and valley seem largely uncultivable and sparsely settled. One's picture of a big empty landscape is mirrored statistically in the estimate that six sevenths of the population have to concentrate on one third of the land. The really inhabited part of China, at a rough estimate, is only about half as large as the really inhabited part of the United States, yet it supports four times as many people. This is made possible only by crowding some 2000 human beings onto each square mile of cultivated earth in the valleys and flood plains. The United States has some 570,000 square miles under cultivation and could greatly increase this area; China has perhaps 450,000 square miles of cultivated land (less than one half acre of food-producing soil per person) with little prospect of increasing this area by more than a small fraction, even if it is used more intensively.

Little is known in statistical terms about the life of the Chinese people upon their crowded land, but sampling studies, in which American investigators once took a leading part, give us some general indications. The great contrast is between the dry wheat-millet area of North China and the moist rice land of the South. These economic regions divide along a line roughly halfway between the Yellow River and the Yangtze on the thirty-third parallel. Let us look at the factors of rainfall, soil, temperature, and human usage which create this striking contrast.

First of all, the rainfall depends upon the continental character of the Chinese climate and the seasonal air flow to which it gives rise. To put it very simply, the Asiatic land

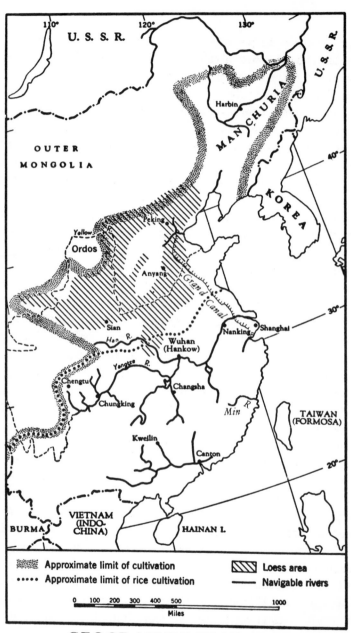

GEOGRAPHIC FEATURES

mass changes temperature more readily than the Western Pacific and its currents, and the cold dry air which is chilled over the continent in the wintertime tends to flow southeastward to the sea, with minimum precipitation. Conversely, the summer monsoon of moisture-laden sea air is drawn inward and northward over the land mass by the rising of the heated air above it, and precipitation occurs mainly during the summer. This southerly wind of summer crosses the hills of South China first, and they receive a heavy rainfall, which remains relatively dependable with a variation of only about 15 percent in the amount of precipitation from one year to the next. North China, being farther from the South China Sea, receives less rainfall, and moreover, the amount of precipitation over the decades has varied as much as 30 percent from one year to the next. Since the average rainfall of the North China plain is about 20 to 25 inches, like the rainfall of the great American dustbowl, it is hardly more than sufficient to maintain cultivation at the best of times. This high degree of rainfall variability from year to year is a most serious problem. North China is normally on the subsistence margin as regards its water supply, and the periodic failure of rainfall threatens to produce drought and famine. In water supply, South China has the better of it.

As regards soil, however, South China suffers by comparison, for the constant seepage of water through its warm earth has dissolved and leached away mineral foods of great importance for plant life. The leached soil resulting is relatively unproductive, and the situation is saved partly by the fact that the constant run-off from the hills brings down new deposits for the cultivated lowlands. Even so, the heavy population centers of the South are to be found mainly on the alluvial flood plains along the Yangtze or on the river deltas, like those inland from Shanghai or around Canton. The soil of North China, on the other hand, thanks to the relative

ANNUAL
RAINFALL

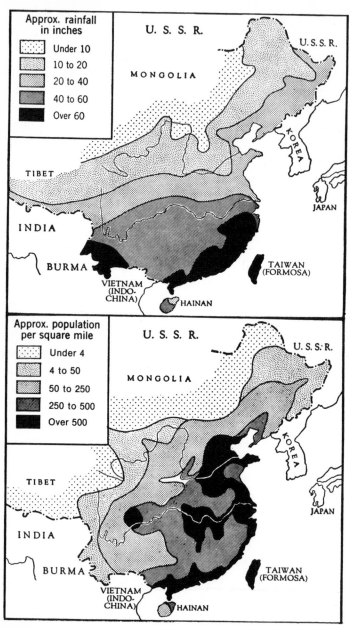

Approx. rainfall in inches
- Under 10
- 10 to 20
- 20 to 40
- 40 to 60
- Over 60

Approx. population per square mile
- Under 4
- 4 to 50
- 50 to 250
- 250 to 500
- Over 500

POPULATION
DENSITY

lack of water, remains unleached and richer in minerals. Sometimes, indeed, as in Mongolia, mineral salts are brought to the surface by evaporating water and, in the absence of rainfall to wash them away, form a saline crust which makes cultivation impossible.

Temperature plays its part in preserving the soil of North China, since the severe continental winters, not unlike those of the American Middle West, limit the growing season to about half the year. In southernmost China crops are grown the year around and rice is double-cropped and even triple-cropped. Too easily we forget that Shanghai is in the latitude of New Orleans and Suez, while Canton is in that of Havana and Calcutta, well into the tropics. This explains why the greater part of the Chinese people live in the more fecund rice economy of the South. Rice culture, with its greater inputs of water and labor, yields more than twice as much food as wheat growing.

Thus the factors of rainfall, soil, and temperature are in a rough balance both North and South, the North having soil which is highly fertile when water is sufficient, but having too often an insufficiency of water and much cold weather; and the South having no lack of water and favorable temperatures but generally infertile soil. In both cases the resources of nature are supplemented by unremitting human endeavor, of which the night soil (human excrement) industry is but one of the more spectacular forms. Without the redolent returning to the land of human waste or equivalent fertilizers no region of China could sustain its present population. It is no accident that Chinese cities from the air can be seen surrounded by a belt of dense green crops which fade out at the periphery. Each urban center sustains its surrounding truck gardens.

A population map will show that the Chinese people are packed into four main regions, which include but a small part of the total area of the country. The first region is the North China plain, the second is the mountain-locked plain of Szechwan in the west, the third is the lower Yangtze valley from the Wuhan cities to Shanghai, including the Hunan rice bowl south of Hankow, and the fourth is the Canton delta in the south. Early travelers compared China to Europe in the variety of dialects and the size of different provinces. For example, three regions along the course of the Yangtze in Central China—Szechwan province in the west, the twin provinces of Hupei and Hunan north and south of Wuhan, and the lower Yangtze delta—are each of them comparable to Germany in area and each bigger in population.

Trade and transport routes in South China have followed the waterways, and the great modern cities—Canton, Shanghai, Wuhan, even Tientsin—have grown up where sea trade can meet the waterborne commerce of the interior. Yet China's foreign trade has never lived up to the foreign merchant's great expectations. Stretching so far from north to south, from the latitude of Canada to that of Cuba, China remains a subcontinent largely sufficient unto herself. As George Washington's contemporary, the great Ch'ien-lung Emperor, put it in his famous edict to King George III, "Our celestial empire possesses all things in prolific abundance and lacks no product within its own borders. There is therefore no need to import the manufactures of outside barbarians."

In spite of the immensity and variety of the Chinese scene, we need not be surprised that this subcontinent has remained a single political unit where Europe has not; for it is held together by a way of life even more deeply rooted than our own, and stretching even farther back uninterruptedly into the past.

China's Origins

The exciting discovery in 1929 of a skull of Peking man (in a big cave at Chou-k'ou-tien near Peking) was of tremendous archaeological significance because the excavators subsequently found skeletal remnants from some forty individuals together with the bones of contemporary animals, human tools, and evidence of the use of fire. Finding all these together in one place was most unusual. Living perhaps a half million or 400,000 years ago, Peking man was a predecessor of *Homo sapiens* with a low skull vault and receding chin but considerable cranial capacity. In 1964 the skull of a more primitive cousin was found near Lan-t'ien south of Sian. The archaeological revolution in the People's Republic has now found many widely scattered sites, skulls, and other remains from later phases of the Paleolithic era.

Meanwhile spectacular Neolithic discoveries at thousands of sites since 1949 have completely remade China's prehistory. As summarized by K. C. Chang, these new finds show a beginning of settled agriculture below the southern bend of the Yellow River, on a border between wooded highlands and swampy lowlands. For example, the villagers of Pan-p'o outside Sian about 4000 B.C. lived on millet supplemented by hunting and fishing, used hemp and silk for fabrics, and built floors and walls of stamped earth (pounded in layers within a wooden frame). They raised pigs and dogs as their principal domesticated animals, and stored their grain in pottery jars decorated with fish, animal, and plant designs as well as symbols that were evidently forerunners of Chinese writing. But this Painted Pottery culture of North China was paralleled by contemporary cultures found at sites on the southeast coast and Taiwan and in the lower Yangtze valley, where rice culture had already begun.

Overlying the Painted Pottery has been found a thinner,

lustrous Black Pottery more widely distributed throughout North China, the Yangtze Valley, and even the southeast coast, indicating a great expansion of neolithic agriculture with many regional subcultures. Thus it seems that neolithic China developed in several centers from paleolithic origins, and the old theory of some Western archaeologists that it was "a civilization by osmosis" basically indebted to cultural traits coming from the Middle East across Central Asia is now outdated. P. T. Ho lists as cultural contributions from outside East Asia: wheat and barley, the horse-drawn chariot, and certain decorative motifs and styles of pottery, all of which seem to have come from West Asia late in the second millennium B.C., long after Chinese society had taken on its enduring shape. Bronze metallurgy raises the general question of influences from the south, since it is found in Thailand before 3000 B.C. (and in the Near East several millennia earlier). But the Near Eastern evidence of early and extensive communication between separate and distinct prehistoric cultures suggests that "diffusion" or the lack of it is a dying issue. Each major culture was by nature a local achievement, but hardly an isolated one.

In racial stock the Chinese have a deceptive homogeneity which does not stand up under anthropological inspection. Peoples from North and Central Asia have continually entered the Chinese scene and have sometimes ruled over it, although never in sufficient numbers to overwhelm Chinese civilization. The arid steppe land north of the Great Wall has been a breeding ground of nomad invaders who could never displace the dense population of agrarian China but who made it more diverse. Consequently the so-called Mongoloid racial type is made up of very mixed strains in which flat noses and hawk noses, black hair and some red hair, beards and lack of beards, all appear, and supposedly common denominators such as the Mongolian eye fold are by no means universal.

The Harmony of Man and Nature

No matter what elements of civilization—peoples or cultural traits—came to China, they all became integrated in a distinctly Chinese way of life, nourished, conditioned, and limited by the good earth and the use of it. To cite but one example, from neolithic times the people of North China have made pit dwellings or cave homes in the fine, yellow, windborne loess soil that covers about 100,000 square miles of Northwest China to a depth of 150 feet or more. Loess has a quality of vertical cleavage useful for such a purpose. Many hundreds of thousands still live in caves cut into the sides of loess cliffs. They are cool in summer, warm in winter, and secure against everything but earthquakes.

The loess of Northwest China seems never to have supported forests. Where forest land occurred, the Chinese, like other early peoples and recent American pioneers, achieved its deforestation. The consequent erosion through the centuries changed the face of their country and erosion today is still a major problem. Through its waterborne loess deposits the Yellow River has built up the broad flood plain of North China between Shansi province and the sea, and the process still goes on. Nothing can so vividly convey a feeling of man's impotence in the face of nature as to watch the swirling coffee-colored flood of the Yellow River flowing majestically within its dikes across, and 20 feet above, the crowded plain 200 miles from the sea; and to realize that this vast yellow torrent is steadily depositing its silt and building its bed higher above the surrounding countryside until the time when human negligence or act of God will allow it again to burst from the dikes and inundate the plain.

Deforestation, erosion, and floods have constantly been met by human efforts at water control. The planting of trees and damming of tributaries in the limitless western watershed of "China's Sorrow" is a recent achievement of the People's Republic. In all previous periods the rulers of China have been periodically confronted with a fait accompli in the debouching of the Yellow River upon the North China plain in full flood and have lacked the scientific knowledge and the means to get behind this pressing fact. In the earliest period, however, flooding of the plain was less of a problem than the reclamation of it from its primitive swamp and fen condition; techniques of water control were developed for drainage purposes as well as for irrigation and the prevention of floods. Thus many generations of labor have been spent upon the land to make it what it is today, protected by dikes, crossed by canals and roads worn into the earth, irrigated by streams and wells, divided by paths and occasional remnants of grave land in their groves of trees, and all of it handed down from generation to generation.

This land which modern China has inherited is used almost entirely for human food production. China cannot afford to raise cattle for food. Of the land which can be used at all, nine tenths is cultivated for crops and only about 2 percent is pasture for animals. By comparison, in the United States only four tenths of the land which is used is put into crops, and almost half of it is put into pasture.

The human implications of intensive agriculture can be seen most strikingly in the rice economy, which is the backbone of Chinese life everywhere in the Yangtze valley and the South. Rice plants are ordinarily grown for their first month in seedbeds, while subsidiary crops are raised and harvested in the dry fields. The fields are then irrigated, fertilized, and plowed (here the water buffalo may supplement man's hoeing) in preparation for the transplanting of the rice seedlings. This transplanting is still done by human hands, the rows of planters bending from the waist as they move backward step by step through the ankle-high muddy water of each terrace. This goes on in the paddy fields of a whole subcontinent—certainly the greatest expenditure of muscular energy in the world. When the rice has been weeded and is mature, the field is drained and it is harvested, again by hand. Given an unlimited supply of water and of human hands, there is probably no way by which a greater yield could be gained from a given plot of land. In this situation land is economically more valuable than labor, or to put it another way, good muscles are more plentiful than good earth. The Chinese farmer could not afford to put his labor into extensive agriculture, which would yield only half as much per acre. He lacked both the land and the capital for mechanized or large-scale methods. Obliged to rely on his own family's labor power, he was obliged to rely on intensive hand gardening in order to feed them. The effort to mechanize farming in the People's Republic today confronts the serious problem of finding alternative employment for the farm population.

The heavy application of manpower and night soil to small plots of land has had its social repercussions, for it sets up a vicious interdependence between dense population and intensive use of the soil whereby each makes the other possible. Population density provides both the incentive for intensive land use and the means. Once established, this economy developed its inertia and set its own human standards, whereby the back-breaking labor of many hands became the accepted norm and inventive efforts at labor saving remained the exception. Early modernizers of China, in their attempts to introduce the machine, constantly ran up against the vested interest of Chinese manpower, since in the short run the machine appeared to be in competition with human hands and backs. Thus railways were attacked as depriving carters and coolies of their jobs, and there was no premium upon invention.

This is only one of many ways in which the ecology of the Chinese, their adaptation to physical environment, influenced their culture. Life on the great river flood plains has always been a hard life, in which man is dependent upon nature more than upon his own initiative. "Heaven nourishes and destroys" is an ancient saying. On the broad stretches of the plain the patient Chinese farmer was at the mercy of the weather, dependent upon Heaven's gift of sun and rain. He was forced to accept natural calamity in the traditional forms of drought, flood, pestilence, and famine. This is in striking contrast to the lot of the European, who lived in a land of variegated topography. Western man, either on the Mediterranean or on the European continent, was never far from a water supply and could usually supplement agriculture by hunting or fishing provided he exercised initiative. From ancient times seaborne commerce has played an immediate part in Western man's economy. Exploration and invention in the service of commerce have exemplified Western man's struggle against nature, rather than a passive acceptance of it.

A different relation of man to nature in the West and in the East has been one of the salient contrasts between the two civilizations. Man has been in the center of the Western stage. The rest of nature has served as neutral background or as his adversary. Thus Western religion is anthropomorphic and early Western painting anthropocentric. To see how great this gulf is we have only to compare Christianity with the relative impersonality of Buddhism, or a Sung landscape and its tiny human figures dwarfed by crags and rivers with an Italian primitive in which nature is an afterthought.

And yet, paradoxically, Chinese man has been so crowded upon the soil among his fellows that he is also a most socially minded human being, ever conscious of the interplay of personalities and social conventions around him; for he is seldom in all his life beyond earshot of other people.

Part One
The Old Order

Chapter 2

The Nature of Chinese Society

Mao Tse-tung's main claim to immortality may lie in his effort to smash the ancient ruling class tradition. His bucolic distaste for the evils of special privilege and urban bureaucracy was deeply felt. It rings a bell in the Chinese mind and touches feelings that go far back; for the old China was the world's great example of upper class government by the few over the many.

Social Structure

Since neolithic times China's governing elite has used vast amounts of manpower for public works. Early in the Shang dynasty (about 1850 to 1100 B.C.) the capital city had a roughly rectangular wall built of stamped earth, 4 miles around and as high as 27 feet. Three thousand years later the capitals of the Ming dynasty (1368-1644 A.D.) at Nanking and Peking were also built of stamped earth. They were some 40 feet high and respectively 23 and 21 miles around, bigger and faced with brick, but still built by massed labor. Of course massed manpower built the Egyptian pyramids and other wonders of ancient empires, but only in China has this custom persisted to the present day.

We can see how Chinese rulers since the dawn of history

have disposed of such resources of manpower if we look at the social stratification evidenced in recently excavated sites of Shang cities. Formerly legendary, known only through ancient literary references, the Shang dynasty became concretely historical with excavations in 1928–37 of its last capital near Anyang and since 1950 at an earlier capital cited above near Chengchow, both on the North China plain not far from the Yellow River. In these cities were royal palaces and upper-class residences of post and beam construction on stamped-earth platforms in the basic architectural style we admire today in Peking's Forbidden City. The extended kinship lineages of the aristocracy had the services of artisans specialized in a highly developed bronze metallurgy, pottery, and many other crafts. The Shang bronzes, never surpassed in craftsmanship, are still one of mankind's great artistic achievements. The Shang king was served by literati who handled the writing system and took the auspices by scapulimancy (applying a hot point to create cracks in bones from animal shoulder blades, interpreting these cracks as the advice of the ancestors, and recording the results), which produced the famous "oracle bones" that first led to excavation at Anyang. The aristocracy lived a superior life, fighting in horse chariots, hunting for sport, performing rites and ceremonies, while served by scribes and artisans and supported by the agriculture of the surrounding village peasants, who lived in semi-subterranean dwelling pits. It was already a highly stratified society. Ancestor reverence on the part of the rulers was a fully ritualized religious observance. Royal tomb chambers deep in the earth were supplied with precious objects and many animal and human sacrifices. As K. C. Chang says, "These burials indicate most vividly a stratified society in which members of a lower class were sometimes victims, perhaps of religious ceremonies."

Thus from ancient times there have been two Chinas: the

Bronze ritual vessels. Note animal mask designs. *Above:* Water buffalo (Shang period). *Below:* Ram with curved horns (Chou).

myriad agricultural communities of the peasantry in the countryside, where each tree-clad village and farm household persists statically upon the soil; and the more mobile overlay of walled towns and cities peopled by the landlords, scholars, merchants, and officials—the families of property and position. There has been no caste system, and the chance to rise from peasant status has not been lacking. Yet China has always remained a country of farmers, four fifths of the people living on the soil they till. The chief social division has therefore been that between town and countryside, between the 80 percent or more of the population who have stayed put upon the land and the 10 or 15 percent of the population who have formed a mobile upper class. This bifurcation still underlies the Chinese political scene and makes it difficult to spread the control of the state from the few to the many. To understand Chairman Mao's problem after 1949 we must get a picture of traditional China as it persisted almost to that date.

The Peasant: Family and Kinship. Even today the Chinese people are still mostly farmers tilling the soil, living mainly in villages, in houses of brown sun-dried brick, bamboo, or whitewashed wattle, or sometimes stone, with earth or stone floors, and paper, not glass, in the windows. At least half and sometimes two thirds to three quarters of their meager material income used to go for food. The other necessaries of life, including rent, heat, lighting, clothing, and any possible luxuries, had to come from the tiny remainder. Today they still lack the luxury of space. Peasant dwellings have usually about four small room sections for every three persons. Sometimes family members of both sexes and two or three generations all sleep on the same brick bed. There is little meat in the diet, and so simple a thing as iron is scarce for tools or for building. Manpower still takes the place of the machine for most purposes. In this toilsome, earthbound existence the hazards of life from malnutrition and disease until recently gave the average baby in China, as in India, little more than twenty-six years of life expectancy. Human life compared with the other factors of production was abundant and therefore cheap.

To an American with his higher material standard of living the amazing thing about the Chinese peasantry has been their ability to maintain a highly civilized life in these poor conditions. The answer lies in their social institutions, which have carried the individuals of each family through the phases and vicissitudes of human existence according to deeply ingrained patterns of behavior. These institutions and behavior patterns have been the oldest and most persistent social phenomena in the world. China has been the stronghold of the family system and has derived both strength and inertia from it.

The Chinese family has been a microcosm, the state in miniature. The family, not the individual, was formerly the social unit and the responsible element in the political life of its locality. The filial piety and obedience inculcated in family life were the training ground for loyalty to the ruler and obedience to constituted authority in the state.

This function of the family to raise filial sons who would become loyal subjects can be seen by a glance at the pattern of authority within the traditional family group. The father was a supreme autocrat, with control over the use of all family property and income and a decisive voice in arranging the marriages of the children. The mixed love, fear, and awe of children for their father was strengthened by the great respect paid to age. An old man's loss of vigor was more than offset by his growth in wisdom. As long as he lived in possession of his faculties the patriarch possessed every sanction to enable him to dominate the family scene. According to the law he could sell his children into slavery or even execute them for improper conduct. In fact, of course, Chinese parents were by custom as well as by nature particularly loving toward small children, and they were also bound by a reciprocal code of responsibility for their children as family members. But law and custom provided little check on parental tyranny if they chose to exercise it.

The domination of age over youth within the old-style family was matched by the domination of male over female. Chinese baby girls in the old days were more likely than baby boys to suffer infanticide. A girl's marriage was, of course, arranged and not for love. The trembling bride became at once a daughter-in-law under the tyranny of her husband's mother. In a well-to-do family she might see secondary wives or concubines brought into the household, particularly if she did not bear a male heir. She could be repudiated by her husband for various reasons. If he died she could not easily remarry. All this reflected the fact that a woman had no economic independence. Her labor was absorbed in household tasks and brought her no income. Peasant women were universally illiterate. They had few or no property rights. Until well into the present century their subjection was demonstrated and reinforced by the custom of footbinding. This crippling practice by which a young girl's feet were tightly wrapped from about age five to fifteen to prevent normal development seems to have begun about the tenth century. The "lily feet" so produced, with the arch broken and lesser toes curled under, meant the suffering of hundreds of millions of young girls but had great aesthetic and erotic value for men. During a girl's childhood and adolescence she endured the pain in her feet in order to attract a good husband. Daily care of her feet, washing them, cutting the nails, maintaining circulation, was a very private matter, since she kept them constantly bound and covered. Eventually a husband's interest in these small sensitive objects made them genuinely erogenous—still another Chinese invention! In daily life bound feet, stumping about on one's heels, also kept womankind from venturing far abroad.

The inferiority of women imposed upon them by social custom was merely one manifestation of the hierarchic nature of a society of status. It exemplified an entire social code and cosmology. Philosophically, ancient China had seen the world as the product of two interacting complementary elements, *yin* and *yang*. *Yin* was the attribute of all things female, dark, weak, and passive. *Yang* was the attribute of all things male, bright, strong, and active. While male and female were both necessary and complementary, one was by nature passive toward the other. Building on such ideological foundations, an endless succession of Chinese male moralists worked out the behavior pattern of obedience and passivity which was to be expected of women. These patterns subordinated girls to boys from their infancy and kept the wife subordinate to her husband and the mother to her son. Forceful women, whom China has never lacked, usually controlled their families by indirection, not by fiat.

Status within the family was codified in the famous "three bonds" emphasized by the Confucian philosophers; namely, the bond of loyalty on the part of subject to ruler (minister to prince), of filial obedience on the part of son to father (children to parents), and of chastity on the part of wives but not of husbands. To an egalitarian Westerner the most striking thing about this doctrine is that two of the three relationships were within the family, and all were between superior and subordinate. The relationship of mother and son, which in Western life often allows matriarchal domination, was not stressed in theory, though naturally important in fact.

Within the extended family every child from birth was involved in a highly ordered system of kinship relations with elder brothers, sisters, maternal elder brother's wives, and other kinds of aunts, uncles, and cousins, grandparents, and in-laws too numerous for a Westerner to keep in mind. These relationships were not only more clearly named and differentiated than in the West but also carried with them more compelling rights and duties dependent upon status. A first son, for example, could not long remain unaware of the Confucian teaching as to his duties toward the family line and his precedence over his younger brothers and his sisters.

Chinese well habituated to the family system have been prepared to accept similar patterns of status in other institutions, including the official hierarchy of the government. The German sociologist Max Weber characterized China as a "familistic state." One advantage of a system of status (as opposed to our individualist system of contractual relations) is that a man knows automatically where he stands in his family or society. He can have security in the knowledge that if he does his prescribed part he may expect reciprocal action from others in the system. It has been observed that a Chinese community overseas gains strength by organizing its activities to meet new situations in a hierarchic fashion.

The life cycle of the individual in a peasant family is inextricably interwoven with the seasonal cycle of intensive agriculture upon the land. The life and death of the people follow a rhythm which interpenetrates the growing and harvesting of the crops. The peasant village which still forms the bedrock of Chinese society is built out of family units; village, family, and individual follow the rhythm of seasons and crops, of birth, marriage, and death.

Socially, the Chinese in the village until recently have been organized primarily in their kinship system and only secondarily as a neighborhood community. The village has ordinarily consisted of a group of family and kinship units (lineages) which are permanently settled from one generation to the next and continuously dependent upon the use of certain landholdings. Each family household has been both a social and an economic unit. Its members derived their sustenance from working its fields and their social status from membership in it.

The Chinese kinship system is patrilineal, the family headship passing in the male line from father to eldest son. Thus the men stay in the family while the girls marry into other family households, in neither case following the life pattern which Western individuals take as a matter of course. Until recently a Chinese boy and girl did not choose each other as life mates, nor did they set up an independent household together after marriage. Instead, they entered the husband's father's household and assumed responsibilities for its maintenance, subordinating married life to family life in a way that modern Americans would consider insupportable. The strength of China's age-old family system has made it a target of the modern revolution. New loyalties to nation and to party have countered the claims of familism, but not always successfully.

From the time of the first imperial unification the Chinese abandoned primogeniture, by which the eldest son would have inherited all the father's property while the younger sons sought their fortunes elsewhere. The enormous significance of this institutional change can be seen by comparison with a country like England or Japan, where younger sons who have not shared their father's estate have provided the personnel for government, business, and overseas empire. The abolition of primogeniture created a system of equal division of the land among the sons of the family. The eldest son retained only certain ceremonial duties, to acknowledge his position, and sometimes an extra share of property. The constant parcelization of the land tended to destroy the continuity of family landholding, forestall the growth of landed particularism among great officials, and keep peasant families on the margin of subsistence. The prime duty of each married couple was to produce a son to maintain the family line, yet the birth of more than one son might mean impoverishment.

Contrary to a common myth, a large family with several children has not been the peasant norm. The scarcity of land, as well as disease and famine, set a limit to the number of people likely to survive in each family unit. The large joint family of several married sons with many children all within one compound, which has often been regarded as typical of China, appears to have been the ideal exception, a luxury which only the well-to-do could afford. The average peasant family was limited to four, five, or six persons. Division of the land among the sons constantly checked the accumulation of property and savings and the typical family had little opportunity to rise in the social scale. The peasantry were bound to the soil not by law and custom so much as by their own numbers.

Yet Chinese peasant life was richly sophisticated in folklore and the civilities and happenings of an ancient folk culture. Life was not normally confined to a single village but rather to a whole group of villages that formed a market area.

The Market Community. This pattern can be seen from the air—the cellular structure of market communities, each centered on a market town surrounded by its ring of satellite villages. The old Chinese countryside was a honeycomb of these relatively self-sufficient areas. Each one, if we visualize it in an ideal model such as that of G. William Skinner, centered on a market town from which footpaths (or sometimes waterways) radiated out to a first ring of about six villages and continued on to a second ring of say twelve villages. Each of these eighteen or so villages had perhaps 75

households and each family household averaged five persons
—parents, perhaps two children, and a grandparent. No village was more than about two and a half miles from the market town, within an easy day's round trip with a carrying pole, barrow, or donkey (or a sampan on a waterway). Together, the village farmers and the market town shopkeepers, artisans, landowners, temple priests, and others formed a community of roughly 1500 households or 7500 people. The town market functioned periodically—say every first, fourth, and seventh day in a ten-day cycle—so that itinerant merchants could visit it regularly while visiting a central market and the adjoining town markets five miles away in similar cycles—say every second, fifth, and eighth day or every third, sixth, and ninth day. In this pulsation of the market cycle, one person from every household might go to the market town on every third day, perhaps to sell a bit of local produce or buy a product from elsewhere, but in any case meeting friends in the tea shop, at the temple, or on the way. In ten years he would have gone to market a thousand times.

Thus while the villages were not self-sufficient, the large market community was both an economic unit and a social universe. Marriages were commonly arranged through matchmakers at the market town. There festivals were celebrated, a secret society might have its lodge meetings, and the peasant community met representatives of the ruling class—tax gatherers and rent collectors. Today the old market communities have been the natural bases for communes and production brigades, just as villages have been organized in production teams to meet tax quotas.

Early China as an "Oriental" Society

Savants of early modern Europe saw in the sweeping prerogatives of Asian potentates a kind of "oriental despotism" which stood at a polar extreme from Western institutions of law and private property. Ancient China, to be sure, had been a contemporary of Egypt and Mesopotamia and in early modern times could be compared also with Mogul India and Persia, where European travelers found impoverished masses and rich, despotic rulers who claimed to own their lands and peoples. European writers thus developed an image of "oriental society" which existed, as Lawrence Krader remarks, "only in the minds of these thinkers, and nowhere else" but still helped shape Marx's little-used concept of an "Asiatic mode of production."

For our purposes here it is enough to note how traditional China was classed with other ancient empires as an "oriental society" basically different from the more recent society of Europe and America. K. A. Wittfogel has even included in this category the empires of the Incas, Aztecs, and Maya in pre-Columbian America. In his analysis they all shared common features of universal kingship, land-based economy, generally ideographic writing, and a monolithic bureaucratic government that dominated large-scale economic activity so that no sanction for private enterprise became established. But of them all, only the Chinese empire survived into modern times.

China's evolution remained comparatively uninterrupted, whereas in the Eastern Mediterranean the Phoenicians and Greeks developed city-states, seafaring, and alphabetic writing. Subsequently, the Greco-Roman world and the European Middle Ages both saw the growth of dominant social classes which were originally outside the framework of government and were based on private property. The Greek city-state, for instance, was dominated by a propertied class which manipulated the government and made every effort to prevent the growth of an independent bureaucracy. In this Greek society of private property, taxes were collected by tax farmers, the mines and customs were farmed out to private individuals, slaves were used as scribes, and the citizens who took office were rotated so rapidly that no one official could accumulate personal power based on official position. Under the Roman Republic the taxes and customs were collected by tax farmers, and public works were made the responsibility of private persons. In feudal Europe the enlargement of the sphere of private activity was of course even more striking. It is no accident that the modern West found the roots of individualism in Greek philosophy and Roman law as well as in the medieval town.

The early Chinese state, in contrast, claimed control over the ingredients of agricultural production—namely, the land, the manpower, and the water supply. The ruler's claim to the disposal of the land and of the people on it was seldom questioned, although it was found through experience that private landowning was a necessary incentive to peasant production and did not impede the collection of taxes. The institution of compulsory corvée labor by the people at the behest of the government became well established and made possible the enormous public works which still amaze us like the Great Wall or the Grand Canal. Finally, administration of the water supply in a region of semi-aridity like North China was part of the government's economic function. Irrigation and flood prevention, to be effective, must be under central control. Both irrigation ditches and river dikes must be maintained throughout their length according to an overall program. So must dikes for land reclamation.

Once established in this pattern the early Chinese state developed further the same principles of administration. The building and maintenance of canals and highways for transport and communication were paralleled by the growth of the civil service. Scribes and administrators were essential to collect the agricultural surplus and superintend the public works. The concentration of population in enormous capital cities at the imperial administrative center went hand in hand with an increased density of manpower upon the land. When urban handicraft industry stimulated exchange between town and countryside, there was no opportunity for the new industrial and merchant class to escape the overshadowing domination of government.

Many of these "oriental" characteristics of the early Chinese empire lasted down to recent times. But modern scholarship has made it plain that China was by no means a fossilized example of the world's early empires unchanging through the ages. Quite the contrary.

The Medieval Flowering. Japanese scholars in particular have helped establish the picture of China from mid-T'ang through the Sung (eighth to thirteenth centuries) as the world's most advanced society. Material progress was indexed by a series of startling inventions—printed books, the abacus, paper money and credit instruments, gunpowder explosives, water pumps, canal locks, water-tight bulkheads and the compass for seafaring, to say nothing of earlier creations like ceramics and "Chinaware," lacquer, silk and cotton textiles, and art objects such as Sung paintings. These were products of a vital society at a high point in history, well ahead of Europe. The urban culture of the Sung reflected advances in farming, craftsmanship, trade, and technology which had their counterparts in philosophy and the art of government. Most important was the growth of domestic and also foreign private trade, a veritable "commercial revolution," which made the Southern Sung government more dependent on trade taxes. Jacques Gernet pictures the Southern Sung capital at Hangchow as certainly the greatest city of its day.

Conditions among China's peasant masses have been variously appraised by historians, depending on the questions asked, sources used, and regions studied. Some Tokyo researchers see the Sung peasantry as virtual serfs on the manors of great landlords. Their critics decry this as Europocentric, adducing evidence that the nature of rice culture favored the small owner—farmer or permanent tenant—for the plowing, transplanting, fertilizing, and weeding of rice fields gets a crop in proportion to the skill, care, and effort of the farmer. "The tiller," as Evelyn Rawski notes, "occupies a more crucial position in rice culture than in the cultivation systems for other grains." By Ming times (1368–1644) she finds agriculture in parts of Central and South China was quite market-oriented: although tenancy had increased with population growth, tenants generally had long-term contracts with fixed rents, which fostered their enterprise and productivity. Farmers could choose seed types best suited to local soils and climate. Instead of double-cropping rice they might grow sugar cane, tobacco (after 1500), or other cash crops or put their household womanpower into handicrafts like weaving silk or cotton. So diversified and sophisticated was this farm production for the market that city merchants could not control it through capital investment, even though a putting-out system and some factory production got started, especially in cotton textiles. As Mark Elvin points out, Chinese cities did not produce a bourgeoisie as a new class of entrepreneurial city dwellers, for "the continuing existence of a unified imperial structure made independent urban development in China as impossible as the development of a true feudal political and military structure."

Instead of a bourgeoisie, China created a new class of a very different type.

The Gentry Class

The gentry dominated Chinese life increasingly during the last thousand years, so much so that sociologists have called China a gentry state and even ordinary people may speak of the "scholar gentry" as a class. But do not let yourself be reminded of the landed gentry with their roast beef and fox hunts in merry England, for "gentry" in the case of China is a technical term with two principal meanings and an inner ambiguity. It requires special handling.

Non-Marxists generally agree, first of all, that the gentry were not a mere feudal landlord class, because Chinese society was not organized in any system that can be called feudalism, except possibly before 221 B.C. While "feudal" may still be a useful swear word, it has little value as a Western term applied to China. For instance, an essential characteristic of feudalism, as the word has been used with reference to medieval Europe and Japan, has been the inalienability of the land. The medieval serf was bound to the land and could not himself either leave it or dispose of it, whereas the Chinese peasant both in law and in fact has been free to sell and, if he had the means, to purchase land. His bondage has resulted from a press of many circumstances but not from a legal institution similar to European feudalism. Nor has it been maintained by the domination of a professional warrior caste. Avoidance of the term feudal to describe the Chinese peasant's situation in life by no means signifies that it has been less miserable. But if the word feudal is to retain a valid meaning for European and other institutions to which it was originally applied, it cannot be very meaningful in a general Chinese context.

The Chinese gentry can be understood only in a dual, economic and political sense, as connected both with landholding and with office holding. The narrow definition, following the traditional Chinese terminology, confines gentry status to those *individuals* who held official degrees gained normally by passing examinations, or sometimes by recommendation or purchase. This has the merit of being concrete and even quantifiable—the gentry in this narrow sense were scholarly degree holders, as officially listed, and not dependent for their status on economic resources, particularly landowning, which is so hard to quantify from the historical record. Moreover, the million or so men who held the first-level degree under the Ch'ing must be seen, as P. T. Ho suggests, as "lower gentry" barely removed from commoner status, whereas the small elite who after further years of effort went on up through the three rigorous week-long examination rounds at the provincial capital and at Peking formed an "upper gentry" of great influence.

The gentry as individuals were public functionaries, playing political and administrative roles. Yet they were also enmeshed in family relations, on which they could rely for material sustenance. This political-economic dualism has led many writers to define the term gentry more broadly, as a group of *families* rather than of individual degree holders only. Both the narrow and the broad definitions must be kept in mind.

The gentry families lived chiefly in the walled towns, not in the villages. They constituted a stratum of families based on landed property which intervened between the earth-bound masses of the peasantry, on the one hand, and the officials and merchants who formed a fluid matrix of overall administrative and commercial activity, on the other. They were the local elite, who carried on certain functions connected with the peasantry below and certain others connected with the officials above.

For the peasant community the gentry included the big landowners, the economic base of the ruling class. Their big

The gentry. Country house of T'ao family, Yun-yang hsien, Szechwan, 1910. Thirty-foot walls dwarf half a dozen human figures.

high-walled compounds enclosing many courtyards, replete with servants and hoarded supplies and proof against bandits, dominated the old market towns. This was the type of "big house" celebrated in both Chinese and Western novels of China. As a local ruling class the gentry managed the system of customary and legal rights to the use of land. These ordinarily were so incredibly diverse and complicated that decided managerial ability was required to keep them straight. The different ownership of subsoil and topsoil, the varied tenant relationships, loans, mortgages, customary payments, and obligations on both sides formed such a complex within the community that many peasants could hardly say whether they were themselves mainly small landowners or mainly tenants. In general, the peasant's loss of title to his land was more likely to make him a tenant and decrease his share of its product than to make him a displaced and homeless wanderer. Peasant poverty was reflected sometimes in the increase of landless laborers in the villages, but it was marked chiefly by the increased payment of land rent.

There have been two schools of thought about China's rural poverty. One school has stressed the exploitation of the peasant by the ruling class through rents, usury, and other exactions, resulting in a maldistribution of income. This idea of landlord class exploitation has of course fitted Marxist theory and is now an article of faith concerning the old China. The other school, as Ramon Myers points out, has been more "eclectic"; it has stressed the many reasons for the low productivity of the old farm economy: farms of two acres per family were too small; even these tiny plots were improperly used; "peasants had insufficient capital and limited access to new technology; there was little control over nature; primitive transport increased marketing costs." Supporters of this interpretation point to the fact that most Chinese farmers owned their land, some were partly owners and partly tenants, and only about one quarter or one fifth were outright tenants, so that landlord exploitation of tenants was far from the general rule and less of a problem than the general lack of capital and technology compared with labor.

Without attempting final judgment, we may suggest one rule: that social status and class prerogatives must have figured in the rural scene along with all the agronomic factors, and any explanation must be social and historical as well as economic. For example, as in all farming, the seasonal need of capital permitted usurious interest on loans, which ran as high as 12 percent a month, depending on what the traffic would bear. Since capital was accumulated from the surplus product of the land, landowners were usually money lenders. The gentry families thus rested in part upon property rights and money power, as well as social prestige. In the early twentieth century, they still dominated the back country in most provinces.

For the officials of the old China the gentry families were one medium through whom tax collections were effected. By this same token they were for the peasantry intermediaries who could palliate official oppression while in the process of carrying it out. The local official dealt with conditions of flood or famine or incipient rebellion and the multitude of minor criminal cases and projects for public works, all through the help of the gentry community. It was the buffer between populace and officialdom.

A poor man, by his educational qualifications alone, could become a member of the gentry in the narrow sense used above, even though he was not connected with a gentry family. Nevertheless the degree-holding individuals were in most cases connected with landowning families, and the latter in most cases had degree-holding members. In general, the gentry families were the out-of-office reservoir of the degree holders and the bureaucracy. The big families were the seedbed in which office holders were nurtured and the haven to which dismissed or worn-out bureaucrats could return.

In each community the gentry had many important public functions. They raised funds for and supervised public works —the building and upkeep of irrigation and communication facilities such as canals, dikes, dams, roads, bridges, ferries. They supported Confucian institutions and morals—establishing and maintaining schools, shrines, and local temples of Confucius, publishing books, especially local histories or gazetteers, and issuing moral homilies and exhortations to the populace. In time of peace they set the tone of public life. In time of disorder they organized and commanded militia defense forces. From day to day they arbitrated disputes informally, in place of the continual litigation which goes on in any American town. The gentry also set up charities and handled trust funds to help the community, and made contributions at official request to help the state, especially in time of war, flood, or famine. So useful were these contributions that most dynasties got revenue by selling the lowest literary degrees, thus admitting many persons to degree-holding status without examination. While this abused the system, it also let men of wealth rise for a price into the upper class and share the gentry privileges, such as contact with the officials and immunity from corporal punishment.

The local leadership and management functions of the gentry families explain why officialdom did not penetrate lower down into Chinese society. Or to put it the other way in terms of origin, the gentry had emerged to fill a vacuum between the early bureaucratic state and the Chinese society that was outgrowing its control. City studies inspired by G. W. Skinner have noted how in the two millennia from early Han to mid-Ch'ing the territorial administrative structure of successive dynasties failed to grow while the Chinese population increased sixfold. The basic-level counties *(hsien)* totaled in the heyday of those regimes "1180 in Han, 1255 in Sui, 1235 in T'ang, 1230 in Sung, 1115 in Yuan, 1385 in Ming and 1360 in Ch'ing," while the empire's population totaled "60 million in A.D. 180, 80 million in 875, 110 million in 1190, 200 million in 1585 and 425 million in 1850." Thus a county magistrate was responsible for 50,000 people in late Han but for 300,000 in late Ch'ing. Skinner submits that the Ch'ing administration simply could not have functioned with 8500 counties managed from Peking. Instead of building up mechanically to such an unmanageable level, the Chinese state as it was expanding consolidated the counties in populous core areas while it created new counties on the periphery. Meanwhile it reduced its local administrative functions. For example, after the T'ang the officially administered city marketing system was given up, the government stopped its "minute regulation of commercial affairs" generally, and it steadily withdrew from "official involvement in local affairs." In its place came the rise of the gentry and their local functions.

In this way the imperial government remained a superstructure which did not directly enter the villages because it rested upon the gentry as its foundation. The many public functions of the local degree holders made a platform under the imperial bureaucracy and let the officials move about with remarkable fluidity and seeming independence of local roots. Actually, the emperor's appointee to any magistracy could administer it only with the cooperation of the gentry in that area. All in all, in a country of over 400 million people, a century ago, there were fewer than 20,000 regular imperial officials but roughly one and a quarter million scholarly degree holders.

Continued domination of the gentry families over the peasantry was assured not only by landowning but also by the fact that the gentry mainly produced the scholar class from which officials were chosen. This near monopoly of scholarship was made possible in turn by the nature of the Chinese language.

The Chinese Written Language—The Scholar

Chinese writing is not only different to look at, it is based on utterly different principles from the phonetically written tongues of western Asia and Europe, many of which look to us just as baffling as Chinese but are in fact closely similar to our own language. Thai children, for example, when they study Thai in school go through much the same process as American children, learning the sounds to associate with a number of otherwise meaningless symbols, or alphabet. As far as their mode of thought and study is concerned, they could just as well learn the English alphabet (with various adjustments to convey Thai sounds) and then proceed to write down words heard in everyday life and develop their vocabularies and powers of self-expression. With a Chinese child it is different. He learns symbols which have meaning because of their appearance, and which exist like pictures or like the figure 5, apart from any sounds. This written language is both pictographic and symbolic, in either case ideographic more than phonetic.

The Chinese language today consists of well over forty thousand characters in the biggest dictionary. But these boil down to about seven thousand necessary for a newspaper font, including about three thousand that one needs to know in order to be really literate. Until recently the form of these characters had hardly changed since the early Christian era. Until a generation ago the Chinese were still getting along with a written language comparable in age to ancient Greek and Latin, so terse that it usually had to be seen to be understood—the sound alone being inadequate. This was one factor helping to keep China, down to the twentieth century, in

The Nature of Chinese Society

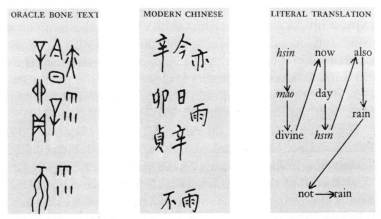

ORACLE BONE TEXT	MODERN CHINESE	LITERAL TRANSLATION

Oracle bones. *Left:* Bone from Anyang with inscribed characters.

Shang inscription on bone. *Above:* The characters are to be read from top to bottom, but the lines in this particular case read from left to right. The meaning of the text is: "[On the day] *hsin-mao*, it is divined whether on this *hsin* day it will rain—or not rain." Most of the characters in the text are clearly identifiable from their modern forms. The second character in the second column is a picture of the sun with a spot in it, while the second character in the third column as well as the lower right-hand character show rain falling from a cloud. The upper right-hand character, showing a man's armpits (the two spots under the arms), was at this time a homophone for the undepictable world "also."

its archaic Confucian mold. The language inhibited easy contact with alien societies, whose students of Chinese found it even harder then than now.

Chinese Writing. Chinese characters began as pictures or symbols. The ancient character ⊙ (later written 日) was the sun, and ☽ (later 月) the moon. Sun and moon together 明 meant bright, illustrious, clear. 木 meant a tree, two trees 林 meant a forest, and three 森 , a dense growth. The symbols 一 二 三 are certainly easier than "one, two, three."　□ indicates an enclosure or "to surround," while a smaller square 口 is the sign for the mouth and by extension means a hole, a pass, a harbor, and the like.

In its early growth the Chinese written language could not expand on a purely pictographic basis (like the joining of "sun" and "moon" to make "bright," noted above). A phonetic element crept into it. As a result most Chinese characters are combinations of other simple characters. One part of the combination usually indicates the root meaning, while the other part indicates something about the sound.

For example, take the character for east 東, which in the Peking dialect has had the sound "tung" (pronounced like "doong," as in Mao Tse-tung's name). Since a Chinese character is read aloud as a single syllable and since spoken Chinese is also rather short of sounds (there are only about four hundred different syllables in the whole language), it has been plagued with homophones, words that sound like other words, like "soul" and "sole" or "all" and "awl" in English. It happened that the spoken word meaning freeze had the sound "tung." So did a spoken word meaning a roof beam. When the Chinese went to write down the character for freeze, they took the character for east and put beside it the symbol for ice 冫, which makes the character 凍 ("tung," to freeze). To write down the word sounding "tung" which meant roof beam, they wrote the character east and put before it the symbol for wood 木 making 棟 ("tung," a roof beam).

These are simple examples. Indeed any part of the Chinese language is simple in itself. It becomes difficult because there is so much of it to be remembered, so many meanings and allusions. When the lexicographers wanted to arrange thousands of Chinese characters in a dictionary, for instance, the best they could do in the absence of an alphabet was to work out a list of 214 classifiers, one of which was sure to be in each character in the language. These 214 classifiers, for dictionary purposes, correspond to the 26 letters of our alphabet, but are more ambiguous and less efficient.

In spite of its cumbersomeness the Chinese written language

was used to produce a greater volume of recorded literature than any other language before modern times. One sober estimate is that until 1750 there had been more books published in Chinese than in all the other languages in the world put together. This was partly because the Chinese invented paper and the printed book some six centuries before they reached Europe.

Perhaps enough has been said to indicate why written Chinese became almost a ruling class monopoly. It had the character of an institution, rather than a tool, of society. Men worshiped it, and devoted long lives to mastering even parts of its literature, which was a world of its own, into which one might gain admittance only by strenuous effort. A major Chinese character was an onion of many layers of meaning accumulated over the ages as it was used for various purposes. For a too simple comparison, suppose the Roman idea expressed as *pater* had come down to us unchanged in written form and today, perhaps combined with other characters, referred to father, patriotism, paternity, patristics, patrimony, patronage, etc., etc. Which meaning to assign to such a character depended on its context. This required one's knowing the classical literature. Many scholars were exhausted simply by mastering it.

The Chinese writing system was not a convenient device lying ready at hand for every schoolboy to pick up and use as he prepared to meet life's problems. It was itself one of life's problems. If little Lao-san could not find the time for long-continued study of it, he was forever barred from social advancement. Thus the Chinese written language, rather than an open door through which China's peasantry could find truth and light, was a heavy barrier pressing against any upward advance and requiring real effort to overcome—a hindrance, not a help, to learning.

The Scholar Class. This class produced by mastery of the

characters was closely integrated with both the gentry families beneath it and the official system above. When successful as a degree holder and perhaps an official, the scholar found his channel of expression and achievement through the established structure of government. He could become an official, however, only by mastering the official ideology of the state as set down in the canonical works of the Chinese classics. These texts were part of a system of ideas and ritual practices in which the scholar-official learned and applied the Confucian rules and attitudes on the plane of verbal conduct while participating in the personal relationships, political cliques, organized perquisites, and systematic squeeze which distinguished the official class on the plane of practical action.

For the scholar who did not rise into official life there was always the alternative of the family system from which he had sprung. His status as a degree holder gave him contact with the lower fringes of official power and through this personal contact he could serve his family by representing its interests. This function again called for the use of Confucian ideas in verbal and literary expression. In this way the scholar, whether in official life or out of it, was wedded to the established order of family and state. His living depended upon them and in practice he served them both. As a cultivated gentleman incapable of manual labor or trade and trained to be the bearer of the family-state ideology, he had no alternative.

It was the security of the individual boy in the gentry family which made it possible for him to take the risk involved in the investment of his time in scholarship. His preparation for the examinations and for official life required usually ten years of study. The average age of acquiring the topmost degree at Peking was the same as for receiving tenure in an American faculty today—about thirty-five. Yet the examinations were a gamble and talented youths could be fed into the system only from sources that had means.

The Nature of Chinese Society

The risk and mobility of official life contrasted with the security and stability of the landed gentry. The point of balance between them was the examination system. In a society which seems to us remarkable for its emphasis upon personal relations, the Chinese examinations appear to have been amazingly impersonal and universalistic. When the system was functioning effectively at the height of a dynasty, every effort was made to eliminate personal favoritism. Candidates were locked in their cubicles, several thousand of which in long rows covered a broad area at each provincial capital. Papers were marked with the writer's number only and were copied before being read by the examiners, all in conditions of strict security. Such precautions were, of course, necessary for the maintenance of any rational and objective standards in the selection of candidates for office. They expressed the Chinese ruler's genuine need of talented personnel to maintain an efficient administration. Once the best talent of the land had been chosen by this impersonal institution, however, it was then perfectly consistent that the officials should conduct a highly personal administration of the government, following a "virtue ethic" which attached importance to the qualities of individual personality rather than a "command ethic" which laid emphasis upon an impersonal and higher law.

The fact and the myth of social mobility in the Chinese state are still matters of debate. Most dynasties which supported the examination system as a mechanism for the selection of talent gave extensive lip service to the myth that all might enter high position, depending only upon ability. Western writers for long assumed that the Chinese examinations were a really democratic institution, providing opportunity for the intelligent peasant to rise in the world. In fact, however, this seems to have happened rather seldom. The many years of assiduous study required for the examinations were a barrier which no ordinary peasant could surmount. The legend of the villagers who clubbed together to support the studies of the local peasant genius has been an inspiring tradition. But it was not an everyday occurrence.

Of the various avenues open to the common peasant, advancement could not usually be sought through the opening up of new land or founding of new enterprises, nor, for most people, through the investment of profits and savings. This fact has given Chinese life a character far different from our own and makes the American doctrine of individualism and free enterprise, when transplanted to China, an almost incomprehensible and rather dubious jumble of slogans. In Chinese circumstances, advancement for the common man has lain in the direction of connections with the bureaucracy. Entrance into the official class or into the penumbra of money handlers and fixers which surrounded it was a goal to be achieved through personal contacts and personal services. This route on the whole led through the gentry and not around them.

Thus landlords, scholars, and officials were all parts of a composite ruling class. Landowning families having some agricultural surplus could give their sons leisure for study to become scholars. Scholars, with a mastery of classical learning, could pass examinations and become officials. Officials, with the perquisites and profits of bureaucratic government, could protect and increase their family landholdings. The structure was flexible, automatically self-perpetuating, and very stable.

Nondevelopment of Capitalism—The Merchant

In Chinese history one urgent question for Americans is why the Chinese merchant class failed to break away from its dependence upon officialdom and create an independent entrepreneurial power.

First of all, the Chinese merchant had an attitude of mind quite different from that of the Western entrepreneur extolled by our classical economists. According to the latter, the economic man can prosper most by producing, and securing from his increased production, the profit which the market will give him. In the Chinese tradition, however, the economic man will do best not by increasing production but by increasing his own share of what has already been produced. He will rise by competing against his fellows directly rather than by creating new wealth through the conquest of nature, or the increased exploitation of her resources, or applications of improved technologies. This is because the Chinese economy has had from early times a maximum of people competing for a minimum of natural resources, instead of great continents and new industries to develop. The incentive for innovative enterprise, to win a market for new products, has been less than the incentive for monopoly, to control a market by paying for an official license to do so. The tradition in China has been not to build a better mousetrap but to get the official mouse monopoly.

The ideal gentleman in China was the man who had risen above the necessity to produce and was able to devote himself to leisure and the scholarly pursuits which symbolized it. The person most esteemed was he who had achieved leisure, not he who outdid his fellows in frenzied business activity. This leisurely ideal could be seen only recently in the Chinese village where a leisure class appeared at the top level of the peasantry although at an amazingly low level of income. The relatively well-to-do peasant, though still bone poor by our standards, would seize the first opportunity to change his status from that of a laborer who uses his back and hands in the fields to that of a gentleman who wears a long gown and affects some literate interest. The long fingernails of old China were certainly the cheapest badge of leisure ever invented.

From the earliest period official position was the key to wealth and leisure, for the official had the greatest opportunity to increase his share of the things already produced. With his official status went the power to settle human affairs and profit thereby. More specifically, the official represented the emperor's power to conscript corvée labor, to levy taxes, to dispense justice, and to regulate the economic and social activities of the people.

Coming from the local gentry, Chinese officials usually brought to their careers the attitude of a rentier class. They sought perquisites rather than opportunities for enterprise. Now the merchant was a competitor of the official, since he also was occupied not in agricultural production but in manipulations and exchanges which would secure a greater share of the goods already available. In theory the merchant from ancient times had been regarded by the scholar-official as nonproductive and parasitic. His transporting produce from place to place was given no credit in the classical literature. He was placed at the bottom of the social scale. In actual fact, however, the merchant was kept in check by the official as a minor ally whose activities could be used and milked in the interest of the official class or of the state. As Etienne Balazs has pointed out, commercial transactions were always subject to the superintendence and taxation of the officials. Government monopolies of staple articles, like salt and iron in ancient times, or like tea, silk, tobacco, salt, and matches more recently, have been an expression of the overriding economic prerogatives of the state. No merchant class was allowed to rise independently and encroach upon these prerogatives.

On the other hand, it was always possible to work out a

close community of interest between the merchant and the official, for official patronage and support were necessary for any big commercial undertaking. Both could profit where neither could succeed alone. Merchants, bankers, brokers, and traders of all sorts were therefore a class attached as subordinates to the bureaucracy. As handlers and manipulators of goods and capital, they assisted the officials in extracting the surplus not only from commerce but also from agriculture.

Merchants indeed could move with some ease into the gentry class through purchase of land and literary degrees and intermarriage. Unlike Europe, China had little foreign trade in which a merchant could invest. Though less profitable than commerce, land was more secure and so remained the great object of investment. The merchant class produced landlords more readily than independent commercial capitalists.

Chinese guild organization, though capable of great feats of passive resistance in the form of strikes or noncooperation, bears out the subservience of merchants to officials. The strength of the guild institution lay in the craft guild by which the artisans of a certain handicraft preserved their monopoly of technical processes and productive rights. Merchant guilds such as led the way in early European trade have been notably weak in China. The Canton Cohong, one of the main examples, was notoriously a tool of court officials.

China's premodern financial system has offered another body of evidence. Savings which represented accumulated capital were ordinarily invested in moneylending because of the high interest obtainable. Usurious rates were an index of the farmer's high seasonal demand for money, both to pay his taxes and for subsistence until the next harvest. Short-term credits to farmers paid higher interest than long-term industrial loans. As a result there was less incentive in China than in America for investment of savings in industrial production.

One sign of the predominance of agriculture in the Chinese economy was the restricted use of money. Creation of credit among the villages was retarded by the relative self-sufficiency of the peasant household and its dependence upon short-term purchases from sources close at hand. Similarly the government used to rely heavily upon taxation in kind and the payments of stipends in grain. The capital at Peking, for example, was fed by grain shipments from the provinces via the Grand Canal. In addition the government had at its command resources of corvée labor which received no money wages.

The old currency system itself was extremely complex, a bimetallic system using both silver and copper. The unit of account for silver (the ounce or tael) varied from place to place and also as between trades and agencies of government. Twenty different silver tael units of account might be in common use in one city at one time, requiring a different "currency" for each major commodity, like salt or cotton cloth, and for payments going to certain other places. It was not possible to maintain a minted currency of fixed value. Reliance had to be placed upon the clumsy circulation of pure silver, each ingot of which had to be weighed and also assayed for its purity. Meanwhile few governments could refrain from debasing the copper coinage. The resulting multiplicity of currency units, and exchange arrangements among them, represented the domination of the money manipulator, who profited by this complexity, over the investor who wanted to put his money into planned productive enterprises. One may surmise that this inefficiency of the money system was tolerated because it helped the ruling class's money operations more than it hindered them, just as the scholars tolerated an ideographic writing system the difficulty of which preserved their semi-monopoly over it. In any case this inefficient money system bespoke a loose, decentralized economy in which commercial activity was mainly in local trade. It was much like medieval Europe.

In short, capitalism failed to grow up in China because the merchant was never able to become established outside the control of the gentry and their representatives in the bureaucracy. In feudal Europe the merchant class developed in the towns. Since the landed ruling class were settled in their manors upon the land, the European towns could grow up outside the feudal system instead of being integrated in it. Medieval burghers gained their independence by having a separate habitat in these new towns, and a new political authority to protect them, in the persons of the kings of national states.

In China these conditions were lacking. The early abolition of feudalism and the dependence of the emperor and his officials upon the local gentry left no political power outside the established order to which the merchant could turn for special protection. In addition the gentry families of China early became the dominant class in the towns, which usually grew up first as administrative centers. The essential connection of the gentry with officialdom drew them into the towns both as cultural centers and as walled havens against bandits or irate peasants. The gentry family's best security lay not in a sole reliance upon landowning but in a union of landowning with official prerogatives. Family property in itself was no security but officials who were family members could give it protection. Thus the gentry class, as an elite stratum over the peasant economy, found their security in land and office, not in trade and industry. Between them, the gentry and officials saw to it that the merchant remained under control and contributed to their coffers instead of setting up a separate economy.

Private enterprise might develop freely in small-scale farming within the grip of government taxation, but this was not a capitalist type of private enterprise. From the peasants' more assiduous cultivation of their privately owned land, the bureaucracy would garner a greater surplus by taxation. By the same principle they also stood ready to collect from the merchant or industrial producer any surplus he might accumulate. Many merchants appear in the records of ancient China but never as a class having political power. Early emperors specifically barred them from taking the examinations for entrance into official life. The growth of commerce was less important to the rulers than continued supervision of the agricultural economy. They depended upon land taxes more than trade taxes.

In the inherited social structure, the upper level or ruling class included several subclasses—the landowning gentry, the scholar-literati, and the officials, as well as merchants, militarists, and hangers-on. This composite upper stratum was the active carrier of China's literate culture in its many aspects. Within this minority segment of the Chinese people, say roughly 10 percent, have been developed most of the literature and the fine arts, the higher philosophy, ethics, the political ideology of the state, the sanctions of power, and the wealth that accompanied them. The values of this higher culture filtered down to permeate the masses and train them in obedience to authority.

Chapter 3
The Confucian Pattern

Confucius and Karl Marx had even less in common than the ideologies which bear their names, and the differences between Confucianism and Marx-Lenin-Maoism are as great as the similarities. Yet both traditional China and the People's Republic have stressed the role of ideology, and no one can understand Mao Tse-tung's thought without knowing something of the Confucian tradition.

Western observers, looking only at the texts of the Confucian classics, were early impressed with their agnostic this-worldliness and their ethical emphasis upon proper conduct in personal relations. In its larger sense as a philosophy of life, we have generally associated with Confucianism the quiet virtues of patience, pacifism, and compromise; the golden mean; conservatism and contentment; reverence for the ancestors, the aged, and the learned; and, above all, a mellow humanism—taking man, not God, as the center of the universe.

All this need not be denied. But if we take this Confucian view of life in its social and political context, we will see that its esteem for age over youth, for the past over the present, for established authority over innovation, has in fact provided one of the great historic answers to the problem of social stability. It has been the most successful of all systems of conservatism. For most of two thousand years the Confucian ideology was made the chief subject of study in the world's largest state. Nowhere else have the sanctions of government power been based for so many centuries upon a single consistent pattern of ideas attributed to one ancient sage.

Naturally, in the course of two thousand years many changes have occurred within the broad limits of what we call Confucianism—periods of decline and revival, repeated movements for reform, new emphases and even innovations within the inherited tradition. The range of variety may be a bit less broad than among the multiple facets of Christianity but it is certainly comparable. Consequently the term Confucianism means many things and must be used with care.

As a code of personal conduct Confucianism tried to make each individual a moral being, ready to act on ideal grounds, to uphold virtue against human error, especially against evil rulers. There were many Confucian scholars of moral grandeur, uncompromising foes of tyranny. But their reforming zeal, the dynamics of their creed, aimed to reaffirm and conserve the traditional polity, not to change its fundamental premises.

That Confucian ideas persist in the minds of Chinese politicians today should not surprise us. Confucianism began as a means of bringing social order out of the chaos of a period of warring states. It has been a philosophy of status and consequently a ready tool for autocracy and bureaucracy whenever they have flourished. Unifiers of China have been irresistibly attracted to it, for reasons that are not hard to see.

When Chiang Kai-shek on Christmas Day 1936 was released by the mutinous subordinates who had forcibly held him at Sian, he returned to Nanking amid unprecedented national rejoicing. Yet four days later he submitted his resignation. "Since I am leading the military forces of the country, I should set a good example for my fellow servicemen. It is apparent that my work failed to command the obedience of my followers; for otherwise the mutiny . . . would not have occurred . . . I sincerely hope that the central executive committee will censure me for my negligence of duties. After the Sian incident, it is no longer fit for me to continue in office."

Nine years later in his famous wartime book, *China's Destiny,* Chiang Kai-shek said: "To cultivate the moral qualities necessary to our national salvation . . . the most important task is to develop our people's sense of propriety, righteousness, integrity, and honor. These qualities are based upon the Four Cardinal Principles and the Eight Virtues, which in turn are based on Loyalty and Filial Piety."

These two examples could be multiplied. They demonstrate the degree to which China down to recent decades remained a Confucian state. In the first case no one wanted Chiang to resign, nor did he intend to do so, and his resignation was elaborately declined. In the second case no one expected that China's national salvation in the midst of Japanese aggression, blockade, and inflation could be achieved through moral qualities alone, nor did Chiang think so. But in both cases his words delineated the traditional Confucian way.

· Countless Chinese leaders before Chiang Kai-shek have quoted Confucius while fighting off rivals or alien invaders, who, like the Japanese, have invoked the Sage on their part while trying to take over China. Peking today sings a different tune, but there are Confucian overtones in the Marxist-Maoist orchestration. The crucial role of ideology under communism lends particular interest to China's ideological past.

Confucian Principles

The principles of Confucian government, which still lie somewhere below the surface of Chinese politics, were worked out before the time of Christ. Modifications made in later centuries, though extensive, have not been fundamental until recently. The past is still just around the corner.

First of all, from the beginning of Chinese history down to the third century B.C. there was a marked stratification into officials and nobility on the one hand, and the common people on the other. We can see this confirmed in the remains of Shang capitals already noted. This social distinction between the ancient ruling class and the common people gave rise to a particular type of aristocratic tradition which was preserved and transmitted through Confucianism. The former aristocrat became the scholar-official, and Confucianism his ideology.

This Confucian aristocracy of merit or talent came closer to the original Greek idea of aristocracy, "government by the best," than did the subsequent European hereditary aristocracies of birth. In the era of warring states, when the empire was not yet unified and philosophers flourished, Chinese thinkers of all major schools turned against the principle of hereditary privilege, invoked by the rulers of the many family-states, and stressed the natural equality of men at birth: men are by nature good and have an innate moral sense—in Donald Munro's phrase, an "evaluating mind." This means that man is perfectible. He can be led in the right path through education, especially through his own effort at self-cultivation, within himself, but also through the emulation of models outside himself. In his own effort to do the right thing, he can be influenced by the example of the sages and superior men who have succeeded in putting right conduct ahead of all other considerations. This ancient Chinese stress on the moral educability of man has persisted down to the present. It still inspires the government to do the moral educating.

Government by Moral Prestige. The Confucian ideology

did not, of course, begin with Confucius (551–479? B.C.). The interesting concept of the Mandate of Heaven, for example, went back to the early Chou period (ca. 1027–770 B.C.). According to the classic *Book of History,* the wickedness of the last ruler of the Shang, who was a tyrant, caused Heaven to give a mandate to the Chou to destroy him and supplant his dynasty, inasmuch as the Shang people themselves had failed to overthrow the tyrant. As later amplified, this ancient idea became the famous "right of rebellion," the last resort of the populace against tyrannical government. It emphasized the good conduct or virtue of the ruler as the ethical sanction for preserving his rule. Bad conduct on his part destroyed the sanction. Heaven withdrew its Mandate, and the people were justified in deposing the dynasty, if they could. Consequently any successful rebellion was justified, and a new rule sanctioned, by the very fact of its success. "Heaven decides as the people decide." The Chinese literati have censured bad government and rebels have risen against it in terms of this theory. It has also reinforced the belief that the ruler should be advised by learned men in order to ensure his right conduct.

Confucius and his fellow philosophers achieved their position by being teachers who advised rulers as to their conduct, in an age when feudal princes were competing for hegemony. Confucius was an aristocrat and maintained at his home a school for the elucidation and transmission of the moral principles of conduct and princely rule. Here he taught the upper class how to behave. He emphasized court etiquette, state ceremonies, and proper conduct* toward one's ancestors and

---

* "When he [Confucius] was in his native village, he bore himself with simplicity, as if he had no gifts of speech. But when in the ancestral temple or at court, he expressed himself readily and clearly, yet with a measure of reserve . . . At court, when conversing with the higher great officials, he spoke respectfully. When conversing with the lower great officials, he spoke

in the famous five degrees of relationship. One of the central principles of this code was expressed in the idea of "proper behavior according to status" *(li)*. The Confucian gentleman ("the superior man," "the princely man") was guided by *li*, the precepts of which were written in the classics.

It is important to note that this code which came to guide the conduct of the scholar-official did not originally apply to the common people, whose conduct was to be regulated by rewards and punishments rather than moral principles.

This complex system of abstruse rules which the Confucians became experts at applying stemmed from the relationship of Chinese man to nature, already mentioned. This relation had early been expressed in a primitive animism in which the spirits of land, wind, and water were thought to play an active part in human affairs. The idea is still prevalent in the practice of Chinese geomancy or *feng-shui* (lit., "wind and water"), which sees to it that buildings in China are properly placed in their natural surroundings. Temples, for example, commonly face south with protecting hills behind them and a water course nearby. In its more rationalized form this idea of the close relation between human and natural phenomena led to the conception that human conduct is reflected in acts of nature. To put it another way, man is so much a part of the natural order that improper conduct on his part will throw the whole of nature out of joint. Therefore man's conduct must be made to harmonize with the unseen forces of nature, lest calamity ensue.

This was the rationale of the Confucian emphasis on right

out boldly . . . When he entered the palace gate, he appeared to stoop . . . When he hastened forward, it was with a respectful appearance . . . When the prince summoned him to receive a visitor, his expression seemed to change . . . When his prince commanded his presence, he did not wait for the carriage to be yoked, but went off on foot . . . He would not sit on his mat unless it was straight." Translated by D. Bodde from *Shih Chi*.

conduct on the part of the ruler, for the ruler was thought to intervene between mankind and the forces of nature. As the Son of Heaven he stood between Heaven above and the people below. He maintained the universal harmony of man and nature by doing the right thing at the right time. It was, therefore, logical to assume that when natural calamity came, it was the ruler's fault. He might acknowledge this by issuing a penitential edict, like that of Chiang Kai-shek quoted above. It was also for this reason that the Confucian scholar became so important. Only he, by his knowledge of the rules of right conduct, could properly advise the ruler in his cosmic role.

The main point of this theory of "government by goodness," by which Confucianism achieved an emphasis so different from anything in the West, was the idea of the virtue which was attached to right conduct. To conduct oneself according to the rules of propriety or *li* in itself gave one a moral status or prestige. This moral prestige in turn gave one influence over the people. "The people are like grass, the ruler like the wind"; as the wind blew, so the grass was inclined. Right conduct gave the ruler power.*

On this basis the Confucian scholars established themselves as an essential part of the government, specially competent to maintain its moral nature and so retain the Mandate of Heaven. Where the Legalist philosophers of the Ch'in unification

---

* In the *Analects* Confucius said: "When a prince's personal conduct is correct, his government is effective without the issuing of orders. If his personal conduct is not correct, he may issue orders but they will not be followed." (See Chiang Kai-shek's statement at the beginning of this chapter.) In the *Great Learning* it was said: "the ruler will first take pains about his own virtue. Possessing virtue will give him the people. Possessing the people will give him the territory. Possessing the territory will give him its wealth. Possessing the wealth, he will have resources for expenditure. Virtue is the root, wealth is the result." Compare Chiang Kai-shek in *China's Destiny:* "So long as we have a few men who will set an example, the people in a village, in a district, or in the whole country will unconsciousy act likewise. As the grass is bent by the wind, so the social tone is influenced by the example of such men."

of 221 B.C. had had ruthlessly efficient methods of government but little moral justification for them, the Confucianists offered an ideological basis. They finally eclipsed the many other ancient schools of philosophy. As interpreters of the *li*, they became technical experts, whose explanations of natural portents and calamities and of the implications of the rulers' actions could be denied or rejected only on the basis of the classical doctrines of which they were themselves the masters. This gave them a strategic position from which to influence government policy. In return they provided the regime with a rational and ethical sanction for the exercise of its authority, at a time when most rulers of empires relied mainly upon religious sanctions. This was a great political invention.

Early Achievements in Bureaucratic Administration. Theory, moreover, was matched by practice in the techniques of government. The bureaucratic ruling class came into its own after the decentralized and family-based feudalism of ancient China gave way to an imperial government. The unification of 221 B.C., in which one of the warring states (Ch'in) finally swallowed the others, required violent dictatorial methods and a philosophy of absolutism (that of the so-called Legalist philosophers). But after the short-lived Ch'in dynasty was succeeded by the Han in 206 B.C., a less tyrannical system of administration evolved. The emperors came to rely upon a new class of administrators who superintended the great public works—dikes and ditches, walls, palaces and granaries—and who drafted peasant labor and collected the land tax. These administrators supplanted the hereditary nobility of feudal times and became the backbone of the imperial regime. They incorporated many of the Legalist methods in a new amalgam, imperial Confucianism.

In the two centuries before Christ the early Han rulers

The Confucian Pattern

firmly established certain principles. First, the political authority in the state was centralized in the one man at the top who ruled as emperor. Second, the emperor's authority in the conduct of the administration was exercised on his behalf by his chief ministers, who stood at the top of a graded bureaucracy and who were responsible to him for the success or failure of their administration. Third, this bureaucracy was centralized in the vast palace at the capital where the emperor exercised the power of appointment to office. His chief task became the selection of civil servants, with an eye to the maintenance of his power and his dynasty. For this reason the appointment of relatives, particularly from the maternal side, became an early practice. (Maternal relatives were the one group of persons completely dependent upon the ruler's favor as well as tied to him by family bonds, in contrast to paternal relatives who might compete for the succession.) Fourth, the early Han rulers developed the institution of inspection which later became the censorate, whereby an official in the provinces was checked upon by another official of lower rank, who was sent independently and was not responsible for the acts of his superior.

In this and in many other ways the central problem of the imperial administration became that of selecting and controlling bureaucrats. It was here that Confucianism gained strength from certain Legalist methods, and ancient China, as H. G. Creel has shown, led the world in developing the basic principles of bureaucratic government: namely, the impersonal use of specifically delegated powers in fixed areas of jurisdiction by appointed and salaried officials who regularly reported their acts during limited terms of office. For more than 2000 years this system of territorial bureaucracy has been epitomized in the walled administrative city of the *hsien* or county.

To find the talent for officialdom the Han emperors subsidized schools and began to set written examinations. This practice continued, and when the imperial structure was reinvigorated under the T'ang dynasty (A.D. 618–907), the examination system became firmly established as the main avenue to office. For more than a thousand years, down to 1905, this imperial institution produced administrators who had established their qualifications for official life by thoroughly indoctrinating themselves in the official orthodoxy—surely another of the great political inventions.

The Classical Orthodoxy

The Confucian doctrines were transmitted through the Chinese classics. As might be expected, these ancient books have formed a canon, the texts of which have been interpreted and reinterpreted through the centuries. In this process later texts, sometimes written for the purpose, have become canonized as more ancient, and books of early importance have fallen into obscurity. In the early Han period the classics usually mentioned were the *Book of Changes* (for divination), the *Book of History*, the *Odes* (ancient folk poems), the *Book of Ceremonies and Proper Conduct*, and the *Spring and Autumn Annals* (chronicles of Confucius' own state of Lu, in Shantung province) with their commentaries. It was not until the T'ang that the ancient book of the philosopher Mencius (ca. 372–289 B.C.) was elevated to the position of a classic. By degrees there was accumulated a canon of thirteen classics, which with their commentaries today fill some 120 volumes. In order to simplify this unwieldly corpus of ancient texts, scholars of the Sung (A.D. 907–1279) selected the famous Four Books (the *Analects* of Confucius, the *Book of Mencius*, the *Doctrine of the Mean*, and the *Great Learning*), which were so brief that any gentlemen could master them.

The apothegms and aphorisms of the Four Books depict paternal government as the key to social order and the defense of the state. "If your Majesty," says Mencius to King Hui, "will indeed dispense a benevolent government to the people, being sparing in the use of punishments and fines, and making the taxes and levies light, so causing that the fields shall be plowed deep, and the weeding of them be carefully attended to, and that the strong-bodied during their days of leisure shall cultivate their filial piety, fraternal respectfulness, sincerity, and truthfulness, serving thereby at home their fathers and elder brothers and, abroad, their elders and superiors—you will then have a people who can be employed, with sticks which they have prepared, to oppose the strong mail and sharp weapons of the troops of Ch'in and Ch'u."

Though eminently rational in form, this official doctrine had its religious side, expressed in the official rites at the Confucian temples, the pantheon of sages and their tablets, and the ritual veneration of them—all forming a state cult closely allied to the veneration of ancestors in the people's homes below and the emperor's ritual acts above. While not anthropomorphic, this was a religious cult. One might call it a cult of state humanism, based on faith in the power of virtuous conduct to capture men's hearts and so lead them in the path of order under wise and benevolent authority.

The vicissitudes of the Confucian creed, like those of Roman Catholicism, are a most instructive study and show how deeply it has penetrated Chinese life. In the third to sixth centuries after Christ, during the decline of central authority which followed the Han Empire, Confucianism was all but eclipsed by Buddhism. But in the second great imperial period of China's long history, under the T'ang and Sung dynasties of the seventh to thirteenth centuries, the Confucian system was re-established and remolded into a form more stable and enduring than ever.

The revival of Confucian government under the T'ang was

part of a general revival of Chinese society in politics, administration, literature and art as well as thought. The T'ang rulers in the seventh century and until the middle of the eighth centruy extended their control in all directions, into Korea and Vietnam (in Chinese called Annam) and over the nomad tribes and the settled oases of Central Asia. Meanwhile the T'ang capital at Ch'ang-an (modern Sian) became a metropolitan center of almost two million persons and a focus of travel and trade from Byzantium and all the Middle East.

It is interesting that in the early period of T'ang strength, when the state and the economy were expanding and both the legal system and the examinations were functioning vigorously, the revived Confucian bureaucracy was remarkably tolerant of foreign creeds. Foreign visitors brought with them all the variety of medieval religions: Judaism, the fifth century Christian heresy known as Nestorian Christianity, and Manichaeism and Zoroastrianism from Persia. But when the first great rebellion threatened the dynasty in the middle of the eighth century, and its problems of revenue and military control continued to grow more pressing, the self-confidence of Chinese power was evidently shaken, and the cosmopolitan spirit declined with it.

After the collapse of the T'ang and the successive incursions of barbarian rulers on the northern frontier, the Sung dynasty failed to recapture the international position which the early T'ang had achieved. Chinese rulers throughout the Sung were on the defensive against the peoples of the steppe. Handicraft production and domestic and overseas trade brought financial well-being to the government, but they were offset by military weakness. The later Sung became a great commercial empire whose exports of copper cash, silk, and porcelain reached all of Eastern Asia and spread into Indonesia, India, the Middle East, and Africa. But through

all this period China's reaction to the invaders from ~~In~~
Asia remained rather unwarlike. Chinese influence abroa~
was based on commerce and culture rather than on military
power.

This experience of foreign aggression in the Sung period of
the eleventh and twelfth centuries (and the Mongol conquest
which followed it in the thirteenth century) strengthened in
Chinese society an ethnocentricity which has remained one of
its chief characteristics. Even today a visitor like Ross Terrill
finds the Chinese "sense of their superiority is rooted in contentment with their own mountains and rivers. Not an active
sense of superiority which pants to convert the world to its
excellence." Of course many other factors also influenced
the thought of this period, but during it the Confucian orthodoxy was reinforced and never lost its grip thereafter.

Neo-Confucianism. This new orthodoxy was an all-embracing system of thought which has been known to the West as
Neo-Confucianism. It was more systematic and more complete than the ancient classics and by a reinterpretation of
them gave Confucianism more metaphysical content than it
had had before. In its new form Confucianism was rounded
out to provide more of the answers which man asks of life.
The absorption of definitely idealistic elements, mainly from
Buddhism, undoubtedly made Confucianism more satisfac-
tory to Chinese intellectuals and so offered Christianity, when
it came to China by sea in the sixteenth century, a good deal
less of a spiritual vacuum to fill. By that time there was more
to Confucianism than met the missionary's eye when he
perused the religiously arid Chinese classics.

The greatest of the Neo-Confucian synthesizers was the
twelfth-century philosopher Chu Hsi (1130–1200), whose historic role in China has sometimes been compared with that of
St. Thomas Aquinas (d. 1274) in the West. As would be ex-

..ie culmination of the efforts of several
....cian writers reaching back to the T'ang
...d large numbers of disciples and whose
....shed a number of philosophical elements
...s able to combine.

....cian system of the Sung, which became or-
thoa.. ..... hundred years thereafter, had its basis in an
absolute firs. ....inciple called the Supreme Ultimate, subsist-
ing beyond time and space. The Supreme Ultimate in turn
was manifest in an infinitude of *li* (not the old Confucian
term) which may be translated here as laws or principles of
form. Each separate type or category of thing has its *li* and
each *li* is a manifestation of the Supreme Ultimate. Physical
matter, on the other hand, consists of the primordial ether or
first substance *(ch'i)*, the stuff of the physical universe. In
each thing therefore, the *li* and *ch'i*, or law and matter, are
mutually essential and complementary. A house, for example,
must be made of bricks *(ch'i)*, but they must be put together
according to a plan *(li)*. The comparability of this system to
the Platonic ideas is plain.

In dealing with the ethical problem of evil, Chu Hsi asserted that the nature of any living creature is the *li* of that creature as found combined with the *ch'i*. The *li* in itself is perfectly good but in the physical world it is always found in
combination with *ch'i*. Evil consists in the obscuring of the
li by the *ch'i*. Thus there is no active principle of evil. It results from situations which arise. (In our modern parlance,
"Dirt is not dirt but only something in the wrong place.")
Man's instincts are fundamentally good. The highest Confucian virtue therefore became an unswerving determination
and honesty expressed in the term *ch'eng*, "complete sincerity." By means of complete sincerity of heart the *li* or principles can be cleansed of the *ch'i* or physical obstructions which
obscure them. This remains today one of the fundamental

The Confucian Pattern

Chinese ideals, and explains why Japanese and Chinese diplomats, or Nationalist and Communist negotiators could hurl no verbal thunderbolt more devastating than the charge of "insincerity."*

The doctrine of original goodness was expressed in the opening lines of the famous *Three Character Classic* which echoed Confucius's *Analects* and was studied first by every schoolboy for generation after generation: "At men's beginning their nature is fundamentally good, by nature they are similar but in practice they grow apart." It is not surprising that the Western missionary's somber conception of original sin had difficulty in overcoming this happier Confucian view.

In politics the Neo-Confucianists believed that the ruler must gain understanding in the true principles of government and become a sage by moral self-discipline. In practice the new Confucian orthodoxy put its primary stress upon the moral development of man. It became an ever more effective mechanism for the inculcation, through the study of the classics and the examination system, of the Confucian doctrines of loyalty and social responsibility and conformity. For the individual this philosophy was essentially monistic rather than dualistic, the *li* and *ch'i* being complementary and harmonious. Hell, heaven, and personal immortality were not conceived of, nor was a personal deity.

After the expulsion of the Mongols and the re-establishment of Chinese control over China under the Ming dynasty

---

* Compare *The Doctrine of the Mean:* "Sincerity is the way of Heaven . . . He who possesses sincerity is he who, without an effort, hits what is right, and apprehends, without the exercise of thought—he is the sage who naturally and easily embodies the right way . . . It is only he who is possessed of the most complete sincerity . . . who can transform others."

Compare Chiang Kai-shek *(China's Destiny):* "Sincerity is the moving spirit of real action. With sincerity, a man works for a just cause in perfect self-possession, pushing steadfastly and calmly onwards, unheedful of difficulties and dangers, until he finally succeeds."

(1368–1644) , the Sung Neo-Confucianism, because of its very inclusiveness, became a strait jacket on the Chinese mind. The Ming rulers used it as a tool of government. Chu Hsi's system became a dogma. Mencius became the greatest sage after Confucius. The Four Books and Five Classics became the intellectual fare of all ambitious men, as though Chinese society could find refuge by turning back into its own cultural heritage and could protect itself by staying within an established framework of ideas. This age saw the introduction of the famous "eight-legged essay," a style which put a premium upon balanced and antithetic forms of writing. Its influence can be seen in the habit of alternating sentences of six and four characters and of presenting no idea without balancing it against an opposite, which characterizes the traditional essay style.

Chinese Militarism

The man of violence was of course looked down upon by the Confucian scholar, who felt that resort to violence demonstrated one's inability to win by reasoning and moral suasion. The dictum perpetuated by civilian chroniclers was that "good iron is not used to make a nail nor a good man to make a soldier." This expressed the idea of the literatus who governs by moral sanctions and uses every opportunity to disparage the warrior who takes power by force. Disparagement of the soldier is deeply ingrained in the old Chinese system of values. Yet few empires in history have had a more impressive military record. Every dynasty has been founded by the sword. In periods of strong government, as under the Han, the T'ang, the early Ming, or the early Ch'ing (see chart, page 140) powerful military expedition have gone beyond China's borders into Vietnam or Korea, or across the wastes of Mongolia and Central Asia. Decades at a time have seen

The Confucian Pattern

an endless succession of rebel hordes, imperial armies, and alien invaders marching across the face of the land. The nomad dynasties of conquest were actually supported by a professional military caste.

Nevertheless the Chinese military tradition is of a different type from the European or the Japanese. Once an imperial regime was set up, civilian government was esteemed over military. It took a soldier to found a dynasty but he and his descendants invariably found it easier to rule as sages, through civilian officials. This is undoubtedly because power over the Chinese economy invariably settled in the hands of administrators, bureaucrats who got wealth in the form of revenues, not warriors who got it in the form of loot. Chinese history has had no counterpart to the Elizabethan or medieval Japanese institutions of maritime adventure and piracy whereby the country waxed strong on its overseas takings. No doubt one factor was the early disappearance of feudalism. In China the fighting man gave place to the administrator some thousand years before he did so in Japan. Just as the commercial society of the United States prefers civilian to military government, so the bureaucratic polity of China sought constantly to avoid domination by any independent military power.

In practice this meant that the problem of force in China was essentially a police problem, how to maintain surveillance over an unarmed and settled population and muster enough strength to suppress those who might turn bandit. Once a dynasty had become well established, armies for the attack and destruction of enemies were not needed within the Wall. This created the constant problem of reconciling the police institutions of China proper with the type of warfare required on the Chinese frontier against the professional fighting men of the steppe. Unlike the Mongols or the Manchus, Chinese farmers could never become a nation in arms in which each

The Old Order

individual had a stake in the tribal or national cause. Like Chairman Mao at a later time, rulers continually dreamed of making every farmer a soldier too, but this created at best a defensive rather than a striking force. Chinese armies until recent times were much more a form of public works, created at times of crisis by the same conscription of cheap manpower that provided the corvée labor gangs for building a Great Wall, a Grand Canal, or a Burma Road.

The Chinese military thus remained a part of the state's bureaucracy, fed by its revenues and a tempting source of corruption. But unlike the technology-based military of industrial states today, the Chinese military machine was not a major component of the economy. It served the dynastic cause of order and unity, which meant peace and even prosperity within the state; but the primary means for preserving the social order was indoctrination in the orthodox principles of social conduct *(li)*, and the secondary means was suasive coercion through rewards and punishments. The use of physical violence to maintain order was seen as a last resort, a confession that indoctrination and suasion had been ineffective and the regime perhaps lacked that popular acquiescence which constituted the Mandate of Heaven. Consequently China's military tradition included many nonviolent methods—mediation by third parties, negotiation, espionage, bribery and subversion, splitting followers from leaders, intimidation and cajolery, and all forms of deception. In short, as the ancient military classic of the fourth century B.C., the *Sun-tzu*, stated, "The acme of skill in warfare is to subdue the enemy, without fighting." The objective was the enemy's submission, not necessarily his destruction, a psychological rather than a physical result. Plainly, this Chinese tradition has a new relevance for the nuclear age of deterrence and mass mobilization.

Individualism, Chinese Style

To Western observers, China has presented a puzzling contrast: a great richness of human personality but little tradition of civil liberties. As in all countries, the creative Chinese writer, artist, or craftsman expressed his individuality, while the hermit or recluse could become a private individualist outside his community. But what was the degree of individualism in the sense of individual rights within the old society?

Instead of simply applying a legalistic Western yardstick, we may well follow W. T. deBary in appraising the actual concerns and solutions of Chinese philosophers. The individual, first of all, had to claim his status or rights within the social scene, among his fellow men. Confucius had said, "If I am not to be a man among men, then what am I to be?" Second, the Confucian emphasis on the individual's conduct supporting the social order was only the outward half of the story. The other, inward half stressed the individual's self-cultivation. But this had meant from early times the fulfillment of his personality by living as "a man among men," in proper relations with those around him and so according to moral principles. Selfishness was to be curbed by duty, and duty defined in social terms. Mencius said, "Between father and son there should be affection; between sovereign and minister, righteousness; between husband and wife, attention to their separate functions; between old and young, a proper order; and between friends, fidelity." Thus Chinese man defined his "self" by his relations to others and to the Tao or Way which made them all interdependent through the "web of reciprocal obligations." This by no means diminished the importance of conscience and morality. On the contrary, trying to stay within the bounds of orthodoxy might intensify the individual's moral problems, but these problems were perceived as "situation-centered," in Francis L. K. Hsu's phrase, not "individual-centered" as in America.

In the sixteenth century a new school of Confucian philosophy arose that gave the individual more scope. Wang Yangming (1472-1529), a high official whose thinking was to have great influence in both China and Japan, led a revolt against the Neo-Confucian orthodoxy by asserting that men have a common moral nature and therefore each individual has intuitive moral knowledge within his own mind. The possibilities of sagehood lie within him. Thus his task is to achieve a moral self-reformation. This is to be done mainly through study, but study must include thought, reflection, and the unending search for truth, not as mere verbal formulas but through personal experience. While it did not attack the traditional social order, Wang Yang-ming's subjective approach urged the individual to achieve a disciplined unity between learning and conduct, thought and action, or in today's terms, between theory and practice. This was a quite restricted form of individualism; in the end, as deBary remarks, it may be "more adaptable to a socialist society than modern Western types of individualism."

Human rights in China are today a wide-open subject—first in our American need to define "human rights" in operational terms of welfare as well as politics; second in the need to find what alternative or equivalent ideas are valued in China. The expected difference in Western and Chinese values makes this study urgent. Richard Solomon, among others, tracing the stages through which Chinese children used to be fitted into their society, has noted the Confucian stress on acceptance of parental authority, the repression of aggressiveness and selfishness, and the following of rituals and emulation of models, all disciplining the child to avoid disorder and depend upon authority at the same time that he resented it. Thomas Metzger, following modern students of

One of the "Twenty-four Stories of Filial Piety." *(From an engraved limestone sarcophagus, c. 525 A.D., Northern Wei Dynasty. In bad times, Kuo Chü's wife bore a son, but Kuo could not both rear a son and feed his widowed mother. "A son we can have again; a mother we cannot get again," he told his wife. Digging a hole to bury his son, he struck a pot of gold. Lower left: Kuo Chü's spade uncovers the gold while the wife holds the baby. Right: A happy ending. The grandmother on a dais feeds the baby, surrounded by food and drink as the filial Kuo Chü and his wife watch respectfully.*

Neo-Confucianism, concludes that the old anxiety due to dependence on authority was tempered by the gratifications of self-assertion and Confucian self-fulfillment. He believes the Confucian individual faced a constant predicament: the possibility or even probability of failure but the need to persevere in moral endeavor nevertheless. Neo-Confucian values, in short, once internalized as authoritative, produced a continual and anxious moral concern for correct behavior. Such studies indicate that we are only beginning to understand the Confucian way; certainly it involved faith, and still underlies Chinese thinking.

The Nondevelopment of Science

The history of technology in China confronts us with still another paradox. Until late medieval times China was at least on a par with and in many ways ahead of Western Europe in technological inventiveness and systematic observations of nature (such as the recording of sunspots). China had led the way in the development of paper and printing, chemical explosives, the mechanical clock, cartography, seismography, the beginnings of pharmacology, discoveries in magnetism (the compass) and in aspects of mathematics, and the perfection of numerous handicraft processes such as bronze-casting, porcelain manufacture, and the making of silk.

During the first thirteen centuries of the Christian era, according to the historian of Chinese science Joseph Needham, successive clusters of technological inventions came to Europe from China. In addition to the more famous items mentioned above, the wheelbarrow and barrow with a sail or sailing carriage, the crossbow, the kite, deep drilling techniques, cast iron, iron-chain suspension bridges, canal locks, the fore-and-aft rig, watertight compartments, the sternpost rudder, the assembly of eccentric, connecting rod and piston rod for the interconversion of rotary and longitudinal motion, among other things, all seem to have been known in China much earlier than elsewhere.

Yet these brilliant early achievements did not lead to the establishment of an organized technology and the formulation of a body of scientific principles—in other words, the creation of science as a persisting institution, a system of theory and practice socially transmitted, consciously developed and used. Europe made this breakthrough by the beginning of the seventeenth century. Why did China not do so? The reader will at once be reminded of other early Chinese inventions, such as the methods of bureaucratic administration, including the examination system (and even the perverse erotic invention of bound feet). In many ways China was ahead of Europe but subsequently fell behind.

In approaching this question, our Europocentric self-esteem may be chastened if we recognize how recent is the Western pre-eminence in many lines of technology and science that we today take for granted. Needham concludes that the knowledge of mathematics, astronomy, and physics in Europe and China had coalesced by the mid-seventeenth century, although China did not catch up in knowledge of botany until the end of the nineteenth century. He argues that in medicine the two traditions have still not coalesced, and that Western medicine for all its tremendous advances in the nineteenth century hardly surpassed the practical therapeutic results of the old Chinese medical system before 1900. (After all, leeches were being used to bleed patient-victims in London down to the 1880s.) Granted the superiority of the West in modern chemistry, surgery, and a multitude of other lines, the question is still a relative one. Why did China lag behind? But even more, why did Europe so dynamically forge ahead? The latter question, perhaps the real mystery, is beyond our scope. Here let us look at factors in Chinese life which seem to have inhibited the independent development of modern science.

In the realm of thought, during the era of Neo-Confucianism from the thirteenth to the nineteenth centuries, the teaching of Chu Hsi urged that sincerity of heart was to be approached by a study of external objects, "the investigation of things," after which one might proceed to the understanding of one's self. This phrase, "the investigation of things," however, was interpreted to mean not scientific observation but rather the study of human affairs. Human society and personal relationships continued to be the focus of Chinese learning, not the conquest of man over nature.

At the end of the seventeenth century under the Manchu dynasty (1644–1911) certain Confucian scholars began to develop a more pragmatic and critical view of the classics and their doctrines. This was called the "Han learning, "as opposed to the "Sung learning." It was part of a general movement of critical scholarship manifest in historical, geographical, and textual studies. But for all their obvious intellectual vigor, these later scholars clearly remained within the Confucian straitjacket, largely unconcerned with material technology. Their enormous and exhaustive compendia (the largest was in 36,300 chapters) stand today as a monument to the vitality of Confucian scholarship in carrying on a great tradition, but not to its creative originality in meeting new problems.

The growth of science was also inhibited by the Chinese failure to work out a fuller system of logic whereby ideas could be tested by ideas, by confronting one statement systematically with another. Philosophers assumed that their principles were self-evident when stated. They made less distinction than the Greeks between grammar and rhetoric, and therefore between abstract and concrete or general and particular. Chinese writers relied more heavily on general ideas of proportion, the balance of opposites, and the harmony of the natural order. Their famous method of chain reasoning, which was a clincher for Chinese scholars of twenty centuries, was from the Greek point of view a fancy series of non sequiturs.*

Underlying this weakness in logic was the physical nature of the Chinese written language. The use of an ideographic script for the transmission of the cultural inheritance from one generation to the next gave the characters themselves an independent status. They seemed to be enduring entities, not mere tools for the expression of ideas. For example, the virtues of which Confucius and Chu Hsi and their millions of disciples have thought and written have been represented in writing by specific symbols to which extensive philosophical connotations have become attached. It is not in the nature of the Chinese language to express these ideas in other terms which are interchangeable or synonymous. The five Confucian virtues of *jen, i, li, chih,* and *hsin* 仁 義 禮 智 信 (roughly equivalent to benevolent love, righteousness, propriety, wisdom, and faithfulness) are not easily expressed by other characters or by circumlocutions. The tyranny of terms is greater in Chinese than in an alphabetic language. The Chi-

---

* Take the following key passage from the *Great Learning:*

"The ancients who wished to be illustriously virtuous throughout the kingdom, first ordered well their own states. Wishing to order well their states, they first regulated their families. Wishing to regulate their families, they first cultivated their persons. Wishing to cultivate their persons, they first rectified their hearts. Wishing to rectify their hearts, they first sought to be sincere in their thoughts. Wishing to be sincere in their thoughts, they first extended to the utmost their knowledge. Such extension of knowledge lay in the investigation of things.

"Things being investigated, knowledge became complete. Their knowledge being complete, their thoughts were sincere. Their thoughts being sincere, their hearts were then rectified. Their hearts being rectified, their persons were cultivated. Their persons being cultivated, their families were regulated. Their families being regulated, their states were rightly governed. Their states being rightly governed, the whole kingdom was made tranquil and happy. From the Son of Heaven down to the mass of the people, all must consider the cultivation of the person the root of everything besides."

nese have been less able to escape from it than Western thinkers. To question the Confucian virtues would have been to deny the existence of the written characters which expressed them.

This tyranny of language was reinforced by an educational method in which the Chinese student traditionally memorized the classics before he understood them. Only after the characters were firmly established in the eye and ear, and in the muscular coordination of the hand in writing them, was their meaning studied and discussed. The enormous weight of the classic texts which had to be mastered put a premium upon memory, which already played an inordinate part in the learning of Chinese characters. The linguistic system of China was a natural matrix for authoritarian thinking.

One concomitant of the tyranny of language and its emphasis upon memory was the nonuse of the hands in connection with intellectual work. To be sure, the scholar sought to develop his calligraphy into a fine art. But once he put on his long gown he entered the ruling class and gave up manual work, which was a sign of a different social level. Chinese life pressed so closely upon subsistence, and learning was so clearly established as a path to economic security, that the scholar set great store upon the badge of learning, his long gown, and the ritual observance of the scholarly life, in which there was no time or occasion for manual labor. People who worked with their hands were commoners, not scholars. Scholars therefore did not work with the artisan in his workshop and the craftsman who needed new techniques. This separation of hand and brain stands in marked contrast to the example of the early European pioneers of science from Leonardo on down, who often came from the tradition of craftsmanship and, although scholars, were not debarred by the mores of their society from setting up their own laboratories. In early modern Europe the heritage of learning and the manual skills of technology might be focused in one man of genius. This seldom if ever happened in China.

Again, China's very use of printed books and written examinations long before Europe may paradoxically have inhibited creative thought. Medieval Europeans were short of written materials but long on oral disputation, and still preferred oral to written examinations down into the nineteenth century. Perhaps this put a premium on wit and reasoning over memory.

In general it appears that the Chinese lag was in motivation rather than ability, in social circumstances rather than innate genius. In short, the nondevelopment of science was an aspect of the nondevelopment of an industrial and military economy. This in turn went back to the essentially agrarian and bureaucratic nature of the Confucian state, and the strength of the ruling class tradition.

Traditional China was not unchanging nor static nor inert. On the contrary there were continual change and great variety, but always within the limits of a distinctive cultural and institutional pattern. This overall pattern persisted so strongly because, within their geographic confines, Chinese institutions—economic, political, social, cultural—over the centuries had developed great self-sufficiency, balance, and stability. Continuity, in short, had created inertia in the sense of momentum, persistence in established channels, not inertness.

The deep-laid inertia of the Confucian pattern in Chinese political life during two millennia explains why China's modern revolution against it has been so grievously long-drawn-out. Yet we can really appreciate the persistent vigor of this pattern only if we realize how nomadic conquest of China, far from destroying, served to reinforce it.

Chapter 4
Alien Rule and Dynastic Cycles

The unfolding of Chinese-Russian relations in the next decades must have overtones of China's past relations with invaders from the north. We should look at the historical record not as a portent of the future but as a source of insight and perspective.

During the last thousand years North China has been ruled more than half the time by alien invaders. This is one of the facts of history which inspired Japanese militarists in their schemes for conquest and rule through Chinese puppets. Alas for the Tanakas and Doiharas—they studied Chinese history all too well, but did not bring it down to date! Modern Chinese nationalism is a new force in history, and the past glories of the Mongol and Manchu conquests cannot be revived today.

Yet the record must be kept in mind, not with the thought that Russia can do tomorrow what Japan could not do yesterday, but in order to understand the complex problems of the Russo-Chinese relationship. For the twentieth-century nationalism of modern China must find its boundaries and achieve expression on a geographical and cultural frontier, between China and Russia, where the centuries have produced distinctive institutions and remarkable patterns.

Nomad Conquest

The great continuing contrast in the life of Eastern Asia has been that between the steppe and the sown, between the pastoral nomads of the plateaus of Inner Asia and the settled villages based on the intensive agriculture of China. This contrast is a striking one in nearly every respect.

On the steppe, population is thinly scattered and there are today perhaps two million Mongols and hardly more than that number of Tibetans in the arid plateau regions which more than equal the area occupied by almost a billion Chinese. The thinness of population in Central Asia in itself makes the life of the steppe nomad vastly different from the crowded life of China. "Nomadism" of course does not mean aimless wandering over the grasslands so much as the seasonal removal of camps and flocks from one known place to another, to the hills in summer and the lowlands in winter, as climate and rainfall make necessary, in search of pasture. Just as intensive agriculture has molded China, so the sheep economy of Central Asia has conditioned the nomad. From his flocks he secures food, sheepskins for clothing, shelter in the form of felt for his yurt, and fuel in the form of sheep dung. Cultivation of the soil being unreliable, he relies upon the management of his animals for a livelihood and upon his horses for a mobility that will save him from the aridity of the steppe. He must therefore be constantly resourceful and ready for new ventures. Custom does not tie him to the land, but he remains inevitably dependent upon a certain minimum of trade with settled regions. He has often been more free than the Chinese farmer and at the same time more poor than the Chinese landlord, since he could not accumulate immobile wealth from generation to generation. He was also a trained hunter and horseman, and so a potential warrior.

Early in the settled history of China the great military striking power of the mounted barbarian archers became a constant problem to the farming peoples of the plain. So powerful were the barbarian invasions of North China that a succession of Chinese states and dynasties were of barbarian origin: the Northern Wei dynasty (A.D. 386–534) in the interregnum after the Han, and the Liao dynasty (907–1127) of the Khitan Mongols, are almost as well known as the Yuan dynasty of the Mongols (1279–1368) and the Ch'ing dynasty of the Manchus (1644–1911).

Chinese defensive efforts in the third century B.C., when the First Emperor of Ch'in joined together existing local walls to make the original Great Wall of China, to keep out the nomads, were followed by constant later efforts to achieve security, either through defensive attack or bribery and payments or through diplomacy and negotiation. In some eras, like that of the Han, the T'ang, or the Ming, native Chinese dynasties have conducted great military campaigns into the steppe. In the process of invasion and counter-invasion during the centuries there has been a great mixing of population. There has also grown up in Chinese society a vast body of lore and tradition concerning the barbarians and how to deal with them. The steppe nomads, in fact, gave China her background in foreign and international relations before the advent of the modern West.

Thus the relations of the Chinese with the nomads of Central Asia have significance not only for China but for us, for in modern times the West has taken the place of the barbarian menace. The modern invasion of China by the Western world, from the point of view of the Confucian way of life, is only the most recent in a long series of invasions of alien cultures carried by alien peoples. There is of course little similarity between the impact of the nomads upon Chinese life and the impact of the West. But the Chinese response to the West has been conditioned by Chinese experience in meeting the nomads.

The fact that China's agrarian way of life could not expand into the steppe and that the nomad herdsmen could never permanently dominate the life of China led to a seesaw of Chinese-barbarian relations in the frontier region beyond the Great Wall. In these border areas, so aptly termed by Owen Lattimore "the Inner Asian Frontiers of China," a mixed economy of marginal agriculture and pastoralism formed the background for mixed political relations. Nomad leaders at times became settled territorial rulers. Chinese officialdom at other times exercised its sway over border tribes.

Lattimore suggests that the alternations of Chinese advance and retreat and barbarian submission and domination on the frontier was a product of interaction between two cycles: the cycle of dynastic rise and decline within China and the cycle of unification and dispersion among the tribes of the steppe. When a nomad leader, drawn by the trade at the border region, extended his power over it, he was obliged to take on settled ways. While this might lead the barbarians further toward domination of China south of the Wall, sedentary life would also in the end lead to a weakening of barbarian vigor and a decline of their new and transitory power over the sown.

Nomad invaders found that it was possible to rule China only in the Chinese way. Usually they achieved power by taking the advice of border collaborators who understood the Confucian system and could maintain an organized state no matter who might have inherited the Mandate of Heaven, so long as the inheritors would abide by Confucian principles.

The First Sino-Foreign Empires

The Khitan Mongols, from whom North China got the name "Cathay," maintained an empire for over two centuries (907–1127) on both sides of the Great Wall, including parts of North China, Manchuria, and Mongolia. Their original way of life, as studied by Wittfogel, had been only semi-nomadic, for they appear to have relied on agricultural crops, especially millet, as well as on sheep, horses, and pigs. Indeed, they rose to power by the very fact that they straddled the frontier between steppe and sown and could thus combine the military force of nomad cavalry with the economic sustenance of peasant tillage. The federation of tribes that founded the empire was led by the imperial Yeh-lü clan, who prolonged their rule by adopting the Chinese institution of hereditary monarchy and many of the forms of Confucian government. The result was a dual state, Chinese in the south, barbarian in the north, the southern half governed through institutions of civil bureaucracy inherited from the T'ang, the northern half by men on horseback. Thus while the Khitan Emperor's officials for one area were being recruited through the classical examination system, the mounted archers of the north were being mobilized and trained to serve in his elite guard, the *ordo* (from which derives our term "horde"). Eventually a dozen *ordos* were set up in separate areas, totaling perhaps 600,000 horsemen, a mobile shock force held in reserve.

Aside from this interesting dualism of government, the Liao Empire of the Khitan contributed little to Chinese culture. Its population was only about four million, less than one tenth, perhaps one twentieth, the size of the Sung Empire to the south, yet the Liao cavalry had such striking power that the Sung finally paid them annual subsidies to keep peace on the border. When the Liao state was taken over by the Jurchen tribes of northern Manchuria, who called their dynasty Chin or "golden" (1127–1234), the same pattern continued: the Sino-barbarian Chin Empire could combine the horses of the grasslands and the grain of North China to mount military assaults and force the Sung southward. (The Northern Sung, 960–1127, had their capital at Kaifeng, on the Yellow River; the Southern Sung, 1127–1279, at Hang-chow, south of the Yangtze.) But these Sino-barbarian achievements were in the realm of power, not of culture, and had historical significance mainly as a foretaste of the disaster to come.

The Mongol conquest and the Yuan dynasty set up by it in China (1279–1368) have been viewed by succeeding genera-tions of Chinese scholars as an unhappy interlude during which the Chinese people were under a foreign tyranny. It is true that the Yuan dynasty lasted less than a century and the Mongol power generated by Chingis Khan (ca. 1167–1227) and spread over China by the great Khubilai (1215–1294) withered and distintegrated with unusual rapidity after the Mongols became rulers of China. This egregious failure of the Mongols to maintain themselves in China stands out in such marked contrast to the later success of the Manchus that it deserves more than passing analysis.

The Mongols finally succeeded in imposing themselves over all China by the sword in 1279 after two generations of fighting and maneuvering, only to be expelled in 1368. The Manchus came to the throne with relative ease in 1644 and maintained a regime which the Chinese literati of the nine-teenth century still stood ready to defend with their lives and fortunes. The key to this contrast lies in the failure of the Mongols and the success of the Manchus in strengthening the Confucian system and using it for their own ends.

Of the factors that operated to prevent the Mongols from ruling China in Chinese fashion, the most immediate was probably their inability to assimilate Chinese culture and make it their own: they were full nomads, unaccustomed to agriculture or settled life. Their background was illiterate, their language different, their daily food and costume out-landish, their moral and legal codes at variance with Chinese tradition. This difficulty was reinforced by the fact that the

Mounted archer at work. By Italian Jesuit lay brother Giuseppe Castiglione (1688-1766), court painter to three Ch'ing emperors at Peking.

Mongols in China were but one part of the great Mongol Empire which was the product of the organizing genius of the Great Khan, Chingis (Genghis, lit., "Emperor within the Seas," the title he took in 1206) , and his sons and grandsons.

It is startling to note that Chingis in early middle age was still a vassal of a minor Mongol chieftain, among a tribal people who did not yet recognize the common linguistic bond later expressed in the name Mongol. His achievement in unifying and inspiring these tribes of the steppe to embark upon the greatest course of territorial conquest in early his-

tory can be understood only by reference to the propitious circumstances of the time in Central Asia.

About the year 1200 there stretched across that region from east to west a belt of settled communities founded on agriculture and connected with one another by trade. China was divided between the Chinese Sung dynasty in the south at Hangchow and the alien Chin dynasty in the north at Peking. In Northwest China was a kingdom founded by a Tibetan people. Westward in Chinese Turkestan were the Uighur Turks and west of them in Russian Turkestan were Turkish

Muslim sultanates such as Bokhara and Samarkand. Finally in Persia there was the Abbassid caliphate with its capital at Baghdad. Commerce among these settled states gave them wealth but none of them was warlike or strong enough to dominate its neighbor. They were a tempting prize for invaders from the steppe.

Another east to west belt of peoples stretched across Central Asia on the north. These were the nomad tribes of the arid plateau country. They were Turkish, Mongolian, and Tungusic in various mixtures and lived by an extensive pastoral economy. They had the nomad's mobility and comparative self-sufficiency; their patriarchal clan organization made them amenable to strong leadership.

Chingis rose through adversity from the lower nobility and built his power on personal loyalty. He asserted his mission to rule the world as the delegate of the eternal blue sky. He gave his tribal name, Mongol, to all the tribes that joined him. He codified their customary law, borrowing the Uighur script for the purpose, and declared it supreme and universal. He organized his warriors on a family principle under clans, tribes, and divisions of the empire. In all these ways he created a nation in arms. His carefully selected personal bodyguard or *ordo* formed an elite corps from which he drew his generals. The war machine thus created depended upon flying columns of Mongol cavalry, disciplined, hard-riding, and ruthless, who lived always for the loot which lay ahead and which gave them a constant incentive to expansion. Their compound bows and armor-piercing arrows and their sudden and deceptive battle tactics made them an irresistible force and the scourge of Asia. The descendants of Chingis set up their khanates in southern Russia, in Persia, and Turkestan, as well as in China.

This international scope of the Mongol Empire makes it

comparable to the expansion of Europe as a cause of cultural and institutional mixing. In both cases the representatives of one kind of society invaded several others. Mongol conquerors who overran settled agricultural states in South Russia, Persia, and China met a bewildering variety of languages, religions, and local customs, yet in each case faced certain general problems—how to maintain order, how to conduct a civil administration through a bureaucracy and secure tax collections, how to retain the Mongol grip on power, and therefore in the final analysis how to maintain their own identity, unity, and vigor. It is truly amazing how far these illiterate warriors succeeded in these exacting tasks. The Mongols of the Golden Horde ruled in South Russia for 200 years and those in Persia for a century. In both countries, as in China, they seem to have built up the political institution of centralized despotism. During the thirteenth century contact among these far-flung domains was kept up by the famous Mongol post routes across the grasslands and oases of Central Asia, the strategic inner core of the empire. This made possible Europe's first direct contact with Cathay.

Unfortunately for the Mongols, their grip proved less strong than their striking power. In China they faced the problem of ruling in a Chinese fashion and yet retaining political control in Mongol hands. To do this it was essential not only that they have force in reserve and that they maintain order which would bring prosperity, but that they also give opportunity for the exercise of Chinese talent in the official system.

Early in their career of conquest the Mongols had learned the necessity of employing experienced civil administrators who knew how to levy taxes, manage finance, and recruit a bureaucracy. For this work in China they relied mainly upon Chinese but they also used in their administration other seminomads of the border region and many foreigners. Marco

Polo (in China 1275–1292) was such a person. There were also others from Europe and a great number of Muslims, both Persian and Turkish, as well as Uighur administrators drawn from the states of Central Asia. The Mongols revived the examination system as a means of recruiting Chinese but it never worked well enough to get the best Chinese talent into the government.

The splendors of the reign of Khubilai, his new capital built at Peking, his extension of the imperial post roads and of the Grand Canal from Hangchow to Peking, and the great commercial development of such centers as Hangchow and Canton, described by Polo, demonstrated the vigor of Mongol rule in its heyday. But Mongol leadership after Khubilai soon deteriorated. The early fourteenth century saw a succession of weak rulers and finally dissension among the Mongol clans. Lamaism, the type of Buddhism developed in Tibet, spread its superstitious practices among the Mongol tribes. Lamaist excesses in China outraged the Confucian literati and stigmatized the Mongols as a people of primitive culture. Yellow River floods, financial difficulties, and at the last an inflation of paper currency undermined the regime. Rebels arose in several southern provinces to compete for the succession, and the strong man who succeeded among them expelled the Mongols and founded the Chinese Ming dynasty in 1368.

From the moment of its establishment one of the chief preoccupations of the Ming was to defend itself against the Mongol power. The first emperor sent big expeditions into the steppe against the Mongols. He recovered Manchuria, secured the allegiance of a new dynasty in Korea, and was finally able to engineer the Mongols' collapse and disintegration into eastern and western kingdoms. The second Ming Emperor personally led four expeditions against them. He assisted the western Mongols to crush the eastern Mongols and later helped the eastern Mongols to crush the western. Even so, the Chinese were not able to wipe out the Mongol threat, for they could not destroy nor could they sinify the steppe society across the Gobi desert. They were therefore forced to fall back on the age-old expedient of using one barbarian tribe against another and preserving the forms of a suzerain-vassal relationship with them all. In the end this led to their undoing, for they could not keep under control the Manchu state which grew up as a vassal on their northeastern frontier.

The Manchu Achievement

The Manchus who ruled China from 1644 to 1911 were a non-Chinese people of different habitat, language, and culture. Yet they succeeded in maintaining their power by traditional Confucian means for as long a period as any Chinese dynasty. The secret of this achievement may lie in the fact that, while they governed in a Chinese fashion, their alien origin and background helped them to retain political vigor within the ruling group. Some understanding of their success may help us to account for the tardy development of Chinese nationalism in modern times.

The essential point about the Manchu conquest of 1644 is that the Manchus by the time they came to power in China had already mastered the Confucian art of government and reconciled their own political institutions with it. Their development to this stage of political sophistication had been made possible by the fact that they were a border people on the frontier of the Chinese state where tribalism and bureaucracy could be synthesized.

Modern Western students of the Chinese frontier under Lattimore's inspiration have worked out an interpretation of

the way in which the Chinese and barbarian societies interacted. In China, intensive agriculture was the basis for a
bureaucratic government, in a region where land was scarce
in relation to manpower and the state depended upon revenue derived from the land. On the steppe, nomad pastoralism
was the basis for a tribal form of government, in a region
where manpower was more scarce than land and the power
of a chieftain consisted in his ability to command the personal
loyalty of the warriors. The Chinese populace had to be governed through an officialdom. The non-Chinese barbarians
could be controlled only through personal vassal relations.
The Manchus were fortunate in coming from a region where
these two systems met and intermixed.

Manchuria in the sixteenth century had been brought
under the Chinese type of intensive agriculture only in the
southernmost region below Mukden (modern Shenyang) on
either side of the Liao River. Northwestern Manchuria was
still a nomad area. The northeast, the original home of the
Manchus, was a partly forested region suitable for hunting
and fishing and the use of horses as well as for some agriculture. The Ming had recognized the frontier nature of South
Manchuria by organizing it in military districts rather than
under a civil administration only. By establishing hereditary
and registered military units at strategic points, separate from
the civil administration of this agricultural area, the Ming
Chinese sought to maintain both a military buffer against
barbarian inroads, and a check upon any separatist tendencies
of local Chinese officials; for they could not overlook the fact
that South Manchuria was a hostage to fortune which could
be cut off from North China at the bottleneck of Shanhaikuan, where the Great Wall escarpment comes to the sea.

In their rise to power the Manchus took full advantage of
their strategic position on a frontier where they could learn

Chinese ways and yet not be entirely subjected to Chinese rule. The founder of the Manchu state, Nurhachi (1559–1626), began as a minor chieftain on the eastern border of the agricultural basin of South Manchuria. Like Chingis among the Mongols, he brought adjoining tribes under his personal rule and early in the seventeenth century set up his capital at Mukden. His successor subjugated Korea on the east and made alliances with the Mongol tribes on the west in Inner Mongolia. In 1636 he gave the name Manchu to his people and proclaimed the Ch'ing ("Pure") dynasty.

The Manchus by this time had made several incursions into North China but had not yet been able to defeat the Ming. The Ming regime in China, however, had grown progressively weaker. Rebellion was already endemic. The leading figure in the disorder of the time was a Chinese rebel named Li Tzuch'eng whose forces had raided widely in Northwest China and even into Szechwan and the Yangtze valley. This leader had finally secured literate advisers and begun to set up a framework of dynastic government. In 1644 he succeeded in capturing Peking and had the dynastic succession within his grasp. But he was unable to consolidate institutionally the position that he had won by force. Chinese officialdom and the scholar-gentry class who provided the personnel of government were not drawn to him. Meanwhile a loyal Ming official in charge at Shanhaikuan invited the Manchus inside the Wall. They came at his bidding, destroyed the rebel Li, and stayed. Within forty years they had completed the conquest of China and their government of the empire remained stable for two centuries thereafter. Their success where a Chinese rebel had failed was essentially an achievement in the creation of political institutions.

The Manchus' first problem had been to develop beyond the state of tribal politics. This they did by creating a territorial administration over their lands, paralleled by a military organization of all the Manchu fighting men in eight divisions, each with a different flag or banner. The Manchu bannermen had lands assigned to them but these lands were kept scattered and the banners did not become territorial units. Mongols and Chinese who came over to the Manchus were taken into the system and organized in their own banner units. Nurhachi appointed his sons to head the banners but their power was brought under central control in a state council. In this way the originally personal relations between the head of the state and his loyal tribal chieftains were put into an impersonal institutional form.

Finally, the early Manchu rulers, like the Liao, Chin, and Yuan Emperors before them, took over the terminology, forms, and ideas of Confucianism and used them, as they were meant to be used, for the support and maintenance of political authority. They promoted study of the classics and the veneration of ancestors, set up the state cult of Confucius, talked and wrote of the "way of the ruler" (like the Japanese in Manchukuo three centuries later), extolled the Confucian virtues, and accepted the idea that the ruler rules by virtue of his moral goodness. More than a decade before their entrance into China, they had created in Mukden a miniature civil administration in imitation of Peking. The Six Ministries and other elements typical of Ming government were formally established and staffed by a bureaucracy in which Manchus, Mongols, and Chinese were represented. When they entered North China and assumed the Mandate of Heaven they were fully prepared to solve their fundamental problem, how to rule in the Chinese way but maintain their identity as Manchus.

Several circumstances aided them in this achievement. For one thing, unlike the Mongols, they had no vast empire to the west to distract them from the all-important problem of China. Having come from the frontier of South Manchuria, rather than from the Mongolian steppe, they did not have to leap the great cultural gap between the steppe and the sown. The unusually long and vigorous sixty-year reigns of two early emperors also provided a strong executive leadership: the K'ang-hsi Emperor (reigned 1662–1722) and the Ch'ien-lung Emperor (reigned 1736–1796) were both hard-working and conscientious sovereigns who commonly saw their ministers every day at dawn, studied the classics assiduously, traveled widely over the empire, and maintained a vigorous personal rule.

The various devices by which the Manchus sought to preserve their dynastic vitality are an interesting study. In order to preserve their identity as a racial group they closed their homeland to Chinese immigration and maintained North Manchuria as a hunting land outside the Chinese agricultural economy. To check Chinese immigration from South Manchuria northward, they built a willow palisade several hundred miles long (a big ditch with willows planted along it) to mark the boundary beyond which the Chinese should not expand. They organized Manchuria under a Manchu military government. In spite of a periodic overflow of Chinese settlers in time of famine, they succeeded on the whole in checking further Chinese settlement. North of the Chinese basin in the south, Manchuria remained a sparsely populated vacuum down to the nineteenth century—a tempting prize for Russian and Japanese imperialists.

In addition to this geographical basis the Manchus sought to preserve themselves by maintaining their racial purity. They banned intermarriage between Chinese and Manchus and fostered differences of custom between the two groups. Manchu women, for example, were not supposed to have bound feet. Manchus were not supposed to engage in trade or labor. The Manchu clan organization was preserved by their shamanistic religious system.

Manchu military control of China was maintained by the establishment of banner garrisons at strategic points. Garrisons in a separate Manchu military quarter in the big cities symbolized force held in reserve. The only Chinese troops given a recognized existence were provincial forces who were used mainly as a constabulary on the post routes and against bandits but lacked any training as a striking force.

In order to preserve strong leadership, the early Manchu emperors arranged that the imperial princes should be pensioned and given wealth but not allowed to become territorial lords. They were kept at Peking out of power. Every effort was made to avoid the historic curse of government by women and eunuchs, which had resulted so often in palace intrigue.

In the civil administration of China the Manchus used a system of dual appointments, whereby both Chinese and Manchus were placed in charge of important functions. Jonathan Spence has shown how at first they relied on Chinese allies from South Manchuria who had been enrolled usually as Chinese bannermen or bondservants, especially dependent upon and loyal to the Manchu rulers. Eventually the formula was to have capable Chinese do the work and loyal Manchus check upon them. At the capital Manchus outnumbered Chinese, but in the provinces Chinese officials far predominated. In order to draw into their service the most able and promising Chinese, the Manchus saw to it that the examination system continued to function with highest prestige and efficiency.

To absorb the energies of Chinese scholars produced by the examination system, the Manchu emperors became great patrons of literature and sponsored enormous projects of criticism and compilation. Spence describes the K'ang-hsi Emperor as a man of "exuberant curiosity." Like Dr. Johnson and the Encyclopedists, he presided over the production of a famous dictionary and of a vast encyclopedia in 5020 chapters. His great successor, the Ch'ien-lung Emperor, sponsored an edition of the twenty-four dynastic histories and a collection of all Chinese literature in "The Complete Library of the Four Treasuries." This compilation included 3462 works. It was too large to print and only seven copies were made by hand. The printed catalog alone ran to ninety-two chapters.

By means of this vast project the Manchu court in fact conducted a literary inquisition, one of their objects being to suppress all works that reflected on alien rulers. In searching out rare books and complete texts for inclusion in this master library, the compilers were able at the same time to search out all heterodox works which should be banned or destroyed. They paid high prices for rare works and even conducted house-to-house canvasses. The works proscribed included studies of military or frontier affairs, criticism anti-barbarian in tone, and chiefly items which extolled the preceding Chinese dynasty of the Ming. Altogether, some 2320 works were suppressed. As L. C. Goodrich has demonstrated, this was thought control on the largest scale.

Recent studies also reveal that the Imperial Household, staffed by the emperor's bannermen and bond servants, took on many aspects of a secret government parallel to the formal ministries at Peking. It collected enormous revenues from lands, trade monopolies, customs taxes, the salt gabelle, silk textile manufactories, loans, fines, and tributes, helping the dynasty to profit from the growth of trade and industry. While it began as a device to keep the palace eunuchs under control, to obviate their inveterate corruption, this inner government in due time became corrupt itself.

By these various expedients and devices the alien rulers of China under the Ch'ing dynasty maintained their racial and social identity, preserved their military and administrative control, and yet gave prestige and opportunity to Chinese of talent. The Manchu possession of temporal power in the Chinese state turned Chinese men of genius to literary and cultural activity. It also preserved in early modern China the nonnationalistic tradition that it makes little difference who governs as long as he governs in the proper fashion.

In Chinese politics this experience of alien rule confirmed rather than weakened the Confucian tradition because it put it on a universal rather than a regional or racial plane. The fact that an alien emperor followed Confucianism confirmed the fact that it was, as it claimed to be, an all-embracing and universal philosophy of government, to which there was no civilized alternative. The Chinese way in politics, like the rice economy of the paddy fields, appeared to be more fundamental than dynasties or races.

The Nature of Chinese Nationalism. Undoubtedly this universalism has meant that culture (the way of life) has been more fundamental in China than nationalism. Early Chinese emperors asserted that they ruled over all civilized mankind without distinction of race or language. Barbarian invaders who succeeded them found it expedient to continue and reinforce this tradition. To any Confucian ruler, Chinese or alien, the important thing was the loyalty of his administrators and their right conduct according to the Confucian code. Color and speech were of little account as long as a man understood the classics and could act accordingly. The successful barbarian rulers were those who acknowledged this fact by becoming assiduous classical scholars, calligraphers, and connoisseurs of Chinese art. They proved their legitimacy by quoting Confucius, conducting the rites, granting amnesties, maintaining the examinations, appointing officials, and issuing edicts in the manner of preceding Sons of Heaven. So long as they did so, they wrought no revolution in the Chinese political system and were accepted. This ability to persist under alien rule was also a measure of the extent to which Confucian government was a "benevolent despotism." It mattered little who was the despot as long as he fitted "benevolently" into the system and kept his grip on power.

Thus the long experience of alien rule has produced a fascinating paradox: the Chinese people in the nineteenth century entered the modern world singularly backward in one of its major qualities, the spirit of nationalism, yet in their twentieth century revolution the inherited pride of culture or "culturalism" has inspired a new cultural nationalism which may in the future outdo the merely political nationalisms that originated in Europe.

This different relationship between culture and political loyalty in China and in the West deserves more study. France and Germany, for instance, became nations only after the time of Charlemagne, who ruled both areas. Though frequently at war, these two nations have shared the common culture of Christendom. Descartes and Bach, Leibniz and Pasteur, Rousseau and Marx are their common heritage. In China, by contrast, the state has remained ideally coterminous with the whole culture. Polity and culture have almost fused. This may be seen in the way that China since the unification of 221 B.C. has clung to two great political myths: the unity of the Chinese empire and its superiority to all outsiders.

Until the Mongol conquest of the thirteenth century the myth of superiority was obviously justified by the facts of China's superior size, technology, wealth, and level of culture. But the idea of the Chinese emperor's supremacy over mankind through his rule-by-virtue was rudely shattered when the unvirtuous Mongols conquered China by sheer power.

However, the Ming Chinese rulers made a comeback and combined virtue and power to reassert the myth of imperial supremacy. In this way the very ancient idea of universal kingship, used by early rulers in Mesopotamia, Egypt, India, and even pre-Columbian America, was able to persist in China down to modern times.

The ideal myth of unity, so long associated in Chinese thinking with the absence of civil war and therefore with domestic peace, order, and prosperity, gained a new lease on life from the Manchu dynasty. When its bannermen in the eighteenth century brought Western Mongolia, Sinkiang, and Tibet under Peking's rule, this meant simply that the "Chinese empire" was in fact the "empire of East Asia" (China and Inner Asia), long a strategic and now a political unit. The consolidation of this whole area under the rule of the Ch'ing dynasty has now been followed in recent decades by its absorption into the expanded Chinese nation, first under the rule of the Kuomintang and then of the Chinese Communist Party. Both parties assert tenaciously even today that only one China, not two Chinas, is conceivable, and that this one China of the Han Chinese rightly includes as cultural minorities the Mongolian, Tibetan, Uighur Turkish, and many other ethnic groups.

The Dynastic Cycle

One basic approach to China's history of the early twentieth century is to regard it as a dynastic interregnum. Viewed in the light of the famous twenty-four histories of Chinese dynastic periods, the successive efforts of Sun Yat-sen, Chiang Kai-shek, and Mao Tse-tung to seize and organize central power are variations on an ancient theme. China's two thousand years of recorded politics have produced apparent rhythms and pulsations. Always, even though the current struggle might ravage the Middle Kingdom, most Chinese have had utter faith that unity would come again.

Anyone who seeks historical uniformities, or who makes societies and civilizations his units of study, will find the Chinese chronicles inexhaustible. Nowhere else are there so many recorded facts of imperial administration waiting to be selected, ordered, and generalized about by philosophers of history or by Marxist and non-Marxist system makers or by ordinary political pundits and historians in off moments. Here if anywhere one might hope to catch History in the act of repeating herself. Only the unimaginative can resist the idea that if we can read correctly the story of China's last two millennia, we can foresee her next two decades—a vain hope but an entrancing one.

Students of several generations have been impressed by the peculiarly parallel sequences in ancient China and in the Greco-Roman world: an age of philosophers and warring states, an age of unification and empire, and an age of disintegration and collapse of central power. Thus Confucius and his disciples are noted to have been roughly contemporary with Plato and Aristotle; Alexander the Great precedes the First Emperor of the Ch'in by only a century; and the imperial systems of Rome and Han flourished contemporaneously. Similarly the barbarians on the northern frontier grew more dangerous as each of these empires declined, and the economic and political disintegration within the "universal state," in Toynbee's phrase, was marked by the spread of foreign religions to which the distressed people turned for solace. The entrance of the northern nomads into China and the spread of Buddhism in the period from the third to the sixth centuries after Christ were actually contemporary with the inroads of the Goths and Vandals and the spread of Christianity, the triumph of "barbarism and religion," in the

West. To all who seek intellectual security in the formulation of laws which govern human affairs, these parallels have been a starting point both for generalization and for further research.

Within Chinese history the most interesting uniformity which strikes the superficial observer is the sequence of phases centering about the Han and the T'ang dynasties. Preceding each of these imperial periods was a time of intellectual ferment marked, respectively, by the philosophers of the late Chou period, and the flourishing of Taoism and Buddhism after the Han. Each phase of imperial greatness was inaugurated by a short-lived powerful dynasty which unified the state, the Ch'in (221–206 B.C.) and the Sui (A.D. 589–618). Both the Han and the T'ang, once established on the basis of a new unity, achieved an expansion of Chinese political power in neighboring regions, especially Central Asia, and a corresponding development of foreign contact.

Stimulated by this parallelism between two major dynasties, students have attempted numerous formulations of cycles. Underlying all these attempts is the fundamental phenomenon observed by Chinese historians and recorded by them so assiduously, namely, the dynastic cycle. In the twenty-four dynastic histories there is naturally a certain recurrence of ideas, since the chroniclers in each case were recording the life history of a ruling family which came to power, had its heyday, and shuffled from the scene. Toward the close of each regime, for example, natural calamities, earthquakes, floods, comets, eclipses, and other heavenly portents become more numerous in the record, evidence that the improper conduct of the ruler is losing him the Mandate of Heaven.

Autosuggestion, indeed, on the plane of public morale and social psychology may have played its part in the dynastic cycle. For so great was the dynasty's dependence on its moral prestige that its loss of "face" in certain instances might set in motion a process in which the ideology, as it were, turned against the regime and hastened its downfall. Once the litera- ti who set the tone of ruling class opinion became convinced that a dynasty had lost its moral claim to the throne, little could save it. This is a factor in Chinese politics today.

Time after time dynastic decline went hand in hand with the increasing inefficiency of the ruling house. The family in power accumulated over the generations a heavy load of dead wood and dead weight, fastened upon it by the family sys- tem. This was most flagrantly visible in the peculations and profligacy of maternal relatives who became entrenched in the imperial household. Wine, women, and song at the court led to increasing personal weakness of the rulers. This dan- ger attended the sinification of barbarian conquerors. The Mongol khans, for example, became effete and were undone by their own excesses.

The economic interpretation of Chinese history has been used even more extensively to explain the dynastic cycle. This approach concentrates particularly upon the land tax, which in the agrarian economy of China has been the chief source of government revenue and power. One process which seems to have appeared in each dynasty was the progressive withdrawal of land from taxation, for the benefit of the ruling official class and to the detriment of the imperial revenues. At the beginning of a dynasty the land and the population were usually estimated and recorded in a rough sort of census. New tax registers could be used as a firm basis for revenue collection. As time went on there ensued a struggle between the interests of the imperial government and of the individ- uals who represented it. Gradually the ruling class were able to increase their landholdings and to remove them from taxa- tion by various expedients such as the destruction of tax registers, official connivance, or legal falsification. This created a vicious spiral in which a greater burden was placed upon the land of the peasantry who still paid taxes, at the same time that the demands of the government for revenue were likely to increase. In this way a progressively smaller proportion of the land was expected to pay a progressively larger amount of revenue. Peasant disorders eventually resulted.

In some cases the final collapse of a dynasty came through peasant rebellion under fanatical religious leadership. Since no dynasty has tolerated an organized opposition, its opponents have had resource to secret societies. For example, as the Mongol administration lost its efficiency and morale in the middle of the fourteenth century, revolt became endemic in many provinces. Some of these revolts were led by secret groups like the White Lotus Society which had a symbolic ritual, esoteric signs and passwords, oaths sealed in blood, and an underground organization. Other revolts were led by religious leaders, usually Buddhist, who might proclaim the imminent advent of the bodhisattva Maitreya. Some rebels claimed to be legitimate successors to the preceding Sung dynasty. Others were content to be mere bandit chiefs who became local warlords and competed in the struggle for the survival of the fittest to receive the Mandate of Heaven. A bandit chieftain in Hupei got control of much of the central Yangtze region, another chieftain seized part of Honan, another rose at the same time in the lower Yangtze, and finally a pirate leader arose in Fukien. Each of them assumed a dynastic title. The eventual founder of the Ming dynasty got himself established in the richest area of the country, around Nanking, and knew how to combine clever politics with the forcible seizure of power. He was himself the son of a laborer and had been a Buddhist monk before seeking his fortune in rebellion. He conciliated the common people, maintained

Alien Rule and Dynastic Cycles

discipline among his forces, and, it is said, prevented plundering. By 1368 he had conquered or absorbed his rivals and was able to seize Peking, where his last successor was not dispossessed until 1644, almost three centuries later.

It is an interesting coincidence that the Ming emperors reigned for 276 years and their successors, the Manchus, for 267 years—spans which attest the stability of the monarchy's political institutions, no matter whether Chinese or non-Chinese were on the throne.

Chapter 5
The Political Tradition

The imperial system survived until 1912, the year Woodrow Wilson was elected President of the United States. The leaders of Republican China grew up under the empire. Those who dominate the Chinese scene today need think back only seventy or eighty years to recall the imperial splendor of the old Empress Dowager, the lavish trappings of despotism, the eunuchs, concubines, and court attendants, palace guards and palanquins, formal audiences, kowtow and lesser rituals, within the high red walls and gold-tiled roofs of the palace at Peking. These things have barely passed away. To look at modern China without seeing them in the background makes no more sense than to look at the United States without any recollection of Washington and Jefferson, Dan Boone and Abe Lincoln, manifest destiny, or the rise of the common man and John D. Rockefeller.

Bureaucracy

One key to the understanding of the People's Republic of China today is the fact that the old imperial government was a bureaucracy of the most thoroughly developed and sophisticated sort. To the American who has confronted the problems of bureaucracy only recently, the effort of modern Chinese to escape from evils and capitalize upon the good points of their own bureaucratic tradition is a matter of absorbing interest.

The old government centered in the capital. Without question the vast symmetrical plan of Peking made it the most magnificently ruler-centered of all capital cities. Paris and London are more diffuse. Washington and Moscow are creations of yesterday and do not attest, in a balance of gate against gate and avenue against avenue, the omnipotence of oriental despots who created their capital city as an outer cover to their palace. Although the great city wall and gate towers were torn down in the 1960s, Peking still centers upon the moated red walls of the Forbidden City. Within it the yellow-roofed throne halls rising from their marble platforms form the main axis of the whole metropolis. Behind them a great man-made hill of earth protects them from the north. Before them were broad avenues, and today a great square stretches south to the old front gate of the city. No Western capital is so plainly a symbol of centralized and absolute monarchy.

At Peking, for the greater part of thirteen centuries the civil administration of China was divided among the famous Six Ministries (or Boards) of civil office (appointment of officials), revenue, ceremonies, war, punishments, and public works (such as flood control). This structure, adumbrated in the first imperial system of the Ch'in and Han, had been formally established under the T'ang. In addition to the Six Ministries there were two other independent hierarchies of administration, the military establishment and the Censorate, as well as a number of minor offices: the imperial academy of literature, a court to review criminal cases, a historiographer's office, the imperial stud, and offices in charge of banquets and sacrificial worship. At the apex of everything the Ming had created the Grand Secretariat, in which high offi-

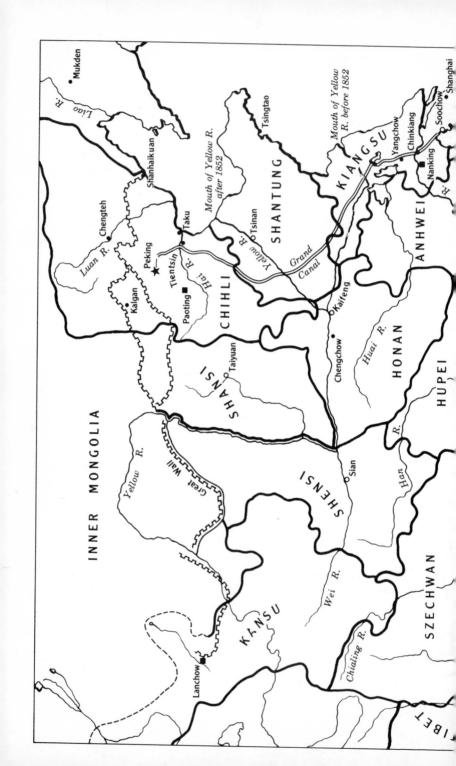

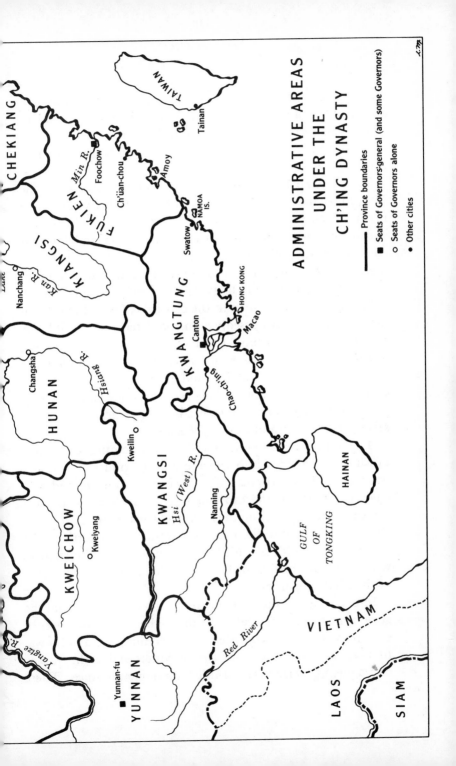

ADMINISTRATIVE AREAS
UNDER THE
CH'ING DYNASTY

— Province boundaries
■ Seats of Governors-general (and some Governors)
○ Seats of Governors alone
● Other cities

cials assisted the emperor in his personal administration of affairs. One of the few Manchu innovations was to add in 1729 a less formal body, the Grand Council, which handled military and other important matters and so became the real top of the administration.

Spread out over the eighteen provinces of China under the Manchu dynasty was a network of territorial divisions (see map). Each province was divided into several circuits *(tao)* and below them into prefectures, departments, and *hsien* or counties in descending order. The mandarins in charge of these divisions with their ubiquitous assistants and subordinates formed the main body of the territorial magistracy. Like civil servants trained in the classics at Oxford and Cambridge, they were supposedly omnicompetent, responsible for the collection of revenue, maintenance of order, dispensing of justice, conduct of literary examinations, superintendence of the official postal service, and in general for all public events within their areas. Theoretically, they stood *in loco parentis* to the people and were called, or rather called themselves, the "father and mother officials."

The imperial civil service was divided into nine ranks, each of which was divided into upper and lower grades. Each rank was entitled to a particular and very fine costume, including a colored button on the cap and insignia such as "mandarin squares" embroidered on the front and back of the gown. Prerogatives, titles, and dignities were minutely set forth in the statutes. High officials might be rewarded with the right to wear a peacock feather or bear the title of "Junior Guardian of the Heir Apparent."

Intervening between the hierarchy of local officials and the government at the capital stood the higher administration in each province. This consisted of a governor-general who was in most cases responsible for two provinces and, as his junior colleague, a governor responsible for a single province. These two officials were of course so placed as to check each other, for they were expected to act and report jointly on important matters. Under the Ch'ing (Manchu) dynasty, frequently the governor-general was a Manchu and the governor Chinese. Beneath them were four provincial officers who exercised province-wide functions: a treasurer, judge, salt comptroller, and grain intendant (who supervised the collection of grain for the capital).

Official business over the far-flung Chinese empire was conducted as in all bureaucracies by a flow of documents of many kinds. In their special forms and designations these multifarious communications mirrored the elaborate proliferation of red tape. A governor addressed his imperial master in certain prescribed forms and addressed his subordinates in others. Every communication began with a clear indication of its nature as a document to a superior, an equal, or a subordinate. Similarly there were special forms for memorials submitted to the emperor and edicts issued from him. Each document also went through a certain procedure of preparation, transmission, and reception. Hundreds of thousands of brush-wielding scriveners were kept busy year in and year out transcribing, recording, and processing official communications. In the imperial archives in the Peking palace are more than one hundred different types of documents which were in common use.

The flow of paper work was maintained by an official post which reached all corners of the empire but was limited to the transportation of official mail, official shipments (as of funds), and persons traveling on official business. This postal system was made up of some two thousand stations stretched out along five main and many subsidiary routes which ran into Manchuria, across Mongolia, westward to Turkestan and Tibet, southeastward through the coastal provinces, and southward through the interior of Central China. Couriers and travelers on these routes were provided with official tallies entitling them to the use of the transportation facilities, which in different areas might be horses, camels, donkeys, chairs (palanquins), or boats. In time of crisis couriers could cover 250 miles a day, using horses in relays. In the early nineteenth century this pony express sent messages from Canton to Peking in less than three weeks and from Shanghai to Peking in one week.

Central Controls. Given this network of officials, connected by a flow of documents and persons along the postal routes, it was the problem of the capital to stimulate the local bureaucrats to perform their functions and yet prevent them from getting out of hand. This control was achieved by the application of techniques common to bureaucracies everywhere, in addition to the special measures (noted above) whereby the Manchus sought to preserve their dynasty.

Among these techniques the first was the appointment of all officers down to the rank of county magistrate by the emperor himself. This made them all aware of their dependence upon the Son of Heaven and their duty of personal loyalty to him. Circulation in office was another device. An official was seldom left in one post for more than three years or at most six years. Ordinarily when moving from one post to another the official passed through the capital and participated in an imperial audience to renew his contact with his ruler.

Thus Chinese officialdom was a mobile body which circulated through all parts of the empire without taking root in any one place. In this it was aided by its reliance upon the Mandarin (Peking) dialect as a lingua franca of universal currency in official circles. Frequently an official would arrive at his new post to find himself quite incapable of understanding the local dialect and therefore the more closely confined to his official level. One means to prevent officials taking local root was the "law of avoidance" according to which no mandarin could be appointed to office in his native province, where the claims of family loyalty might impair devotion to the imperial regime.

Another custom which interrupted an official's rise to power was the rule of three years' mourning (actually some twenty-five months) after the death of his father, during which an official retired to a life of quiet abstention from worldly activities. As Arthur Waley says, this was "a sort of 'sabbatical' occuring as a rule toward the middle of a man's official career. It gave him a period for study and reflection, for writing at last the book that he had planned . . . for repairing a life ravaged by official banqueting, a constitution exhausted by the joint claims of concubinage and matrimony."

In general the bureaucratic principle was to set one official to check upon another. This was done particularly through the system of joint responsibility. The Six Ministries each had two presidents, one Manchu and one Chinese, who watched each other. It was common to appoint one man after he had gained prominence to several offices so that he was not able to master any one of them, and at the same time to appoint many men to perform one job so that no one of them could completely control it. Indeed many offices were sometimes created to carry on the same function, checking each other through their duplication of activity. The result of this duplication of offices and mutual responsibility was to hedge each official about with a multiplicity of commitments in each of which others were concerned. It was something like the unlimited liability of a partnership in which there were dozens of partners. Over and above all these immediate checks created by the involvement of many officials in a common responsibility, there was the system of the Censorate. Under it some fifty-six censors selected for their loyalty and uprightness were stationed in fifteen circuits through the provinces with the duty of keeping the emperor informed upon all matters concerning the welfare of the people and the dynasty. The early Ch'ing rulers even invented an eyes-alone type of "palace memorial" by which designated officials could send secret reports, to be opened only by the emperor and returned with his comments only to the sender. The ruler thus had his informers throughout the bureaucracy.

The evils inherent in bureaucracy were all too evident. All business was in form originated at the bottom and passed upward to the emperor for decision at the top, memorials from the provinces being addressed to the emperor at the capital. The higher authority was thus left to choose alternatives of action proposed, and yet the proposal of novel or unprecedented action was both difficult and dangerous for the lower official. The greater safety of conformity tended to kill initiative at the bottom. On the other hand the efficiency of the one man at the top was constantly impaired by his becoming a bottleneck. All business of importance was expected to receive his approval. All legislation and precedent were established by his edict. Modern China still suffers from this tradition.

In view of the complete and arbitrary power which the imperial bureaucracy asserted over the whole of Chinese life, it is amazing how few and how scattered the officials were in number. The total of civil officials for whom posts were statutorily available, both at the capital and in the provinces, was hardly more than 9000. The military officials were supposed to number only about 7500. It is true, of course, that there was an increasing number of supernumerary or "expectant" officials who might be assigned to various functions without receiving substantive appointments. There was also the vast body of clerks and factota necessary for the copying, recording, negotiating, and going and coming in each Chinese official's establishment or yamen. Down to the gatemen, runners, and chairbearers, these human elements in the official machine no doubt totaled millions. But if we look for the men of genuine official status who could take official action and report it in the hierarchy as representatives of his imperial majesty, we find them few and thinly spread, totaling at a rough estimate hardly more than 30 or 40 thousand "officials" at most, ruling over a country of about 200 million which grew to perhaps 400 million by the middle of the nineteenth century. Of the nine ranks, for example, the seventh rank near the bottom of the scale began with the county magistrate who was responsible for a population on the order of 300,000 persons. This relative smallness of the imperial administration reflected the fact that it depended upon the gentry class to lead and dominate the peasantry in the villages, as already noted.

Government as Organized "Corruption." Another anomaly of the bureaucracy was its low salaries. According to the official redbook, a governor-general in charge of two provinces as big as European countries received from his imperial master a salary equivalent in our terms to $300 a year. To this nominal sum was added a larger payment drawn from the provincial rather than the imperial treasury. For the governor-general in question this supplementary salary (*yang-lien*, lit., "to nourish honesty") would be equivalent to some $41,000 a year. But still, when added together from all sources, such salaries could not begin to meet the needs of an officer who had to employ a great retinue of private secretaries and special assistants.

The imperial officials were held responsible for all public events within their jurisdiction but not for all public funds. Budgeting and accounting procedures were rudimentary. The bureaucracy lived by what we today would call systematized corruption which sometimes became extortion. This was a necessary concomitant of the system of intricate personal relationships that each official had to maintain with his superiors, colleagues, and subordinates.

Among the bureaucracies of history, the Chinese has been distinguished by the way in which the twin institutions of "squeeze" and nepotism reinforced each other. The former operated through forms of politeness rather than secrecy. Junior officials in the course of their duties gave their superiors customary "gifts." But like all prices in old China, the amount of such a gift resulted from the working out of a personal relationship. The squeeze system was no more cut and dried than any other part of the man-to-man bargaining which pervaded Chinese life. The extralegal sums which passed between officials were larger but no different in kind from the small commissions extracted until only recently from every money transaction by underpaid houseboys.

Nepotism supported the squeeze or "leakage" system by giving an added sanction for personal arrangements contrary to the public interest. Even classic texts extolled duty to family, and particularly filial piety, as superior to any duty to the state. Thus the interest of the imperial administration at the capital, which needed the sustenance of revenue from the provinces, was constantly in conflict with the multifarious private interests of all the officials, each of whom had to provide for his relatives and his further career. High office commonly meant riches. The favorite minister of the Ch'ien-lung Emperor, when tried for corruption and other crimes by that emperor's successor in 1799, was found to have an estate worth in our terms of that period more than one billion dollars—probably an all-time record. Another high Manchu, who fell into disfavor at the time of the Opium War in 1841, was found to have an estate of some 425,000 acres of land, $30,000,000 worth of gold, silver, and precious stones, and shares in ninety banks and pawnshops. I would not suggest that Westerners have been backward or less adept in the art of graft. But in China corruption remained longer into modern times an accepted institution, unashamed and unafraid.

The vast new bureaucracy of the People's Republic must be seen against this tradition. Though utterly unprecedented in its total effect, it has ancient foundations to build on. It also faces the age-old problem of how to keep the bureaucrats energetic, efficient, and honest.

Law

In the Western tradition bureaucracy has been tempered by law. Against the tyranny of officialdom the individual has had recourse to legal protection. Our civil liberties rest upon this. But the law in Chinese life has not been similarly developed to protect the individual either in his political rights or in his economic position. The early use of law by the Legalist school of the third century B.C. was as a tool of absolutism to aid in administrative unification. Later the imperial government under the Han continued to use certain Legalist practices, like that of mutual responsibility among family members. Thus the "Confucian state," for all its exaltation of the name and teachings of Confucius, came to incorporate elements of the Legalist tradition as well. This tradition has lingered on and been reasserted from time to time ever since.

Modern students of legal history have only begun to look at the enormous and ramified documentation of Chinese law. The great T'ang code of the eighth century and its successors in the Sung, Yuan, Ming, and Ch'ing periods still invite analysis by Western scholars. It is plain that by any premodern standard the Chinese codes were monuments of their kind. As with so many other aspects of Chinese society, the old legal system was "unmodern" yet in the context of its times we should be slow to call it "backward." Early European observers had been well impressed with Chinese justice. It was only after the eighteenth and nineteenth century reforms of law and punishments in the modern West that China was left behind.

Nevertheless the Chinese concept of law was fundamentally different from legal conceptions in the West. It began with the ancient Chinese idea of the order of nature, the necessity of human actions harmonizing with it, and the ruler's function of maintaining this harmony. Since the ruler swayed the people by his virtuous conduct and moral example, not by law, it was felt that enlightened and civilized persons would be guided by such an example and by the norms of proper conduct without the need of regulations. Punishment was necessary in this theory only for barbarous and uncivilized persons who could not appreciate the teachings of the sages and the ruler's example and so must be intimidated. Rewards and punishments were useful in order to make clear the activities proper to each person according to his status. But they were always considered in theory a secondary means of securing people's right conduct. The object was to "punish only to be able to stop punishing."

Certain generalizations can be attempted about this Chinese legal system. First of all, the law was not regarded as an external and categorical element in society; there was no "higher law" given to mankind through divine revelation. Moses received his golden tablets on a mountain top, but Confucius reasoned from daily life without the aid of any deity. For his rules of propriety, he did not claim any metaphysical sanction. Rather disingenuously, he merely said they came from the moral character of the natural universe itself, from this world, not from another world beyond man's ken. It followed that legal rules were but one expression of this morality—models or examples to be followed, or working rules of administration or ritual observance. So the breaking

十一月　飛雪撲　人面日　暮風又北　寒此時甚　方知己乗白　有功少壯重　繡髮俱豐　衣織婦裏深　閨堂上煖　爐煖氣　融陳餚禮　醉與翁姻無　子號街頭寒　總屬空

The Confucian ethic. Frugal and assiduous householders sip wine by the fire in winter while in the street below the indolent suffer from the cold. (From an eighteenth-century work illustrating the rewards of virtue.)

of such rules was a matter of practical expedience rather than of religious principle. Law was subordinate to morality. Its sanction lay in reason or the common social experience which underlay morals. This avoided the unhappy dualism which grew up in the West between the letter of the law and the dictates of common sense morality.

In practice the Chinese imperial code was chiefly penal, a corrective for the untutored. It was also administrative, and prescribed the details of the rites. In other words, the code was partly accumulated out of administrative decisions. It was nearly all public law, referring to procedures, marriage, inheritance, and other matters relative to and important in government administration. The law occupied a comparatively small share of the public scene. The people avoided litigation in the magistrate's court, where plaintiffs as well as defendants could be interrogated with prescribed forms of torture, and everyone would have to pay fees to the yamen underlings. The magistrates hired personal law secretaries to advise them; aside from these there was no legal profession, no private lawyer class to represent clients. Justice was official, weighted on the side of the state and social order. It operated vertically, from the state upon the individual, more than it did horizontally, to resolve conflicts between one individual and another.

Within its limited sphere, the Ch'ing legal system, as analyzed by Derk Bodde and others, was elaborately organized, and it functioned, once it got into action, with a good deal of exactitude. The five punishments (beating with the light and heavy bamboo, penal servitude, exile, and death) were imposed by a hierarchy of courts running from the county magistrate's yamen up through the prefecture and province to the capital and eventually, for death sentences, to the emperor. Cases were reported to and reviewed by superiors. Appeals could be made. Magistrates were under deadlines to apprehend criminals and could be severely disciplined for wrong judgments.

The great Ch'ing code listed 436 main statutes and about 1900 supplementary or substatutes, which provided specific penalties for specific crimes. The magistrate's problem was to find the statute most applicable to a given case. In doing so he might follow precedent or reason by analogy, but the law was not built up by cases, and although thousands of cases were collected and published with private commentaries to help the magistrates, there was rather little development of generalized doctrine and principles. The statutes were sometimes contradictory and their applicability uncertain. In general, the law was neither primary nor pervasive within the state, and it was felt that to appeal to the letter of the law, like Shylock, was to disregard true morality or to admit the moral weakness of one's case. The law had to be tempered by circumstance in order to achieve justice. Legality was an inferior substitute for morality. As the traditional saying put it, "when a state is about to perish, the regulations increase in number."

One major aim of this legal system was to preserve the Confucian hierarchy of relationships, the social order. Thus penalties for the same act varied according to the social and especially the kinship status of the actors. Filial disobedience was the most heinous crime. A son who merely struck his parent could be decapitated where a parent who beat his son to death, if provoked by the son's disobedience, would deserve only 100 blows (by custom "100" was normally 40 blows) of the heavy bamboo and might be let off entirely. A wife's striking her husband deserved 100 blows, whereas a husband's striking his wife was punishable only if she was badly injured and lodged a complaint. A younger man's scolding his paternal uncle was more heavily punished than his scolding the grandson of his great grandfather's brother. Back of such provisions lay a concern for ritual to maintain social harmony and for punishment as necessary retribution when the social order had been violated. Contributing to the death of one's parent was a capital offense even when quite unintended. T. T. Ch'ü cites a case: "Teng Feng-ta fell while engaged in a fight, his opponent on top of him. The latter picked up a stone and Teng's son fearing that it would be hurled at his father grabbed a knife and made for the attacker. The latter moved and the knife entered Teng's father's belly, killing him. The authorities considered that the son had sought to rescue his father. They presented his case to the emperor and asked that his sentence be reduced from 'dismemberment' to 'immediate beheading.' This was granted."

In short, the law was not an independent specialty, like modern law in America, but part of the functioning of administration in general. Within the broad view of the Confucian philosophy in which the ruling class was educated, the law was a means to be used in the ceaseless struggle to sustain a moral order. Many Chinese officials, in Thomas Metzger's insight, "felt themselves to be poised between harmony and chaos . . . Confucians perceived the society around them as corrupted and in tension with ideals almost beyond the possibility of implementation." But this was a moral problem. They could find no refuge in the mere letter of the law.

Since formal law mainly served the interests of state and society, private law remained underdeveloped in this legal system. Resolution of conflicts among the people was therefore achieved through various nonofficial channels. Conflicts arising from business deals and contracts might be settled within craft or merchant guilds. Disputes between neighbors might be mediated by village elders, neighborhood associations, or gentry members. In particular, the heads of extended family (lineage) or clan organizations, so-called "common descent groups," in addition to maintaining the religious rituals of ancestor reverence, supporting schools for clan members' children, and arranging their marriages, would make every effort to keep their members out of court by assuring their tax payments and settling disputes among them. After all, the legal system was part of the government, which remained superficial, far above the level of daily life in the villages. Most conflicts were therefore resolved extralegally by mediation and appeals to old custom and local opinion.

This nondevelopment of Chinese law along lines familiar to the West was plainly related to the nondevelopment of capitalism and an independent business class in the old China. There was no idea of the corporation as a legal individual. Big firms were family affairs. Business relations were not cold impersonal matters governed by the general principles of the law and of contract in a world apart from home and family. Business was a segment of the whole web of friendship, kinship obligations, and personal relations which supported Chinese life. In old China the law, sanctity of contract, and free private enterprise never became a sacred trinity.

In brief, "the law" in China was an arm of the state and something to avoid—a very different institution from that which has nourished political leadership, guided legislation, trained statesmen, served corporations, and protected individual rights among the legal-minded and litigious American people.

Religion

Another part of China's heritage from her past, which lies behind modern authoritarianism, was the peculiarly passive attitude of the common people toward government, the apparent irresponsibility of the individual citizen toward affairs of state. Sun Yat-sen once complained that his people were like "a heap of loose sand." Many writers during the century of Western contact from the 1840s to the 1940s deplored the selfish opportunism, competitive jealousy, and disregard for others which they discerned in individual conduct outside the bonds of family, clan, and personal relations. It was a perennially fascinating paradox—this contrast, to the Western way of thinking, between loyalty to family and friends and disregard of the public interest, between the most meticulous sense of responsibility when responsibility was customarily expected and clearly undertaken, and a callous irresponsibility regarding the suffering of strangers or public evils that concerned no one in particular.

Obviously this less than ideal conduct sprang partly from the fact that the Chinese family outweighed the community both as an object of loyalty and a source of benefits, particularly during a dynastic interregnum when the government itself did not command popular loyalty or at least respect. But the secret of the paradox undoubtedly lies also in the passive and individualistic aspects of China's religions. This passivity complements, and also conduces to, authoritarian government. To understand it we should look briefly at the religious alternatives to the Confucian doctrine.

Taoism. Taoism (*tao* means "the path," "the way") expressed the common people's naturalistic cosmology and belief in the unseen spirits of nature. It also provided an escape from Confucianism, profiting by each revulsion of scholars against the overnice ritualism and detailed prescriptions of the classics. It was a refuge from the world of affairs. It is aptly said that the Chinese scholar was a Confucian when in office and a Taoist when out of office.

Traditionally Taoism stemmed from Lao-tzu (lit., "The Old Master") who was claimed by his followers to have been an elder contemporary of Confucius. The school of thought ascribed to him became a repository for a variety of beliefs and practices which Confucianism had refused, including early popular animism, alchemy, ancient magic, the search for the elixir of immortality and the Isles of the Blest, early Chinese medicine, and mysticism generally, both native and imported from India. Finally the Taoist church as an organization in China was influenced profoundly by Buddhism.

In general the Taoist philosophical writers who followed the brilliant literary example of Chuang-tzu (fl. 339–329 B.C.) raised their doubting questions from what we would now call a relativistic point of view. It was Chuang-tzu who delighted succeeding generations by writing that he had dreamed that he was a butterfly playing in the sunshine and after he awoke he could not be sure whether he was still Chuang-tzu who had dreamed that he was a butterfly, or actually a butterfly dreaming that it was the philosopher Chuang-tzu. The early Taoists were bright people. Applying the idea of the unity of opposites, they argued that human moral ideas are the reflection of human depravity, that the idea of filial piety springs from the fact of impiety, that the Confucian statement of the rules of propriety is really a reflection of the world's moral disorder. Following this line of thought, the typical Taoist took refuge in a philosophy of passivity expressed in the term *wu-wei*, meaning "action by inaction" or "effortlessness." This took the form of laissez-faire, of following one's unrationalized inner nature and accepting without struggle the experience of life. This was plainly the philosophy of those who condemned government meddling and moral crusading and who sought to be resigned to the burdens of life, since they could not be avoided. The famous "Seven Sages of the Bamboo Grove" got a great reputation for bibulous irresponsibility in pursuit of the elixir of life and a good time. One practical Taoist contribution came from their protoscientific experiments. Their search for elixirs and herbs built up the great Chinese pharmacopoeia, on which the world is still drawing, and also contributed to the technology of porcelain, dyes, alloys, and other Chinese inventions like the compass and gunpowder.

The Taoist church, as distinct from the philosophers, reached the masses with an imposing pantheon and many sects but failed to build up a worldly organization or appeal to the literati. Monasteries and temples remained disconnected units, catering to popular superstition. By its nature Taoism could not become a vigorous organized force in Chinese politics. It expressed an alternative to Confucianism but left the field of practical action to the Confucians.

Buddhism. The Buddhist element in Chinese life is difficult for Westerners to assess because of our ignorance of Buddhism. Its influence in setting the tone of oriental life is familiar to us through Buddhist art, but its ideas are little studied.

In retrospect we can see that the Buddhist age in China, roughly from the fourth to the ninth centuries after Christ, when a foreign religion from India with a new system of values and institutions became dominant in Chinese life, is the chief prototype of the modern invasion of China by the West. What example does China's experience of this foreign religion set before us? Neither Christianity nor Marxism form exact parallels. Yet China's acceptance of foreign faiths today has overtones of the past. Religious enthusiasm among Chinese rebel movements is an ancient thing. In the case of Buddhism the new faith was taken up first by the barbarian invaders who were entering China from the north. But it was never a political tool of a foreign power.

To understand the appeal of Buddhism in China, we must note its major conceptions. One of the most ancient tenets of Buddhism is that life is painful and that it is not limited to the mortal span with which we are familiar; this is the concept of transmigration.

The Buddha, who lived probably during the sixth century B.C. in Nepal, was born of a noble family and began life as an aristocrat. After renouncing his palace and its harem and luxuries he achieved through meditation an illumination in which he realized the great principle of the wheel of the law or the wheel of the Buddha.

This may be defined as a theory of the "dependent origination" of life: that everything is conditioned by something else in a closed sequence, so that in effect the misery of life is dependent upon certain conditions, and by eliminating these conditions it is possible to eliminate the misery itself. Thus desire originates in dependence upon sensation, which in turn originates in dependence upon contact and the six senses, and so on. The Buddhist objective therefore becomes to cut the chain of conditions which bind one into this sequence of passions, desires, and attachments. From this premise that misery is conditioned and that the conditions can be destroyed, the early Buddhists developed many theories.

One central idea of peculiar interest today is that of the dharmas. This is actually a theory of elements or atoms, according to which an entity does not exist in itself but is made up of its parts. The old Buddhist monks believed that man himself is composed merely of these many parts or dharmas; he has no personality, soul, or self. The dharmas are of several types. Some relate to form and substance, others to sensation, and others to mental activity. Taken together they make a very neat explanation of experience and form a basis for the denial of the existence of self. This is just what the Buddhist sought, as a way of escaping life's misery. Since all the elements of experience could be analyzed to be disparate, unconnected, and atomic, both in space and in time, it was held that a proper realization of this truth could lead to elimination of the self and a release from the wheel of the law. This sort of escape or enlightenment, as you prefer, has been sought by mystics the world over and was eagerly pursued in medieval China.

Early Buddhism was institutionalized in a monastic order that developed its rule on lines which may be compared and contrasted with the monasticism of Christianity at a later date. By these early Buddhist monks the sutras (traditional sermons and teachings of the Buddha) were finally written down.

By the time of its expansion from North India to the Far East the Buddhist school of the Mahayana (the "greater vehicle") had wrought profound changes in the ancient doctrines and made them more likely to appeal to the masses of the population. One of these developments was the idea of salvation, which became possible through the intercession of the bodhisattva (or "enlightened ones") who had attained to the enlightenment of the Buddha but continued their existence in this world in order to rescue others. Probably the most famous of these deities has been the so-called Chinese Goddess of Mercy or Kuan-yin, who is an abstraction of the principle of compassion. Another is the Buddha of Endless Light, Amitabha (in Chinese, O-mi-t'o-fo). Salvation of others through the efforts of these enlightened ones was made possible on the theory that merit could be transferred. Along with this went the concept of charity, which supplemented the original Buddhist faith and has made it in China and Japan a more positive social force.

The Mahayana school also developed a positive doctrine of nirvana, the state which it was the object of Buddhist effort to attain but which the Buddha himself had regarded as so completely indescribable that he had said nothing about it.

The Buddhist teachings were set forth in the great Buddhist canon or tripitaka. Translation of sutras from this can-

Buddhist sculpture. Stone bas-relief of the empress as a donor with attendants, from the Lung-men rock temples (near Loyang) of the Northern Wei Dynasty (about 522 A.D.).

on became the chief work of the first Buddhist monks in China. They and their followers faced enormously complex linguistic as well as intellectual problems—how to translate from Sanskrit, which was polysyllabic, highly inflected, and alphabetic like English and other Indo-European languages, into the monosyllabic, uninflected, ideographic script of China; how to convey, in that rather terse and concrete medium, the highly imaginative and metaphysical abstractions of Indian mysticism.

In attempting to transfer or "translate" their new and alien ideas into terms meaningful for their Chinese audience, the early Buddhist missionaries ran into the problem that has faced all purveyors of foreign ideas in China ever since: how to select certain Chinese terms, written characters already invested with established meanings, and invest them with new significance without letting the foreign ideas be subtly modified, in fact sinified, in the process. For example, the Chinese character *tao* ("the way"), already so much used in Taoism and Confucianism, might be used variously for the Indian dharma or for yoga or for the idea of enlightenment, while *wu-wei*, the "nonaction" of Taoism, was used for nirvana. The result was at least ambiguity, if not some watering down of the original idea.

Abstract ideas from abroad when expressed in Chinese characters could hardly avoid a degree of sinification. In addition, exotic values were resisted. As Arthur Wright remarks, "The relatively high position which Buddhism gave to women and mothers was changed in these early translations. For example, 'Husband supports wife' became 'The husband controls his wife,' and 'The wife comforts the husband' became 'The wife reveres her husband.' "

Barbarian invaders of North China, in the fourth century and after, accepted Buddhism partly because, like themselves, it came from outside the old order which they were taking over. Buddhist priests could be allies in fostering docility among the masses. For the Chinese upper class who had fled to the south, Buddhism also offered an explanation and solace, intellectually sophisticated and aesthetically satisfying, for the collapse of their old society. Emperors and commoners alike sought religious salvation in an age of social disaster. When the rulers of the brief Sui dynasty (589–618) and of the early T'ang (618–907) revived a strong central government, they patronized Buddhism as a state religion. Great works of art, statues and rock-cut temples, have come down from this period. Fruitful comparisons and contrasts can be made between the roles of clergy and monasticism, the growth of sects and relations of church and state, during this age of faith in China and its later counterpart in medieval Europe. Buddhist monasteries, for example, served as hostels for travelers, havens of refuge, and sources of charity. They also became great landowners and assumed quasi-official positions in the administration.

The early period of borrowing and domestication had been followed by one of acceptance and independent growth. The native Buddhism was influenced extensively by Taoism, and influenced it in return. New sects arose in China, catering to Chinese needs. Best known to us today through its influence on Oriental art was the school which sought enlightenment through practices of meditation (called in Chinese Ch'an, or in the Japanese pronunciation, Zen). Perhaps enough has been said to indicate the very complex interaction between such elements as Indian Buddhism, the barbarian invaders, native Taoism, and the eventual growth, flowering, and decay of Chinese Buddhism.

A comparison of Buddhism's role in China with that of Christianity in Europe shows one striking difference on the political plane. After the revival of strong government in the T'ang, under Buddhist influence Confucianism was gradually reinvigorated in the form of Neo-Confucianism. But the imperial bureaucracy eventually sought to bring the Buddhist church under firm control. So little had Buddhism disrupted the political tradition that the government had relatively little difficulty in reducing the economic power of the Buddhist monasteries. The several persecutions of Buddhism culminating in the ninth century were in part a struggle to keep land out of the hands of the church and more easily amenable to taxation. But no struggle between church and state developed in medieval China comparable to that in the West. The church—whether Buddhist or Taoist—was quite unable to achieve independence of the temporal power. Their priesthoods and temples in recent centuries have remained loosely decentralized, dependent on modest local support but without organized lay congregations or any nationwide administration, and passive in matters of politics.

By its persistent proscription of religious organization, Confucianism more easily succeeded in dominating both the field of ethics and one major aspect of religious life, notably the family cult of ancestor reverence. Thus, as C. K. Yang points out, the weakening of Buddhism and Taoism as "institutional" religions was compensated by "diffused" religious activity within secular institutions. Not only did every family lineage and clan conduct ceremonies of reverence or "worship" of its ancestors, so also did guilds and communities toward their patron deities, while officials and gentry performed the cultic rituals of the state. It was quite natural therefore that in modern times China's resistance to Christianity has been not only ideological but also institutional—against any organized church independent of official control.

The preceding pages have stressed certain political and social institutions which on the whole tended toward authoritarian government in traditional China. Since most imperial governments, East and West, have been authoritarian down

Buddhism in the Sung. Polychromed wooden sculpture of the Bodhisattva Kuan-yin.

to recent times, this should be neither a surprise nor a stigma. The pertinent questions today are whether China's political experience can offer inspiration for democracy as well as for dictatorship—assuming that these terms will have to be understood and specifically defined in a Chinese way. Two traditions are pertinent here, one from the scholar literati, one from the peasantry.

Chinese Humanism

Among the educated upper class there was a strong and indeed inspiring tradition that the Confucian scholar had a moral responsibility to speak out against misgovernment. The famous maxim (Buddhist-tinged, to be sure) was handed down from a Sung reformer: "A scholar should be the first to become concerned with the world's troubles and the last to rejoice in its happiness." Scholar-officials in disfavor at the late Ming court were publicly beaten with the bamboo; no laws protected them. Nevertheless those of the Tung-lin ("Eastern forest") Academy in the early seventeenth century inveighed against the misrule of the eunuchs, suffering torture and death accordingly. Chinese history has not lacked heroes who attacked evil in terms of principle—only the principles have been a bit different from our own. If we speak of a Chinese tradition of humanism, we must note the difference in values which sets it apart from our Western tradition.

These different values can be perceived in the rich heritage of China's art and literature. T'ang poetry and Sung landscape painting represent a society which in its day outshone that of Europe, an aesthetic level which the West has not surpassed. But even a superficial glance at the status of the individual in Chinese art and literature will disclose that his place is less prominent than in the West. The Chinese tradition was humanistic, in short, in its concern for man-in-society, in its preoccupation with human relations in this world, especially the problem of conduct.

China's long experience of crowded community and family life produced a body of accepted norms of conduct. The individual had first of all to accept the austerity of a bamboo-and-vegetable (as opposed to our iron-and-meat) standard of material wealth. This fostered in him the virtue of frugality. As in most peasant societies, he esteemed personal honesty, industry, and thrift. He also accepted the Buddhist virtue of contentment with little and limitation of wants. The old saw ran, "Acknowledgment of limits leads to happiness." Chinese life was marked, finally, by a special concern for propriety. The individual acknowledged the strength of social conventions and subordinated himself to them. He paid special respect to the old, he revered past generations, he yielded to family. In all these social forms there was a heavy discipline.

The Chinese type of humanism included a concern for the dignity of the individual, but from a social point of view. "Face" has been a social matter. Personal dignity has been derived from right conduct and the social approval it has secured. "Loss of face" came from failure to observe the rules of conduct so that others saw one at a disadvantage. Personal worth was not considered innate within each human soul, as in the West, but had to be acquired. Chinese humanism recognized that some persons had more gifts than others—human beings, though by nature good, were not equal in their capacities; there was no theory that each had an immortal soul.

On the contrary, right conduct was attuned to a hierarchic society in which some people dominated others because of their status. The center of Confucian moral life, *jen* or "benevolent love," was a distinctly un-Christian though logical doctrine which called for loving others in a graded fashion, beginning with one's own father, family, and friends. Chinese humanism, indeed, was something of an upper-class luxury. The niceties of right conduct in social relations were less to be expected from the unlettered.

All this meant that the acts of a person were to be judged mainly by their contribution to social welfare and stability. The individual as such was not exalted. He was neither unique, immortal, nor the center of the universe. The proper study of mankind was mankind. Emphasis upon individual self-expression tended too often toward license and anarchy, and so the Chinese tradition emphasized social conduct. Compromise and tolerance, perspective and sense of humor, wisdom concerning human nature, character achieved through self-discipline, were all parts of a structure of goals and sanctions which gave each individual his motivation within his community.

Certainly this code may be called humanistic, in its concern for human affairs, yet it fostered paternalism in government and permitted a high degree of authoritarianism. The official's task was to manipulate the people, not to represent them. The emperor and his officials had sweeping prerogatives over the goods and persons of the economy. They created at will state monopolies of salt and iron, controlled production or distribution of various goods, conscripted labor gangs and soldiery on a vast and merciless scale, forbade social gatherings and all unlicensed organizations, and generally ruled without fear of any higher law. Yet this absolutism was tempered by an all-pervading concern with human relations and social stability. In spite of the theories and devices of autocracy, the Chinese tradition distinctly did not put the state above mankind. It was not *étatisme*. But the main reason for this, less a matter of theory than of circumstance, was that the government and ruling class remained superficial, merely the top layer of the whole society. They had always to remember that "Heaven sees as the people see." Meanwhile another political tradition survived among the masses, not of paternal manipulation but of violent rebellion.

Folk Sects and Peasant Rebellion

Modern studies in China and abroad are just beginning to penetrate the vast ocean of the Chinese people's religious experience below the level of the Confucian ruling class who left the written record of it. This is the area that today's Marxist ruling class contemns as "popular superstitions," a truly bewildering variety of beliefs and practices, the more various because so locally fragmented, by which villagers through faith and ritual sought meaning and security amid life's uncertainties. Peasant religion as part of China's popular culture of course was much influenced by the higher culture. For example, of the three main types of supernatural spirits, as Arthur Wolf points out, *ancestors* were everyone's concern; the local *gods* of many kinds had all the characteristics of "supernatural counterparts of the imperial bureaucracy," managing their affairs in a hierarchy of duties and proper procedures; while the *ghosts* were supernatural equivalents of misfits, wanderers and strangers, usually dangerous, often malicious.

The popular sects might borrow Taoist, Manichaean (good versus evil, light versus darkness) or Buddhist beliefs or make a syncretic mixture of them, but they usually featured a shamanistic leadership of inspired masters in touch with the spirit world who foretold that a great disaster and judgment day would come, a "chiliastic" or "millenarian" idea (by analogy to the medieval belief in the second coming of Christ after 1000 years). In this future cataclysm only the sect believer would attain salvation and rebirth. Meantime he enjoyed membership in a special in-group community.

These folk religions can be studied both for their valid

religious beliefs and for their social significance as escapism, protest, or sometimes rebellion. The Buddhist sects studied by Daniel Overmyer, for example, were intent on salvation, typically through the messianic advent of the Maitreya or Buddha of the Future. Some sects were open voluntary associations and made no attempt at secrecy, quite different from secret societies. While they usually accepted state authority, they typically countered the hierarchic social order of Confucianism by a strong egalitarianism. Within a sect, women might be leaders of men, and youth of age. Unlike the illegal secret societies such as the Triads and its offshoots, who were anti-dynastic but had rather orthodox ideas of social order, the illegal religious sects were generally heterodox, with wild ideas of social leveling, destructive and anarchic.

When times grew hard, a popular faith with leaders from the bottom fringes of the upper class might produce the fanaticism to mobilize violent rebellion. Since Chinese history had seen this many times, officials and gentry regularly proscribed heterodox sects. When lying low under persecution, the teaching might be transmitted orally and secretly from master to disciple, impossible to eradicate. Moreover, sects proliferated in great variety: in the modern era the Great Way of Former Heaven, the Way of Pervading Unity, the Heavenly Principle Sect, the Eight Trigrams, all had a common tincture as scattered groups of believers in a common religion, "normally diffuse, potentially cohesive" as Susan Naquin puts it. She has traced the process of mobilization by which leaders of the Eight Trigrams Sect, millenarian believers in the White Lotus cult of the Eternal Mother, plotted a North China revolt in 1813 that even invaded the Forbidden City for a few hours. Utilizing the generally illiterate members of a fragmented religious cult for armed uprising was not easy. Such a movement, to succeed, had to create or join with a military force (see Chapter 7).

The Political Tradition

Recent decades have seen a collapse and transformation of China's ancient polity. But in looking at the advent of nationalism, liberal democracy, Marxism, and other dynamic elements of a worldwide civilization, we should not forget the still largely unexplored resources of the Chinese people's own experience. The Chinese tradition is rich and various. Tomorrow other elements may emerge from it.

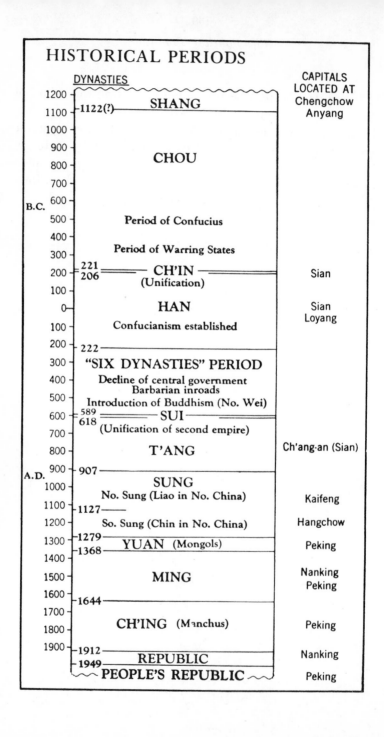

HISTORICAL PERIODS

DYNASTIES	CAPITALS LOCATED AT

1200		Chengchow
1100	1122(?) SHANG	Anyang
1000		
900	CHOU	
800		
700		
B.C. 600		
500	Period of Confucius	
400		
300	Period of Warring States	
221	CH'IN	Sian
200 206	(Unification)	
100		
0	HAN	Sian
100	Confucianism established	Loyang
200 222		
300	"SIX DYNASTIES" PERIOD	
400	Decline of central government Barbarian inroads	
500	Introduction of Buddhism (No. Wei)	
600 589	SUI	
618	(Unification of second empire)	
700		
800	T'ANG	Ch'ang-an (Sian)
A.D. 900 907		
1000	SUNG	
No. Sung (Liao in No. China)	Kaifeng	
1100 1127		
1200	So. Sung (Chin in No. China)	Hangchow
1300 1279	YUAN (Mongols)	Peking
1368		
1400		
1500	MING	Nanking Peking
1600		
1644		
1700		
1800	CH'ING (Manchus)	Peking
1900		
1912	REPUBLIC	Nanking
1949		
PEOPLE'S REPUBLIC	Peking	

Part Two
The Revolutionary Process

Chapter 6

The Western Invasion

Powerful invaders were nothing new to the Middle Kingdom in the nineteenth century. The unprecedented novelty of the Western invaders was their technological superiority, for it constituted a claim to institutional and cultural superiority also. A people who had regarded themselves during four millennia as the originators of material culture and the center of civilization, could not acknowledge this Western claim. Yet the invading British devoted themselves throughout the Victorian era to asserting their superiority worldwide. Progress in all its forms seemed to be on their side. As the record steadily accumulated against China, her ruling class suffered a profound demoralization.

The Western impact of the 1840s and 1850s was a stunning blow. To the next generation, however, from the 1860s through the 1890s, the West became a model to imitate, the better to strengthen China to deal with the West. Finally, in the twentieth century the West has been an inspiration for China's three revolutions, Republican, Nationalist, and Communist. Clearly its "impact," whether blow, model, or inspiration, has been both varied and changing.

Indeed, "the West" includes even more variety and complexity than our pet generality "China." Since 1840 the West has gone through revolutionary changes as profound as those

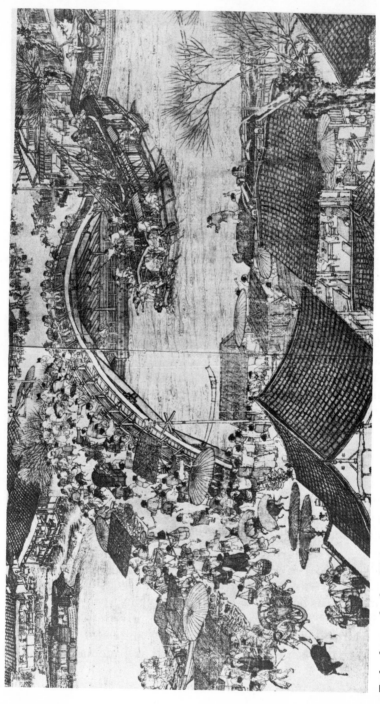

Technology and urban life in the Sung. At the Northern Sung capital boatmen lower their mast to pass under the cantilevered beams of a bridge. (From the long scroll painting "Going up the River at the Spring Festival," ca. 1125.)

in China. Neither the West nor its impact has been a single, simple thing. Why even speak of the multiform impact of a multifaceted West? Why be so simplistic?

Yet one basic fact remains: the West was the homeland and inventor of the technological and other kinds of progress that convulsed the globe in the nineteenth and twentieth centuries. The West could therefore modernize from within its own civilization, one nation learning from another—and the peripheral giants, America and Russia, learning from them all—without shame or self-doubt. China, however, given her own distinctive tradition, had to modernize from without. Steamships and railways came in foreign hands. The center of modern innovation was obviously outside China. All things Western came by sea and to Chinese recipients were indiscriminately "foreign" (*yang*, "oceanic," "from overseas"). Thus the ordinary friction match was called foreign fire; kerosene, foreign oil; cement, foreign mortar; rifles, foreign guns; galvanized iron, foreign iron. Modern man in China could never forget the West, and since his civilization had consciously developed on the basis of its own central superiority, he could never overlook the self-confident Western claims to Western superiority. China's sense of identity could hardly be impaired, but her self-confidence could be severely shaken. In this rather general, pervasive sense there certainly was a Western impact. Similarly China's "response" to the West was also an enormous fact, a mixture of many processes, complex and interacting.

Perhaps the best starting point is to note how the beginnings of Sino-Western contact have cast long shadows over later events. The American role in China has had exotic nuances which came not from American life but from the precedents established by our European predecessors in the East. Sino-American relations developed within the shadow of older Sino-European relations.

European versus Chinese Expansion

The expansion of Europe which brought Western civilization into direct contact with China can be described in general terms under the headings of capitalism, nationalism, and Christianity. These headings may serve to remind us of the characteristics of Western society. The growth of capitalism can be traced from the time when the crusades aided in the revival of trade between Western Europe and the Eastern Mediterranean through waters which had been closed off by Arab domination. This revival was accompanied by the development of commercial techniques and eventually the rise of towns with their urban classes, stimulation of industrial production, the accumulation of investment capital and its use through new techniques of banking and finance. This economic development during the later Middle Ages was paralleled by the gradual rise of the national states.

Except by hindsight it cannot be said that either of these phenomena, capitalism or nationalism, was inevitable. Neither of them followed patterns that were familiar to the ancient world. Older societies, for example, had been organized in city states or else in universal empires. The nation state was something new. It appears to have had many roots—in the self-consciousness and the kingship institution of the Germanic tribes, in the economic needs of new enterprises growing beyond the limits of the city-state type of economy, in the growth of representative institutions as a means of bringing people into larger political groupings than had been possible in the direct assemblies of the ancient world.

Once the national states for these and other reasons had become self-conscious units, the rivalry and warfare among them encouraged economic expansion and technological innovation. Capitalism and nationalism, which are of course no more than convenient overall abstractions for descriptive purposes, thus appear to have interacted upon each other as aspects of a single expansive process. In doing so they stimulated learning, science, and invention. None of these developments had equal counterparts in China.

The expansive energy of Christian evangelism, particularly that of the Jesuits and other orders in the time of the Counter Reformation, may no doubt be compared more easily with Chinese experience in the time of the Buddhist expansion. But the crusading zeal of the Spanish and Portuguese against the infidel Moors in Spain and later overseas represents a type of religious enthusiasm foreign to the Confucian mind. Taken with the other factors mentioned above, the proselytizing energy of early modern Europe came from a social growth quite different in its nature and processes from the traditional society of China.

The West approached China through the medium of China's foreign trade. The sixteenth-century Portuguese and the seventeenth-century Dutch and British adventurers and merchants who opened the China trade discovered unknown regions, just as their contemporaries were opening up the New World. The all important difference was that East Asia, far from being a virgin continent, was already the center of an enormous and ramified commercial life of its own. The early Western ventures were but small increments in channels of commerce already centuries old. It is a striking fact that British trade was opened at Canton in 1637, within a very few years of the founding of New England. Yet British trade with China was not able to expand outside Canton until the nineteenth century, when New England had long since become part of a new nation ready itself to aid in expanding the Canton trade.

The contrast between European expansion in America and its retardation in China must be understood from the Asian as well as the European side. It was not solely that European expansionist hopes and rivalries became more easily focused upon the wide open opportunities of the New World. The very size and richness of the Far Eastern empires, China and Japan, made them at first too strong to coerce, too sophisticated and too self-sufficient to best in trade.

The Arab Role. Except for brief intervals the trade between medieval China and the West down to the modern period was mediated through the Arabs. It is not always remembered that the Arab expansion of the seventh and eighth centuries across North Africa and into Spain, which made the Mediterranean a "Muslim lake," was paralleled by a similar expansion to the east. The battle of Tours (732) at which the Arabs were turned back in France may be compared with the battle of Talas (751), at which Arab forces in Central Asia north of the Pamirs defeated a Chinese army of the T'ang dynasty. The spread of Islam into Chinese Turkestan, and the accession of Muslim dynasties in India in the twelfth century and later, were part of a continuing expansion toward the east which carried Arab merchants all the way to China and eventually set up Muslim sultanates on the Malay Peninsula and the islands of Indonesia. The Indian Ocean in late medieval times became equally a "Muslim lake," in which the spice trade from the East Indies to the Levant formed but one of the staples. China was a participant in this Arab trading world.

The Chinese records show early "tribute missions," by which we may understand traders, arriving from the Roman East in the Han period, but refer only vaguely to Chinese trading expeditions to the south or west. Chinese ships no doubt reached India, perhaps even Arabia, by the fifth century, and by 756 Islamic Arab traders were present at Canton in numbers sufficient to burn and loot the city. When the Sung dynasty in the twelfth century was forced by the barbarian invasions to withdraw to South China, there was an increased concern for the maritime trade, which already had a history of a thousand years and yet had not to that time become a major focus of Chinese energies. Under the Sung, trade was already confined to certain ports and foreign traders to a certain quarter of the city. Sung ceramics, whether carried by Chinese or Arab ships, are found throughout the Middle East and far down the east coast of Africa. In the Mongol era, Khubilai Khan, asserting his claim to rule all mankind, sent a dozen missions to Southeast Asia to secure the vassalage of the native rulers. While these costly efforts led to no permanent results for the Mongols, they acknowledged the existence of a well-established Chinese trade. This commercial background makes sense of the otherwise startling and inexplicable Ming expeditions into and across the Indian Ocean in the early fifteenth century.

The Ming Explorations. These amazing expeditions between 1405 and 1433 took Chinese ships to India, the Persian Gulf, and the East African coast almost a century before the more famous Portuguese navigators reached those places by sea around Africa. China's precedence over Europe at that time in naval architecture, navigation (the magnetic compass had been a Chinese invention), and the nautical arts in general was clearly demonstrated. But it is quite plain that this achievement had little significance in the Chinese scheme of things. Perhaps there is no more telling point of contrast between the China and Europe of the fifteenth century than their respective attitudes toward maritime exploration.

The Ming expeditions were under the superintendency of the chief court eunuch of the time, a Muslim named Cheng Ho, who acted for the court, not the government bureaucracy. There were seven separate ventures. The first in 1405 was composed of sixty-two ships carrying 28,000 men. The fourth voyage in 1413–1415 sent ships as far west as the terminus of navigation in the Persian Gulf and to Aden. Seven Chinese reached Mecca. Chinese vessels touched the coast of Africa as well as Arabia. So-called tribute missions came to China from these places—from Bengal eleven times in this period and from a score of other states. The King of Malacca came to the Chinese court four times in person.

The motive of the Ming court in supporting these vast undertakings is by no means clear. It is true that the eunuchs were able to use the tribute missions and strange gifts from faraway potentates as a means of flattery and ingratiation at court. Elephants and ostriches, strange products and stranger tales could be used to gain imperial favor. Giraffes brought from Arabia were touted as unicorns—in Chinese mythology a symbol of imperial virtue and an occasion for flowery congratulations to the ruler.

A traditional Chinese explanation of these voyages, that they were intended to seek out a deposed emperor who still claimed the throne, hardly seems like the full story. Perhaps their motivation was a combination of political and commercial interests: their political sanction lay in the desire of the Ming court to perfect its claim to rule all men by bringing the maritime trading nations of the world into the traditional suzerain-vassal relationship which was demanded by Confucian theory as an alternative to the direct rule of the Son of Heaven. Ming suzerainty was vigorously asserted over the tribes of Central Asia in the early fifteenth century. The Cheng Ho expeditions seem to have been equally an effort to assert Chinese suzerainty over rulers accessible by sea.

The comparison between these Ming expeditions through the Indian Ocean and the contemporary Portuguese expeditions down the coast of Africa is both spectacular and instructive. Portuguese exploration of the African coast had begun as early as 1270. From 1418 Prince Henry the Navigator sent out expeditions almost every year. But Cape Verde was not reached until 1445, by which time the Ming court had already ceased its activity. In size the Chinese fleets were much larger than the Portuguese and were undoubtedly comparable if not superior in technical abilities of seamanship. Yet the Chinese fleets, for all their competence, lacked any incentive to reach Europe around Africa or even to establish trading posts. The similar capabilities of the Chinese and Portuguese voyagers make the contrast between their motivations all the greater. The Chinese simply lacked the expansive urge which the Europeans had, and this fact made all the difference. Strategically, the Ming court was obliged to face a recrudescent Mongol threat and ward off repeated invasions of the northern frontier. Maritime expeditions were no help against the Mongols. But the main point demonstrated by the Ming voyages and their cessation fifty years before Vasco da Gama was China's self-sufficiency.

Early Maritime Contact. After the Portuguese entered the channels of China's maritime commerce, from 1514, they began a process of trade and evangelism which was to culminate three centuries later in the unequal treaty system of our own day. The chief focus of the new Sino-European relationship was trade. The Portuguese carried the silks of China to Japan as well as the spices of the Indies to Europe. Their commercial empire was built on a far-flung network of fortified trading posts, in India, at Malacca, at Nagasaki, and after 1557 at Macao near Canton. Development of bigger ships and guns and of skill in navigating by compass, astrolabe, and written sailing directions gave the Portuguese their century of supremacy in the eastern seas. They were eclipsed in the seventeenth century by the Dutch and British, whose East India Companies were better organized and financed, but a similar network of trading posts continued to facilitate European penetration of the Far East. Each outpost contained the seeds of empire—claims to national sovereignty, zeal for Christian evangelism, demands for Western legal practices, plus fluid capital funds, and superior military technology—all planted on Oriental shores and ready to sprout when conditions permitted.

The Spanish from Manila and the Dutch from Batavia soon expanded over the adjacent territories to create colonial domains. But Japan and China, under new centralized regimes in the seventeenth century, were able to keep the Europeans quarantined for the time being at designated ports like Nagasaki, Macao, and Canton, which became the predecessors of the nineteenth-century treaty ports.

The striking contrast between the Japanese and Chinese responses to Western contact was one of timing as well as degree: Japan reacted more rapidly and extremely, though China eventually followed a somewhat similar pattern. Within forty years after the first Portuguese reached Japan in 1542, the Jesuits had seventy-five priests at work there and some 150,000 converts. After a century, however, by 1640, Japan was closed to Western intercourse and Christianity was proscribed. In China the process went more slowly. St. Francis Xavier, one of the founders of the Jesuit order, had entered Japan in 1549 but he died off the coast of China in 1552. During the next two centuries he was followed in the effort to Christianize China by some 463 selected and highly trained evangelists whose devotion and pertinacity have seldom been surpassed. The great Jesuit pioneer Matteo Ricci (1552–1610) took twenty years to work his way step by step from the Portuguese community at Macao to the court at Peking.

The Jesuit Success. The Jesuits came to China opportunely, when late Ming society was in disarray and bright minds craved new ideas, even from abroad. Ricci quickly saw how to make his way into the scholar-official elite. He gave up his original Buddhist monk's costume for a scholar's gown. He gave up preaching in a chapel and held conversations with small, select groups. He accepted the early classics of Han Confucianism, quoting them for Christian purposes, and disputed only the more systematic tenets of Sung Neo-Confucianism. He permitted reverential kowtows to one's ancestors or the emperor as secular rites compatible with Christian faith. All this cultural accommodation, combined with his own impressive personality, his command of Chinese, and a display of Western technology—a clock, prisms, a map of the world, Euclidean geometry—won him acceptance. Like a Chinese scholar, he found patrons among the officials, living and traveling in their entourages. He and his colleagues established friendships, based on the art of learned discourse and polite etiquette, with several high officials of the late Ming, including some in the Tung-lin Academy group of moral reformers. In the end Ricci had an imperial stipend at Peking and was buried in a plot granted by the emperor.

His successors served as Chinese officials heading the astronomical bureau in charge of the imperial calendar under both the late Ming and the early Ch'ing. Indeed they were the first technical experts from the West, retained by the Manchu rulers as useful courtiers who could map the empire or build fountains for the Summer Palace in imitation of Versailles. Several hundred Jesuit publications in classical Chinese made available much of the scientific learning of Europe, while representing Christianity as a system of wisdom and ethics compatible with Confucius' original teaching.

After functioning at Peking for more than a hundred years, interpreting China to Europe and Europe to China, the Jesuits were undone by the Rites Controversy, a long altercation in which the rival Dominican and Franciscan friars, coming to China from their success in far different circumstances in the Philippines, accused the Jesuits of a permissiveness that flouted the positive laws of the Church. When the Pope supported this attack, the great K'ang-hsi Emperor supported his courtiers the Jesuits. Between two such potentates, each superior to the other, no compromise was possible. K'ang-hsi's successor proscribed Christianity as a heterodox subversion. Eventually the Pope suppressed the Jesuit order.

Through this early contact the elite of Chinese scholarship at Peking had been made acquainted with the best of Western learning. With what result? One of the greatest seventeenth century literati (Ku Yen-wu) could only repeat the old wives' tale recorded in the official Ming History: "Portugal is south of Java . . . She sent an envoy for the purpose of buying small children to cook and eat." The imperial encyclopedia of 1747 called Ricci a liar: "His description of the five continents is nothing more than a wild fabulous story." After all, Cheng Ho's ships had sailed west seven times in the Ming dynasty and never come across Italy, Portugal, or Europe. The early knowledge of the West in China had little influence, and although trade continued, it was kept under control at Canton, on the southern edge of the empire.

Meanwhile the early Russian contact by land across Siberia was slower to develop, though in the end more permanent. Cossack bands penetrated North Manchuria in the middle of the seventeenth century, but the power they could muster there, across the barren continental reaches of Siberia, could not yet compare with that of European warships on the China coast. After the treaty of Nerchinsk in 1689 the Manchus obliged the Russians to remain outside the Amur watershed for a century and a half. A trade treaty in 1728 let Russia maintain a nondiplomatic ecclesiastical mission—a few priests and language students—at Peking, while her traders were kept tightly controlled at Kiakhta, an emporium far off on the Siberian border of Mongolia, a cold counterpart to Canton on the southern seacoast of the empire. Thus Russian commercial relations were controlled like those of all other foreigners, but from the first the Russian political contact by land was different from that of the Europeans by sea. Russia gradually became a territorial neighbor, like the Mongol tribes of Inner Asia, but more distant.

China's Impact on Europe

Europe was the aggressor in opening relations with China. The impact of the new relations was therefore felt first in Europe. This is really no paradox, for the responsiveness to stimuli which led Europeans overseas made them sensitive to what they found there. Until a century and a half ago, China played a greater part in Western life than the West did in China. American understanding of Chinese society today is still colored and a bit befuddled by this inheritance from our own past.

The Europeans' discovery of Asia by sea in the sixteenth and seventeenth centuries revolutionized their view of the world. Before the great sea voyages, and except for the brief contact with Cathay in the time of Marco Polo, the only other contemporary society known to Europe had been that of the Muslims and Turks, the infidel on the border of the known world against whom medieval Christendom had struggled. Even in the sixteenth century in Europe there were still more books published on the Turks than on the New World. But the discovery of mighty kingdoms and ancient societies in Asia which were non-Christian and had actually survived for centuries without benefit of Christianity eventually had a profound effect on Western thought.

The implication of these new facts was fully developed only in the eighteenth-century Enlightenment. In it the conflict between natural morality and revealed religion came to a head. And China was taken as evidence to support the argument that the deity could be found through the natural order without revelation. The favorable picture of Cathay so brilliantly sketched by the Jesuit letters of the seventeenth century from Peking tended to show that virtuous conduct, in many ways adequate to Christian standards, could be achieved without revealed religion. This afforded a basis for the separation of morality and religion as sought by the Enlightenment. The translation of the Confucian classics into Latin at Paris in 1687 provided textual evidence. Writers like Leibniz, who had already been profoundly influenced by China, asserted that the Chinese were actually superior in the practical organization of their society and the administration of its affairs, even though Europe remained superior in theoretical studies. For a generation which sought to show how the natural law underlay human institutions even in the absence of religion, China provided a perfect answer. In the China portrayed in the classics, a philosopher-king indeed appeared to be the benevolent father of his people.

Among the writers of the Enlightenment, Voltaire gave enormous prestige to Chinese government by his discussion of it in his *Essay on Morals* published in 1756. He stated that the highest achievement of China was "morality and law." The Chinese officials were benevolent guardians of the people, the whole kingdom a family, and the public weal the first duty of government. As evidence of this he pointed to the Chinese officials' concern for public works, roads, and canals, and other activities fostering economic prosperity. He pointed out that the laws not only punished crime but also recompensed virtue, as when the emperor honored virtuous persons.

The physiocrats in seeking the reform of administration in France and other countries also got inspiration from China. As prophets of the industrial revolution and the rise of the modern middle class, the physiocrats stressed the inviolability of private property. In their reaction against mercantilism they argued that the private individual should be able to accumulate wealth without government supervision. The leader of the physiocrats, Dr. Quesnay, who was known as the "Confucius of the West," published his book *The Despotism of China* in 1767. He argued that the emperor of China, although an absolute monarch, ruled within the framework of natural law. Chinese society approached Quesnay's idea of perfection. There was no hereditary nobility. The son succeeded to the goods of his father but could succeed to his father's dignity only by study and self-improvement. China seemed to him a deistic society which worshiped the Supreme Being. Property rights seemed well assured. Taxes were regulated by the emperor and no lands except temples were exempt. Quesnay did observe that commerce was not sufficiently encouraged and that corruption among the officials and the despotism of the ruler were only partly tempered by fear of rebellion. But on the whole his estimate was favorable and had wide influence.

Eighteenth-century Europe also had a vogue of chinoiserie, the use of Chinese motifs in art, architecture, landscape gardening, ceramics, and other household furnishings such as wallpaper and latticework. Blue-and-white Ming porcelain, both imported and imitated, graced the mansions of the well-to-do. Chippendale furniture and Wedgewood china used Chinese patterns. The Chinese vogue in England reached its height in the ten-story pagoda built in Kew Gardens in 1763.

China's impact on early modern Europe was thus highly selective, mediated through thinkers and craftsmen who found in the example of China certain things that they wanted to find. This set a style that still persists among travelers who take to China, prefabricated, their later impressions of the place.

In the nineteenth century this secondhand idealized view of China held by the Enlightenment was rudely shattered by the maledictions of treaty-port merchants and consuls not interested in philosophy.

The Tribute System

During a full century, from 1842 to 1943, China labored under the handicap of the unequal treaties by which she was opened to Western commercial and religious enterprise. Although the unequal treaty system was finally abolished before the Communist victory, it still meets the need for a focus of patriotic resentment in retrospect. National disasters in the United States, like the Civil War or the Great Depression, have commonly been utilized in the appeals of domestic politics; so the leaders of modern China have found the treaty system a valuable symbol of national humiliation. Chiang Kai-shek, in his book *China's Destiny*, attributed to it all modern China's ills—economic, political, social, psychological, and moral—and the Communist denunciations are even more vigorous and comprehensive.

To understand the one-sidedness and inequality of the unequal treaties which the Western powers imposed upon the Chinese empire, one must look at the ancient tribute system which China first imposed upon Western visitors. This old Chinese system was just as unequal as the treaty system that supplanted it.

The tribute system was an application to foreign affairs of the Confucian doctrines by which Chinese rulers gained an ethical sanction for their exercise of political authority. Just as the virtuous ruler by his moral example had prestige and influence among the people of the Middle Kingdom, so he irresistibly attracted the barbarians who were outside the pale of Chinese culture. To a Confucian scholar it was inconceivable that the rude tribes of the frontier should not appreciate China's cultural superiority and therefore seek the benefits of Chinese civilization. Since the emperor exercised the Mandate of Heaven to rule all mankind, it was his function to be compassionate and generous to all "men from afar." The imperial benevolence should be reciprocated, it was felt, by the humble submission of the foreigner.

Once the foreigner had recognized the unique position of the Son of Heaven it was unavoidable that these reciprocal relations of compassionate benevolence and humble submission should be demonstrated in ritual form, by the ceremonial bestowal of gifts and of tribute respectively. Tribute thus became one of the rites of the Chinese court. It betokened the admission of a barbarian to the civilization of the Middle Kingdom. It was a boon and privilege, and not ignominious. As the original Chinese empire spread its influence through the centuries, over the rest of East Asia, the formalities of tribute relations were developed into a mechanism by which barbarous regions outside the empire might be given their place in the all-embracing sinocentric cosmos.

When Europeans first came to China by sea these formalities were naturally expected of them. According to the collected statutes of the Manchu dynasty, a tributary ruler of a foreign state should receive an imperial patent of appointment which acknowledged his tributary status. There should also be conferred upon him a noble rank and an imperial seal for use in signing his memorials, which should be dated by the Chinese calendar. When his tribute missions came, they should be limited in size to one hundred men, of whom only twenty might proceed to the capital, by the imperial post. At the capital the mission was lodged, carefully protected, and entertained. Eventually it was received in audience by the emperor. This was the time of all others when the tribute envoys performed the kowtow.

Early European envoys, like the unhappy Hollanders who presented tribute at the Manchu court in 1795, were inclined to feel that this calisthenic ceremony more than offset the imperial benevolence which filtered down to them through the sticky hands of the officials who had them in charge. The full kowtow was no mere prostration of the body but a prolonged series of three separate kneelings, each one leading to three successive prostrations, nose upon the floor. The "three kneelings and nine prostrations" left no doubt in anyone's mind, least of all in the performer's, as to who was inferior and who superior. Egalitarian Westerners usually failed to appreciate that this abasement of the individual who kowtowed was a normal aspect of the ceremonial life in a society of status. The emperor kowtowed to Heaven and his parents, the highest grandees kowtowed to the emperor. In a less formal way friends might kowtow to each other, as polite Japanese almost do today. From a tribute bearer it was therefore no more than good manners.

The secret of the tribute system was the fact that it had become a vehicle for trade. The Ming chroniclers, by including the long defunct Roman East, fictitious principalities, and border tribes, had listed more than 120 tributaries. The Manchus put the border tribes under a special office and reduced their list of genuine tributaries to less than a dozen including the still shadowy countries of the "Western Ocean," whose merchants had already appeared at Canton. Because the Manchu empire chiefly sought stability in its foreign relations, it dealt only with neighboring countries or with those who came to China. If foreign merchants came and their ruler wanted to promote their trade, he could present tribute. It was as simple as that.

The trading states of East Asia presented tribute to the Chinese court in order to maintain their trade and friendly relations and were duly enrolled as tributaries. Certain ports and markets were designated for them. Thus tribute and trade from Korea came by land through Shanhaikuan, from the Liu-ch'iu (Ryukyu) Islands through Foochow, from Siam through Canton. When the first Europeans reached Canton, they were similarly enrolled and almost without realizing it became part of China's tributary firmament. Until the nineteenth century the diplomatic missions sent from Western powers to China, although they totaled more than a score, did little or nothing to shatter the Chinese institution of tribute and the conviction of superiority which it signified. It was still possible for the Ch'ien-lung Emperor, in his famous mandate of 1793 to King George III, to compliment the barbarian ruler on his "respectful humility" while at the same time refusing to permit any exchange of diplomatic representatives or expansion of British trade outside Canton.

The Canton System and Its Collapse. The old Canton trade in its heyday (c. 1760–1840) was carried on under a working compromise between the Chinese system of tributary trade and European mercantilism. During the Napoleonic wars one of the great survivors of the mercantilist era, the British East India Company, based on India, beat out its Continental competitors and brought the growing tea exports of Canton into a profitable triangular trade between England, India, and China. Fleets of East Indiamen voyaged annually from London to Canton, where the company by its charter monopolized all British trade and dealt with a comparable monopoly on the Chinese side—a licensed guild of about a dozen firms or "hongs." These Chinese hong merchants were responsible to the imperial officials for the foreign trade and traders. The foreigners in turn were restricted by various regulations which, for example, confined them largely to their factories and kept them outside the walls of Canton. Thus by mutual agreement during most of the eighteenth century, in spite of continual disputes, the old Canton trade proved mutually profitable within the limits imposed by two, Chinese and foreign, systems of trade regulation.

Western expansion, and free trade in particular, disrupted the Canton system after the East India Company lost its monopoly of Britain's China trade in 1833. Unfortunately for the repute of private enterprise in the Orient, it reached the China coast at this time chiefly in the form of the opium trade conducted by private traders. This historical circumstance has poisoned Sino-Western relations ever since.

The opium was supplied mainly by British Indian government manufacture for more than a century down to 1917, surely one of the longest-continued international crimes of modern times. It was carried to China by private British and Indian traders, as well as by Americans who competed as best they could by buying opium in Turkey. The traders usually found Chinese merchants and mandarins eager to flout the emperor's prohibition of smoking and importation. The result until 1858 was an illegal trade—openly connived at by British, American, Chinese, and other merchants and officials—too valuable to the British Indian exchequer to be refrained from, too necessary to the balancing of the tea export trade to be given up by the merchants, and too profitable to them and to venal Chinese officials and distributors to be easily suppressed.

In the retrospect of Chinese patriots today it makes little difference that the opium traffic was a fully bilateral activity, or that its evils hardly exceeded those of the contemporary smuggling of Africans for sale in the United States. In China the opium trade remains a classic symbol of Western commercial imperialism—foreign greed and violence demoralizing and exploiting an inoffensive people. British humanitarians denounced it as such at the time.* A century later we can see it as part of an unavoidable conflict, Western expansion clashing head-on with China's traditional order. Conflict was bound to come. Opium provided the first occasion, though not the last. Similarly, the West was bound to win. (Whether that was a good thing depends on what you think of modern life.)

In the Chinese view, the Western barbarians were outlandish in their physical characteristics, generally uncouth and smelling of mutton fat. In slang they have been called "foreign devils" (*fan-kuei* or *yang-kuei-tzu*), "big noses" (*ta-pi-tzu*), or "hairy ones" (*mao-tzu*). The official history of the Ming had described in some detail the Portuguese method of boiling and eating little Chinese children. Nineteenth-century mission orphanages were thought to make medicine out of children's eyes and hearts. Foreign diplomats seemed to the mandarins wily and inscrutable, unpredictable "as dogs and sheep." Peasant mothers used to shield their babies from a foreigner's unlucky glance and especially the black magic of his camera. All in all, the white peril in nineteenth-century China was a good deal more sinister than the yellow peril of the 1900s in America.

Moreover, since the white barbarians came by ship, the traditional Chinese defensive strategy was completely reversed. The sea now took the place of the steppe. China's frontier was no longer on the Great Wall or at the Jade Gate in Kansu, but at Canton and Shanghai. Age-old conceptions had to be reversed accordingly, but this was not easy.

The Treaty System

The legal structure established by the unequal treaties in

---

* One devout Scottish opium captain noted in his journal on December 2, 1832: "Employed delivering briskly. No time to read my Bible."

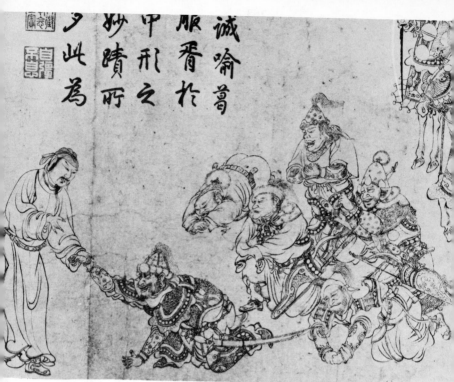

Civilizing the barbarians. Sung painting of a T'ang general (Kuo Tzu-i) making peace with Uighur Turks.

Accommodating the invaders. Ch'ing and foreign officials, Foochow, ca. 1905. The Manchu general Ch'ung-shan is flanked by Japanese, French, and American consuls and the American commissioner of Chinese Maritime Customs.

the period 1842–1860 was forced on China by the two wars fought by the British against the Ch'ing government. The Opium War of 1840–1842 resulted directly from the doughty Commissioner Lin Tse-hsu's vain effort to suppress the drug trade at Canton. Opium was the life-blood of the British invasion. British opium traders helped work out the war aims and strategy, leased vessels to the fleet, lent pilots and translators, provided hospitality and intelligence, and cashed the quartermaster's bills on London. But the British expeditionary force was sent to Canton and thence up the coast to secure privileges of general commercial and diplomatic intercourse on a Western basis of equality, and not especially to aid the expansion of the opium trade. The latter was expanding rapidly of its own accord and was only one point of friction in the general antagonism between the Chinese and British schemes of international relations.

The principles embodied in the Treaty of Nanking in 1842 were not fully accepted on the Chinese side and the treaty privileges seemed inadquate from the British side. Consequently the treaty system was not really established until the British and French had fought a second war and secured treaties at Tientsin in 1858. Even then the new order was not acknowledged by the reluctant dynasty until an Anglo-French expedition had occupied Peking itself in 1860. The transition from tribute relations to treaty relations occupied a generation of friction at Canton before 1840, and twenty years of trade, negotiation, and coercion thereafter.

Although the new treaties were signed as between equal sovereign powers, they were actually quite unequal in that China was placed against her will in a weaker position, open to the inroads of Western commerce and its attendant culture. By the twentieth century, after three generations of energetic Western consuls had developed its fine points, the treaty structure was a finely articulated and comprehensive mecha-

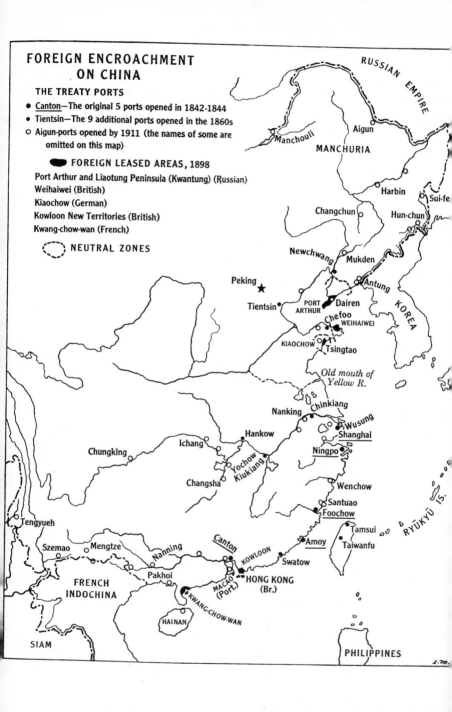

FOREIGN ENCROACHMENT ON CHINA

THE TREATY PORTS

- Canton—The original 5 ports opened in 1842-1844
- Tientsin—The 9 additional ports opened in the 1860s
- Aigun-ports opened by 1911 (the names of some are omitted on this map)

■ **FOREIGN LEASED AREAS, 1898**

Port Arthur and Liaotung Peninsula (Kwantung) (Russian)
Weihaiwei (British)
Kiaochow (German)
Kowloon New Territories (British)
Kwang-chow-wan (French)

⊂⊃ **NEUTRAL ZONES**

RUSSIAN EMPIRE

Manchouli

MANCHURIA

Aigun

Harbin

Sui-fe

Changchun

Hun-chun

Newchwang

Mukden

Peking ★

Antung

Tientsin

PORT ARTHUR

Dairen

KOREA

Chefoo

WEIHAIWEI

KIAOCHOW

Tsingtao

Old mouth of Yellow R.

Chinkiang

Nanking

Wusung

Hankow

Shanghai

Ichang

Ningpo

Chungking

Yochow

Kiukiang

Changsha

Wenchow

Santuao

Foochow

Tengyueh

Tamsui

Szemao

Mengtze

Nanning

Canton

Taiwanfu

KOWLOON

Amoy

Pakhoi

Swatow

FRENCH INDOCHINA

MACAO (Port.)

HONG KONG (Br.)

KWANG-CHOW-WAN

HAINAN

RYŪKYŪ IS.

SIAM

PHILIPPINES

nism. It was based first of all on treaty ports, at first five in number and eventually more than eighty (see map).

The major treaty ports had a striking physical and institutional resemblance to one another. Each had a crowded, noisy bund and godowns (warehouses) swarming with coolies (a foreign word for cheap Chinese laborers) who substituted for machinery, under the supervision of Chinese compradors (business managers), who managed affairs beneath the overlordship of the foreign taipans (firm managers). Each treaty port centered in a foreign section newly built on the edge of a teeming Chinese city and dominated by the tall white flagstaff of Her Majesty's Consulate. Its institutions included the club, the race course, and the church. It was ruled by a proper British consul and his colleagues of other nations and protected by squat gunboats moored off the bund. At Canton, Amoy, Swatow, and Foochow this foreign community got further protection by being established on an island adjacent to the shipping. At Ningpo, Shanghai, and other places the foreign area was separated from the Chinese city by a river, canal, creek, or other waterway.

Extraterritoriality. This legal system, under which foreigners and their activities in China remained amenable only to foreign and not to Chinese law, was not a modern invention. In a manner rather like that of the Turks at Constantinople, the Chinese government in medieval times had expected foreign communities in the seaports to govern themselves under their own headmen and by their own laws. This had been true of the early Arab traders in China. The British and Americans at Canton before the Opium War demanded extraterritoriality because they had become accustomed to the protection of their own laws in their relations with the Muslim states of North Africa and the Ottoman Empire and had suffered from Chinese attempts to apply Chinese criminal

The Revolutionary Process

law to Westerners, without regard for Western rules of evidence or the modern Western abhorrence of torture. But most of all the foreign traders needed the help of their own law of contract.

As applied in the treaty ports, extraterritoriality became a powerful tool for the opening of China because it made foreign merchants and missionaries, their goods and property, and to some extent their Chinese employees, converts, and hangers-on, all immune to Chinese authority. France in particular undertook the protection of Roman Catholic missions and communicants. All this was, to say the least, an impairment of Chinese sovereignty and a great handicap to China's self-defense against Western exploitation. The Japanese, who were saddled with the same system after 1858, made tremendous efforts to get out from under it and did so by the end of the century.

A further essential of the treaties was the treaty tariff, which by its low rates prevented the Chinese from protecting their native industries. Since, for various reasons, the administration of the low treaty tariff was not effective in Chinese hands, a foreign staff was taken into the Chinese customhouse. This Chinese employment of foreigners followed ancient precedents and was one of the most constructive features of the treaty system. Under Sir Robert Hart as Inspector General, the Westerners who served as commissioners of Chinese Maritime Customs became leading figures in every port, guardians both of the equality of competition (by enforcement of the regulations for foreign trade) and of the modest Chinese revenue of about 5 percent derived from it. The growth of trade gave Peking important, because uncommitted, new revenues which could be used for modern needs.

Under the new dispensation of the treaties Western civilization brought to China a rich fare of good and evil. Legalized in 1858, the opium trade supplied 10 or 15 percent of the revenue of British India while the Protestant missionary movement was nourished by the shillings and dimes of devout congregations in the Christian West. Beginning in the 1830s British and American Protestant missionaries found that modern medicine carried more weight in China than the scriptures. Missionary hospitals were soon attempting to repair the ravages of disease, including the effects of opium. In Chinese eyes this was no more anomalous than the general gap between Christian precept and imperialist practice.

By the most-favored-nation clause (the neatest diplomatic device of the century) all foreign powers shared whatever privileges any of them could squeeze out of China. The treaty system kept on growing as the fortunes of the Manchu dynasty deteriorated. The dynasty became increasingly dependent upon British administrative and diplomatic support. During the century of the treaties the Chinese people were consequently subjected to a gradually accelerating, cumulative, and often violent process of change. The opium trade that had begun as a joint sino-foreign traffic was taken into the country. After the 1880s China's native opium production began to supplant the Indian product, importation of which ceased in 1917. From the treaty ports along the coast and up the Yangtze, Western ways as well as goods spread into the interior, aided in the remote centers by zealous evangelists like those of the China Inland Mission. Christianity opened the way for the acceptance of Western values, which upset the old order entirely.

Today this influx of Western goods, ways, and ideas during the treaty century is rather indiscriminately condemned by Chinese patriots in retrospect as simple "imperialism"—military, commercial, financial, or cultural as the case may be. Indeed, all sino-foreign contact of this period almost without exception is now termed "imperialistic," so that the term covers everything and thereby ceases to mean much for analytic purposes. Missionary hospitals, for example, are classed as "cultural imperialism." But this blanket use of "imperialism" to malign even the noblest motives of Western philanthropy may well remind us of one basic fact: the West expanded into China, not China into the West. The foreigners even in their best moments were in this sense aggressive; they were agents of change, and thus destructive of the old order. Americans of today, feeling themselves catapulted forward by technological progress, have no one but their forebears to blame for it; but the Chinese can blame the outside world for having forced modern changes upon them, and for having done it in a certain way. How it was done is thus the question at issue.

The degree of China's victimization and exploitation by the treaty powers is no problem for politicians or true believers, who believe what they prefer, but it will be endlessly debated by historians. The question is so difficult to decide because it involves both objective facts and subjective feelings and neither alone can settle it. A degree of Chinese humiliation can be assumed, though it seems to be greater now in retrospect than it was at the time in fact. But what actually happened under the treaty system?

Here we confront new evidence from researchers in economic history which may alter the picture of China's victimization. This new perspective is derived from work in China, Taiwan, Japan, the United States, and Britain. It stresses the vast size and long-developed maturity of China's domestic trade and the growing power of the merchant class in the Ming and early Ch'ing periods, a power only indirectly acknowledged in the official records. As Rhoads Murphey has pointed out, even Adam Smith could perceive that China's "home market" was as big as that of "all the different countries of Europe put together." The extensive interprovincial trade meant that China was already highly commercialized and, as always, self-sufficient. Lancashire textiles, for example, failed to sweep the Chinese market simply because China's handwoven cotton cloth was a superior and on the whole cheaper product for local purposes. It still supplied most of North China's needs at late as 1930. After all the long struggle to "open" the Chinese market, the chief Western import for Chinese mass consumption turned out to be kerosene—a product more of geological conditions than of Western industrial preeminence. Modern economy when it did develop, mainly in the treaty port sector, was to a large extent in Chinese hands. Chinese compradors of course had long managed nearly all the foreigners' business within China. It now appears that much of the nominally foreign enterprise in the treaty ports was a convenient cover for investment by Chinese entrepreneurs. Meanwhile the honeycomb pattern of the rural market towns and their surrounding villages continued to handle the Chinese people's largely self-sufficient commercial life. The foreigner, his trade goods and investment funds, were unable to compete or have much effect at this level. The great rural sector of the economy ran into crisis conditions for many reasons after 1911 and rescue has been under way only since 1949, but the foreign impact and the treaty ports were only one element in this crisis. This new picture does not fit into the framework of Leninist imperialism, although it rather suits Chairman Mao's anti-urban stress on the self-sufficiency of the Chinese countryside.

The Demographic Disaster

China's ills in the nineteenth and twentieth centuries have been intensified by the unhappy conjunction of two processes: Western invasion and dynastic change. At the same time that Western contact began to undermine the Confucian social order, an accumulation of domestic problems was weakening the government. From the end of the eighteenth century the Manchus, already 150 years upon the throne, had begun to experience all the difficulties which had undone preceding dynasties. In particular, peace and prosperity had brought an unprecedented increase of population, so tremendous as to constitute almost a new type of crisis in itself, with disastrous repercussions on livelihood, administration, and public morale. Today, as Ping-ti Ho puts it, "China's population is a world problem."

The imperial registration of A.D. 2 recorded a population of 59.9 million, concentrated mainly in the Yellow River area with relatively little habitation south of the Yangtze. In the next millennium and a half these figures were hardly exceeded. The Manchu dynasty in 1651 recorded 10 million families or households, each of which was estimated at six persons. But we know that the official population estimates of dynasties erred on the short side. This was because tax payments were due from an administrative area partly according to the estimated population total. This created an incentive for short reporting both by the people and by the authorities responsible for tax payments. There never was a genuine census of the modern type, recording precise data as of a given date on age and sex distribution, marital status, migration, and the other minutiae necessary for scientific analysis. The Chinese figures, on the contrary, resulted from registration and estimation for government purposes, to find out the numbers capable of cultivating land, laboring on public works, bearing arms, or paying taxes. Popular cooperation was not to be expected. Whole categories of persons were omitted. Uniform schedules, accurate maps, trained enumerators, all were lacking. The estimates were often products of bureaucratic ritual. Honan province, for example, during much of the nineteenth century reported an increase of 1000 persons every other year.

One may guess that the Chinese population in Sung times may have been 80 million. Possibly by 1600 it was close to 150 million. From 1741 to the outbreak of the great rebellion in 1851 the annual figures rose steadily and spectacularly, beginning with 143 million and ending with 432 million. If we accept these totals, we are confronted with a situation in which the Chinese population doubled in the fifty years from 1790 to 1840. If, with greater caution, we assume a total of 200 million in the early eighteenth century and only 400 million by 1850, we still face a startling fact: something like a doubling of the vast Chinese population in the century *before* Western contact, foreign trade, and industrialization could have had much effect.

To explain this sudden increase we cannot point to factors constant in Chinese society but must find conditions or a combination of factors newly effective during this period. Among these the most obvious is the almost complete internal peace maintained under Manchu rule during the eighteenth century. There was also an increase in foreign trade through Canton and possibly some improvement of transportation within the empire. But of most critical importance was the food supply.

Confronted with a multitude of unreliable figures, economists have compared the population records with the aggregate data for cultivated land area and grain production in the six centuries since 1368. Assuming that China's population in 1400 was about 80 million, Dwight Perkins concludes that its growth to 700 million or more in the 1960s was made possible by a steady increase of the grain supply, which evidently grew five or six times between 1400 and 1800 and rose another 50 percent between 1800 and today. This increase of food supply was due perhaps half to the increase of cultivated area, particularly by migration and settlement in the central and western provinces, and half to greater productivity, the farmers' success in raising more crops per unit of land. This technological advance took many forms: most important was the continual introduction from the south of earlier ripening varieties of rice, which made possible double-cropping. New crops were also introduced from the Americas such as corn and sweet potatoes as well as peanuts and tobacco. Corn, for instance, can be grown on the dry soil and marginal hill land of North China, where it is used for food, fuel and fodder, and provides something like one seventh of the food energy available in the area. The sweet potato, growing in sandy soil and providing more food energy per unit of land than other crops, became the poor man's food in much of the South China rice area. Productivity in agriculture was also improved by capital investments in irrigation works, farm tools, draft animals, and human fertilizer (nightsoil), to say nothing of the population growth, which increased half again as fast as cultivated land area and so increased the ratio of human hands and of nightsoil available per unit of land. Thus the rising population was fed by a more intensive agriculture, applying more labor and fertilizer to the land.

In this broader perspective, population growth over the last 600 years has averaged only about four tenths of one percent a year, not a rapid rate overall. But the eighteenth- and early nineteenth-century doubling and redoubling of numbers, something like the contemporary European population explosion triggered partly by the spread of the potato, spelled disaster for the Manchu dynasty. As the whole economy grew, the government tax rate failed to keep pace. Trade increased along with the population, but the Ch'ing administration lagged behind. All the devices so astutely contrived by the ruling class over the centuries to maintain social stability (described by K. C. Hsiao) became undermanned and less effective: police control by household registration and mutual responsibility among neighborhood groups, the so-called *pao-*

chia system; the corvée labor service and village tax collections according to registered quotas; famine control by maintaining reserves in official granaries; thought control by having local lecturers expound the emperor's *Sacred Edict* of edifying precepts and by officially honoring virtuous persons and condemning heterodox writings—all were weakened by the administration's failure to keep up with the growth of population and economy. Instead, the massive enlargement of the Chinese body politic was accompanied throughout the nineteenth century by a continual increase of unsolved problems, official corruption, endemic disorder, and widespread demoralization.

This pervasive crisis greatly exacerbated the usual difficulties of dynastic decline, rebellion, and reunification. Pressure of numbers has equally menaced the whole effort at economic modernization. Industrialization elsewhere has generally involved a rapid population increase. But China's population greatly expanded before industrialization. This has set the stage for the most serious population problem of all time.

The People's Republic faces this problem today. The registration of 1953–54, still not a genuine census in our terms, gave a grand and appalling total of 586 million in mainland China. At 2 percent net increase a year, by no means an unlikely rate, the Chinese people were estimated to total roughly 630 million by 1957, 820 million by 1970, and 880 million by 1974. Even if the growth rate should drop to 1.5 or even 1.0 per cent a year, China will reach more than one billion by the 1980s.

Chapter 7
Rebellion and Restoration

The breakdown of the old way of life in China and the building of new ways is the least known story of modern times, and one of the most dramatic. It has been marked during the last century by a series of phases. Each phase has seen the collapse of certain old forms and the emergence of new ones. The major periods of change, considered as a single revolutionary process, may be grouped to form two main stages: a period of anti-dynastic rebellion along traditional lines which was suppressed in a rather traditional fashion, and a period of reform and Westernization which merged into revolution. Indeed, rebellion, reform, and revolution have been intermixed, and the division of the revolutionary process into stages is merely an analytical device, to indicate how the elements of Chinese society have been remade and reorganized during the last century. Behind them all may be seen two types of change at work, one cyclical and one permanent.

By cyclical change I mean simple pendulum-like fluctuations, for example, from unity to disunity and back to unity again. This kind of change has occurred often in Chinese history with the rise and fall of dynasties, many of which ended with great rebellions provoked by the corruption of the bureaucracy, the rise of provincial warlords fighting civil wars, and the eventual reunification of the country under another strong founder of a dynasty. This process may be seen in the decline and fall of the Manchu dynasty, the warlord period which followed (1916–1928), and the rise of regimes under Chiang Kai-shek and Mao Tse-tung in succession.

By permanent (or secular) change we mean the reshaping of Chinese life through seemingly irreversible trends like the emancipation of women, inauguration of government by parties instead of dynasties, the increasing use of machines, and the spread of new ideas.

Here let us recall briefly that when the modern revolution began a century ago, the old China was still a society containing two main strata, the literate upper class and the mass of the peasantry. The gentry families included most of the local degree holders. Some of their sons became scholars, some of whom in turn became officials. Government was conducted by the bureaucracy selected mainly from the literate upper class, who were knit together by the Confucian ideology which they imbibed from the classics. Thus an authoritarian monarchic government had for centuries held sway over a universal empire which embraced the world of Chinese culture. But it rested upon intensive cultivation of the soil by an earthbound peasantry who did not participate in the higher life of government and the arts. The politics, economy, and ideas of old China were still dominated respectively by bureaucratic authoritarianism, the landlord, and the Confucian ethic.

The first phase of the revolutionary process consisted of rebellion in the traditional pattern from the bottom up, against both the local elite and the alien Manchu dynasty. But the fanatical religious leadership of this rebellion was anti-Confucian in ideology and failed to enlist the support of the Confucian literati, who instead supported a restoration of the traditional administration.

The Reform Movement at the end of the century was led by gentry-literati, who sought to retain Confucian values while strengthening the Chinese state by adopting Western methods. But these scholar reformers sought change through the emperor, from the top down, and had no thought of mobilizing peasant support.

The Republican revolutionary movement was led by students of the West and supported by the new merchant-gentry and military classes. The transition from the Manchu Empire to the Chinese Republic in 1912 marked both the end of a dynastic cycle in the traditional pattern and a permanent change away from monarchy. But leadership in the new Republic was taken by provincial gentry and the new military. Western ideas of parliamentary government did not take firm root and the peasantry still did not participate in politics—China relapsed into warlordism.

In the ensuing decade the student class, imbued with a new patriotism, became leaders of a true nationalist movement in politics and espoused social and cultural reform under the slogan of "Science and Democracy." The modern student class for almost the first time began to try to give political leadership to the common people. Out of this came the nationalist revolution of the 1920s.

This abbreviated preview of the summary which follows is offered here to indicate one thing—that political change in modern China has been part of fundamental social developments in class structure as well as in the economy and system of values.

The White Lotus as a Prototype

Military power in agrarian China rested on the control of the countryside, its manpower and its food supply. These were the sinews of warfare, which might be mobilized to unseat the reigning dynasty. Domestic rebellions therefore saw a struggle between competing groups, as to which side could control and use the men and crops in the villages. The dynasties relied first upon their professional striking forces, like the Manchu bannermen, and ultimately upon local gentry initiative in supporting the established order. The rebels usually found their initial organization in a secret society or religious cult.

This age-old pattern emerged once again, before the expansion of Western contact, in the savage rising of the White Lotus Society, 1796–1804. This secret religious cult went back to the Mongol period. It appealed to the superstitious faith of poverty-stricken peasants by its multiple promises that the Maitreya Buddha would descend into the world, that the Ming dynasty would be restored, and that disaster, disease, and personal suffering could be obviated in this life and happiness secured in the next. In the late eighteenth century the cult had spread through the border region where the provinces of Hupei, Szechwan, and Shensi join, in the region north of the Yangtze gorges and on the upper waters of the Han River. This mountainous area, rather inhospitable to agriculture, had been opened to cultivation and settlement under official Ch'ing auspices only recently. Migration of poor settlers into these mountains, although encouraged officially, had not been accompanied by an equal development of imperial administration over them. The communities of settlers lived on the very margin of subsistence and tended to be a law unto themselves. The fanatical leaders of the White Lotus cult soon added to their popular appeal an anti-Manchu racial doctrine.

The rebellion began in 1796 as a movement of protest against the exactions of minor tax collectors. Though the imperial garrisons were able to come in and get each small uprising under control in turn, new outbreaks continued to erupt and became too numerous to control. The populace had already organized self-defense corps against the aborigines to the south and had collected arms and food. The insurgents could move into easily defensible mountain redoubts and had time to establish their positions before the imperial forces could arrive. The systematic corruption permitted by the senile Emperor Ch'ien-lung handicapped the imperial military effort. While the rebels had little strategic plan and remained merely roving bands, the imperial forces lacked supplies, morale, and incentive as well as vigorous leadership. Both sides ravaged the populace instead of fighting.

The White Lotus Rebellion was suppressed only after the Chia-ch'ing Emperor assumed real power in 1799 and supported vigorous Manchu commanders, who restored discipline to their forces. By pursuing the rebels tenaciously, on the one hand, and getting control of the manpower and food supply of the area, on the other, the Manchu generals eventually achieved an old-style suppression of the rising. Their methods, which have been analyzed by Philip Kuhn, indicate certain persistent problems in the military control of a densely populated countryside.

First of all, they mobilized the villagers to build several hundred walled enclosures in which the local peasantry could be concentrated. These walled villages were then protected by newly organized local militia, who could by this time more easily be enrolled because the devastation of the countryside had seriously hindered their farming and sustenance. Thus the populace was brought under imperial control. Meanwhile militia were trained to join in the campaign of extermination against the rebels, although it was found that these troops when properly trained became professional soldiers, warlike and dangerous, and subsequently an effort had to be made to recover their arms from them. At the same time a policy of conciliation was pursued toward the men the rebels had impressed into their bands, so as to secure their surrender; and other measures were taken to prevent refugees from continuing to join the rebels. By this combination of force and administrative arrangements, the imperial commanders gradually starved the rebels of their new recruits and food supplies. The policy of "strengthening the walls and clearing the countryside" eventually sapped the strength of the rebellion and it died out. It had cost the imperial regime the rough equivalent of five years' revenue (200 million ounces of silver).

This pattern is reminiscent of many earlier uprisings and is even relevant to North China during the Japanese invasion of the 1930s, the Chinese Communist expansion of the 1940s, and the war in South Vietnam in the 1960s. But the White Lotus, though an omen of dynastic decline, lacked one ingredient of power: the ideological and administrative leadership of scholars. In this respect it was a mere curtain raiser for the greatest struggle of the nineteenth century world, a civil war in China which in numbers dwarfed our own Civil War.

The Chinese revolution of today really goes back to the Taiping Rebellion of 1851–1864, a full lifetime before Marxism entered China. The Taiping rebels were mainly peasants. Although Karl Marx learned about them, they never heard of the Communist Manifesto. Yet modern China's revolution is unintelligible without reference to the Taiping effort to destroy Confucianism, and why it failed.

The Taiping Heavenly Kingdom

This great upheaval arose from a background of population pressure, which had increased the insecurity of life and the vulnerability of the populace to drought, flood, famine, and disease. These in turn presented the creaking machinery of government with problems it could not meet—flood control, famine relief, increased need for taxes, increased difficulty in getting them. These larger burdens combined with official self-seeking to produce inefficiency in government and loss of confidence among the people. The emperor's inability to subdue the British barbarians in 1842 had shaken the imperial prestige. In 1846–1848 flood and famine were widespread among China's expanded population. It is not surprising that a great uprising finally began in 1850.

We can also understand why it should have begun in the southernmost provinces. The Canton region and its hinterland had been longest connected with the growing foreign trade, not only of the Western merchants at Canton but of Chinese traders with Southeast Asia. Disorder grew through the connivance of Chinese merchants and pirates with the foreigner in the import of Indian opium. This area, moreover, had been last conquered by the Ch'ing, and their military hold was relatively weak in the very region which had been most fully subjected to the upsetting effect of foreign trade. The local society, as analyzed by Fred Wakeman, Jr., was dominated by large landowning clans, whose militia bands in this era of weak government often carried on armed feuds between clan villages or groups of villages. Such local wars were fostered by ethnic fragmentation, due to the fact that South China had received infusions of migrants from the north, such as the Hakka people, whosee customs set them apart both from the earlier Han Chinese inhabitants and from the tribal peoples in the hills. Finally, as population grew and conditions worsened, the foreign opium trade gave a key role to the anti-dynastic secret societies, those sworn brotherhoods that offered mutual help and a social subsystem to the alienated and adventurous, especially on the trade routes. In the traditional pattern the natural candidates to lead rebellion were the branches and offshoots of the Triad Society, whose network was already widespread among Chinese overseas and in foreign trade. The fact that the Taiping Rebellion did not join with these established agencies of revolt springs directly from the personality of the Taiping founder, Hung Hsiu-ch'üan.

How this disappointed scholar had visions and became a rebel emperor of half China is a remarkable saga. Hung was born into a Hakka family in 1814. Three times he tried and failed in the provincial examinations at Canton. After one failure he suffered an illness and delirium. He believed that he saw a venerable sage who commanded him to defeat the demons and save humanity. After this vision he returned from Canton to continue as a village schoolmaster, bringing with him a Christian missionary tract entitled "Good Words to Admonish the Age." Curiously enough, Hung appears to have read this tract and its biblical quotations for the first time only six years later, in 1843. The correspondence between its teaching and his earlier vision gave him the conviction that God had called him. He became a traveling preacher and made converts in villages along the West River in Kwangsi, where his followers soon organized a sect, the God Worshipers' Society.

A subsequent visit to a Protestant missionary at Canton, in whose house he spent two months, added to Hung's store of religious tenets and confirmed him in his sense of mission. For his followers he wrote hymns and religious tracts. With them he performed the rite of baptism, broke the idols in the local temples, and prayed to God. He soon had between one and two thousand baptized converts and began to give his religious teaching an anti-Manchu tinge. Already his lieutenants had created a military organization for protection against bandits, and to fight in village feuds or against local gentry-armed militia groups, in this era of growing disorder. By this concatenation of seemingly chance elements, Hung's movement grew in strength. In 1851 the leaders gave it a dynastic title, *Tai-p'ing t'ien-kuo*, "The Heavenly Kingdom of Great Peace," and thus raised the standard of open rebellion.

Once launched, the rebellion rapidly expanded and its leaders conducted their forces on a great northern expedition into the Yangtze valley. The troops of the established dynasty held out in the Hunan capital, Changsha, but otherwise were routed or beat strategic retreats. Their "victories," which every imperial commander was bound by custom to report to the throne, occurred closer and closer to Peking. In the beginning of 1853 the Taipings captured and burned Wuhan and started down the Yangtze by boat, half a million strong. In March 1853 they captured Nanking and made it their capital. Expeditions continued northward and got within 30 miles of Tientsin but failed to capture the symbol of dynastic authority, Peking. The Taipings thus established their base in the lower Yangtze but at first made no effort to seize Shanghai. The next decade saw much bloodshed but a continuing stalemate between the imperial and the rebel forces.

So great a rebellion has naturally demanded explanations of its rapid rise and long drawn out failure. In the present state of research more can be said about its ideology and leadership than about its actual administration.

The Taiping Religion. In creating his new religion, Hung selected elements of Christianity from missionary translations mainly of the Old Testament: the uniqueness and omnipotence of God the creator, his spiritual fatherhood of all men, the efficacy of prayer, baptism, keeping the Sabbath, the Ten Commandments, the rewards of Heaven, together with stories of the creation, the flood, the flight from Egypt, and the like. But he found little use for Jesus' teaching of the spiritual power of love, forgiveness, and concern for one's neighbor. Instead, Hung set himself up as Jesus' younger brother, the second son of God, sent down by him to create a new heaven on earth. Thus he became a new fount of pseudo-Christian revelation.

Having studied the Confucian texts so long in preparation for the classical examinations, Hung in his theology inevitably expressed Confucius' values more than Christ's. As analyzed by Vincent Shih, the Taipings' sacred writings are studded with quotations from the *Analects*, the *Mencius*, and classical authors, often unacknowledged or slightly modified. They rejected the basic Christian concept of original sin in favor of the more optimistic Chinese belief in the fundamental goodness of human nature, which of course made repentance less meaningful. The Taipings stressed many traditional moral concepts: the importance of maintaining basic social distinctions and relationships, and of proper conduct according to status, the need to accept fate, the ideal of the Great Harmony.

Most interesting was their choice of the term for God, a key decision confronting all advocates of monotheism in China. The early Jesuits had settled on *t'ien* ("Heaven") and *shang-ti* ("Lord on High") but their opponents in the famous Rites Controversy had secured a papal decision in 1715 in favor of *t'ien-chu* ("Lord of Heaven"). Protestant missionaries in the mid-nineteenth century remained split between *shang-ti* and *shen* ("Spirit,"), so irreconcilably indeed that they produced two versions of the Bible. Hung chose *t'ien* ("Heaven") as his principal term and so his God at once acquired traditional attributes such as conferring the Mandate of Heaven.

Thus the Taipings' religion had an apparently Christian framework, but it was distorted to meet their needs. Their religious literature added in many bits and pieces of the Confucian classics, but played down a key element like filial piety. In short, they made their own mixture.

Fanaticism, the priceless ingredient in their sudden success, was supplied partly by another Taiping leader, a former charcoal burner, Yang Hsiu-ch'ing. Though less educated than Hung, Yang showed considerably more genius as a political organizer and military leader. Very early he developed a capacity to receive direct visitations from God, who in a crisis would speak through his lips in no uncertain terms. Hung never found this capacity and was left literally speechless. Yang became commander-in-chief, the third son of God as well as the Holy Ghost, and the chief power at Nanking until Hung got him assassinated in 1856.

All in all it seems plain, as Chinese scholars of all camps have pointed out, that the great rebellion failed primarily from inadequate leadership. In spite of their tremendous fervor and the early devotion of their followers, Hung and Yang and the other leaders were blinded by their religion and incapable of setting up an effective government. The Hakka leadership were displaced persons, from a minority group. At Nanking they soon imitated earlier dynasties in creating a nobility, the Six Boards, examinations, levels of bureaucracy, and sumptuary laws to distinguish gradations among this elite according to costumes and ceremonies. But they never developed an effective civil service or administration over the countryside, and were therefore quite unable to lead a genuine social revolution in the villages. As Kuhn remarks, the Taipings "remained, in effect, besieged in the cities" while their enemies, the Confucian gentry elite, continued to control and eventually to mobilize the countryside against them.

The Taipings' failure to win the adherence of any body of Confucian literati was a primary element in their political failure as a whole. Meanwhile their failure to join forces with the anti-Manchu secret societies, particularly the Triads, seems to have come partly from the antithesis between the "Christian" rites and doctrines used by Taiping fanatics and the Triad ceremonies derived from Chinese folk religion.

The Triad ritual, for example, used esoteric characters not to be found in a Chinese dictionary, Triad members worshiped the Dipper, recited thirty-six incantations, stabbed their fingers to achieve a blood brotherhood, and performed ceremonies to represent the forces of heaven, earth, and man.

Since the Triad Society was widely organized in South China in five main lodges, of which the head was in Fukien and others in Kwangtung and Kwangsi, with a great number of followers among the lower military and civil officials, their aid to the Taiping cause could have been substantial. The Triads also had many members among the petty merchants and seafaring people connected with foreign trade at the southern ports. In 1853 rebels connected with the Triads actually seized the walled city of Shanghai, next door to the young Foreign Settlement, and held it for seventeen months. Yet in this time the Taiping movement at Nanking failed to join forces with them. They also failed to court the friendship of the foreign trading powers at Shanghai.

Taiping Communism. The gropings of the Taiping leaders in the direction of a social and economic reorganization of Chinese life were visible in their use of ancient utopian ideas from pre-Confucian classics like the *Rites of Chou*, schemes to which earlier Chinese reformers had also appealed. These ancient texts called for a sort of primitive communism in which each twenty-five households among the peasantry were to form one communal unit, each with its treasury and temple and two superintendents. In these communities the fields were to be tilled in common, as on a Communist collective farm today. Food, clothing, and money were to be used in common. The surplus from the harvest was to revert to the communal treasury. While this system seems to have been actually put into effect only in Taiping military organization, it expressed their egalitarian interest.

In the same vein they advocated, although they could not make it effective, the redistribution of land so as to have it used according to need. Farm land was to be divided into nine classes and distributed among the people, with preference to men above sixteen and under fifty. At the same time the farming population was to be redistributed. In this way it was proposed to distribute land and people so that all would be equally well off. This was essentially a policy of equalization of land use, reminiscent of traditional reform efforts. It may be compared with the doctrine later put forth by the Chinese Communists, in the agrarian reform which preceded collectivization.

In other social teachings the Taipings advocated equality between the sexes. They inveighed against slavery, concubinage, foot binding, arranged marriage, cruel punishments, and the use of opium. These doctrines reflected popular desires which have found fuller expression in later decades.

Their military policy suffered from a lack of controlling leadership. The chief leaders usually acted on their own and became prey to feuds and jealousy. After 1854 they too often remained on the defensive and time after time squandered strategic opportunities. All the original leaders were eventually murdered or expelled, except Hung, whose fanaticism verged upon insanity. He killed himself when Nanking fell in 1864, after a revival under new leadership in the early 1860s had proved unavailing.

The final collapse of this great rebellion, with all its latent potentialities, was an inevitable result of its early failures. Securing the support neither of scholar-gentry nor of anti-Manchu secret societies, it could not achieve a dynastic revolution of the traditional type. On the other hand its religion was too thin and its social and economic doctrines inadequate to take the place of Confucianism.

The Nien and Other Rebels

During the period of Taiping control of the lower Yangtze region there arose on their north between the Huai and the Yellow rivers another movement, of rebel bands called "Nien." Based on fortified earth-walled villages on the southern edge of the North China plain, these bands followed the White Lotus tradition. They organized cavalry forces in their own banner system for raiding abroad and controlled their territorial base by taking over the local militia corps. Though lacking dynastic pretensions, the Nien movement from 1853 to 1868 supplanted the imperial government in a sizable region and harassed it with raids to plunder food supplies from neighboring provinces.

Imperial efforts to root the Nien out of their fortified nests repeatedly failed. Walls were leveled only to rise again. The scholar-generals who had defeated the Taipings tried to deprive the Nien of their popular support in the villages by promising security to the populace, death to the leaders, and pardon to the followers. But other risings flared up in many parts of North China. They and the Nien were eventually put down by new provincial armies with modern weapons. They cut the rebel cavalry off from their supplies of food and manpower and eventually, with blockade lines and counter-cavalry, destroyed them on the plain.

In the aftermath of these revolts which convulsed Central and North China there were also sanguinary risings of Chinese Muslims in the Southwest and Northwest during the 1860s and 1870s—bitter struggles which are only now beginning to be studied. All in all, the movement for change in modern China began by following traditional patterns of peasant-based rebellion and produced little but disorder and disaster, bequeathing to later revolutionists an egregious example of intellectual failure in popular leadership.

The Restoration of Confucian Government

The constructive alternative to rebellion was to combine some degree of Western means with an old-style revival of imperial administration. In 1860 the Ch'ing dynasty seemed on the point of collapse, beset by a recrudescence of Taiping military vigor in the lower Yangtze region and by the Anglo-French invasion and capture of Peking. Yet just at this point there emerged new Manchu leaders under the regency of the young Empress Dowager (Tz'u-hsi). By accepting the Western treaty system and supporting the conservative Chinese scholar-generals in the provinces, they achieved the suppression of the Taipings by 1864 and gave their dynasty a new lease on life. A small Sino-foreign mercenary force, called in Chinese style the "Ever Victorious Army," was led by an American and then a British commander (F. T. Ward of Salem and the famous C. G. "Chinese" Gordon). It helped defeat the rebels around Shanghai; but the victory was essentially a Chinese one.

As a result the 1860s saw a genuine conservative effort at a "Restoration," similar to those which had occurred after the founding of the Later Han dynasty or after the great mid-T'ang rebellion of the eighth century. During the 1860s the components of the traditional Confucian state were energized to function again: a group of high-principled civil officials, chosen by examination in the classics and loyal to the reigning dynasty, sternly suppressed rebellion and tried to minister benevolently to the agrarian economy and the popular welfare. Order was restored in the central provinces, taxes remitted, land reopened to cultivation, schools founded, and men of talent recruited for the civil service, even though more was advocated by the top officials than could be actually achieved at the rice roots. While reviving the traditional order in this fashion, the Restoration leaders also began to

Westernize. They set up arsenals to supply modern arms, built steamships, translated Western textbooks in technology and international law, and created a prototype foreign office in the form of a special committee (the Tsungli Yamen) under the Grand Council. Soon their new provincial and regional armies with modern arms made peasant risings impossible of success. In these efforts they were aided by the cooperative policy of the Western powers, whose imperialist rivalries did not become intense until the 1870s. Yet in the end this renewed vitality within the Ch'ing administration showed both the strength and also the inertia of the traditional Chinese polity—it could not be Westernized but could function only on its own terms, which were growing out of date. As studied by Mary Wright, this successful revival within a context of inevitable failure makes an absorbing story.

The personal embodiment of the Restoration was the scholar-general Tseng Kuo-fan (1811–1872), who has been revered or condemned ever since as the great protagonist of Chinese conservatism. Tseng was loyal to the Manchu dynasty because it was an integral part of the Chinese social order. He was not racially nationalistic in the modern fashion but was patriotically culturalistic in the old tradition of the Middle Kingdom. Although trained as a classical scholar and civil official at Peking, during the 1850s he became a general in the provinces, organizing the famous Hunan Army which suppressed the Taipings along the central Yangtze by a strategy of gradual envelopment and mobilization of provincial resources. This first regional army of modern times was officered largely by local gentry-literati who followed Tseng Kuo-fan's example in leading peasant troops by the force of their personal moral character, their paternalistic sense of duty, and their faith in the Confucian principles of social order. Both in civil war and in later reconstruction, Tseng

Moral example. A memorial arch to a virtuous widow, Chiung-chou, Szechwan, 1908. Of the eight inscriptions, the topmost reads "chaste and filial."

and his colleagues stressed the pre-eminence of "human abilities" or talent and character, which were partly inborn but partly could be cultivated by individual devotion to principle. They therefore stressed the revival of the examination system as a means of choosing talent and, for this purpose, the founding of academies and reprinting of classic texts.

In spite of the influx of Western trade and the evident commercial power of the foreigners, the Restoration leaders clung conservatively to the economic principle of the pre-eminence of agriculture as the basis of state revenue and popular livelihood. They had no conception of economic growth or development in the modern sense but were austerely anti-acquisitive and disparaged commerce, including foreign trade, as nonproductive. Rather, they tried to set before the peasantry and bureaucracy the classical ideals of frugality and incorruptibility, so that the product of the land could more readily suffice to maintain the people and the government. To assist agriculture, they tried without much success (as K. C. Liu has shown) to reduce land taxes in the lower Yangtze region but did not try to lower rents or limit landlordism. They tried to revive the necessary public works for water control, but could not control the Yellow River any better than their predecessors.

The Restoration lost vitality after the 1860s for many reasons. Its leaders were conscientiously reviving the past instead of facing China's new future creatively. They could not adequately inspire the lower levels of their bureaucracy nor handle the specialized technical and intellectual problems of Westernization. The very strength of their conservative and restorative effort inhibited China's responding to Western contact in a revolutionary way.

"China's Response to the West" in Retrospect. Since "China" and "the West" were complex variables in the nineteenth

century, both terms need careful definition if they are to help our thinking and not hinder it. As Paul Cohen has pointed out, Chinese leaders had to respond to the total situation confronting them, "of which the Western impact was only one ingredient." As in so many countries, the foreign menace evoked initially a nativist reaction that asserted traditional values. But the domestic menace of rebellion was also of a traditional sort. Basically the Taiping movement was a response to local problems of livelihood and authority. It was influenced by the West only superficially, in its pseudo-Christianity. "The 'slowness' of China's response was due not only to the nature of Chinese society but to the extraordinary problems facing it . . . There was no time to respond to the West." In short, we confront again the concept that China's center of gravity lay deep within the country, and the treaty ports and treaty system, though important in the eyes of their Western creators, remained for a long time peripheral and marginal to the main concerns of the Chinese people and even of the ruling class.

Meanwhile, however, the great rebellion created profound changes in the Chinese political structure, primarily by shifting the center of initiative from the capital to the provinces both in financial and in military affairs. With Peking cut off from its richest provinces, local Chinese gentry leaders had to raise the funds and the armies with which to suppress the rebels. This local militarization under the gentry was a new thing. One result was that local trade taxes began to compete with the land tax as the government's staff of life, while personally led regional armies began to supplant the effete imperial forces. As the Manchu dynasty weakened, the Chinese local gentry enhanced their position, a trend which continued into the twentieth century.

The chief new trade tax instituted at this time was *likin* (literally, a tax of "one-thousandth"). Beginning in 1853 in the lower Yangtze, provincial officials set up *likin* stations on the main routes of domestic commerce. These soon proliferated in all the provinces as a source of local revenue, available for the support of regional armies. Meanwhile the new foreign-staffed Imperial Maritime Customs began to give the central government an increased revenue from foreign trade, which could be used partly to support the new office under the Grand Council for handling foreign affairs, the Tsungli Yamen. Once the major rebellion was brought under control, the new trade revenues could finance fresh efforts, both in the provinces and at Peking, to deal with the Western invaders.

Chapter 8
Reform and Revolution

During the decades following the Ch'ing Restoration of the 1860s, a whole generation of leading Manchu and Chinese officials worked to strengthen the Chinese position by imitating and adapting Western devices and institutions. This movement for "self-strengthening," studied by Albert Feuerwerker, Kwang-Ching Liu, and others, was posited on the attractive though fallacious doctrine of "Chinese learning as the fundamental structure, Western learning for practical use"—as though Western arms, steamships, science, and technology could somehow be utilized to preserve Confucian values, instead of destroying them. In retrospect we can see that the latter was inevitable—gunboats and cotton looms bring their own philosophy with them. But the generation of 1860–1900 clung to the frustrating shibboleth that China could leap halfway into modern times.

The Self-Strengthening Movement

Under the slogan of self-strengthening Chinese leaders therefore began the adoption of Western arms and machines, only to find themselves sucked into an inexorable process in which one Western borrowing led to another, from machinery to technology, from science to all learning, from acceptance

Reform and Revolution

Status of women. A Canton shopkeeper family, wife and daughter with bound feet. (Photo by M. Miller, 1861-64.)

of new ideas to change of institutions, eventually from constitutional reform to republican revolution. The fallacy of halfway Westernization, in tools but not in values, was in fact apparent to many conservative scholars, who therefore chose the alternative of opposing all things Western.

The leaders in self-strengthening were those who had crushed the Taipings, scholar-officials like Tseng Kuo-fan and his younger coadjutor, Li Hung-chang (1823–1901). These men set up the arsenals to make guns and gunboats. They supported the translation of Western books on science and spread the idea that Western methods must be learned and used for defense. As early as 1864, Li explained to Peking that the foreigners' domination of China was based on the superiority of their weapons, that it was hopeless to try to drive them out, and that Chinese society therefore faced the greatest crisis since its unification under the First Emperor in 221 B.C. Li concluded that in order to strengthen herself China must learn to use Western machinery, which implied the training of Chinese personnel. This simple line of reasoning had been immediately self-evident to the fighting men of Japan after Perry's arrival in 1853. But the movement for Westernization in China was obstructed at every turn by the ignorance and prejudice of the Confucian literati. This lack of responsiveness in China, during the decades when Japan was being rapidly modernized, provides one of the great contrasts of history.

China's difficulties were repeatedly illustrated. To make Western learning available, for example, some eighty Jesuit missionaries during the seventeenth and eighteenth centuries had produced Chinese translations of over four hundred Western works, more than half on Christianity and about a third in science. Protestant missionaries of the early nineteenth century published about eight hundred items, but nearly all as religious tracts or translations of scripture, mainly directed in simple parlance at the common man, not the Chinese literati. At Tseng Kuo-fan's arsenal at Shanghai during the last third of the century one gifted Englishman (John Fryer) collaborated with Chinese scholars to translate more than a hundred works on science and technology, developing the necessary terminology in Chinese as they went along. But the distribution of all these works was limited, rather few Chinese scholars seem to have read them, and their production depended on the initiative of foreigners or of a few officials concerned with foreign affairs, not under guidance from the throne.

At the capital an interpreters' college had been set up in 1862 as a government institution to prepare young men for diplomatic negotiation. With an American missionary as head and nine foreign professors and with Robert Hart's prompting and support, this new college soon had over one hundred Manchu and Chinese students of foreign languages. Yet this innovation had to be defended vigorously against the attack of anti-foreign literati who objected to the teaching of Western subjects. The erroneous excuse had to be offered that "Western sciences borrowed their roots from ancient Chinese mathematics. Westerners still regard their mathematics as coming from the Orient . . . China invented the method, Westerners adopted it."

The jealousy of a scholar class whose fortunes were tied to Chinese learning was most vigorously illustrated in the case of the first Chinese returned student. This man, Yung Wing, had been taken to the United States by missionaries in 1847 and graduated from Yale in 1854. When he returned to China after eight years abroad, he had to wait almost a decade before he was used by Tseng Kuo-fan as an agent to buy machinery and as an interpreter and translator. Yung Wing's proposal to send Chinese students abroad was not acted upon until fifteen years after his return. In 1872 he headed an educational mission which brought some 120 long-gowned Chinese students to Hartford, Connecticut. Old-style Chinese teachers came with them to prepare these prospective Westernizers of China for the examinations in the classics, a preparation still essential to their becoming officials. Yung Wing was also given as colleague an obscurantist scholar whose mission was to see to it that Western contact did not undermine the students' Confucian morals. In 1881 the whole project was abandoned.

Similar attitudes handicapped the early industrialization effort. Conservatives feared that mines, railroads, and telegraph lines would upset the harmony between man and nature *(feng-shui)* and create all sorts of problems—by disturbing the imperial ancestors, by assembling unruly crowds of miners, by throwing boatmen and carters out of work, by absorbing government revenues, by creating a dependence on foreign machines and technicians. Even when modernizers like Li Hung-chang could overcome such fears they still faced enormous practical difficulties such as the lack of entrepreneurial skill and capital. Major projects had to be sponsored by high officials, usually under the formula of "official supervision and merchant operation." This meant in practice that enterprises were hamstrung by bureaucratism. Merchant managers remained under the thumb of their official patrons. Both groups milked the new companies of their current profits instead of reinvesting them. An ongoing process of self-sustaining industrial growth through reinvestment was never achieved.

Thus China's late-nineteenth-century industrialization proved generally abortive in spite of the early promise of many officially sponsored projects. For example, the China Merchants' Steam Navigation Company founded in 1872 was subsidized to carry the tribute rice from the Yangtze delta to feed the capital. Almost every year since 1415 long flotillas of grain junks had moved these shipments up the Grand Canal. Now they could go quickly by sea from Shanghai to Tientsin. To provide coal for the steamer fleet the Kaiping coal mines were opened north of Tientsin in 1878. To transport this coal, China's first permanent railway was inaugurated in 1881. Yet by the end of the century these mutually supporting enterprises had made comparatively little progress. The China Merchants' Company, plundered by its patrons, managers, and employees, lost ground to British steamship lines. The Kaiping mines, heavily in debt to foreigners, were taken over by Herbert Hoover and others in 1900. Railroad building was neglected by China and promoted by the imperialist powers in their spheres of influence after 1895.

How far China's slowness in industrialization was due to

Reform and Revolution

Curiosity about the foreigner. Ta-ning hsien, Szechwan, 1910.

foreign privilege and exploitation under the unequal treaties
is a question awaiting impartial study. As Western imperialism in the Far East intensified in the late nineteenth century,
Japan succeeded in throwing it off while China succumbed
further and further. Certainly one main cause in this period
was the nature of Chinese institutions, including the fact of a
big country with a comparatively weak central government. ✓

Imperialism and Reform in 1898

During the four decades from 1860 to 1900 China was
opened increasingly to foreign commercial exploitation and
missionary endeavor. Foreign trade grew though it never
realized the persistent Western hope that if every "China-

man" would only add an inch to his shirttail, the mills of Lancashire might be kept humming indefinitely. China proved less attractive to foreign capital investment than newer lands in the Americas or the British empire. Likewise the Western evangelist found China remarkably self-sufficient and spiritual converts rather few.

The opening of the country in the 1860s facilitated the great effort to Christianize China. Building on old foundations, the Roman Catholic establishment totaled by 1894 some 750 European missionaries, 400 native priests, and over half a million communicants. By 1894 the newer Protestant mission effort supported over 1300 missionaries, mainly British and American, and maintained some 500 stations—each with a church, residences, street chapels, and usually a small school and possibly a hospital or dispensary—in about 350 different cities and towns. Yet they had made fewer than 60,000 Chinese Christian converts. Plainly, China was not destined to become a Christian nation. But the influence of mission schools and hospitals, of missionary ideals and activities in seeking out the common man, translating Western literature, initiating women's education, and assisting in ancient tasks of charity and famine relief, was considerable. This influence was highly disruptive to the old Chinese society, even though it was eminently helpful to the Chinese people.

On a small scale, the missionaries were the Communists' predecessors, but the Peking fashion today is to belittle the good works of the missionaries as "cultural imperialism." The argument that they were carried on by self-righteous foreigners under the protection of extraterritorial privileges backed by gunboats is undeniable. So is the fact that there were hundreds of anti-Christian riots, sometimes with loss of life, including at least fifty cases that required top-level diplomatic attention, up to the Boxer massacres of 1900. Yet the fact remains that the missionary movement, whatever its spiritual-doctrinal result in this period, was a profound stimulus to change. The riots against it seem to have been generally inspired less by the superstitious fears of the populace in the first instance than by the jealousy of the Chinese gentry, whose privileged status in society was directly threatened—socially, ideologically, and in the end politically—by the new class of privileged cultural invaders from abroad.

As long as the dynasty and its traditional institutions survived, the penalty for China's complacent self-sufficiency and inertia became apparent mainly on the frontiers where the lesser states, traditionally tributary to China, were taken over by imperialist powers. Japan took the Liu-ch'iu Islands, Russia moved for a time into the Ili region in Central Asia, France seized Annam and created French Indochina, the British took Burma, and Korea was opened to foreign intercourse. As these ominous developments continued to whittle away the Middle Kingdom's once-proud hegemony in Eastern Asia, the pressure for drastic action gradually accumulated.

Its most vigorous expression was in the righteous memorials of "literati opinion" *(ch'ing-i)* submitted to the throne by officials who invoked lofty moral principles for often extremist policy ends. These Confucian superpatriots were particularly incensed during the 1870s against Russia in Ili and during the 1880s against France in Tongking. Their fiery denunciations of foreign contumely supported Peking's intransigence and made compromise difficult.

Institutional reform became fashionable only when disaster was imminent. Not until Japan had unexpectedly defeated the Chinese empire in 1895 and the European powers had extorted leaseholds and concessions in the three years following were genuine institutional changes attempted. Even then, the objective was still not fundamental change but merely intensified "self-strengthening" by the use of foreign methods.

The reformers still took the position that the fundamental values in Chinese society should remain unchangeable but that the laws and institutions were changeable and must be made to take account of the West.

Thus the reformers of 1898 were merely reformers and not revolutionaries. They still wanted only "change within tradition." With great courage and even greater optimism they hoped that the bearers of the Chinese tradition could renovate it to suit modern needs.

Most famous of these men was the fiery Cantonese K'ang Yu-wei, a scholar of high standing who startled the literati with his study *Confucius as a Reformer*. This iconoclastic interpretation pictured Confucius as standing for the rights of the people as a check upon the authority of the ruler. By quoting ancient texts of a minor tradition, K'ang also smuggled the idea of progress into the classical heritage. He was in fact well acquainted with Buddhist, Christian, and translated Western writings and espoused the then popular doctrine of Social Darwinism about the survival of the fittest in the struggle among nations.

K'ang Yu-wei's chief argument was that China must reform or perish and that moderate reform was not enough to save her. In reforming, he believed China should learn particularly from Japan, whose experience was closer in time and space than that of Western countries. This led K'ang to advocate constitutionalism. He organized a rudimentary political party, the Society for the Study of Self-Strengthening, to spread this point of view. His collaborator at this time was another Cantonese literary genius, Liang Ch'i-ch'ao, who edited a self-strengthening newspaper.

This group gained adherents after the disastrous defeat of China by the Japanese in 1895 and attracted the attention of the emperor, for whose information K'ang prepared memorials and wrote two books. So convincing was his presentation that the young emperor for a brief period of one hundred days in the summer of 1898 with his assistance issued a cataclysmic series of reform edicts.

These famous documents in the name of the emperor ordered the remaking of the examination system, the administration, and many of the government institutions. The edicts aimed to inaugurate all the new services of a modern government and at the same time to wipe out the sinecures and corruption of the old. There were edicts dealing with medicine, agriculture, education, the penal code, the police, postal service, mining, commerce, the army, the navy, inventions, and study abroad. Seldom has the untrammeled power of an emperor been more vividly exemplified, at least on paper.

The Hundred Days of 1898 produced consternation among officials high and low. It mattered little that the constitution envisaged by the reformers would hardly limit the ruler's power, even though it espoused the rule of law—the fact was that too many officials felt themselves too closely endangered by these sudden changes. The Manchu Empress Dowager, Tz'u-hsi, who had been in retirement for the past decade, was able with military support to effect a coup d'état, depose the unfortunate emperor, declare herself regent, and rescind his edicts. Six of the reformers were executed. K'ang and Liang fled to Japan.

No incident could have dramatized more effectively the hopelessness of updating China through gradual reform from above. The defeat of 1895 and the fiasco of 1898 together gave the first great impetus toward revolutionary change. From then on, efforts at political revolution ran parallel to those for constitutional reform.

Revolutionaries versus Reformers

Sun Yat-sen. Dr. Sun came from the modern fringe of China and was the most Westernized of her revolutionary leaders, educated in Western medicine, fluent in English, much traveled abroad. His career symbolized the rise of nationalism, which grew up strongest among treaty-port merchants, overseas Chinese, and students abroad, on the frontier of foreign contact where Chinese were most aware of the power and achievements of foreign nations. Operating in this no-man's-land outside the bonds of the old society, Sun was devoted to his nationalist cause and ready to try anything that would help it, a sincere opportunist. His sincerity was charismatic, his opportunism quite practical, even when he pursued inconsistent alternatives at the same moment. Perhaps equally important for his career was the fact that he early became a symbol and subsequently kept on trying. In the course of his efforts, as traced especially by Harold Schiffrin and C. Martin Wilbur, Sun Yat-sen dealt with all the revolutionary social forces of his time: Cantonese emigrants to foreign lands, Christian missionaries in China, treaty-port compradors and journalists, reforming officials of the Manchu dynasty, antidynastic secret societies, overseas Chinese merchants, Japanese expansionists, Chinese students abroad, New Army officers at home.

Sun was born near Macao in the region from which so many Cantonese emigrants have gone overseas. He got his first contact with the West in 1879 when at the age of fourteen he went to Honolulu to join his elder brother there. He attended a Church of England boarding school. He studied English, mathematics, and English history and even sang in the choir. When he returned to his native village at the age of seventeen, he was a radical. Partly because he attacked the images in the local temple, he was sent away to study at Queen's College, Hong Kong. There he became a baptized Christian in the Congregational Church.

The crushing French defeat of China in the undeclared war of 1885 roused Sun Yat-sen's interest in reform and national salvation. He appears already to have made some contact with the Triad Society. Having studied medicine from 1887 to 1892, he began to practice at Macao but could not continue without a diploma from Portugal. Sun abandoned his new profession and finally embarked upon a revolutionary career. He had already helped organize a secret society, the Hsing Chung Hui (lit., "Revive China Society"). The members were sworn to secrecy by oaths written in blood, and Sun began to organize branches. Thus by the time the Japanese victory of 1895 precipitated the efforts at reform as well as the heightened imperialism of the powers, Sun had already become a leader in the cause of revolution.

In 1895 using Hong Kong as a base, his group attempted to seize the Canton provincial government offices. The plot was discovered. Several of Sun's colleagues were executed. He himself escaped with a price on his head. He went into disguise, cutting his queue and adopting foreign dress. With a mustache he thenceforth passed easily as a Japanese. When in Japan he used the name Nakayama (meaning literally "central mountain"), pronounced in Chinese "Chung-shan," a name later applied to numerous institutions, streets and even a style of clothing in modern China. As Marius Jansen's fascinating study makes clear, Sun during the next decade got repeated and substantial help from Japanese patrioteer expansionists, including the Black Dragon Society and politicians of the Liberal Party. This help included funds, arms, advice, and protection.

In 1896 Sun underwent in London an experience which confirmed him in his revolutionary mission. He was recognized at the Chinese legation and locked up there incommunicado for twelve days. The legation prepared to ship him back to China to be executed, but through British intervention, Sun was saved. He found himself at the age of thirty world-famous as the leader of the anti-Manchu revolutionary movement. During the next two years he studied in London and on the Continent, acquiring more background of political and social theory. From 1900 to 1911 he was on the move organizing revolutionary activity and seeking funds in the Far East and around the world. However, Sun Yat-sen was only one of the new breed of revolutionaries, and his political work was only one of the long-term developments that led to revolution. In the decade preceding the birth of the Chinese Republic in 1911, intensive reformist activity prepared the ground for it.

Liang Ch'i-ch'ao. After the fiasco of 1898, K'ang Yu-wei had remained a monarchist. He was left behind in the development of the reform movement while Liang Ch'i-ch'ao through his writing and editing in Japan became one of the founders of the modern Chinese liberal tradition. Liang was a classical scholar, a graduate of the provincial examinations, and a powerful writer, essentially a reformer of ideas rather than a political revolutionist. His pre-eminent literary abilities made him the man to reinterpret the Chinese tradition by importing Western ideas. Yet as Hao Chang makes clear, Liang at the same time was well-grounded in the modern reform tradition of the so-called New Text movement for reappraisal of the classics and for practical statesmanship in administration.

After travel in the West Liang began in 1902 in Yokohama to publish the *New Citizen,* a journal devoted to the theme of the "renovation of the people" *(hsin min).* In the first few issues were articles by himself on Hobbes, Spinoza, Montesquieu, Bentham, Rousseau, and the history of Western political thought. He extolled Anglo-Saxon individualism and pointed out that personal freedom is possible only under the disciplined acceptance of law and order. The new Chinese citizen, said Liang, should learn to be public-spirited, to have a spirit of enterprise, to assert his rights and forget the emperor's benevolence; he should achieve and maintain his independence of social custom, take an interest in his community, and demand self-government. This was a direct attack upon the ancient dogma of the Confucian relationships.

Liang's reinterpretation of the Confucian ethic may be illustrated by his use of loyalty and filial piety. Since the state had now become the community in which the fortunes of the people were involved, it, he said, instead of the monarch, should now become the focus of loyalty. Confucian loyalty should be metamorphosed into modern patriotism through the redirection of human feeling, not by coercion.

Thinking along these evolutionary lines, Liang argued that a republican form of government in China was still impossible; the educational standard of the Chinese people was still too low to permit their participation in representative government. Moreover a revolution would bring great dangers of dictatorship and invite foreign aggression and the partition of China. He therefore advocated a benevolent constitutional monarchism under which education for the new citizenship and the establishment of provincial and national assemblies would permit gradual progress. The political group which Liang organized in Japan advocated the setting up of a national assembly with a cabinet government responsible to it, new law codes and an independent judiciary, local self-government, a division of powers between local and central government, and the achievement of diplomatic equality through abolition of the unequal treaties. This enlightened and gradual program represented the most humane and sophisticated political thought of the period and had wide influence, competing for the support of student youth.

Liang's liberal gradualism lost out, in competition with the revolutionaries, because it had little program of action and could not offer immediate results or satisfy the passion of patriotic youth to smash the old order and save China overnight. The sweeping blueprints of the revolutionaries appealed to a scholar class trained in abstract principles more than in action. Republicanism was also the latest style in governments, and a Manchu emperor could not possibly symbolize the new Chinese nationalism. Thus the ancient Chinese monarchy was doomed along with the Manchu dynasty, even though the monarchy showed considerable vitality and adaptability even in its last decade.

Dynastic Reform and Republican Revolution

The activity of revolutionists and reformers abroad was paralleled in the 1900s by the belated reform efforts of the dynasty at home. In this effort to save itself by changing its spots, the Manchu government was given a compelling impulse by the Boxer uprising of 1900, which had the makings of a traditional peasant rebellion but lacked even the social objectives of the Taiping movement. It was led by fanatical members of a secret society, who eventually got support from xenophobic officials and gentry. The gentry violently resented both the obvious aggressions of imperialism and the less spectacular rise of a new class of Christian converts and protégés under the wing of foreign missions and the protection of extraterritoriality. Manchu princes finally supported this bitter and superstitious effort to expel the foreigner by relying on the magic "invulnerability" of Boxer braves.

In the end armed provocation by foreign troops was partly responsible for the outbreak of violence against foreigners. In this sudden frenzy the Boxers killed many thousands of Chinese Christians and some 242 missionaries and other foreign civilians in North China and Manchuria. For two months in the hot summer of 1900 they besieged the foreign community

Old Peking. *Above:* Traffic through archway on Hatamen Street, ca. 1900. *Below:* Shop fronts.

in the Peking legations, yet the attack was never pushed home because leading Manchus realized its suicidal futility. Chinese officials in the southern provinces quickly asserted that this was a domestic rebellion, not the anti-foreign war which Peking declared it to be. By this fiction the dynasty was preserved for another decade, though further humbled by the Boxer Protocol and indemnity of 1901. But the powers egregiously failed to demand or support genuine reform. Once again they used their influence to prop up a profitable though decadent status quo.

The Empress Dowager, on her return early in 1902 from her flight on a "tour of inspection" to the western provinces, took full responsibility for the Boxer trouble and announced a reform program. During the next decade the Manchus attempted, too late, to carry out many of the reforms which had been proposed during the famous Hundred Days of 1898. But history left them behind. The net effect of their reluctant reform efforts was to prepare the ground for the revolution.

The apparent inevitability of this process, in which the incompetent leadership of the Manchu dynasty seemed capable only of leading it to disaster, is well illustrated in its program for educational reform, which succeeded just enough to undermine the established order.

In 1905 the ancient examination system was abolished, marking the end of an era. New schools and new studies were hopefully planned to take its place, though the funds and the teachers were alike inadequate. Students were sent abroad, principally to Japan, both by Peking and by the provincial governments. An elementary school system was inaugurated, modeled on that of Japan. Colleges were opened in many centers. By 1911 there were said to be 57,000 schools with 1,600,000 students (out of perhaps 65,000,000 young people of school age). In higher education the Imperial University at Peking was formally established, incorporating the inter-

preter's college founded in the 1860s. As of 1911 there were in
the United States some 800 Chinese students and in Europe
about 400. Meanwhile, however, Japan had been the chief
training ground for modern China. During the decade of
the 1900s and particularly after Japan's great victory over
Russia in 1905, every year saw 10,000 or even 15,000 Chinese
students securing a modern education in Japan. Much of
the top leadership of China in the next generation came from
this group. But from the point of view of the Chinese government the net effect of this decade of educational beginnings was to create in China a student class with radical ideas.

The students' dangerous thoughts came from their having
a little learning and a great deal of patriotism, without finding anyone at home or abroad who could give them blueprints for the economic development and social restructuring
of their homeland. Many of them on their return to China
were appointed to official positions. Others became teachers
in the new colleges on which local authorities prided themselves. A considerable number joined the revolutionary movement secretly.

In yielding to the pressure for reform the court accepted
the idea of constitutionalism, an idea the ruling oligarchy in
Japan had actively pursued a generation earlier. The constitutional commission sent abroad after 1905 quickly copied
the Japanese constitution. A reorganization of the government's ministries in 1906 established a cabinet system. Reorganization of provincial government in 1907 was followed
in 1908 by the proclamation of a set of principles looking
toward full constitutional government at the end of a nine-
year period of preparation. It was proposed to establish assemblies in the provincial and central governments, which,
however, should be purely consultative. When they met in
1909 they became natural centers of agitation for change, and
produced new provincial leaders, men trained in the classics

who often combined their elite status with business activities as "gentry-merchants"—entrepreneurs, reformers, and politicians of a new type, loyal to their provinces as a first step in saving China.

Many of the Manchu reform efforts got no further than the paper stage. This was particularly true of the navy and the Western-type legal system, both so foreign to Chinese ways. Tariff revision provided in the Boxer protocol was impeded by the difficulty of securing agreement among the powers. Currency reform made little progress. Of all these efforts perhaps the most significant was the development of the New Army, under a vigorous official, Yuan Shih-k'ai. Following the precedent of Tseng Kuo-fan and Li Hung-chang, he became in effect the head of a personal army organization, the commanders of which felt loyalty to him as much as to the state.

The New Nationalism. The awakening of patriotism in the 1900s, roused by the acts of imperialist aggression in the decades preceding, was only one of the many processes of social change now under way. The rise of the treaty ports, together with steamship and some railway travel, the telegraph, newspapers and magazines, the imperial post office set up under Hart in 1896, had all greatly enlarged the literate Chinese political community. Education was spreading, literacy increasing. Local citizens, often led by Christian converts, now lent support to reform movements against opium smoking, foot binding, servant-girl bondage, prostitution, gambling, and other evils. Urbanization and the gradual discrediting of Confucianism had weakened the "three bonds" of the old society, for as soon as the Manchu emperor's right to rule came into question, the subordination of youth to age and of women to men was questioned equally. The emancipation of women, that great revolution quietly effected by an unsung silent majority, began to gather momentum. Youth came to the fore, and merchants responded to their agitation for boycotts of foreign goods—against the United States over exclusion of "oriental" immigration in 1905 and against Japan because of an incident in 1908.

What had happened to the gentry class? Several new studies (by Wellington Chan, Joseph Esherick, Charlton Lewis, Mary Rankin, Edward Rhoads, and others) trace its diversification in a new provincial leadership—the rise of officials as industrialists, of reform-minded scholar-gentry and scholar-publicists, and ardent young army officers as well as vigorous conservatives. Most of this new leadership was still working within the established order.

As recounted by Mary Wright, these social stirrings of the New China were accompanied by the demand for "recovery of sovereign rights," in effect, the rolling back of the whole unequal treaty system. Peking's vigorous reassertion of sovereignty in Manchuria, Mongolia, Tibet, and along the southern frontiers in the decade of the 1900s represented a Chinese at least as much as a Ch'ing dynasty program. But the revolutionaries, like the dynasty, avoided stressing the theme of anti-imperialism for very practical reasons. The "foreign omnipresence" was a principal fact in the Chinese political scene: not only British and American gunboats in the ports and on the Yangtze patrol but also Anglo-American, Japanese, and European business enterprises both in the treaty-port concession areas and in the interior provinces. This was a pervasive influence. For instance, a great part of the central government revenues now went to meet just the interest payments on the foreign loans for the Japanese indemnity of 1895 and the Boxer indemnity of 1901, without reducing the principal still to be paid off. In the shadow of this semi-permanent imperialist intervention in Chinese life, the revolutionary movement could more easily concentrate on being anti-dynastic, anti-Manchu, than on being anti-imperialist. In any case, paradoxically, the revolutionary effort was in large part inspired and aided from abroad.

By using Japan as their base in the early 1900s, Sun and his corevolutionaries were well situated to enlist both the idealists and the adventurers among the thousands of Chinese students who came there. Sun's main problem, now that a new generation of student youth were flocking to Tokyo, was how to offer them intellectual leadership, something more than putschist plotting, no easy task when he was not himself a classically trained literatus. His first statement of the Three Principles of the People *(San-min chu-i)*, which still form the dogma of the Kuomintang (National People's Party), was made in 1905. Roughly translated, they are Nationalism, Democracy, and the People's Livelihood, which included some rather vague ideas of non-Marxist socialism, particularly Henry George's proposal to expropriate future increases in land values, effecting an "equalization of land rights." In 1905, with Japanese help in bringing disparate Chinese student groups together in Tokyo, Sun amalgamated his own revolutionary society with leaders from Hunan, Shanghai, and elsewhere to form a secret revolutionary league (the T'ung Meng Hui). Four hundred members at the first meeting took an oath to overthrow the Manchus and establish a republic.

This new and more powerful organization continued its secret activity using traditional techniques. Members were known by number only and communicated verbally rather than in writing. They made themselves known to one another by such devices as lifting a teacup with a thumb and two fingers. Using Japan as their base, they began publication in 1905 of a monthly newspaper, *The People (Min Pao)*, smuggling two thousand copies regularly into China to feed the discontent of the student class. By early 1911, ten revolutionary outbreaks had been engineered, all in vain.

As this subversive movement gained strength, the Ch'ing government had been able to strike against it. The revolutionary attempt of 1906 in Hunan province failed. Diplomatic representations from Peking moved the Japanese government to refuse further shelter to the revolutionists. Dissension arose within their ranks against Sun himself, who was finally expelled by the Japanese. When Sun set up headquarters in Hanoi, he was expelled by the French in turn. By 1909 the organization was in danger of disruption and demoralization. Its attempted putsches had failed.

The Revolutionary Leadership. A revolutionary attempt at Canton in April 1911 was put down with the loss of seventy-two martyrs. This constituted the tenth failure. The next plot was planned in Hankow in October 1911. Its accidental discovery precipitated the uprising of October 10, since celebrated as the birthday of the Republic, the "double ten" (tenth day of the tenth month). This was the signal for similar risings in most of the other provinces. The Manchus' mandate had been exhausted, and the lead in declaring the independence of one province after another was taken by two principal elements: the military governors who commanded the New Army forces and the gentry-official-merchant leaders of the provincial assemblies. These elements had more power and were more conservative than the youthful revolutionists of the T'ung Meng Hui. The anti-Manchu movement swept the country with comparatively little bloodshed, but the ease with which it overthrew the dynasty was deceptive, for many who joined in the movement soon proved to be less for revolution than simply against the Manchus.

Sun Yat-sen and his many revolutionary colleagues had derived their main support from the new merchant class among the overseas Chinese and from parts of the new student and officer classes within the country. In revolt, they joined with the larger movement, inside China, which sought provincial autonomy particularly in economic development. On this issue the leading landlord gentry and commercial interests active in the provincial assemblies had united in opposition to the belated efforts of the Manchu central government when it tried to reform China from the top down. The whole issue of provincial autonomy against monarchic centralization of power had been raised in the provincial assemblies and also in the provisional national assembly at Peking. It had been brought to a head by the dispute over railroad development, particularly the financing of railroads through Hankow and into Szechwan. On this railroad issue the provincial leaders had ranged themselves in public statements against the element of foreign control implicit in Peking's railway loan agreements. They had been jealous of the prospect that central government officials would chiefly profit from the new developments.

The revolution of 1911 thus represented a good deal more than the revolutionary leadership supplied by Sun Yat-sen and his colleagues. By the same token, Sun, though the nominal leader of the revolution, had relatively little power to control the forces behind it. He was inaugurated as provisional president of the new republic on January 1, 1912, at Nanking. But several considerations combined to make him decide to step aside within a few weeks in favor of Yuan Shih-k'ai, as a strong administrator better fitted to succeed to the top position.

Yuan, the builder of the New Army in North China, had been called to run the Peking government when the Manchu regent resigned in December 1911. With this beginning he was able to improve his position as the only man prospectively capable of maintaining order in the country. He negotiated with Sun but used delaying tactics. Time favored Yuan, for it became increasingly apparent to all that a China which continued divided would invite foreign aggression. The foreign trading powers, led by Great Britain, encouraged peace within China because they feared the possibility of intervention by her territorial neighbors, Japan or Russia. The revolutionists themselves were aware of this danger and tried to secure from Yuan assurances which would safeguard the Republic.

Agreement was soon reached in the negotiations between Yuan at Peking and Sun at Nanking. On February 12, 1912, the Manchu Emperor formally abdicated to Yuan Shih-k'ai as provisional president of the Republic of China. In this new post Yuan was to work with a parliament, and a cabinet vaguely responsible to it, under the terms of a new constitution. In this way the Chinese Republic was inaugurated to succeed the Manchu dynasty without any settlement of the fundamental institutional problems which confronted it. A political institution of 2133 years' standing had come to an end.

While all this occurred within the ruling class, what of the Chinese common people? The late Ch'ing reforms had usually been gentry-led and required more taxes from the people, among whom therefore they were often unpopular. Revolution when it came was led by reform gentry and new military, who jointly set up provincial governments that maintained order. Social change was under way but mainly still within the ruling strata.

Chapter 9
The Rise of the Kuomintang

The end of the monarchy in 1912 marked the beginning of a prolonged crisis of authority and central power in the world's most ancient state. While not exactly theocratic, the Son of Heaven had been indubitably placed above mankind. The significance of the Revolution of 1911 thus lay in its negative achievement—the extinction of the monarchy, which was not just a national kingship of the European type but the universal kingship of the Son of Heaven. This abandonment of China's age-old focus of political life was possible because nationalism had arisen to provide a new loyalty to the Chinese state, culture, and people. But this new nationalism had not yet found institutional expression.

The Search for a New Order

Once the Son of Heaven vanished from the scene, China's political life inevitably deteriorated because the chief of state now lacked the customary ideological sanction for the exercise of final authority. The sovereignty that resided in a dynasty had been far more concrete and tangible than the newly alleged sovereignty of the people, especially when there was as yet no election process to give it form. In the absence of either a dynastic succession or a party election, how was an adminis-

tration to be legitimized? Just at the moment when nationalism had triumphed in theory, the Chinese Republic suffered a
decline of central power in fact, and modern patriots in addition to the continued burden of China's semi-colonial status
under the unequal treaties now had to bear the further humiliation of political chaos.

Two foreign circumstances colored the decade after 1911.
First, the imperialist powers became absorbed in World War
I, and industry in China had a breathing space in which to
develop in relative freedom from the pressure of foreign commercial competition. Second, the World War gave Japan an
opportunity for political aggression. After ousting the Ger-
mans from Shantung in 1914, the Japanese presented to China
in 1915 the notorious Twenty-one Demands. This brazen
diplomacy backed by the threat of force consolidated the Japanese position in Shantung and Manchuria but failed to
achieve a Japanese protectorate over China. In the process
it roused Chinese nationalist sentiment to a new height.

The Collapse of Parliamentary Democracy. Yuan Shih-k'ai,
the provisional president in 1912, had been a leader of the
late-Ch'ing government reforms. A strong administrator, he
drew together an able staff but had trouble securing revenue
from the newly autonomous provincial governments. Meanwhile for more than a year he confronted what Ernest Young
aptly terms "the liberal republic"—new-style institutions of
an elected parliament and a cabinet which were to represent
the people after the fashion of Western democracies. But
these new institutions had little or no foundation in Chinese
political practice.

The idea of political parties, for example, was contrary to
the tradition by which the emperor had ruled through his bureaucracy with a monopoly of political organization while opposition groups had had to become secret societies in order to

survive. Not only were party programs a new alternative to personal leadership as a principle of group organization; the very idea of a cabinet responsible to parliament was a further anomaly, since the cabinet ministers at the same time in the Confucian tradition felt a fundamental loyalty to the head of the state. The old-style landlord interests in the provinces were not accustomed to participating in the settlement of national problems, and the new commercial interests of the treaty ports were not strong enough to dominate their society. The genuinely modern-minded revolutionists formed but a slight leaven in the Chinese political public.

Having no faith in the Western liberal model, Yuan as president steadily built up his position and moved toward dictatorship. He got his own men into the cabinet, disregarded the spirit of the constitution, and attacked the newly organized Kuomintang. The Kuomintang had been created as an open, electioneering political party, out of the revolutionary T'ung Meng Hui and other groups, by a brilliant young Hunanese, Sung Chiao-jen. The Kuomintang candidates in February 1913 won China's first and only national election, based on a very limited franchise. Sung's campaigning to mobilize local gentry support in Central China showed such promise of political leadership that Yuan promptly had him assassinated. This demonstrated a principle (that the ruler is above the law) and a tactic (that opponents can best be checked by eliminating their leader) which have strangled democracy in China ever since. Sung's murder inspired a "second revolution" of several provinces against Yuan in 1913 but he was able with foreign backing to suppress it by force.

Yuan finally dissolved the parliament entirely, got control of the major provinces militarily, and secured the foreign powers' support as China's necessary strong man. His police conducted a reign of terror. He abolished the national and provincial representative assemblies as well as the new local assemblies and councils and tried to reassert civilian bureaucratic control over the whole state. But this effort at centralization torpedoed the initiative and participation of the composite gentry ruling class as local and provincial leaders. Yuan's dicatorship thus lacked a social base.

Led on by his entourage, he eventually attempted in 1915 to establish himself as emperor; he was thwarted in this by the opposition of the revolutionists, abandoned the project, and died in June 1916. After his death China broke up into rival warlord areas and for more than a decade, from 1916 to 1928, suffered disunity even though the government at Peking continued to receive international recognition.

Why did the 1911 revolution fail to build a new Chinese state on Western lines? First, there was no common goal. As already noted, the elements that combined at the time of the uprising had few common objectives beyond the overthrow of the Manchus. Second, there was little body politic, little participation. The revolutionists in their secret plots had not been able and indeed had seldom attempted to mobilize mass support either in the cities or in the countryside. The provincial gentry who cooperated against Peking were at heart the opposite of revolutionary. They soon acknowledged the superior armed force that Yuan commanded. Third, all patriotic Chinese at this time feared foreign intervention. As an alternative to Japanese troops at Peking they acquiesced in the stabilizing efforts of other foreign powers led by the British, who backed Yuan Shih-k'ai. The reorganization loan of £25,000,000 in 1913 (from which the United States abstained) represented the powers' inveterate support of stability, which Yuan then embodied. Against this combination of foreign finance and domestic arms, the revolutionaries could do little. Finally and most important, the ideas of political organization through a constitutional parliament and cabinet, which the Chinese Republic had borrowed from the West, could not be linked up with the Chinese political tradition.

The Republic's Decline into Warlordism. Warlordism was in part an old-style political phenomenon, regionalism carried to the level of power struggle. It was based on the fact that coolie armies were easy to conscript and feed and that most Chinese provinces have natural geographic boundaries and can be made into military satrapies relatively independent of outside authority. Shansi province with its mountain escarpment on the east, the Yellow River on the west and south, and the Great Wall on the north is a prime exemplar of a unit based on geographic boundaries. It is not surprising that it remained continuously from 1911 to 1949 under the domination of a single warlord, the so-called "model governor," Yen Hsi-shan. Other warlord areas were centered about key economic regions such as the Canton delta, the Chengtu plain in Szechwan, the lower Yangtze valley around Shanghai and Nanking, or southern Manchuria. Using these geographic bases it was the aim of each warlord to train and enlarge his army, secure economic resources, and defeat his rivals.

At this point, however, warlordism departed from the old pattern of a dynastic interregnum with its struggle to claim the Mandate of Heaven; for the monarchy was gone, dynasties were out, and a new basis for political unity had to be found. The warlords struggled in an ideological vacuum. To have the commanding personality of a would-be Son of Heaven was not enough. As C. M. Wilbur points out, a warlord must now claim to be acting for "the people," and if possible secure his legitimacy from a civilian parliament. His new officer corps, trained in specialties like artillery, engineering, and signals, might form a nascent, literate bureaucracy with some capacities for administration. But several factors made for continual rivalry among regional commanders. One was the foreign omnipresence, the fact that arms, funds, and even sanctuary might be obtained from treaty ports, if not actually from treaty powers like Japan, which backed the Anfu clique in North China. Another factor was the new transportation, the steamship and railway, which gave the warlord forces a new mobility and tended to uproot them from any one region. As rivals for power, they could not leave one another alone, and so their armies ended up as peripatetic scourges upon the landscape.

Many warlords were military parvenus of lowly origin— bandits, coolies, peddlers, privates risen from the ranks. The most famous was the "Christian General," Feng Yü-hsiang, studied by James Sheridan. He was converted to Methodism and set his men an example of puritan living, physical fitness, and strict discipline. A man of unusual height and physique, Feng prided himself on his peasant origin. He recruited and trained his troops with care, stressing vocational education, recreation clubs, and even conversion to Christianity. It may be untrue that he baptized them with a fire hose. But the folklore concerning him testifies to an unusual vigor of personality. It was symptomatic of the current bankruptcy of politics that Feng had only the vaguest political program and became a pure opportunist, switching allies and fighting first on one side and then on another among the shifting warlord factions. In 1925–26 he accepted Russian aid. In 1927 he joined Chiang Kai-shek but in 1929 was arrayed against him. In the end he became an honored captive of the Kuomintang.

During the height of the warlord period Sun Yat-sen tried repeatedly to achieve his revolutionary objectives through warlord channels. He had soon become disillusioned as to the efficacy of the Western parliamentary system. In 1914 he had withdrawn from the futile competition of the cliques in Chinese politics and had organized again a secret revolutionary party, loyal to himself personally, through which to complete the unfinished task of revolution. In 1917, accompanied by much of the Chinese navy, he went to Canton and sought to cooperate with the local warlords. Thwarted at first, he nevertheless continued his efforts to unify China through military means. In the summer of 1920 Sun was cooperating with the Kwangtung governor to fight the Kwangsi governor. In early 1922 he launched his first, but abortive, northern campaign to invade Hunan, like the Taiping rebels seventy years before.

In these old-style efforts to compete with the warlords by cooperating with some against others, Sun opposed the idea of federalism which was then current. This conception has sometimes been raised in modern China, by analogy to the experience of the United States. In 1922 there was a widespread "federated provinces self-government movement." Intellectuals at this time argued that democracy in China must develop on the level of the provincial assemblies, after which a national government could be built on federal lines. Warlords supported the idea of a federal constitution as a basis for their own local autonomy. It is a striking fact, however, that the logic and apparent expediency of this federalist movement were quite unavailing, for two main reasons. First, the great weight of tradition, that there is "one sun in Heaven, and one ruler on earth," dominated political thinking. Second, the dangers of foreign intervention mobilized all the forces of nationalism in support of unity, to be attained under a strong central government.

The Growth of Urban Nationalism. The rise of patriotic sentiment was fostered in this period by the spread of industry in the great Chinese cities. World War I gave Chinese industrial production an opportunity to expand. Building on earlier beginnings, China developed her own industries in cotton textiles, flour milling, and the production of matches, cigarettes, cement, canned food, and similar mass commodities. Heavy industry and highly technical processes were still retarded. But the use of cheap hand labor to tend cotton spindles or sort tobacco developed steadily. Newly important towns like Tsinan, Hsüchow, and Chengchow grew up at railroad junction points. Shanghai, Tientsin, and Wuhan (including the three cities of Wuchang, Hanyang, and Hankow) became genuine industrial centers with a large factory labor class.

The growth of industrial cities, large and small, offered alternative opportunities of employment for the peasant masses of the countryside. The new cities and the railroads leading to them opened a way of escape from the strait jacket of peasant life. The son of a farmer, for example, no longer had to depend so completely upon his family situation and particularly upon his filial rectitude toward his father as the only road toward a good life. Similarly, peasant women, customarily dependent on male domination, were offered an alternative in the form of factory wages. The old Chinese family system began to crack.

The vital significance of this process will be apparent if we recall how the family had been not only a social but also an economic institution, each peasant household functioning ideally as a self-sufficient unit. The members of the family, tilling their soil and managing their home in common, had had to accept the personal relationships of status, in which each individual found himself placed by fate. The new life of the industrial cities, however, was based on utterly different principles of organization, on function rather than status. There the wage-earning individual could be the economic unit of subsistence, not the family. Moreover, individuals were hired and fired by impersonal criteria of the labor mar-

Muscle power. *Above:* Making lumber in the old way. *Right:* Transporting 267 pounds of wooden bowls, near Ichang, Szechwan, ca. 1909.

ket without reference to personal or family connections. No
one should idealize the life of unskilled laborers in an industrial city. The point is that with all its evils this new life provided an alternative to the old. More than that, it created a
new class of people to whom the old loyalties and customs no
longer applied, a nascent proletarian class ready to give their
allegiance to mass movements such as nationalism and communism.

The growth of the cities had its most immediate effect
upon China's merchant class, for whom the treaty ports of the
nineteenth century had opened a new era of opportunity.
The term comprador (of Portuguese derivation) had become
well established in the pidgin English of the China coast to
designate the "general manager" who represented a foreign

merchant in all his operations in China. Following the example of the celebrated hong merchants who had monopolized the Chinese side of foreign trade at Canton until 1842, the compradors of foreign firms in the treaty ports soon became merchants in their own right. This new merchant class grew up under the wing of the foreigner. It was trained in his ways, and frequently protected by the operation of his laws under the system of extraterritoriality. Chinese merchant capital was amassed in the treaty ports. Absorbing Western ideas, these merchants began to share the concern for national independence and unity which have typified the modern bourgeoisie in other countries. This modern Chinese business class rose to prominence in Shanghai during World War I but, as M. C. Bergère has shown, it soon met political and economic constraints that checked its growth.

Patriotism among Chinese merchants led to the increasing use of boycotts against foreign goods. Boycotts had been a widely used form of passive resistance, or nonviolent coercion, by which organized groups such as merchant guilds could exert their influence upon officialdom. In the twentieth century they began to be used as expressions of anti-foreignism. The Twenty-one Demands in 1915 provoked a nationwide movement to boycott Japanese goods and to encourage the purchase of Chinese goods and the growth of Chinese industries.

The May Fourth Movement

This is the name given in China to the intellectual movement which crystallized in the Peking student demonstration of May 4, 1919. By extension the term has come to represent the whole development of thought and activity among the Chinese scholar class in the years immediately before and after that date. This intellectual movement, so well surveyed by T. T. Chow, was a necessary preparation for the successful Nationalist revolution of the years 1925 to 1928. To be properly understood, the May Fourth Movement must therefore be seen against the background of warlordism, industrialization, and rising patriotism sketched above. In the May Fourth Movement the scholar class now for a brief time assumed the active leadership of the Chinese revolution. This reflected the fact that China's problems lay so deep that the analysis and understanding of them were more than ever prerequisite to effective action. The failure of the constitutional reform movement of 1898 and of the parliamentary movement after 1911 had demonstrated that no mere imitation of the West would suffice to remake China. Yet the national humiliations of the Japanese victory of 1895, the Boxer Protocol of 1901, and the Japanese demands of 1915 had strengthened the realization that Chinese society must be somehow revived and reorganized by the most fundamental changes.

One point of attack upon this problem of change was the classical written language. In the twentieth century a script and even a vocabulary which had been largely created by about 200 B.C. were still being used. In the minds of Western-educated Chinese it inevitably became a question whether this language, like Latin in the West, had not become outmoded and insufficient for modern needs. Like all languages, Chinese has been the creation as well as the creator of those who studied it. Like Japanese, it had begun to absorb modern technical terms. The fundamental question was not the technical one, whether the classical language could be used for modern purposes of scholarship, but the social one, whether its use could be spread among the great mass of the Chinese people as a written medium.

Since the Chinese written language has been one of the tools by which the upper class has enjoyed the fruits of Chinese culture and maintained its social dominance, language reform and the mass literacy which it might make possible have been a fundamental problem in China's revolution.

The first stage in the linguistic revolution was to use the everyday speech in written form—the step taken in Europe at the time of the Renaissance, when the national vernaculars supplanted Latin. Protestant missionaries had pioneered in this effort, to make the scriptures available to the common man. Among the new scholar class the time was ripe. Leadership was taken by Hu Shih, a student at Cornell and Columbia during World War I, who advocated the use of the *pai-hua*, or Chinese spoken language, as a written medium for scholarship and all purposes of communication. Many others joined in this revolutionary movement, which denied the superior value of the old literary style and made the Confucian classics into works of reference rather than textbooks to be memorized by every student. The use of *pai-hua* spread rapidly; the tyranny of the classics had been broken.

Hu Shih, a student of John Dewey and of pragmatism, also became a leader in the advocacy of scientific methods of thought and criticism. The value of science in technical studies had long been incontrovertible. Its application, as a way of thought, to Chinese literary criticism and historical scholarship now marked a further step. The new scholarship vigorously attacked the myths and legends of early Chinese history and reassessed the authenticity of the classics.

With science came democracy as the other watchword of the new learning. Leadership in the propagation of the new doctrine of Science and Democracy was taken by the son of a rich family, Ch'en Tu-hsiu. He had absorbed in France the tradition of the French Revolution and returned to found a magazine in Shanghai in 1915 called *The New Youth (Hsin Ch'ing Nien,* or *La Jeunesse).* In this and a score of similar journals which soon sprang up in the cities, the scholars of this revolutionary generation debated and discussed the application of Western ideas to China's ancient culture. Hu Shih stood for a critical attitude toward all things and the necessity of persistent, long-term efforts to change Chinese thinking bit by bit, solving problems, not marching to slogans. Ch'en Tu-hsiu, in the name of human rights and social equality, attacked Confucianism. Like Liang Ch'i-ch'ao, these scholars pointed the way toward an ethical revolution at the very roots of China's ancient society. Beginning in 1917 this intellectual ferment centered in the University of Peking (commonly abbreviated in China as Peita), where the chancellor, Ts'ai Yuan-p'ei, a courageous advocate of freedom of thought and expression, added Ch'en Tu-hsiu and Hu Shih to his faculty.

The Student Movement and New Literature. The incident of May 4, 1919, was provoked by the decision of the peacemakers at Versailles to leave in Japanese hands the former German concessions in Shantung. After learning of this decision, some five thousand students from Peita and other Peking institutions held a mass demonstration at theT'ien-an men, the gateway leading to the palace. They burned the house of a pro-Japanese cabinet minister and seized and beat the Chinese minister to Japan. Police attacked the students. They thereupon called a student strike, sent telegrams to students elsewhere, and organized patriotic teams to distribute leaflets and make speeches among the populace. Similar demonstrations were staged in Tientsin, Shanghai, Nanking, Wuhan, Foochow, Canton, and elsewhere. A few students were killed and others were wounded. The prisons were soon full of demonstrators.

The spirit of protest spread among the merchants, who joined the movement by closing their shops in a merchants' strike which spread through the major centers in June of 1919. This developed into a boycott of Japanese goods attended by clashes with Japanese residents. For more than a year student patriots continued the agitation for the destruction of Japan's market in China, with an appreciable effect upon it. Meanwhile strikes were staged among the recently organized labor unions, which joined in the broadest demonstration of national feeling that China had ever seen.

The startling thing about this movement was that it was led by intellectuals who brought both the new cultural ideas of science and democracy and the new patriotism into a common focus in an anti-imperialist program. More than ever before the student class assumed responsibility for China's fate. They even began through their student organizations to reach the common people in the villages, to bring scholars into touch with peasants in a common cause. But their main influence was still city-bound.

Literature led the way in this effort, in novels and short stories in the new written vernacular. Most writers were well educated and from the upper class. Leading figures had studied in Japan, but once returned to China they lived in urban poverty and often under police harassment. Their audience was mainly young students in the cities who were caught up like the writers themselves in the social revolution. They opposed the bonds of the family system and stood for individual self-expression including sexual freedom. Leo Lee, Merle Goldman, Harriet Mills, and others have shown how the romantic individualism and self-revelation of some pioneers, telling all in a first-person narrative or diary style, was quite shocking to strict Confucian mores. In the later 1920s a less sentimental, more socially conscious concern arose, as individuals struggled to find a cause and serve society.

The outstanding writer of the 1920s, Lu Hsün (1881–1936), came from a Chekiang gentry family that fell into disgrace. He took the first-level classical examination, studied science at naval and military academies, began medical training in Japan and finally settled upon his interest in literature as a means of social reform. But his early efforts to rouse his countrymen with translations of Western, especially Slavic, literature (which he read in German) met no response. Lu Hsün returned to a government job in Peking thoroughly depressed. He leaped into prominence only in 1918 by publishing in *New Youth* his satire "The Diary of a Madman," who finds between the lines of "benevolence, righteousness, truth, virtue" in his history book two words repeated everywhere: "Eat men." Chinese culture, he wrote, was "a culture of serving one's masters, who are triumphant at the cost of the misery of the multitude."

The Nationalist Revolution

In a general way the Nationalist revolution of the 1920s combined the traditional trend toward reunification of the country under a strong leader (in this case Chiang Kai-shek) with a new trend toward modern government through the use of Western administrative methods, the inculcation of a new loyalty to the nation, and the monopoly of power by a party dictatorship (rather than a dynasty). The dominant sentiment behind the revolution was a nationalism which sought both unity within China and independence from foreign domination. Its class basis was still, however, the literate upper stratum. Essentially, the Nanking government in the decade after 1927 led the way in establishing upper class institutions. But it turned against the idea of revolutionizing the life of the common peasant.

This part-way nature of the Nationalist cause, its limited aims in the reorganizing of Chinese society, emerged quite clearly in the 1920s. The occasion was provided by Sun Yat-sen's decision in 1922 to learn from, and Chiang Kai-shek's decision in 1927 to break with, Soviet Russia.

The Kuomintang-Communist Alliance. The Chinese Nationalist revolution, in its effort to shake off the unequal treaties and other bonds of imperialism, was of course deeply influenced by the doctrines of Marxism-Leninism and the example of Soviet Russia. Leninist theory put anti-imperialism on a more than national basis and made it a part of the worldwide trend of history. Since political thinking in China had always been based on universal principles, and the Chinese empire had traditionally embraced the civilized world, Chinese revolutionists readily sought to base their cause on doctrines of universal validity. Ch'en Tu-hsiu became one of the founders of the Chinese Communist Party, which was organized in the summer of 1921 in Shanghai. Sun Yat-sen, while not subscribing to the Communist idea of class struggle, in the last years before his death (in March 1925) fully recognized the usefulness of Communist methods and accepted Communist collaboration in his Nationalist cause.

The Russian Bolsheviks had organized the Comintern (Communist International) out of scattered groups in various countries. Their first Comintern congress in 1919 was followed by six other international congresses before World War II. Immediately after World War I the Comintern encouraged active revolution in many countries in Europe. But after 1921, when Lenin turned the Soviet Union to his new economic policy, though the Comintern still competed with the revived socialist parties of Europe, it was less actively revolutionary, except in China.

Lenin held that Western capitalism was using the backward countries of Asia as a source of profit to bolster the capitalist system. Without imperialist exploitation of Asia, which allowed continued high wages for the workers of the West, capitalism would more rapidly collapse. Nationalist revolutions in Asia, which would deprive the imperialist powers of their profitable markets and sources of raw materials, would therefore constitute a "flank attack" on Western capitalism at its weakest point—that is, in Asian economies where imperialist domination exploited the working class most ruthlessly. From the very beginning the Bolsheviks had therefore called upon the colonial peoples to rise against their Western masters. From this time on, Lenin's explanation of imperialism was to gain increasing acceptance among Asian intellectuals.

In China the Soviet government had capitalized upon its own impotence by grandly renouncing the privileges of the tsar's unequal treaties. But it subsequently proved a hard bargainer over the old tsarist rights in Manchuria, and its Foreign Office continued to deal diplomatically with the Peking government and warlords in North China while the Comintern worked subversively for revolution. The Comintern picked China as the chief area of foreign struggle and British imperialism as its chief target in the years from 1922 to 1927.

On his part Sun Yat-sen by 1922, after thirty years of agitation, had reached a low point in his fortunes. He had been proclaimed president of the Chinese Republic only to see his country disintegrate into warlordism. His effort to unify China through warlord means had led him into dealings with opportunist military leaders at Canton. In June 1922 a Cantonese militarist whom he had attempted to outmaneuver turned the tables upon him. Sun was forced to flee, and reached Shanghai in August. It was just at this moment, when Sun had demonstrated his pre-eminence as China's Nationalist leader but his incompetence to complete the revolution, that he joined forces with the Comintern. In September 1922 he began the reorganization of the Kuomintang on Soviet lines.

This was purely a marriage of convenience. The entente announced in a joint statement by Dr. Sun and a Soviet representative in January 1923 was a strictly limited arrangement.

It stated that Sun did not favor communism for China, since conditions were not appropriate to it, that the Soviets agreed that China needed unity and independence, and were ready to aid the Chinese Nationalist revolution. As Sun Yat-sen wrote to Chiang Kai-shek at the time, he had to seek help where he could get it. The Western powers offered no aid. But although Sun now sought and accepted Soviet Russian aid, communism in his mind did not supplant his own Three Principles of the People as the program for the Chinese revolution—even though he found it useful to incorporate in his ideas the Communist emphasis on a mass movement fired by anti-imperialism.

On the basis of this uneasy alliance, Soviet help was soon forthcoming. Chiang Kai-shek spent three months in Russia in late 1923 and returned to head the new Whampoa Military Academy at Canton in 1924. Meanwhile a Soviet adviser, Michael Borodin, an able organizer who had lived in the United States, became the Kuomintang's expert on how to make a revolution. He helped to set up a political institute for the training of propagandists, to teach Kuomintang politicians how to secure mass support. On the Soviet model the Kuomintang now developed local cells, which in turn elected representatives to a party congress. The first national congress was convened in January 1924, and elected a Soviet-modeled central executive committee as the chief authority in the party. Borodin wrote its new constitution.

In addition to aiding the Nationalist revolution, the ulterior objective of the Comintern was to develop the Chinese Communist Party and get it into a strategic position within the Kuomintang, so as eventually to seize control of it. Members of the Chinese Communist Party were, by agreement with the Kuomintang, admitted to membership in it as individuals, at the same time that the Chinese Communist Party continued its separate existence. This admission of Communists seemed feasible to Sun Yat-sen because they were still so few in number, the two parties were united on the basis of anti-imperialism, and the Kuomintang aimed to lead a broad, national multi-class movement avoiding class war. Sun also felt that there was little real difference between the People's Livelihood and communism, that the Chinese Communists were only a group of "youngsters" who hoped to monopolize Russian aid, that Russia would disavow them if necessary to cooperate with the Kuomintang.

On their side the Chinese Communists were seeking definite class support among urban workers, poor peasants, and students. But they recognized that this class basis was still weak. They therefore sought to go along with and utilize the Nationalist movement without antagonizing the major non-Communist elements within it. It should not be forgotten that the Communist Party in China at this time was still in its infancy. It numbered hardly more than 300 members in 1922, only 1500 or so by 1925, whereas the Kuomintang in 1923 had some 50,000 members. As in other countries the Chinese Communists of this period were significant for their ideas and methods of organization rather than their numbers.

Thus from the beginning the Kuomintang-Communist entente was a precarious thing, held together by the usefulness of each group to the other, by their common enemy, imperialism, and, while he lived, by Sun Yat-sen's predominance over the more anti-Communist elements of his party.

The Nationalist Accession to Power. After Dr. Sun's untimely death in March 1925, his followers achieved, in 1926–27, the successful northern expedition from Canton to the Yangtze valley. The newly trained propagandists of the Nationalist revolution preceded the armies of Chiang Kai-shek, who was aided by Russian arms and advisers. This military effort was the climax to the great wave of nationwide anti-imperialist sentiment which had been roused by student demonstrations and police gunfire in incidents at Shanghai and Canton (May 30 and June 23, 1925, respectively). These provocative and dramatic proofs that the unequal treaties and the foreigners' privileges still persisted had been followed by a prolonged boycott and strike against the British at Hong Kong.

Thus Chinese nationalism in the years from 1925 to 1927 had reached a new height of expression and was focused against Britain as the chief imperialist power. To defend their position the British on the one hand restored to China their concessions at Hankow and Kiukiang on the Yangtze and on the other hand, with the support of the powers, built up an international force of 40,000 troops to protect Shanghai. In fear of anti-foreignism, most of the missionaries evacuated the interior. In March 1927, when the revolutionary troops reached Nanking, foreign residents were attacked, six of them killed, and the others evacuated under the protecting shellfire of American and British gunboats.

It was at this point in the spring of 1927 that the latent split between the right and left wings of the revolution finally became complete. For two years the right and left within the movement had generally cooperated, although as early as March 1926 Chiang Kai-shek had arrested leftist elements at Canton allegedly to forestall a plot to kidnap him. His three-month view of Russia in 1923 had left him aware of Soviet methods and suspicious of Communist aims. The success of the Northern Expedition finally took the lid off the situation.

In brief, the left wing of the Kuomintang together with the Communists by March 1927 dominated the revolutionary government, which had been moved from Canton to Wuhan. Here were collected, among other leaders, Madame Sun Yat-sen and Wang Ching-wei, the widow and the chief disciple of

The Rise of the Kuomintang

the founder, and Borodin, the chief adviser on revolution. Wuhan had been proclaimed the new national capital. This suited Communist strategy because it was a large industrial center. Two members of the Chinese Communist Party had actually been made cabinet ministers. But this government was weak in military strength.

Chiang Kai-shek with the support of the more conservative leaders of the Kuomintang had aimed at the rich strategic center of the lower Yangtze. Once the Shanghai-Nanking region was in his grasp, Chiang was able by military force to forestall the Communists, and consolidate his position. In April 1927 at Shanghai foreign troops and warships confronted the Communist-led labor unions, which had seized local control. Under Comintern orders they awaited Chiang as their ally, only to be attacked and decimated by his forces once he had got in a position to do so. He set up his capital at Nanking and shortly afterward a local general seized power at Wuhan and broke up the left-wing government. Some of its leaders fled to Moscow. The new Nanking government expelled the Chinese Communists from its ranks and instituted a nationwide terror to suppress the Communist revolution. In this effort it was, for the time being, largely successful. Small contingents of Communist-led troops revolted, and in December 1927 the Communists attempted a coup at Canton. But after this failure to seize power they withdrew to the rural mountain area of Kiangsi province in Central China.

This ignominious failure of the Comintern's laboratory experiment in revolution in China had been affected by a power struggle in Moscow. Trotsky and his followers had criticized the Comintern effort to work through the Kuomintang. They foresaw Chiang Kai-shek's "betrayal" and urged an independent program to develop workers' and peasants' soviets in China under purely Communist leadership. Stalin and his supporters, however, had argued that an independent Communist movement in so backward a country would invite suppression all the sooner. They had looked forward to the time at a later stage of the revolution when, in Stalin's phrase, the Communists could drop their Kuomintang allies as so many "squeezed-out lemons." Whatever the merits of these competing strategies, it is plain that the right-wing Kuomintang squeezed first.

Much of the Comintern's ineptitude undoubtedly came from its remoteness from the scene of action. Lacking instantaneous radio communication, Stalin and his colleagues could hardly succeed in masterminding by the aid of Marxist dialectics the confused and unprecedented stirrings of revolution in a place like Shanghai. The Comintern plot in China was also frustrated by the Comintern's own prior act in giving the Kuomintang a centralized Soviet-style party apparatus, which was much harder to infiltrate and subvert than an open Western-style parliamentary party. In the end the Comintern made Ch'en Tu-hsiu, who had been a founder and leader of the Chinese Communist Party, the scapegoat. He was expelled in 1929.

Chiang Kai-shek's break with the Communists represented an effort to consolidate the gains of the national revolution at a certain level in the revolutionary process, stopping short of class struggle, social revolution, and the remaking of peasant life in the villages. This consolidation in the Nanking government, combined with military campaigns to check revolt, enabled Chiang and the Kuomintang leaders to achieve a superficial national unity, secure the recognition of the powers, and begin the process of administrative development, which would be a necessary prerequisite to the abolition of the unequal treaties. In the spring of 1928 Chiang led a further northern expedition from the Yangtze to Peking, which was occupied in June and renamed Peiping ("Northern Peace"). In November the young warlord of Manchuria completed the nominal unification of all China by recognizing the jurisdiction of the Nanking government. Meantime the foreign powers one by one made treaties with it and so gave the Nationalist revolution international recognition.

In historical perspective, these achievements can be viewed as a phase in a long process which has not even yet been finished—the gradual mobilization of the Chinese people in their national political life. The fact that the Nationalist revolution went only part way in realizing this potentiality of popular mobilization gave the Communists their later opportunity.

Chapter 10
The Nanking Government

History is regularly colored by the age-old rule that any regime stands condemned by its successor. Nanking said little in favor of Yuan Shih-k'ai and the warlords. Today in the People's Republic, the Kuomintang era is seen as a dark age, the acme of feudal backwardness, imperialist aggression, and social evils. Yet in the long course of China's struggle for regeneration, the Nanking decade began as the time of greatest promise since 1912. Let us view it for itself, as an interlude between the earlier evil of warlordism and the later evil of Japanese invasion.

The most poignant feature of the Nanking period as we look back at it is the superficiality of modern things in China up to that time. The modern China with which we Americans then had contact was a thin veneer spread lightly over the surface of an ancient civilization. Beneath it the old China still endured, in the peasant villages of half a continent. But it was cut off from us by barriers of language, material standards, and social taboos. Americans had no direct contact with the profuse remnants of this old culture. Our knowledge of it was mediated through modern China, which included the educated elite, the routes of rail and steamship communication, books and newspapers in the modern language, the new conceptions and interests assimilated from the West. All this agglomeration of modern life in China—financiers, students, urban proletariat, ricksha coolies (a new profession), and trained soldiers—were participants in the new society which represented on Chinese soil the new world culture of literacy, telecommunications, factory industry, world markets, and mass movements. But beneath and behind this new China whose life interpenetrated with ours abroad lay the old Chinese society, rooted in an alien cultural tradition, which Westerners, and often the modern Chinese, failed to understand.

Our failure in understanding sprang partly from our mistaking the modern veneer of China for the whole of Chinese life. This was particularly easy because the top stratum of Chinese society—the moneyed, official, and literate classes —almost monopolized the machinery of power. The government, the banking structure, education and the press, the bureaucracy, were dominated by the new generation, many of whom indeed knew English and could the more easily deal with China's alien problems in a Western way.

In short, Chinese society was still dominated by a small ruling class, and foreigners in China by their unequal treaty privileges had become a part of this ruling class establishment.

Political Development

It was deceptively easy during this generation for a new class of Chinese scholars, merchants, and officials to use foreign techniques—financial, military, and ideological—in order to erect a new Chinese nation on the ruins of the old Chinese society. Yet how superficial a thing this new nation was may be seen in a few statistics. In mileage of highways, China (78,850 miles in 1943) was about the size of Spain (77,574 miles in 1941). In mileage of steam railroads, China in 1942 (12,036 miles including Manchuria) was smaller than Illinois (12,967 miles) or Italy (14,384 miles). In cotton spindles China was also about the size of Italy. The telegraph lines at the disposal of an administration governing in China (59,275 miles in 1943) exceeded those available in Italy (41,354 miles in 1938) but were less than a third of those in France (229,000 miles in 1937). If we turn to less material matters, the total of 1,163,116 students in secondary schools in China (population say 450 million) hardly exceeded the total of 1,077,000 students in high schools in the two states of Illinois and New York (population roughly 23 million).

However we look at it, Kuomintang China in its equipment and modern plant was a small show. In industrial production it was smaller than Belgium, in air and sea power negligible, in the gadgets and equipment of American life not as big as a middle western state. Yet this small and relatively insignificant modern state was spread out over the protean body of a vigorous people in a vast and ancient land. Nanking's problems were therefore formidable from the start.

Party Dictatorship. The Nationalist government at Nanking in the decade from 1927 to 1937 was the most modern that China had known. It was controlled by the Kuomintang on the basis of party dictatorship. The Kuomintang had inherited from Sun Yat-sen his five-power division of the government among executive, legislative, judicial, civil service, and censorial agencies *(yuan)*. Of these, the Executive Yuan with its dozen ministries of Foreign Affairs, Economics, Communications, War, and the like at once became dominant and overshadowed all the others. The last two agencies, the Examination Yuan and the Control Yuan, were derived by Sun from the imperial traditions of the examinations and the censorate. In practice this censorate tradition was carried further by the extensive growth of the secret police, both of the government and of the party. Sun's theory of the three stages of the revolution (military unification, political tutelage, and constitutional democracy) was put into effect by the proclamation in 1929 of the beginning of the period of political tutelage under the Kuomintang dictatorship.

Ever since the first Party Congress had met in January 1924 and adopted a Soviet-style organization, the Central Executive Committee had become the chief repository of political authority. High officials of the government were chosen by the Central Executive Committee and usually from it. Constitutional government was postponed. Party ministries, such as the Ministries of Information, Social Affairs, Overseas Affairs, or Party Organization, functioned as part of the central administration and yet were in form under the Kuomintang, not the government. Party and government thus became indistinguishable.

But in this way the Kuomintang became a wing of the bureaucracy and lost its revolutionary mission. The earlier party supervision of local administration, its political work in the army, its special criminal courts to try counterrevolutionaries, all were reduced or abandoned. So also were the mass organizations of workers, peasants, youth, merchants, and women. These mass movements had mobilized popular support for the Northern Expedition, but the Nanking power holders now looked askance at processions, demonstrations, and mass meetings. They discouraged student movements, looking back upon all these activities of the mid-twenties as useful tools to beat the warlords but no longer of value, now that power was theirs to organize for purposes of control. With this attitude the Kuomintang suffered an actual drop in numbers. By late 1929 its membership totaled barely 550,000 of whom 280,000 were military. Members in Shanghai were mainly officials or policemen.

Rights Recovery. Nationalism received its first expression after the unification of 1928 in the "rights recovery" movement. This was an effort to wipe out the unequal treaties bit by bit. The Washington Conference in 1922 had provided for modifications in extraterritoriality and the customs tariff. By 1930 the Nanking government had secured treaties which placed many minor foreign nationalities under Chinese legal jurisdiction. New civil and criminal codes had been issued. The old Sino-Foreign Mixed Court at Shanghai had been abolished, although the major powers, Britain, the United States, France, and Japan, had not yet given up extraterritoriality. This promising beginning came to a halt when the Japanese aggression of 1931–32 gave both the Chinese and the other foreign powers a common interest in the preservation of the powers' legal position in China.

Similarly the new Nationalist government sought to realize the promise of the Washington Conference regarding tariff reform. Under the unequal treaties China had been prevented from protecting her native industries or taxing foreign trade for revenue beyond nominal rates of about 5 percent. Most of the available customs revenue had become earmarked to pay foreign loans and indemnities. After 1911 the customs duties had been collected, in effect, for an international commission of bankers. The Nanking government at once moved to recover tariff autonomy and by 1930 had done so. Boxer indemnity payments by that time had also been largely remitted by the powers, on the understanding in the cases of Britain and the United States that the sums due would continue to be made available by China mainly for educational purposes.

The foreign concessions which had been the embodiment of the unequal treaties began to return to Chinese sovereignty. By the outbreak of the war with Japan in 1937 the maximum of thirty-three concession areas leased to foreign powers had been reduced to thirteen, in addition to the continuing International Settlements at Shanghai and Amoy. The rights of the foreign powers to station troops and warships in China and navigate her inland waters still persisted. But this was mainly because they had become measures of international opposition to Japanese encroachment. In general the Nanking government had begun to satisfy the demands of Chinese nationalism for the assertion of Chinese sovereignty and international equality. By 1937 the chief impairment of China's national independence came not from the unequal treaties (which were finally abolished in 1943) but from Japan.

The Rise of Chiang Kai-shek

One long-term factor in the Chinese Communist rise to power was Japan's continuous effort at military conquest, which roused the Chinese people for patriotic political action but weakened the Nationalist government's capacity to lead them in other than military ways.

By defeating Russia in 1905, Japan had acquired a strategic and patriotic stake in the area now known as China's Northeast, which except for the Liaotung ("east of the Liao River") region in the south had been the Manchu dynasty's homeland. Having inherited Russia's imperialist privileges in this part of China, Japan and its South Manchurian Railway Company fostered export trade, especially in soybeans, and heavy industry around Mukden. When Chinese nationalism increasingly resisted this expansion, young officers of the Japanese army with the knowledge of their superiors staged an incident at Mukden in September 1931 and soon took over most of Manchuria. In March 1932 it was proclaimed the independent state of Manchukuo ("the Manchu kingdom") with the last Ch'ing emperor (P'u-yi) as ruler.

Japan's attack, from 1931 on, obliged the Kuomintang to

continue militarizing in self-defense. Its resources went into its armies, its leadership into the hands of a generalissimo, its policies became more defensive and militaristic—"unify before resisting" rather than "unify by resisting." Whampoa generals and party organizers came to dominate its councils and control its actions as they might not otherwise have done.

In Chiang Kai-shek the government had a military leader who met the demands both of ancient tradition and of warlord politics. Born in 1887 in a gentry family near Ningpo, Chiang had entered China's first military academy at Paoting near Peking in 1906 and then spent four years at a military college in Tokyo. A convert of Sun Yat-sen's, he participated in the revolutionary efforts of 1911 and 1913. During the first World War he led an obscure existence as a small broker in Shanghai. His career really began when Sun sent him to Moscow in 1923. He provided the Nationalist movement, through his political astuteness and ruthless determination, with a strong man who could deal with and outdo the warlords. In this respect he was the traditional hero who founds a dynasty by skill and violence. To get around the constraints of extraterritoriality he had seized Shanghai in 1927 through alliance with the organized underworld of the Green Gang. Its reign of terror began as anti-Communist but later became anti-capitalist also, when threats, kidnappings, and assassinations squeezed massive funds out of the business class for Nanking's use. Chiang Kai-shek in power was a party member, austerely and fervently devoted to the cause of Chinese nationalism, which he came to regard as indistinguishable from his own career. After sharing power in the early 1930s with Wang Ching-wei and other party stalwarts senior to him, Chiang eventually emerged as the one indispensable man. Japan's aggressions, combined with Nanking's domestic problem of suppressing warlord and Communist armies, made him essential. Chiang has been aptly characterized as a "military politician," supremely capable of holding power in a country where armies and generals, not electorates, provide the final sanction. In the larger context Diana Lary views him as representing "party militarism" of a centralized type, "needed to dispose of regional militarism."

In the end the Generalissimo's power rested on a tripod of army, party, and government. Surviving graduates of the first classes at the Whampoa Military Academy formed a "Whampoa clique" of generals personally loyal to him, which dominated China's new armies. In 1939 he became permanent Party Leader. Any office he held was the point of government decision making. All this reflected not merely Chiang's ability but even more the demand of the Chinese political scene for personal rule by a modern Son of Heaven.

Echoes of Confucianism. The growth of political controls through local gendarmerie, secret police, press censorship, subsidizing of education, the *pao-chia,* and other devices, all supervised by the local party office, was accompanied in Kuomintang China by a Confucian revival. This doctrinal metamorphosis began by stressing the principle of nationalism and from it going back to the national heritage to find political doctrines which would support central power. Even as commandant at Whampoa in 1924 Chiang Kai-shek had taken as his model the victor over the Taipings, Tseng Kuo-fan. As Mary Wright has shown, the example of revived Confucian government in the 1860s had a fatal fascination for the Kuomintang leaders of the 1930s, even though the Restoration had failed to preserve the traditional Confucian order.

By 1934 the state cult of Confucius was nominally revived. In the same year Chiang launched his New Life Movement to instill in his people a new social consciousness and martial spirit through a revival of the ancient moral virtues: proper behavior according to status, right conduct, integrity, and the sense of shame. Since these classical concepts were now vague at best, ninety-six specific rules applied them to the categories of food, clothing, shelter, and action: for example, do not eat noisily, correct your posture, stop smoking, keep your gown buttoned, do not spit, kill rats and flies, be prompt, use native products. Through a nationwide network of some 1300 local associations, the movement sought paternalistically to lead each individual to practice orderliness and cleanliness. Many other activities proliferated under it in 1934–1937.

Roots of Totalitarianism. Unnoticed by his American admirers, Chiang also became a devotee of fascism, the apparent wave of the future in the 1930s. As Lloyd Eastman has pointed out, Nazi German officers were training Chiang's troops. Sensing that the Kuomintang revolution had lost its vitality, he tried to revive it by borrowing from abroad, creating a secret faction within the party, known as the Blue Shirts, an elite mainly of Whampoa graduates, sworn to follow him as leader. The Blue Shirts opposed Western capitalist materialism, democracy, communism, self-seeking individualism, corrupt bureaucratism and all other sources of national weakness. Like their European counterparts, they were ready to use violence, in utter devotion to the nation and its leader. With some 10,000 members, this fascist secret society set up a network of branches with small-group units that met for weekly discussion. The New Life Movement we can now see was only a public manifestation of this pervasive effort to save China by militarization and dictatorship. Another and more formidable offshoot was the Special Services (*t'e-wu*), a secret anti-Communist intelligence-terrorist organization headed by the faithful Tai Li, who specialized in assassination.

Chiang Kai-shek's thought was a syncretism derived from many sources: Tseng Kuo-fan's view of moral purpose as the arbiter of human affairs, Lenin's interpretation of imperialism, the Methodist piety of a practicing Christian, influences from Japan, Russia, America, and the Axis powers, all within the framework of a conservative nationalism. Much of this appears in the book that he published in Chinese, not for foreign consumption, in 1943, *China's Destiny*. This volume celebrated the abolition of the American and British unequal treaties in 1943 and became required reading for Free China's youth in the compulsory study of "party principles." It attributed China's national humiliation and other modern ills almost entirely to the unequal treaties. The treaty ports caused the spread of famine, stock market panics, the breakup of the family, selfishness, the use of narcotics, profit-seeking materialism, Chinese self-abasement, and the slavish copying of Western ways. While publishing this work to urge national revival by moral regeneration, Chiang also produced in 1943 a work restricted to official circles entitled *Chinese Economic Theory*. In it he derived from the ancient philosophers a sanction for the state control of economic life. Against Western free enterprise this work called for an anti-Marxist Confucian totalitarianism. It sought to direct China's industrialization toward building a defense state, rather than toward mass welfare. Specifically, Chiang asserted that Western economic theory is unsuited to China and so he tried to reconstruct China's traditional economics by quoting the sages. This opened the door to several non-Western conceptions—for example, that land and labor are factors of production in China, but not capital. Chiang proposed to conscript China's farmers onto collective farms where they would also be soldiers. If the masses were farmer-soldiers, China would be strong. In general, Chiang castigated the liberal tradition in economics as advocating government noninterference in the people's economic life. In China he believed the government should not only plan the people's livelihood but also control and

Treaty port life. *Above:* Returned students from Britain, France, and the United States. *Below:* Sikh policeman directing Shanghai traffic.

restrict their wants, thus combining "benevolence" with "justice."

The revival of Confucianism was most actively promoted by Ch'en Li-fu, whose uncle had been Chiang Kai-shek's patron and who became Chiang's most loyal political organizer. Ch'en Li-fu had studied at the Pittsburgh School of Mines. He specialized in party personnel management, together with his elder brother, Ch'en Kuo-fu, the patriarch of the Central Political Institute for the training of civil servants. The Ch'en brothers led the "CC" clique which dominated the right wing of the Kuomintang. In general Ch'en Li-fu called for the fusion of Western technology and Confucian social values. "The spirit of Confucianism is the means of adjusting our culture to the modern age." He urged that the dicta of famous Confucian scholars be systematically arranged and explained to the people. "Confucianism belongs to no specific class." It is actually in keeping with Sun's Three Principles.

These ideas of Chiang and his henchman made no contribution to Chinese thought but had importance because they were held by the wielders of Kuomintang power. Modern-minded Chinese could not find in their confused atavism any solution to the fundamental problems of China's adaptation to modern life.

The resulting alienation of student intellectuals during the Nanking decade was indexed by Communist success in dominating the field of modern literature. For example, Lu Hsün during the 1920s had been hounded out of Peking and disillusioned by Nationalist Canton. Eventually he accepted the Chinese Communist Party's aims, though never becoming a party member, and in 1930 helped found in Shanghai the League of Left-wing Writers, whose widespread activities marked the beginning of Communist ascendancy in the literary world.

The progression among modern writers during the 1920s

from subjective self-expression to the discipline of socialist realism was epitomized by Ting Ling. Her early writings had revealed a liberated woman's most intimate feelings, and she won fame and notoriety. But her husband was shot, and she was imprisoned by the KMT. As Yi-tsi Feuerwerker says, literature was her "response to the horrors of what was happening" around her; just as for the whole May 4 generation, writing was an "answer to the insoluble problems of their times." But in the 1930s increasingly, "as total revolution seemed the only way out," literature became subordinated to political action. And the revolution treated literature as a tool, not an art. Typically, Ting Ling maintained that "no matter how literary creation is guided, a work is created through the individual" (but in 1958 her personal life was to be denounced with puritanical outrage and she was to be expelled from the Communist party for "bourgeois individualism"). Meanwhile, despite Nanking's failure to win the allegiance of literary talent, beginnings were under way in the long process of China's economic development.

Progress toward Industrialization

Transportation. The major means of transport in Central and South China was the ancient system of waterways, which make the great Yangtze River still the lifeline of the country. The old China was not able to defend herself on these routes, and the opening of China had begun with the British and American steamship invasion of the junk trade along the coasts and up the Yangtze. Foreign treaty rights of inland navigation gave British firms like Jardine Matheson and Company for a time almost a monopoly of modern waterborne commerce. Even as late as 1936 two fifths of the steam tonnage in China's domestic coastal and river trade was still un-

The railway at Peking. Coalyard of the Peking-Hankow line outside the Tartar city wall, ca. 1903. The frozen moat is a thoroughfare. *Background:* Inner and outer towers and barbican wall of Ch'ien Men, the "front gate."

der the British flag. Chinese vessels carried less of this domestic trade than did those flying the Union Jack.

Railways had been delayed as long as possible because officials of the Manchu period were fully aware of their strategic importance and wanted them, when built, to be under Chinese control. The first railroad, from Shanghai to Wusung, was proposed in 1865, constructed by foreign merchants in 1876, purchased and destroyed by Chinese authorities in 1878. By 1894 China had only 195 miles of railroad in the whole country. After the imperialist powers' scramble for concessions in 1898, this mileage was increased to 2700 by 1903 and 5800 by 1911. The decade before the revolution saw the completion of the network from Shanghai to Nanking and thence to Tientsin and Peking and the parallel line on the west from Hankow to Peking, which provided two main north-south arteries north of the Yangtze. The first Chinese-built line had also been started along the southern border of Inner Mongolia, west from Peking. A beginning had been made on the Lunghai Railroad, the main east-west line just south of the Yellow River (see map).

As Arthur Rosenbaum has pointed out, this slow growth showed the inhibiting effect of imperialism. The foreign contracts to finance China's railways commonly required foreign supervision, which in turn led to separate administrations and to overinvestment in foreign materials to meet "Western standards." This prevented creating a national rail system that could, for example, pool rolling stock and share shop facilities. Moreover, each line charged high rates in order not to default on its foreign loan payments, and its public service was limited accordingly.

After 1911 the combination of warlord rivalry, foreign absorption in the World War, and the international bankers' consortium arrangements (which tended to act as a brake on the investment both of Japanese and other foreign capital),

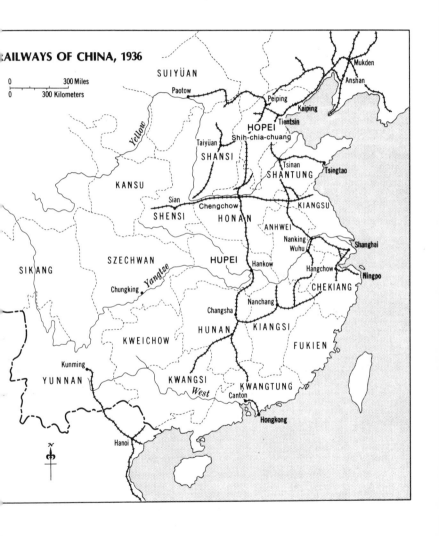

RAILWAYS OF CHINA, 1936

0   300 Miles
0   300 Kilometers

SUIYÜAN

Paotow

Yellow

Peiping

Kaiping

Tientsin

HOPEI

Shih-chia-chuang

Taiyüan

SHANSI

KANSU

Tsinan

SHANTUNG

Tsingtao

Sian

Chengchow

KIANGSU

SHENSI

HONAN

ANHWEI

Nanking

Wuhu

Shanghai

SZECHWAN

Yangtze

HUPEI

Hankow

Hangchow

CHEKIANG

Ningpo

Chungking

Nanchang

SIKANG

Changsha

KIANGSI

HUNAN

FUKIEN

KWEICHOW

Kunming

YUNNAN

KWANGSI

West

KWANGTUNG

Canton

Hongkong

Hanoi

Mukden

Anshan

all contributed again to the retardation of railroad development. By 1926 the total mileage in China including Manchuria was only 7683 and by 1935 it was still under 10,000 miles. The railway accompanied the expansion of the frontier of Chinese settlement into Manchuria more easily than it could be introduced into the crowded countryside and rough terrain of South China. As a result, more than a third of all China's railways were in Manchuria, serving less than one tenth of China's population. (By 1945 Japan's heavy investment in Manchukuo's strategic and economic rail network made the total mileage roughly equal to that in China proper.)

Railroad construction in Chinese hands was held back by lack of capital. When provincial gentry had demanded control over railroad construction before the Revolution of 1911, they had put forward projects in fourteen provinces, but were unable to mobilize the requisite capital. The Nationalist government program after 1928 was stalemated by the patriotic aversion to foreign financial control and the foreign hesitation to invest without more definite security. In the end foreign firms were asked to finance the foreign-built equipment for new roads while Chinese sources financed the local building costs. Foreign loans, which had been in default were refinanced and a new period of growth was just beginning when Japan struck. The major achievement of the Nationalist government in preparation for its struggle against Japan was to complete the Canton-Hankow Railway, connecting the Yangtze with Hong Kong, and build an east-west (Chekiang-Kiangsi) line from Shanghai south of the Yangtze westward to meet the Canton-Hankow line.

Industry. As a power resource for industry, China's coal reserves were conservatively estimated during the Nationalist period as perhaps the fourth largest in the world, comparable to those of Germany and surpassed only by Canada, the United States, and the USSR. China's iron resources were variously estimated, by pessimists and optimists. The higher estimates made China's reserves comparable in quantity to those of the Lake Superior district in the United States or about half those of European Russia. But oil seemed very scarce in China.

An industrial complex using coal and iron had been inaugurated in Central China near Wuhan in the 1890s, but it became dependent on Japanese financing and markets. British interests developed the Kailan coal mines north of Tientsin. But the chief industrial development before 1949 was left for the Japanese in the Mukden region of Manchuria.

While Manchuria was unquestionably a part of China, inhabited over 95 percent by Chinese people, it was very different indeed from the more settled regions south of the Great Wall. Except for the Chinese pale south of Mukden, it had remained in large part a Manchu preserve down to the late nineteenth century and therefore became a focus of rivalry among Russia, Japan, and China. As an undeveloped area Manchuria profited by its low density of population. Its 500,000 square miles (including Jehol, the mountainous province north of Peking) are one quarter the size of China proper, yet the population as estimated in 1900 was only 17 million. Its subsequent rapid growth was aided by migration of Chinese farm labor from North China.

When the Japanese grabbed Manchuria in 1931 and made it their puppet state of "Manchukuo," it accounted for one fifth of all China's trade. The trade in soybeans and Japanese coal and iron exports had made Dairen the second port to Shanghai. This was only a beginning. The Japanese rapidly developed a communications network, reformed the currency, and pushed industrialization for strategic purposes. In the fourteen years of their occupation, they invested something like US $2 billion, a large amount considering Japan's resources. Manchuria acquired some 60,000 miles of roads in addition to about 6000 miles of railway. Dairen, Changchun (Hsin-king), and Mukden (now Shenyang) all became big cities. Coal production reached 30 million tons a year. The steel works at Anshan near Mukden could produce 2 million tons of pig iron and 1.5 million tons of steel. On the basis of an efficient coal and iron combine, great factories arose where machinery, chemicals, automobiles, and even aircraft were produced. As an industrial base Manchuria under Japanese exploitation outstripped all the rest of China put together.

Meanwhile in China proper, textiles and light industries had concentrated in Shanghai and a few other treaty ports like Tientsin and the Yangtze cities. Here again, foreign and Chinese finance and entrepreneurship combined with cheap Chinese labor to produce a mixed Sino-foreign management of the modern economy, with "semi-colonial" features. The cotton mills, silk filatures, small shipyards, cement works, canneries, and cigarette factories of Kuomintang China did not add up to a heavy industrial base. Machines to make machines were still lacking. The nearest thing to the contemporary Soviet, German, and Japanese economic plans was a program for developing arsenals and military production under Nazi tutelage.

Banking and Fiscal Policy. China's old-style "native" banks had been local institutions, usually partnerships, which existed for the purpose of handling money—lending, saving, transmitting, or exchanging it—but not for productive investment. Although organized in guilds, the native banks were decentralized and conducted a form of small private business, mainly in supporting small merchants with unsecured personal loans. Countrywide remittances had been handled by the famous Shansi banks and their many branches. But after 1911 these traditional institutions proved inadequate. The native banks generally had depended on methods of personal contact under the wing of official patronage.

Foreign banks had grown up in the treaty ports under the protection of extraterritoriality to finance foreign trade and handle foreign exchange. By 1936 there were some thirty-three foreign banks in China; many had issued their own bank notes. The most important was the Hongkong and Shanghai Banking Corporation, established in 1864 with a capital of Hongkong (HK) $2.5 million. By the 1930s its paid-up capital was HK $20 million with a reserve of HK $100 million and assets of HK $1 billion. The foreign banks had dominated the Chinese financial scene not only because they financed foreign trade and after 1911 held the official funds derived from the Chinese Martime Customs and other sources to pay off foreign debts and indemnities, but also because they served as repositories of the private funds of politicians and militarists. Fundamentally, their position rested on their monopoly of foreign exchange and international transactions. At times they held as much as half the silver stocks in Shanghai.

In 1905 the Manchu government had finally opened a Board of Revenue Bank to issue notes and conduct modern central banking operations. This early institution became the Bank of China in 1913. Its chief competitor was the official Bank of Communications set up in 1907. During the warlord period new provincial banks had often issued great quantities of rapidly depreciating bank notes. By 1926 the total of modern government, provincial, and private banks had grown to 102 institutions, most of them mercantile in character and dealing in short-term liabilities rather than long-term investments. As part of their chief business these modern banks began to finance the government both by issuing loans and by direct advances.

The Kuomintang had begun in Canton in 1924 by setting up the Central Bank of China to finance the Nationalist revolution. Its first manager was T. V. Soong (Harvard '15), brother of Madame Sun Yat-sen (Soong Ch'ing-ling) and of Soong Mei-ling (Wellesley '17), who married Chiang Kai-shek in 1928. After first extorting funds from the Shanghai business class by terror, the Chiang government with T. V. Soong as finance minister 1928–1933 got cooperation from Shanghai's modern Chinese banks by issuing government bonds to them at very favorable discounts. Under H. H. Kung (who married Soong Ai-ling) as finance minister from 1934, the Nanking government took control of the Bank of China and Bank of Communications in addition to the Central Bank of China and the Farmers Bank set up in 1933. These four government banks all issued bank notes, and the functions performed by a single central government bank in most European countries were distributed among them. The flow of silver funds to the treaty ports led to a heavy concentration of capital in Shanghai and a consequent deflation in the rural economy. By 1935 the four government banks had two fifths of the total capital and reserves of all the modern Chinese banks and more than half of the total deposits.

Thus in its first years the Nanking government, led by T. V. Soong as Minister of Finance until 1933, had succeeded in creating a government banking mechanism which greatly aided its program of unification. The readjustment of internal loans and external debts, reforms of taxation, and the suppression of the tael (the old unit of account) in 1933 were all aspects of a program whereby the modern sector of the economy was brought increasingly under the financial domination of the central government. By 1937 there was a marked concentration of the national capital resources under government influence, which could pave the way for government control of credit.

The monetary reform of November 1935, with the support of Britain and the United States, was a final essential step in creating the modern banking structure. The American silver-buying program had already exacerbated the depression in China and was sucking out her currency in a most disastrous manner. This reform now nationalized all the old silver currency in China, thus taking it out of circulation, and substituted a managed currency. The foreign banks, even with extraterritoriality, were put in a position of "necessary cooperation" with the Chinese government. The latter was now able to unify and administer the financial reserves which it held against note issue. These reserves were gradually changed from silver into foreign exchange. The effort was to nationalize control of foreign exchange and build a national banking system independent of foreign powers. The notes of the four government banks were substituted for silver and other notes. In 1936–37 there was still no inflation.

But it must be admitted that this progress was most rapid on the fringe of China where the money economy centered, in the treaty ports. For four fifths of the people the greater problem was agricultural credit and how the government or the modern banks could take the place of the rural moneylender. Some city banks attempted to counter the preference for financing treaty-port activities and tried to channel bank credit into rural areas through credit cooperatives. This had been aided by the China International Famine Relief Commission, which by 1927 had set up more than 500 cooperative credit associations in the province around Peking. In 1937 the government organized the Agricultural Credit Administration. Many expedients were tried. But the tendency was to use rural bank credit for seasonal short-term needs, in the same way as the loans of old-style usurers, not for long-term productive investment. Moreover, the official class who controlled bank credit flowing through government channels had many common ties at the local level with the landlord moneylenders.

Public Finance. The halfway nature of the Nationalist regime was nowhere more evident than in its fiscal policies. The central government from the first renounced its claim to the land tax, the chief potential source of revenue, and left it for provincial administrations to exploit. Instead, Nanking financed its regime by taxing the trade and industry of the modern sector of the economy, thus living off that very sector that it should have tried by all means to develop.

About 50 percent of the revenue came from the Maritime Customs (as compared with about 1 percent in the United States). The second source was consolidated excise taxes on consumer staples like tobacco, kerosene, and flour, and the government salt monopoly. This was regressive taxation, reducing the purchasing power of the masses at the lower income levels. The ancient tradition of bureaucratic revenue grabbing still continued, for example, in the form of export duties which penalized native industry instead of subsidizing its development.

In this context, the fiscal reforms remained superficial and indeed took on an ambiguous air. The *likin* tax on local trade was finally abolished along with the intricate tael system, and the currency was unified. But it proved impossible to install an effective budget system or keep military expenditures anywhere within bounds. Constant deficits were met by borrowing about 25 percent of the sums expended from the four government banks, which in turn issued bonds on the domestic market. Debt payments to domestic bondholders soon exceeded those to foreigners, which had been extensive, and the service of these debts took a third of the government expenditures.

The net result was to tax the consumption goods of the poor

in order to pay interest to the rich bondholders, many of whom were Nanking bureaucrats. Productive investment at home and capital loans from abroad were both discouraged by these anti-development policies. The Nanking decade probably saw continued stagnation in the agrarian economy, with no appreciable increase of production. This was accompanied, moreover, by a stultifying growth of "bureaucratic capitalism," that is, domination of industry and finance by officials and political cliques who feathered their private nests by manipulating government monopolies, finances, development schemes, and agencies.

As a result of these aims and practices in the immemorial tradition of *sheng-kuan fa-ts'ai*, "become an official and get rich," Nanking was unable to achieve a healthy and solvent fiscal regime, much less a breakthrough into a genuine process of self-sustaining reinvestment and industrialization. The unified government banking structure was used not to provide cheap credit for purposes of economic growth but to pay high interest rates (20 to 40 percent after allowance for discounts) to government bondholders, and to finance the very heavy military expenditures. Savings were thus channeled into current government use or private speculation, while the nation's capital resources were not mobilized, even for military purposes.

Local Government

Local administration under the Kuomintang spread downward from the counties *(hsien)*, which had now increased to about 2000. It was here that the Nationalist regime faced the central task of any Chinese government, how to govern a rural society from an urban base.

In imperial times the county magistrate had had as his chief task to collect the revenue: land tax, grain levies, salt revenue, customs duties, and miscellaneous duties including taxes on goods in transit. Only a small fraction of this revenue which the official collectors secured from the villages ever reached Peking. Regular quotas went to the capital annually, and transfers were made to other provinces as Peking might require. But Peking received no more than a proportion, perhaps a quarter, of the reported tax collection; and the collection reported was no more than a part, possibly one quarter, of the revenue actually received. In short, the officials lived on their take. The magistrate was a tax farmer who had to support himself, his collectors and personal staff, and his relatives out of the public funds passing through his hands.

As times grew harder in the nineteenth century, influential gentry-landlord households could usually make better deals with the collectors; small households therefore often sought their protection, and the big gentry thus wound up as unauthorized tax farmers themselves, collecting and turning in the taxes of commoners while taking a commission. Big landlord families might also set up bursaries to collect their rents from tenants and get the help of the local magistrate's underlings in coercing rent defaulters. Thus the local elite and local officials joined forces to squeeze rents and taxes out of the villages, with no benefit to the government treasury and increasing damage to its image among the populace.

A similar enlargement of the gentry role in maintaining order had occurred during the suppression of the mid-century rebellions: the local elite then took the initiative to mobilize militia, first as officially authorized local defense forces and then, at a higher level of militarization, as mobile battalions of professional mercenaries or "braves" who were organized in striking forces personally recruited, trained, and led by scholar-official commanders. Tseng Kuo-fan had been only the most famous of this class of gentry-military.

The gentry class in the twentieth century became fragmented. After the ancient examination system was abolished in 1905, official degree holders were no longer produced, while the new secondary school and college graduates flocked into city life. Absentee landlordism presumably grew and the educated elite became diversified and probably fewer in the countryside. Under the warlords local administration deteriorated along with peasant livelihood. The landed ruling class, no longer the top elite of the country, no longer indoctrinated in Confucian ideals of community leadership, became even more narrowly self-seeking. Secret societies like the Red Spears in Shantung or the Society of Brothers and Elders (Ko Lao Hui) in Szechwan became tools of the local families of property, helping to protect them against both popular disorder and official exaction. Organized in a network of branches, each with its secretariat, treasury, and directorate capable of mobilizing the clandestine brotherhood, such agencies could help the big family lineages dominate the villages in a rich enclave like the Chengtu plain. For a secret society had its executive arm in the person of professional thugs, as well as its income from the protection of illicit activities—gambling houses, brothels, opium dens, or illegal markets where government taxes were evaded. This darker side was combined with the protection of respectable rank-and-file members in their daily pursuits, and with clandestine leadership by some of the wealthiest landlords and officials.

When the Kuomintang came to power the telephone and telegraph, motor roads and bus routes, linking local areas with the cities, enabled Nanking and later Chungking to convey their orders at once to the smallest hamlet. The regime continued the trend toward bureaucratizing the countryside. In place of the magistrates and gentry of imperial times, the new administrators from Nanking tried to spread their reforms, and the police organized their anti-Communist security net. Both came further into the local scene than had been the custom under the empire. Where the emperor had appointed the county magistrate but left him under the provincial authorities, the central government now developed direct contact with him. Magistrates were a chief element among the trainees brought to the capital for indoctrination in Chiang Kai-shek's Central Training Corps. Meanwhile the central government established local administrative organs in charge of military, customs, transportation, or other matters, independent of the regular structure of county government. The Kuomintang also set up its local cells under central party control, parallel to the official system. Below the county were new levels of wards, districts and subdistricts, groups of towns and villages, leading down to the groups of households which formed the revived *pao-chia* system: families organized in decimal units for mutual guarantee, each unit responsible for the acts of all the others—a surveillance system which set neighbor to spy upon neighbor and kith upon kin.

The Kuomintang theory was that through this hierarchy of subunits the government could train the people during the period of political tutelage to prepare them for local autonomy. In 1939 the Nationalist government issued a new statute to reorganize local government. Families were to be grouped more flexibly, on community lines, to form *chia* and *pao*. Villages and towns were now to become incorporated legal persons able to operate their own local administrations. Each *pao* should form an assembly and elect two representatives, who would in turn function in a village or town assembly to assist the head of the village or town government, who would himself be elected. On paper the law of 1939 was put into effect in nearly all the counties in Free China. Yet in the same period the military and police authorities dominated the scene. There is little record of the election process taking hold.

The Rural Problem. Looking back on the Nanking decade, we can see that, ideally, the new government should have attacked the key problem of agricultural production with programs to improve farm technology. Nanking early sought technical aid from the League of Nations for public health work. Many fine blueprints were offered in the 1930s and 1940s for China's economic regeneration. Land reclamation, reforestation, water conservancy, hydropower, crop and animal breeding, better tools, improved land use, pest control, crop storage facilities, land redistribution, rent reduction, light and heavy industrialization, rural industry and cooperatives, cheaper farm credit, mass education, public health, transportation, law and order—all had their advocates and their obvious rationale. The first and foremost object of all such efforts was to increase the productivity of the farmer. This was the crux of China's problem but the government was unable to get at it. No comprehensive plan was ever devised, much less given effect. The Nanking decade was the time for Western aid to China's vigorous economic growth. But America was absorbed in the Depression and New Deal. Kuomintang China in these years made halting and spotty progress along many lines, to no particular end.

The brilliant social anthropologist Fei Hsiao-t'ung described the quagmire of old agricultural conditions and practices as an "economy of scarcity." This long established low-level manpower economy was perpetuated by the Chinese emphasis upon the virtue of contentment and limitation of wants. This age-old acceptance of the institutionalized penury of peasant life, for want of any alternative, was a means by which the individual could fit himself into his kinship group, sustain his lot in life, and actually achieve a high degree of "social integration" of himself in the community. Indeed the narrow horizon, low efficiency, poor diet, and chronic diseases of the Chinese peasant, which struck the eye of the modern in-

Manpower taxis. *Above:* Chinese family wheelbarrow with front and rear handlers, Hankow foreign concession area, late nineteenth century. *Right, above:* Ricksha puller evacuating a Nationalist officer from Nanking, 1949. *Below:* Pedicab on Nanking Road, Shanghai, 1966.

vestigator, were always an integral part of the old society, just as they were part of premodern society in Europe.

Not only did the old farm economy produce a relatively small surplus. The surplus, once produced, was poorly distributed—little or none of it could be invested in improvements. Landholding relationships in China were generally complex; tenantry, sharecropping, and various forms and degrees of indebtedness were intermixed. Landlordism was generally small-scale and there were few large baronial estates. Probably the majority of peasants were independent landowners, not tenants at all. Yet they were handicapped by the minuscule size of their holdings and by their lack of capital and were consequently vulnerable in time of stringency vis-à-vis the small-scale landlord moneylender with his extra, though meager, resources. One careful American estimated that rents in China took from 45 to 60 percent of the crop, not counting other payments. Indebtedness was endemic, but probably half or more of farm loans were for unproductive purposes, to buy food or repay debts, or to meet the compelling social obligation of ceremonial display and hospitality on occasions of marriage and death.

During the Nanking decade the lack of large-scale government aid for the villages was highlighted by a widespread and growing private interest in "rural reconstruction." Many programs were set going in selected areas where the problems of peasant life were studied and methods developed for the promotion of literacy and improvement of living standards. In some of these efforts, as James C. Thomson has shown, Christian missionaries had led the way. Best known to Westerners was the experiment financed partly by the Rockefeller Foundation at Ting-hsien in North China under the leadership of the dynamic Christian, Dr. Y. C. James Yen. A model county was cautiously developed by the government near Nanking. Perhaps the most interesting pioneer effort of this type was made in Shantung by the scholar Liang Shu-ming, whom Guy Alitto rightly calls "the last Confucian." Fundamentally, these were all reform efforts which tried to give the peasantry some education for citizenship, some public health service, and scientific improvements in crop and animal breeding.

The movement for rural reconstruction discovered very soon that the problems of economic livelihood were deeply imbedded in social and political institutions. A higher standard of living was a prerequisite for any democratic processes of a Western type. Improvements in living standards in turn depended upon social change. For example, the scientific reforms attempted at Ting-hsien needed financial support greater than the peasantry could provide, peasant organizations in support of local improvements required official permission, the improvement of crops raised questions of rent and land tenure, an increase of literacy was likely to make the populace more vocal in the pressing of grievances.

In short, any real change in one aspect of the old order on the land implied fundamental changes in the whole system. The problems of the Chinese countryside were so far-reaching and the pressure for change so great that reforms seemed likely to set off a chain reaction toward revolt.

Chapter 11
The Rise of the Communist Party

The simple facts of Mao's career seem incredible: in a vast land of 400 million people, at age 28 with a dozen others to found a party and in the next fifty years to win power, organize, and remold the people and reshape the land—history records no greater achievement. Alexander, Caesar, Charlemagne, all the kings of Europe, Napoleon, Bismarck, Lenin—no predecessor can equal Mao Tse-tung's scope of accomplishment, for no other country was ever so ancient and so big as China.

Indeed Mao's achievement is almost beyond our comprehension, unless we note the trends which culminated in his career: first, the new growth of Chinese mass nationalism in response to Western and then Japanese invasion; second, the movement of upper-class literati to lead the peasant masses toward a better life; third, Soviet Russia's transmission of its theory and practice of revolution, including united front tactics, through the Communist International (Comintern). Sun Yat-sen got Comintern help only at the end of his career in 1923, two years before his death. Mao and his colleagues began with it. They got started also with Kuomintang help.

Vicissitudes of the First Decade
The Kuomintang and the Chinese Communist Party experienced a curious parallelism in their early histories. After

its formation in 1912 as successor to the revolutionary league or T'ung Meng Hui and its proscription by Yuan Shih-k'ai, the Kuomintang spent the next decade largely in eclipse and came to power only sixteen years after its founding. After the founding of the Chinese Communist Party in 1921 and its early effort to seize control of the Nationalist revolution, the split of 1927 drove it out of the cities into the mountains of South China. Its final triumph came twenty-two years later. It had a long preparation in the wilderness.

The early Kuomintang and Communist leaders differed less in social than in geographic origin. Dr. Sun's followers were city men, often from merchant families and hence from the big coastal treaty ports, particularly Canton. More of the Communists were from rural areas, particularly the central Yangtze basin. As time went on, the Communists recruited leaders of true peasant origin, the Kuomintang did not. One main difference between them was chronological. The founding fathers of the Kuomintang grew up in that ancient time before World War I. The Communists belonged to the wartime and postwar generations of an entirely different age, responsive to new pressures and new ideas. It is not surprising that the older generation of republican revolutionists was destined to do a partway job, leaving the potentialities of change in modern China to be exploited more thoroughly by a younger group.

The Attractions of Communism. Several aspects of China's past favored the Communist approach. Confucian tradition gave the modern student the sanction and indeed the moral imperative to take the lead in public affairs as a member of the scholar-elite and in terms of ideological principles of universal validity. The authoritarian tradition by which the official class monopolized all overt political activity made it natural that an opposition movement must be secretly organized. Rebellion in the past had usually been energized by utopian and messianic doctrines (usually of Buddhist derivation but in the case of the Taipings pseudo-Christian). Rebels had usually found in their sworn brotherhood a substitute for the support given each individual, in the absence of legal safeguards, by the old family system. Chinese folklore and literature had a romantic Robin Hood tradition of banditry in the cause of the downtrodden.

China's experience in modern times reinforced traditional tendencies. As the economic plight of the farmer grew more apparent, if not in fact steadily worse, it was naturally assumed that government action should be taken to remedy it. The job was too big for individuals and must be the primary responsibility of those in power—all of which suggested some kind of state socialism. Sun Yat-sen had vaguely pointed in this direction. However, as Don C. Price has shown, Russia's example down to 1911 had encouraged Chinese interest in revolution but not specifically in Marxism. The Marxian social ideal in China was from the first a Communist Party monopoly. No social-democratic movement preceded it, to spread the socialist creed as in Europe on a gradualist, reformist basis. For those attracted to socialism there was nowhere to go but into a Leninist party.

Leninism, finally, provided an explanation of the great fact in any Chinese patriot's political life—the foreign omnipresence, "imperialism." When it proceeded to identify those ancient twin evils of landlords and warlords as "feudalism," the Marxist-Leninist scheme of history seemed to many sufficiently applicable to China to deserve their belief and faith. It claimed to be "scientific" and strictly "modern." It would allow China to expunge her modern humiliations by leaping over the capitalist phase of universal development to stand as she would in the forefront of the nations. For the faithful believer the party would provide. A new China would result.

China's early Marxists, like their contemporaries in Japan, began the process of choosing what Marxist beliefs to stress as most appropriate to their country's situation. Li Ta-chao, the pioneer Marxist at Peking University and Mao's mentor there, had an activist faith in man's ability to change his environment or, in Maurice Meisner's phrase, "the power of the human conscience to mold social reality." This voluntarism went with an intense patriotism and a faith in the Chinese people, the peasantry, as potential revolutionaries—beliefs that became typical of Mao Tse-tung.

On the other hand, there were several reasons why the Communist movement was checked and almost suppressed, before the Japanese war facilitated its resurgence. One reason was the success of the Kuomintang at Nanking in mobilizing latent talent and support for its new government. Another was the Kuomintang effort at suppression, which killed thousands, if not tens of thousands, of leftist youth. But perhaps the most fundamental reason for retardation lay with the Chinese Communist Party (hereafter CCP) and the orthodox urban orientation on which it generally agreed with the masterminds of the Comintern in Moscow. Roy Hofheinz comments that the early CCP had "no precocious commitment to rural work." This can be seen if we trace the early vicissitudes of the party line—that ingenious device for maintaining basic aims while choosing allies and isolating enemies by "class analysis" according to "laws of history."

The Comintern's Difficulties. After the Comintern agent Gregory Voitinsky in 1920 had prompted Ch'en Tu-hsiu to call together a mixed group of intellectual revolutionaries to form a Communist party, it required some time to mold them into a genuinely Bolshevik organization. They early became active in the labor movement but, as C. M. Wilbur points out, their membership remained less than a thousand until the

May Thirtieth Movement of 1925 roused a great surge of anti-imperialist feeling and gave them a tenfold increase of numbers. The greater size of the Kuomintang (KMT) intensified the Communists' persistent problem: how to seize political opportunities on a basis of theoretical principles, thereby avoiding a mere unprincipled opportunism. This necessity for rational flexibility, for reasoned opportunism, is what makes the party line so interesting a study.

The Chinese Communists had begun by dividing Chinese society into the classes of workers (proletariat), peasants, petty bourgeoisie, national bourgeoisie (capitalists), and other, reactionary, classes (militarists, feudal landlords, and others). Their first manifesto of June 1922 (a year after the formal founding) called for a united front against the militarists in which the CCP would represent the workers (assuming with Marx that a party can really be an organ of only one class) and also poor peasants, while the "democratic party" (the KMT) would represent bourgeois elements.

This concept countered Lenin's early decision that the CCP must work through the existing revolutionary movement rather than risk destruction on its own. Consequently the Comintern shortly declared that the KMT was actually, and quite anomalously, a "bloc of four classes" (national bourgeoisie, petty bourgeoisie, workers, and peasants) and that the CCP, instead of seeking a united front with it as a "bloc without" (that is, from outside), should do so as a "bloc within," that is, by having CCP members as individuals become KMT members while still remaining part of the CCP apparatus. The CCP Third Congress in June 1923, in confirming this ingenious idea, echoed the Comintern declaration that the KMT "should be the central force of the national revolution." When dual membership was accepted by the KMT in January 1924, the race began to see which party apparatus could make more use of the other. Communists gained key posts in the KMT organization.

Adhering to this approach (advocated by Stalin, criticized by Trotsky), the Comintern in December 1926 ordered the CCP to join the left wing of the KMT in the Nationalist government at Wuhan, which it now defined to be a bloc of three classes (workers, peasants, and petty bourgeoisie). The aim was to effect a transition by which the national bourgeoisie (big capitalists) would be excluded from the revolutionary movement. As a result the CCP continued to seek power as a "bloc within," even though its subordination to Wuhan prevented its exploiting the peasant unrest of the time. The final fiasco of the Comintern's "bloc within" strategy was signalized first by the split between the left KMT at Wuhan and the right KMT at Nanking (February–April 1927) and then by Wuhan's expulsion of the Communists (July 1927).

Under Comintern orders the CCP now reoriented itself (August 1927). It condemned Ch'en Tu-hsiu (who later was expelled) and "the Party's leading cadres" (who themselves participated in the condemnation) for "opportunism." "Their constant vacillation, their false, unrevolutionary theories . . . in complete contradiction to the resolutions and instructions of the Comintern . . . in reality betrayed the revolution." At the same time the CCP accepted Stalin's view that the revolution was entering a "higher" stage, which must be marked by secret conspiracy and armed insurrections in city and countryside. Yet lip service was still paid to the necessity of achieving "hegemony within the Kuomintang," a statement without meaning except as support of Stalin against Trotsky.

Following this new line the CCP staged the Autumn Harvest uprising in Hunan (led by Mao Tse-tung) and seized the South China port of Swatow for a week, in September 1927. In December it contrived a four-day uprising in Canton (the "Canton Commune"). These and similar efforts all failed.

The Sixth Congress of the CCP, meeting in Moscow with eighty or more members present in June and July 1928 and carefully manipulated by the Comintern, tried to set a new line. While condemning Ch'en Tu-hsiu's "opportunist" right deviation, it now equally condemned his successor for the "putschist" left deviation, which had resulted in unsuccessful uprisings. The new line stated that the revolution was in a "trough between two waves" and the CCP must prepare for armed insurrections in view of the inevitable arrival of a new "revolutionary rising tide." The agrarian revolution was the main "content" of the Chinese revolution as a whole, but it could be achieved only under "proletarian hegemony." Stalin in 1928 urged preparatory organization and struggle in both city and countryside to win mass support. The united front effort to take over the KMT now gave way to the building of independent CCP power as a state within a state to be partly based on rural soviets.

The young CCP leadership was scattered between Moscow, Shanghai, Kiangsi, and other small bases, and its organization had been shattered. Unanimity was difficult. As Richard Thornton has shown, Li Li-san, the new secretary general appointed by Moscow, had his own ambitions and in 1928–1930 continued the extremist insurrectionary line that had already led to disaster. He had the CCP apparatus try to organize city workers for political strikes and armed uprisings, exploiting the labor union members for party ends rather than representing their economic grievances. In the face of the KMT white terror and its competing "yellow" (anti-Communist) labor union movement, Li Li-san and his ally in this period, Chou En-lai, got nowhere. No tide rose, least of all in the cities. In 1924 two thirds of the party had been classed as proletarian and another fifth as intellectuals. In 1930 Chou En-lai reported that out of 120,000 party members, only about 2000 were industrial workers. Chou now opposed

Li and went again to Moscow, where the Comintern became alarmed at Li's plans. Mao Tse-tung, on the other hand, at first showed sympathy for Li's fervor; as Stuart Schram suggests, this period brought a first confrontation between the Comintern and its Chinese section.

The summer of 1930 saw large-scale fighting between KMT armies under Chiang Kai-shek and warlord forces both north and south. In the midst of this turmoil came the climax of Li Li-san's insurrectionary effort to seize major cities. In July Communist forces made front page news by seizing Changsha, the capital of Hunan, only to be expelled a few days later. Li Li-san's downfall followed and he went to Moscow "for study" (to reappear in Manchuria in 1946). Chou En-lai, after confessing his "cowardly rotten opportunism," remained on the Central Committee. It was now dominated by a "returned student" group of twenty-eight comrades newly trained in Moscow, who purged and rebuilt the party apparatus but found the KMT-controlled cities inhospitable and therefore moved to take over the rural soviet bases.

The mixed record of the first decade of Chinese communism reflected the difficulty of importing and adapting a foreign ideology and its institutions. In Chinese politics the CCP leadership was something new, a band of professional revolutionists, disciplined and trained to concentrate in Leninist ideological terms upon the organization and seizure of power. The decisive feature of their party was that, unlike the Kuomintang, which had borrowed a similar Leninist structure, it was committed to functioning as an ideological entity. Ideally the line set by the leadership on reasoned "dialectical" grounds was capable of shifts and reversals, resilient in adversity and flexible when opportunity offered, always sacrificing individuals as expendable in the total cause. In practice, Comintern directives, often devised with one eye on Stalin's enemies in Moscow, regularly included contradictory alternatives, which allowed ambitious executors of policy in China to bend the line so as to outdo their rivals in the inevitable struggle for power.

Thus by 1931 the first decade of communism in China had created a Leninist party, in spite of the failure of the united front policy. The second decade was to see a further adaptation of Marxism-Leninism to Chinese potentialities.

The Rise of Mao Tse-tung

Mao came from Hunan, a seedbed of Chinese nationalism that produced not only the scholar-gentry-generals who suppressed the Taiping rebellion and led the Restoration of the 1860s but also several leaders of the 1911 revolution—Huang Hsing, the military commander under Sun Yat-sen, and Sung Chiao-jen, who organized the Kuomintang, among others. Mao's father, with two years of schooling, became a middle peasant owning two acres of land, eventually a rich peasant owning more than three acres. After five years of primary school from ages eight to thirteen, Mao had to work full time on the farm, where he fought with his father. By the time he got to a higher primary school, he was sixteen, and the Revolution of 1911 was at hand. To his early reading of Chinese novels like *All Men Are Brothers (Shui Hu Chuan,* also translated as *Water Margin)* he now added the writers of the reform movement, especially Liang Ch'i-ch'ao and the ideas of nationalism. In 1911 he entered middle school in Changsha, older than his classmates, already a leader and a rebel. After six months as a common soldier, Mao got his real education between the ages of twenty and twenty-five at a provincial normal school. His first article published in *The New Youth* in 1917 was on the necessity of physical culture through systematic exercise and firmness of will.

Mao spent six months at Peking University in the winter of 1918–19, not as a regular student but as an assistant to the librarian, Li Ta-chao, in whose Marxist study group he participated. After Mao returned to Changsha early in 1919 and became a leader of the May Fourth Movement there, his article on "The Great Union of the Popular Masses" stressed the revolutionary role of the whole Chinese people. He was not yet thinking in Marxist categories but was an eclectic espousing a broad range of ideas then current. By the time Mao participated in the organization meeting of the CCP in July 1921, he was twenty-eight years old, had organized labor unions and led strikes, edited journals and written articles. He was a vigorous leader but lacked a systematic grounding in Marxism and had never been abroad or received Soviet indoctrination. He was very much a nationalist-Marxist from the beginning.

During the first United Front of 1923–1927, Mao was a leading collaborator with the Kuomintang. Already outstanding as an organizer, for a time he worked in the Shanghai bureau of the KMT with leaders like Wang Ching-wei and Hu Han-min. After recovering from an illness in Hunan in the winter of 1924–25, he went again to Canton and became the executive head under Wang Ching-wei of the KMT propaganda department and even presented its report to the second KMT Congress in January 1926. Mao became an alternate member of the KMT central executive committee as well as editor of a party weekly. He served as principal of the Kuomintang's Peasant Movement Training Institute from May to October 1926, long after tension had increased between the KMT and the CCP organizations and long after the Northern Expedition had commenced under Chiang Kai-shek's command. In this period, in short, Chiang and Mao were working in parallel organizations in the same general cause of national revolution. When Mao investigated the peasant movement in Hunan early in 1927, he addressed his report to the Kuomintang at Wuhan. In this report, at age thirty-four, Mao put forward his vision that the revolutionary passion and energies of the common people could be harnessed to liberate the peasantry and overthrow the old ruling class. Under the United Front government at Wuhan, he became the chief advocate of land reform. After the KMT–CCP split, Mao commanded the 1927 "Autumn Harvest" attack on Changsha but was defeated and took his surviving forces into the mountains. He was dropped from the CCP central committee because of his "military opportunism."

From his collaboration with the Kuomintang, Mao had learned a great deal; after the split he learned the importance of military force and guerrilla tactics.* In neither period was

---

* Mao's guerrilla style had ancient roots. The *Sun-tzu* says, "By discovering the enemy's disposition and remaining invisible ourselves, we can keep our forces concentrated while the enemy must be divided. We can form a single united body, while the enemy must be split into fractions." Mao in 1936: "We can turn a big 'encirclement and suppression' campaign waged by the enemy against us into a number of small, separate campaigns of encirclement and suppression waged by us against the enemy . . . This is what we call exterior-line operations within interior-line operations, encirclement and suppression within 'encirclement and suppression,' blockade within blockade, the offensive within the defensive, superiority within inferiority, strength within weakness, advantage within disadvantage. and initiative within passivity. The winning of victory in the strategic defensive depends basically on this measure —concentration of troops . . . We use the few to defeat the many—this we say to the rulers of China as a whole. We use the many to defeat the few—this we say to the enemy on the battle field."

The *Sun-tzu* had said: "All warfare is based upon deception. Hence, when able to attack, we must seem unable; when using our forces, we must seem inactive; when we are near, we must make the enemy believe that we are far away; when far away, we must make him believe we are near . . . If he is superior in strength, evade him. If your opponent is of choleric temper, seek to irritate him. Pretend to be weak that he may grow arrogant. If he is inactive, give him no rest . . . Attack him where he is unprepared; appear where you are not expected." In Kiangsi the Red Army developed defensive principles from a position of weakness: "The enemy advances, we retreat. The enemy camps, we harass. The enemy tires, we attack. The enemy retreats, we pursue." See Stuart Schram's basic study, *Mao Tse-tung*, pp. 142–145.

he an organization man working primarily within the Communist party; indeed, as Maurice Meisner remarks, Mao's "faith in the revolutionary wisdom of the party was a good deal less than absolutely Leninist."

The Maoist Strategy. The Comintern had reiterated that only the proletariat could lead the peasantry. It regarded peasants, in orthodox Marxist-Leninist fashion, as capable only of auxiliary action. But rural soviet bases had long been a Comintern and a Stalinist concept. The issue was their relative priority. Mao Tse-tung's famous report on the peasant movement in Hunan foreshadowed what Benjamin Schwartz long ago called "the Maoist strategy." Mao asserted heretically that the "revolutionary vanguard" in China was not the proletariat but the "poor peasantry." Convinced that revolution in China must be based on the peasantry, he began to build up rural guerrilla forces, and to create "soviets" (as Trotsky had advocated) even before the Comintern sanctioned it. With Chu Teh as his military commander he took refuge in the winter of 1927–28 in the mountainous Chingkangshan region on the Hunan-Kiangsi border, collecting some 10,000 men, together with arms for perhaps 2000.

Here developed a territorial base, to be fused with the other components—a Leninist party, support from the peasant masses, a Red Army. The territorial base, Mao declared in 1928, must have a good food supply and a strategic location, preferably on the rugged natural border between two provinces. Collecting here the traditional sinews of rebellion, manpower and grain, Mao kept his program ideologically orthodox in form, even though he could not prevent the Moscow-trained central committee members who arrived from Shanghai gradually pushing him out of power in the CCP apparatus.

The Chinese Soviet Republic was proclaimed at Juichin,

Kiangsi, in November 1931 as a "democratic dictatorship of the proletariat and peasantry," using Lenin's formula of 1905 in utterly different circumstances. The nonexistent "proletariat" were favored by excellent labor laws on paper and given greater representation than the peasantry in the system of soviets, the same as in Russia. The Red Army was specially privileged as a political class army. Land was violently redistributed, both in the time-honored fashion of peasant uprisings and also in the name of class warfare, for purposes of establishing political control. But collectivization, then the Russian fashion, was not pushed. In fact the Soviet Republic in Kiangsi was in no position to coerce all the soviets organized in and around its base area. Some rich peasants and landlords organized soviets so as to make peace with it.

Kuomintang arrests and executions forced the Central Committee to abandon Shanghai for Kiangsi in the autumn of 1932. Chiang Kai-shek's first four extermination campaigns, in late 1931, May–June and July–October 1932, and again in 1933 were checked by guerrilla tactics which drew KMT columns into the mountains and concentrated superior force against isolated units. In late 1933–34, however, a systematic, German-devised, KMT blockade and penetration along roads lined with blockhouses began to invade the Soviet base. The Red Army's efforts at positional defense proved disastrous. After receiving permission from Moscow by radio, over 100,000 CCP personnel in October broke out of their Kiangsi redoubt, moving swiftly by night on the beginning of the Long March.

Only now, when Chinese communism was out of touch with Moscow and irrevocably committed to survive in the countryside or not at all, was the Moscow-trained element obliged to acknowledge Mao's leadership, which CCP official history now dates from the Tsunyi conference of January 1935. Even so, as John Rue has noted, they continued to oppose him in party councils for several years longer. The outer anti-KMT struggle was as usual combined with the intra-party power struggle, which involved both persons and policies, so that party history, as Tetsuya Kataoka has pointed out, "was an instrument of internal struggle." Mao, who survived, has left us his version of how he did it.

Yenan and Wartime Expansion. The Long March was just that—a retreat under continual harassment that lasted a full year and covered 6600 miles. As James P. Harrison says, "Mao's group marched 235 days and 18 nights, averaging about 17 miles a day for the year (or 26 if rest periods are excluded)." "By keeping our two feet going," as Mao said later, they went through eleven provinces, crossing eighteen mountain ranges and twenty-four rivers. After surviving perils and hardships now legendary, most of the CCP leaders and fewer than 20,000 troops reached northern Shensi province in the latter part of 1935, transferring their headquarters to Yenan at the end of 1936. This arid, sun-drenched, dusty region of loess soil broken up by eroded gullies and not easily penetrated on wheels was a natural setting for an egalitarian, do-it-yourself way of life, far from the evils of the city. During the Yenan decade, Mao set the tone for the CCP leadership. Here in the Northwest, not far from the border of Soviet Outer Mongolia, a new chapter opened with the second united front, this time against Japan.

Since general Chinese resistance to Japan would serve a dual purpose, diverting Japan from attacking Russia and Nanking from attacking the CCP, it is not surprising that at the beginning of August 1935 both the CCP and the Comintern called for nationwide resistance in a new united front. The CCP now offered to join with the archenemy, Chiang Kai-shek; but he remained deaf to this proposal until after his spectacular kidnapping at Sian in December 1936 by Manchurian troops who chafed to fight Japanese invaders, not Chinese rebels. Chou En-lai on Russian orders mediated to secure the release of Generalissimo Chiang, who now reached the zenith of his career as the indomitable symbol of China's national resistance.

The Japanese invasion of China in 1937, like the subsequent effort of the Nationalist government to quell the Communist rebellion was dominated strategically by the problem of transport. In each case the higher striking power of modernized armies could be made effective only over a transportation network. So the Japanese campaign in China during its first year and a half was a railroad campaign. The Japanese first brought their troops in over the Peiping-Mukden line and advanced from Tientsin southward and from Peiping both south and west along the main trunk lines. They overran Shantung and Shansi provinces. They moved from Shanghai up the railway to Nanking and then up the Yangtze to Wuhan.

Japan's war machine, conquering cities with torture and rapine, burning villages, bombing Free China, roused the student youth and the peasant populace for a movement of resistance and national survival which went far beyond the military sphere. Millions of persons were displaced, some 14 million men conscripted, families were broken up, vested interests destroyed—the social order over wide areas was thoroughly disrupted. The student youth and the peasant populace were subjected to violent social changes and so prepared for revolutionary programs of action.

The outbreak of hostilities near Peiping on July 7, 1937, had led to a second KMT-CCP marriage of convenience, an uneasy armed truce which began in an atmosphere of patriotic enthusiasm but soon deteriorated. The Communists now met Nanking's demands and promised to support Sun's Three

Principles, to give up overthrowing the KMT by force and abandon the soviet campaign against landlordism, to democratize their local regime, and to put their troops under Nationalist command. These were of course tactical expedients by which to expand CCP power in the wholly new context of a national war of resistance.

This process of expansion was first of all military. The Red Army in 1937 was put nominally under the central government, which named it the Eighth Route Army. Its forces pushed into the mountain-ringed province of Shansi and thence out onto the North China plain. In the second year of the war the Communists organized the New Fourth Army from remnant forces left in the lower Yangtze region and extended their organization also into the seacoast province of Shantung. The war bases which they organized centered in the less accessible border areas between provinces, beginning with the Shansi-Hopei-Chahar Border Region set up in 1938, which eventually contained roughly 20 million people. By 1941 the old area of the Nien rebellion of 1853–1868 on the Shansi-Hopei-Honan-Shantung borders was unified as another such region with a population of perhaps 30 million. By war's end there were said to be 19 bases, mostly called Liberated Areas, with a total population of 70 to 90 million, protected by about 2 million militia and by Communist armies claimed to total 910,000 troops.

The Nationalist government, never locally dominant in much of North China, could not prevent this expansion. Its modernized forces, absorbed in stemming the main Japanese war effort in such areas as the Hunan rice bowl, were trained for positional, nor guerrilla, warfare. Chiang Kai-shek's troops were also handicapped by the Chinese military tradition which kept the army separate from the people.

Throughout Chinese history an armed populace had invariably endangered the established order, while the soldier had been held in low esteem, kept ignorant, used wastefully, and bought and sold as a mercenary. Armies had lived off the countryside and been the scourge of the people. Politically indoctrinated armies were a new thing in modern China. Typically the Kuomintang had modernized its military machine to the point of giving social prestige to a patriotic new officer corps and giving new arms and training to their peasant soldiers, but it had not reached the point of indoctrinating the ordinary rifleman to fraternize with the farmer and fight in his behalf, because this would have been revolutionary. For that very reason Mao and Chu from the beginning had trained their troops to be defenders of the populace. This meant paying for supplies, helping the households on whom they were quartered, and making the Eighth Route Army the friend of the people. As the Communists put it, "the soldiers are fish and the people water"—the army depended upon popular support. Contrast the philosopher Hsün-tzu (ca. 300–235 B.C.): "The people are the water and the ruler is the boat: the water can support the boat but it can also sink it." By being immersible among the people the Communists added a dimension to their movement.

This fraternization with the populace meant that the Communist troops could largely dispense with the modern paraphernalia of a central commissary. By using local civilian labor and intelligence networks they could more easily decentralize their military organization. This enabled the Eighth Route Army to operate as a scattered, mobile force, appearing and disappearing in the populated farm land behind the Japanese-held rail lines.

As Chalmers Johnson has demonstrated, Japan's attack created a vacuum of leadership. Local politicians had been the first to go as the Japanese advanced, and in some cases had gone over to puppetry. New leadership had arisen locally, teachers in some cases becoming chairmen of guerrilla government. Intellectuals from Peiping, inheritors of the spirit of the May Fourth Movement, packed their belongings in a bundle and joined the guerrillas. Living close to nature and the common people, they emulated the adventurous heroes of Chinese folklore, daring all with loyal comrades in a righteous cause to succor the downtrodden.

The migration of patriots was common to both South and North, but in the more modern centers of the unoccupied Southwest, the students became symbols of the country's future technological development and remained in the universities-in-exile. In the Border Regions and Liberated Areas of North China, where universities were lacking, they were recruited to be Communist cadres. The Communist area during the early united front period attracted venturesome idealists who sought action.

Organization of Popular Support. In their land policy the Communists temporarily abandoned their program of land confiscation and redistribution in favor of rent reduction. This merely carried out the Kuomintang law of 1930 which limited rent to $37\frac{1}{2}$ percent of the crop. Landlords were very generally left in possession, guaranteed a reduced rent, and also allowed to vote in local elections, so that there was no great flight of the propertied class from the Communist area. Instead of their former soviet system, the Communists announced direct elections by the so-called three thirds system, in which they would confine their own representation to one third and seek to retain Kuomintang and independent participation in the other two thirds of the offices. This was based on the united front theory that in a community unified against the Japanese the Communists would provide leadership most effectively by refraining from a monopoly of government. In practice the Communist movement and the

Chairman Mao at Yenan. Thinking things out.

Eighth Route Army could prosper only in proportion as the populace actually supported them, for the war period was one of free political competition, in which the Japanese and their Chinese puppets as well as the Kuomintang offered some alternative to the Communist regime.

The key to popular support lay in the CCP leadership of a patriotic war of resistance and, at the same time, in the Communists' economic program. This included production drives both by troops and by farmers which sought to achieve the self-sufficiency of each area in food supply and, with more difficulty, in cotton production. The Communists were not well supplied with improved seeds and farming techniques, but they made up for this lack by their emphasis upon cooperation in land reclamation, labor exchange among farmers, mutual aid in transport, and small-scale industrial cooperatives. Since the old order had inveterately discouraged the cooperative association of peasant households in any way that might threaten authority, the immense potentialities of peasant cooperation at the village level were ready at hand for Communist exploitation.

Compared with the years of struggle and disaster in the wilderness after 1927, the Yenan decade of the united front after 1936 was full of vitality, growth, and innovation. While not renouncing their orthodox Communist aims, the CCP now stressed "agrarian reform," though far from being "mere agrarian reformers." When an enterprising American journalist, Edgar Snow, interviewed Mao and his colleagues after the Long March, he found a self-confident and even jovial band of veteran revolutionaries, whose homespun earthiness and evident devotion to the peasant's cause, brilliantly portrayed in *Red Star over China*, captured the imagination of readers around the world. During World War II the electric optimism and sunny atmosphere of Yenan impressed foreign visitors, who invariably arrived there from the clammy fog and frustration of the capital at Chungking. Communist propaganda in this period sang a liberal tune, for "national independence, democratic liberty, and the people's welfare" (paraphrasing Sun's Three Principles), with no further stress on soviets, bolshevization, class war, dictatorship, or even the absent proletariat. This facade for outside observers, however, did not disclose the party's inner aims and methods, nor its problems of organizing central power during its wartime growth.

Wartime Ideological Development

The three goals set forth by Mao in 1940 were to pursue the united front, armed struggle, and party-building. A fourth goal, not advertised, was to build a million-man army. The basic problem was to maintain a Leninist party with its long-term revolutionary aims while finding as many allies as possible in the dual effort to fight Japan and reform China.

For this purpose the CCP united front tactics became sophisticated, flexible, and efficient. As Lyman van Slyke puts it, they "defined the enemy in terms as manageable as possible and sought to isolate him," separating out all possible allies and neutrals, appealing to their interests, cultivating their friendship, caring for their specific needs almost like a ward politician, and yet never compromising the ultimate independence, power, and aims of the CCP. The United Front Work Department at Yenan had its "united front cadres" in the KMT areas pose as non-Communist, pursue overt, constructive, liberal-type careers, make their own friends, and never expect CCP help or acknowledge any connection. Free China's cultural and political life was accordingly infiltrated by able, dedicated, and hard-working patriots who kept their secret faith in China's Communist future but had contact with the CCP only occasionally and at a high level. Similarly the "friendly armies" program penetrated the KMT forces with military men who rose by merit and acquired influence while awaiting future opportunities. But the united front was much more than secret infiltration and recruitment among the unorganized. It was also a wartime attitude of friendly cooperation and exemplary sacrifice in the common cause of Chinese partriotism.

Armed struggle was first of all against the Japanese invader. The Communists had declared war on Japan when in Kiangsi. In North China their mobile warfare culminated in the

"Hundred Regiments" attack on Japanese forces in five provinces simultaneously by 400,000 troops in August 1940, a damaging blow which roused savage and comprehensive Japanese retaliation in 1941. Meanwhile CCP troops on occasion fought KMT forces, for example, in North Kiangsu, north of the Yangtze from Shanghai, where the CCP was intent on establishing a base area. When Nationalist forces wiped out part of the CCP New Fourth Army south of the Yangtze in January 1941, they made them into martyrs, for the CCP had come to seem more anti-Japanese than the government, notwithstanding their flouting of its orders. Thus the war provided the great overt sanction for the CCP's innate militancy. Armed struggle could be integrally combined with the united front, against either Japanese invaders or KMT diehards, once they had been sufficiently isolated. In united front politics, as in guerrilla warfare, one maneuvered to isolate and outnumber the enemy before attacking.

The third ingredient of CCP power was party building, and this was essential because CCP expansion had created decentralization. Party membership grew from 40,000 (claimed by Mao in 1937) to 80,000 (claimed by Chou in 1943) to 1,200,000 (claimed by Mao in 1945). Strenuous efforts were required to keep the CCP a disciplined, centrally controlled Leninist party. Its membership was new. It was less than ever a party of the proletariat, even though peasants were now called "rural proletarians." At the same time its activities were spread over a quarter of a million square miles where travel was mainly by foot of man or beast and communication was quick only by radio. Control could be exercised only by Communists working with proper ideological coordination in the four parallel hierarchies of party, local government, army, and mass organizations (for women, youth, labor, and the like). Veterans of the Long March usually headed these hierarchies. P'eng Te-huai, Lin Piao, and others commanded armies, Liu Shao-ch'i headed the labor federation. But to retain central direction it was essential to indoctrinate the new cadres (party workers) in Leninist assumptions and principles of organization.

For this purpose party schools processed thousands of students at Yenan and in 1942 Mao inaugurated an ideological reform movement for "correcting unorthodox tendencies" *(cheng-feng)* in thought, in personal relations inside and outside the party, and in speech and writing. Borrowing heavily from Russian and Comintern sources, he and his colleagues produced a body of documents for intensive study and discussion—"How To Be a Communist Party Member," "In Opposition to Liberalism," "Liquidation of Menshevik Thought," "On the Intra-Party Struggle." Prolonged criticism and self-criticism in small groups, confessions of guilt and repentance in public meetings became standard procedures. The aim was to maintain the party's militancy and dedication during all the distractions of a united front period, to keep its membership prepared for future tasks. Behind the jargon of "subjectivism, sectarianism, and formalism" (the three main evils attacked), one can perceive a strenuous effort to re-educate and discipline new followers still contaminated by a liberal background, an individualistic temperament, or traditional morality. In particular Mao's dicta on art and letters required that artists and writers subordinate their personal creativity to the political aims of the CCP. "Art for art's sake" was out.

Simultaneously the *cheng-feng* movement marked the eclipse (though not a physical purge) of the doctrinaire "returned student" group who had behind them more training in Moscow than work in villages. Part of their wrong ideas no doubt was that they were not on Mao's team. In other words, the winnowing of personnel in the ideological reform was simultaneously a hunt for talent and for loyalty to Mao, as the leader built up his echelons of followers and put forth his doctrinal guidelines. Henceforth Marxist-Leninist theory must be tested in action, applied to rural China's concrete realities: this became the basis of "Mao Tse-tung thought." As the new CCP constitution of 1945 put it, "the ideas of Mao Tse-tung, the combined principles derived from the practical experience of the Chinese revolution" were now added to Marxism-Leninism as the party's guiding principles. While not calling for an independent national communism like that of Tito in Yugoslavia, this growth of Maoism represented the sinification of communism in China, in a period of wartime nationalism and minimal Russian influence. Henceforth it was no longer an alien creed. Its principal achievement had been to build a Leninist party on a peasant base, demonstrating (contrary to its own theory) that the Communist order is in fact independent of the proletariat.

This inversion of Marxism implied that a man's ideological tendencies did not come from his class affiliation, as posited by historical materialism. His class was now determined by his ideology; a bright peasant could become a "proletarian." This was a triumph of subjective and political considerations over the influence of the economic mode of production.

The New Democracy. The party line for public consumption in the Yenan period was laid down in Mao's essay *On the New Democracy* of 1940, a persuasive propaganda document which justified the united front as a temporary phase and yet reaffirmed the party's long-term mission. Mao divided the Chinese revolution into two stages: first, a "democratic revolution" (the New Democracy) and then a "socialist revolution." The New Democracy must first change the old "semi-feudal" society into an independent "democratic" society, which the Chinese people had been attempting ever since the Opium War. The 1911 Revolution, though a step in this direction, was only bourgeois-democratic, whereas the New Democracy would be part of the worldwide proletarian-socialist revolution in which China could win her freedom from imperialism only with the aid of international socialism represented by the Soviet Union. Thus the New Democracy aimed to develop a type of "democratic" state suited to China's semicolonial situation, ruled by an alliance of several revolutionary classes (unlike the "dictatorship of the proletariat" in Russia), before proceeding to a second stage of socialism.

In form the New Democracy should have a government of "democratic centralism," based on elections in which all participated but graded through a hierarchy of people's assemblies from the village on up to a national congress. In economic life the new government should own and operate largescale and monopoly activities including big banks, big industries, railways, and the like, in accord with the declaration of the first Kuomintang Congress of 1924. On the land the New Democracy would confiscate and distribute the holdings of big landlords in order to realize Sun Yat-sen's slogan, "Land to those who till it." By turning the land into the private property of the peasants, this reform, said Mao, would produce something quite different from a socialist agricultural system.

In the cultural revolution, said Mao, the May Fourth Movement had been chiefly significant for the introduction of Communist cultural thought. For the current phase the new culture should not try to be socialist, since socialism was not yet achieved but should be based upon nationalism, science, and the masses of the people. Thus Mao Tse-tung toward his non-Marxist audience blandly claimed to inherit the mantle of Sun Yat-sen and May Fourth, while for Marxists he put himself on the level of Marx-Engels-Lenin-Stalin as an original contributor to Communist theory. In actual fact Mao's "innovations" had been in the realm of practice, not theory. All his dicta could be found in earlier literature. His real contribution had been the creation of a state within a state—a party, an army, and mass support in a territorial base. But this was not something to boast of in 1940. The ambiguity of Mao's terminology catered to the liberals' hopes while actually building a framework in which to organize them.

Liberation. The semi-totalitarianism of wartime in any country, when life is mobilized by the state under the sanction of a common struggle for survival, may create high morale in the midst of suffering. With Japanese armies in the land, the Communists' organizational know-how, their current reasonableness and moderation, their militant and messianic faith, set the stage for a new cult of the common people. Liberation aimed at the awakening and activation of the Chinese peasant masses. The cultural movement stressed pictorial art in the form of the woodcut, which could be cheaply reproduced by wood-block printing for mass distribution. Choral singing was another wartime development in all parts of China. In the Communist areas it was combined with an ancient type of country dance to create a new art form in the *yang-ko* ("seedling song"), an all-talking-singing-dancing poor man's opera which used simple rhythms, folk tunes, a chain dance step, propaganda stories, and the subject matter of everyday life to provide entertainment which indoctrinated as it liberated. Getting the common man and woman to express themselves in public in country dancing and choral singing was part of their social integration.

Popular participation in cultural, economic, and political programs created a new psychological atmosphere. Participants in this wartime order were moved by a new creed, a humanitarian love of the peasant masses. This religion of the common man embraced the revolutionary ideal that modern technology and a new social organization could be used to remake and enrich the life of the peasant. This cult of the com-

Teaching public health. Instructor uses chart to stress principles of hygiene and proper preparation for child delivery. (Woodcut, Yenan period.)

mon people animated the cadres and the military forces. In order that the revolution might draw perpetual sustenance from the masses, the party worker was taught that he must live in the villages, work with the peasant, eat his food, lead his life, think his thoughts. Only thus could party cadres lead the peasant masses in their regeneration.

This spiritual concept of liberation became a dynamic element in the Communist movement and, by the inexorable logic of events, became also the sanction for the new party dictatorship. The reasoning in this paradox proceeded on orthodox lines: the revolution aimed to give the masses a new life, beginning with their economic betterment; this betterment could be achieved only through the exercise of absolute political power, sufficient to change the old order; political power could not be achieved by uncoordinated individuals but only through organization in a centralized party; a party could be effective only if its members submitted to absolute party discipline—in party councils all might have a voice, but once the party decision was taken, all must obey it. By this logical progression the party took on the character of an ongoing, living entity with a historic mission, transcendent over individuals who expended themselves in its cause. With its alleged scientific foreknowledge of the historical process, it became (or rather its leadership became) a law unto itself.

When the CCP held its Seventh Congress in April–June 1945, the first since 1928, it perfected its strategy for the postwar period by adopting the flexible line of "coalition government." After the New Fourth Army incident of January 1941, when Nationalist troops had fought a CCP force south of the Yangtze, the government had blockaded the CCP area more intensively, partly to prevent contact with Russia through Central Asia. Henceforth it had focused its attention as much on the Communists as on the Japanese, who in any event were plainly going to be dealt with by the United States. A general fear arose in China that World War II would be followed by civil war. Both Chungking and Yenan responded by promising to seek a "political" rather than military solution of their differences, and negotiations began early in 1943.

Building on his New Democracy line, Mao now declared that, being still in the stage of "bourgeois-democratic revolution," China needed a "New Democratic government of a coalition nature embracing all parties and nonpartisan representatives." Depending on expediency, this could mean a coalition including the Kuomintang, as was to be proposed in

1946, or a coalition with minor parties and liberals against the Kuomintang, as was to be achieved in 1949. Meanwhile this line appealed particularly to the modern-minded but frustrated intellectuals of Free China—professors, students, journalists, the literate and technically trained, who formed a basic resource for postwar reconstruction.

By war's end in 1945 the CCP had created a dynamic centrally controlled movement in its own areas and exerted a great attraction upon intellectuals in all China. Having done less of the fighting against Japan than the Nationalist government and having avoided the burdens of city administration and modern services, it was prepared to bid for power in the countryside. Only at this point did it become an immediate and inescapable problem for United States policy.

Part Three

*The United States and
the People's Republic*

Chapter 12
Our Inherited China Policy

Vietnam made it plain that we need a new perspective on our past relations with East Asia. Have our relations there always depended in the last analysis on bombs and bullets or at least the threat of bombs and bullets held in reserve? Or has our reliance on military firepower been a new thing, a recent aberration? The answer is mixed. The Western position in East Asia during the past century was maintained by force, but the force was usually European, seldom American. And before the spread of nationalism and modern technology to East Asia, not so much force was needed to maintain a Western position, and not so much firepower was available. Our use of violence in Vietnam was not unprecedented or aberrant so much as tragically out of date, disastrously out of proportion, as though the nineteenth-century principle of gunboat diplomacy (using superior firepower to impose one's will on local authorities) could be inflated to the level of coercing whole peoples from outside.

A new perspective on ourselves requires first a framework of conceptions. This, I think, must come from the academic disciplines because they represent the way our minds are organized for analytic purposes. We think in the terms of economics, politics, psychology, sociology, literature, fine arts, and so on. When we picture the past, the insights of all these approaches contribute to our historical synthesis. To an inquiring mind, no monocausal system is likely to be sufficient. Neither original sin nor the class struggle is the one key to understanding our past behavior.

A new perspective requires, second, that we recognize certain basic features of our past relations with East Asia, beginning with our own dynamism as part of the Western imperialist expansion in general.

American Expansion and Britain's Empire

In the early decades of the Republic, before the railroad opened up the Middle West, the United States was a small nation on the western fringe of the Atlantic civilization. Its revolutionary doctrines of democracy were designed to give the individual maximum freedom of enterprise in trade, travel, proselytism, and general self-development within the protective framework of the Bill of Rights and rule by law. Government and special political privilege were to be strictly limited, and opportunity thereby enhanced for all who could make the most of it. Our early trade was mainly by sea. James A. Field, Jr., has described how our early traders got around the British and French empires by trading in the eastern Mediterranean. Boston merchants who bought Turkey opium at Smyrna to ship to Canton were part of a three-pronged expansion of merchants, naval officers, and missionaries who were at first more active in the Mediterranean than in the Far East. The United States Navy's Mediterranean squadron, usually based on Majorca, conducted gunboat diplomacy with the "Barbary Pirates," meaning the local rulers of Morocco, Algiers, Tunis, and Tripoli, primarily to protect American traders there. Our earliest missionaries abroad were mainly in the Levant and the Ottoman empire beginning in the 1820s.

Our Inherited China Policy

Thus developed several features of the American expansion which were to be repeated in East Asia. First, we were country cousins of the British and righteously condemnatory of their empire; but we also relied upon their facilities, like the ports of Malta or Hong Kong, and imitated many of their methods. After all, London was the center of world trade, in which we were eager participants. Second, we were ready to demand the privileges of extraterritoriality. For example, we joined in the system of capitulations which exempted Europeans from the legal jurisdiction of the Ottoman empire. Third, we demanded equal opportunity and therefore most-favored-nation treatment, so that we could show the British and other imperialists what American enterprise and ingenuity could do in a fair field.

Finally, in dealing with local peoples, American democrats, proud of our new democracy at home, were ever ready to assist local rebels with doctrines of national independence, reform, and social equality. We felt ourselves to be on the giving end and enjoyed the feeling. Foreign missions, which grew steadily throughout the nineteenth century, were only one expression of this general attitude. Since Britain was master of India, the Ottoman empire was at first our main field of missionary enterprise. Toward the end of the century, with the decline of the "sick man of Europe," we found our chief evangelical opportunity in the Chinese empire, the sick man of Asia.

This missionary endeavor, in both Near East and Far East, was distinctly culture-bound, an expression of American home values. It used methods developed in the early missions of the seventeenth and eighteenth centuries to the American Indians. As summarized by R. Pierce Beaver, these methods "included the primary emphasis on preaching, the founding of churches, the assumed unity of evangelization and civilization, general education, Bible translation and the production

Missionaries and mandarins. *Above:* A civil official and his wife photographed in 1873. *Right:* The Reverend Calvin W. and Mrs. Julia B. M American Presbyterian educators, Tengchow, Shantung.

of vernacular literature, the recruiting and training of native pastors, evangelists and teachers, the mission station, and to some extent the Christian colony or community." All these features characterized our missions in the Near East and in China.

Our expansion across the Pacific had begun with the Canton trade, the whaling industry, and the fur trade of the Northwest coast, all handled from New England and the Middle Atlantic states by sea. But as we moved westward to explore and settle the American continent, we began in the 1840s to see our trans-Pacific contact as a natural extension of America's "manifest destiny." Orators pictured the westward course of empire, from the ancient Near East through Greece, Rome, Western Europe, and on across the Great Plains. Eventually in the 1880s the frontier began to disappear at home at

the same time that student youth volunteering for foreign missions felt challenged by a new frontier in China.

The American frontier in Asia was very different from that of the Great Plains: instead of open spaces and natural resources, we found Cathay. This new and strange type of human society aroused our curiosity and eventually our sympathy quite as much as our greed or avarice. Toward it we proceeded to apply attitudes developed at home. These were expansive, adventurous, and acquisitive. They included conceptions of individualism, progress, growth, and improvement as the law of life. The American merchant in Shanghai spoke of the beneficent role of commerce; the missionary, of saving the heathen from their state of sin. The American expansion into China was not solely economic, religious, or nationalist, but a combination of them all.

This American activity was largely carried on by individuals or private agencies; the United States government seldom led the way. Instead of the joint-stock trading companies with their armed fleets and semi-official merchant-administrators who had conducted the European expansion in the age of mercantilism, our early New Englanders went as commercial adventurers, a few boys and men in one tiny ship at a time. They took with them the peculiar philosophy of the young American nation—an eye for profit, innovation, and invention; concern for the moral worth and salvation of the individual; energy and self-confidence. Beginning with Peter Parker's celebrated eye hospital in Canton in the 1830s, American missionaries soon rivaled the British in numbers and in resources, decades before the American merchant caught up with his British counterpart. Missionary constituencies have been the seedbed of our humanitarianism toward China, a sentiment that sometimes set policy and sometimes ran into frustration.

America's Role within Britain's Informal Empire. Our traders at Canton after 1784 had found Britain the dominant Western power there. They continued to condemn British imperialism while making use of its banking facilities. The concept of "informal empire" is of course only a semi-concept; it describes a partway situation in which a foreign power dominates some aspects but by no means the whole of a local situation. But the British-sponsored unequal treaty system in East Asia made foreigners a privileged class on a par with the local ruling class, and certainly had some attributes of empire. The system was maintained by the presence of foreign naval firepower and gunboat diplomacy. The fact that our Commodore M. C. Perry, who had risen to fame as a gunboat diplomat on the Barbary Coast, was the man who opened Japan merely proved the rule: the Americans were a minor part of Britain's informal empire but could sometimes take the lead in its expansion.

This Anglo-American relationship was at first quite unequal. Britain was a bigger and more powerful country, covering the globe. America's economic absorption after the Civil War in her own domestic growth left her quite subordinate in the China trade, and her naval power in East Asian waters remained equally small. Consequently the Americans got the fruits of informal empire without the hard work and experience of using power. British diplomacy had to learn how to make difficult decisions, calculate the consequences, and live with them afterward. For example, when Harry Parkes, the chief British negotiator, was seized under a flag of truce in 1860, Lord Elgin felt he had to retaliate against the Ch'ing government but not hurt Chinese people. His solution was to burn the Ch'ing Summer Palace outside Peking. This was only one of many thousands of British imperial decisions that had to be made, day in and day out. The Americans had little similar experience.

Historians have been misled by the fact that our junior partnership with the British in China was not always apparent in the American archives. To a student of the American end of the record, American policy in China before John Hay is poorly documented and dull as dishwater. The scanty correspondence of our diplomats was chiefly enlivened by the anti-British fulminations of doughty and oratorical amateurs like Humphrey Marshall, American commissioner in 1853. Mr. Marshall has been often quoted by students of the American record because he asserted our duty to support the Chinese Empire against British machinations. But he was there so briefly, knew so little of the facts, and had such inadequate assistance that his dispatches express an attitude rather than a policy. British imperialism in its commercial phase on the China coast was not particularly exclusive. The real American policy in this early period was usually to acquiesce, sometimes querulously, in British policy.

When Robert Hart, in building up the Chinese Imperial Maritime Customs Service, enlisted E. B. Drew of Cambridge,

Massachusetts, and Drew in turn enlisted four members of the Harvard class of 1874 to go to China and as customs commissioners superintend the foreign trade of the treaty ports, it had nothing to do with American policy. It was private American participation in British policy, mediated through Manchu policy at Peking.

After 1922, when the Anglo-Japanese alliance, that prolongation of British Far Eastern naval dominance, came to an end, American influence and activity in China began to outstrip Britain's. The Shanghai Municipal Council and the Hong Kong docks were still British preserves, but the dozen Christian colleges of the 1920s and 1930s were primarily American achievements, and some big commercial distributors like the British-American Tobacco Company were joint Anglo-American efforts. The rise of Nazi Germany in the 1930s made it plain that foreign help to stop Japanese expansion would have to come mainly from America rather than Britain. America was also becoming the chief source of Chinese returned students, superseding Japan as well as Europe. The decade of the Nanking government was the height of American peacetime influence, and it was followed by the big American military effort in China during the 1940s. The balance shifted, and the United States inherited the British position as the principal Western power active in China.

The American Ambivalence about China

The way in which we first entered the Chinese scene, on the morrow of our war of independence against the British empire, still inveighing against its evils while demanding equal enjoyment of its benefits, contributed to a curious ambivalence in our China policy, a gap between thought and reality. The principal reality was the unequal treaty system, but since this had been fought for and was still maintained by British and French arms, the United States government felt little primary responsibility for it. Our principal thought was to get our share of privilege and opportunity, a me-too policy.

In politics, for example, by our own revolutionary tradition we were conscientiously opposed to colonialism, suspicious of European machinations, a bit holier-than-they in our early abstention from empire and even from power politics. Yet at the same time by demanding most-favored-nation treatment we were quick to enjoy all the semi-colonial fruits of extraterritoriality. In daily life, even the most undistinguished American citizens—deadbeats escaping their failures, remittance men sent abroad for their families' sake, stowaways, and adventurers—once they disembarked at Shanghai had upperclass status thrust upon them. Like the Chinese gentry, they were set above the masses, not subject to local police coercion. Embarrassed at first to be pulled by a human horse in a ricksha, the average American soon accepted his superiority and found Oriental life and its inexpensive personal services enjoyable. Even the most egalitarian missionary had to compromise with Chinese hierarchic realities.

From this ambivalent experience, I suggest, emerged the sometimes startling contrast between the vigor of our verbal pronouncements and the limitations of our official actions. We would not abandon our ideals of national self-determination and individual freedom for the Chinese people, but somehow we could never take action to get these values realized in fact. The ideals we treasured as part of our own culture; the facts were part of China's. They remained incompatible. The result was to encourage in our traditional policy a disconcerting split between humanitarian ideals and strategic realism. The moral righteousness which long distinguished American Far Eastern policy was remarkable for its omission of any idea that war is a practical tool of policy. We were ready to pronounce vigorous moral judgments condemning Japanese aggression at the same time that we refused absolutely to contemplate going to war in support of our moral and diplomatic position. This resulted in anomalous situations, as when the Stimson doctrine after 1931 upheld our honor by refusing to recognize Manchukuo, while we still sold war supplies to Japan.

Our inability to translate our moral ideals into active policy in China, our tendency to talk grand and act small, sometimes almost irresponsibly, has been affected by another pattern, one of fluctuation between energy and apathy. The long-term fluctuations in our interest in East Asia have been a function of many complex factors in American life, including the fact that we were never as dependent as Britain upon overseas trade. We were latecomers at Canton and even later in California. Both the Spanish and for a time the Russians were on the Pacific coast ahead of us. (One incentive to the Monroe Doctrine of 1823 was the Russian ukase of 1821, which declared the Pacific coast from 51 degrees northward to be a Russian preserve.) Our efforts in the period 1818–1824 had given us a continental position stretching to the Pacific; but the Mexican War, the California gold rush, Perry's opening of Japan, and the general American westward expansion of the forties and early fifties were followed by another period of apathy. Washington remained profoundly uninterested in trans-Pacific expansion. Repeated plans and proposals by Americans in the Orient left the American home government unmoved. In Taiwan (Formosa), Americans from Canton explored the island, built a port, raised the American flag, loaded some seventy-eight vessels with cargoes worth half a million dollars, and got the American commissioner to China to advocate annexation. The State Department did not even reply to the proposal. When the Russians in the 1860s decided to sell Alaska as indefensible in war and unprofitable in peace, Secretary Seward had great difficulty in getting congressional approval to buy it. The House of Representatives passed the appropriation bill only after nine months' delay and after the Russian minister had paid out thousands of dollars in bribes.

Underlying the gap between word and deed, and the waxing and waning of interest, perhaps we can discern the intractable problem of cultural differences. Our folklore and public attitudes concerning China have included several discordant images—exotic, idealized, or disillusioned—which have co-existed but remained unreconciled in our inherited thinking.

The exotic approach used to emphasize cultural oddities —men's pigtails, women's bound feet, scholarly long fingernails, opium smoking, and other trappings of the premodern age. Reader interest in man-bites-dog items was satisfied by tidbits like "Chinese eat rats." The exotic approach also made much of all things "Chinesey" (an adjective denoting Westernized versions of things Chinese) like "Chinese chow," moon gates, and the cunning handicraft curios produced for the tourist trade. Emphasis was on dissimilarity. "Everything in China is opposite." The men wear gowns and the women trousers. They read from up to down and right to left. The soup comes last. Mourners wear white and brides red. The last name comes first. The compass points south. Left is the seat of honor, and so on. Quips like "Confucius say" and "Damn clever, these Chinese" belong in this category, as well as the inscrutable Dr. Fu Manchu. Other sources of exoticism were the supposed Chinese indifference to suffering and the tradition of fiendish oriental tortures, associated respectively with lower economic and lower political standards of living.

The idealized approach to China had more substance. It went back to the eighteenth-century vision of China's rational and enlightened despotism as a model for Europe. This favorable view included our reverence for the wisdom of the

East, which interested Emerson and the New England transcendentalists. China traders and Christian missionaries nourished the thought of a "special relationship" between Americans and Chinese, a supra-cultural friendship based on common traits and values and mutual respect. In real life our penchant for idealization was applied to such contrasting persons as Madame Chiang Kai-shek, on her famous grand tour of the United States in 1943, and the Communist guerrillas of the Eighth Route army, during the earlier stages of the anti-Japanese war—both of whom were assigned incredible virtues by the obvious predilections of the American public. Idealization of Chinese resistance against Japan, at a time when the United States was still supplying war materials to the latter, no doubt sprang from a guilty conscience; but other factors of American mass psychology also entered into our periodic enthusiasms about China—particularly our sympathy with the underdog.

In 1894 when China was still a vast archaic empire and Japan an up-and-coming pupil of the West, American opinion favored Japan in her war against China, and on the same underdog principle, also favored Japan against Russia in 1904. We began to fear Japan only after 1905 when Japan gave promise of being top dog in the Far East. In the 1930s American opinion supported the valiant but ill-equipped efforts of Chinese patriots to withstand Japanese aggression. This sentiment was particularly evident in the American support of Chiang Kai-shek during the early war years. Yet the same sentiment operated in favor of the Chinese Communists when they represented a minority cause among the peasantry, struggling against the weight of Chiang's legions. Our concern for the underdog led us to shift our emotional support from one contestant to another depending on the apparent justice of their cause and the circumstances of their relative strength. It may be doubted whether the Japanese or Chiang Kai-shek or the Chinese Communists changed as greatly as American opinion concerning them changed.

The disillusioned view of China bulks large in the record, for nineteenth-century Americans as fresh apostles of progress found a China in decay, actually sunk in poverty, filth, disease, corruption, thievery, and disorder, and apparently unwilling to do anything about it. Reform-minded Americans, always ready with suggestions, were overwhelmed with the size of China's problems, annoyed by Chinese apathy. In the United States the picture of Chinese drug addiction, prostitution, foot binding, concubinage, and unspeakable vices excited the morbid, while heathen idolatry and sin appalled the devout. Chinese immigrant laborers, brought to help develop California, by 1880 formed a twelfth of the population there, and scores were killed in anti-Chinese riots in California and other western states in the 1870s and 1880s. But the Chinese exclusion acts of 1882 and later years were supported by East Coast sentiment as well. These laws expressed many fears: that Chinese were culturally and racially unassimilable, that their lower living standard was a positive menace to public health, that their presence would promote the spread of slavery, as well as the new labor unions' fear of their economic competition. The exclusion laws made racism our national policy. The big city Chinatowns became all-male ghettos. Upper-class Chinese visitors, the only kind allowed, met humiliation and harassment.

Meanwhile in China American farm boys who had received the call and become missionaries, when they met the hostility of the elite and indifference of the masses, found their Christian forebearance sorely tried. The Reverend Arthur H. Smith in his *Chinese Characteristics* (1890) expressed the tolerant but sometimes acerbic frustration of missionaries who found the Chinese villager impervious to progress and the gospel. Smith's analysis of Chinese psychology was admired in both the United States and Japan. Its great-grand-child in social science garb may be found in Lucian Pye, *The Spirit of Chinese Politics: A Psychocultural Study of the Authority Crisis in Political Development.* Meanwhile disillusionment was epitomized in the "Shanghai mind" of the treaty-port businessman, whose low view of Chinese character was summed up in the 1920s in Rodney Gilbert's *What's Wrong with China.* During World War II, this disillusionment was distilled in the GI hatred of Chinese filth and poverty, heightened by the boredom and complaints of wartime. In 1950 the Chinese Communists' manufacture of the germ warfare charge and their treatment of American prisoners in Korea seemed to exemplify the super-evils produced by modern totalitarianism in a backward country. The Cold War made our earlier mood of patronizing enthusiasm for a land of sturdy peasants and attractive students fade into the background.

Americanists have only begun to study our ambivalent images of China. Their variety is confusing, but one thing stands out: in Sino-American relations to 1949, China was always the weaker party, in trouble, the recipient of our interest and philanthropy. America was always the superior party, not in such trouble, able to help. It was not an equal relationship, which is no doubt why we enjoyed it.

In 1972 President Nixon's spectacular trip to China began still another cycle of ultra-enthusiasm tapering off into mixed feelings. Now our problem is dual: to accept China's irreducible differentness and yet to treat China as a mature and independent equal.

The Evolution of the Open Door

In the circumstances of 1899 John Hay's Open Door notes take on a significance quite different from the tradition of benevolence toward China which later became associated with them. They came right in the midst of a territorial expansion that gave us Hawaii by annexation and Puerto Rico, Guam, and the Philippines by the peace treaty with Spain in 1898, and part of Samoa in 1899. While Germany had got a foothold in China's Shantung province and Russia in South Manchuria, we acquired in the Pacific not one but several naval bases and an archipelago to boot.

The idea of preserving an Open Door for trade in China by the "collective influence of the trading nations" was originally British. Secretary of State John Hay borrowed it. When he asked W. W. Rockhill in August 1899 to draft the notes, Rockhill got the advice of a British commissioner of Chinese Maritime Customs, A. E. Hippisley, who had been one of the closest coworkers and assistants of Robert Hart, who was at this time the chief proponent of equal taxation of, and commercial opportunity for, the trade of all nations in China. His policy as Inspector General of Customs in Peking differed from that of the British Foreign Office.

Following Hart's views, Hay's Open Door notes of September 1899 made no reference to the integrity of China and interposed no bar to the extension of imperialist spheres of influence. The notes were primarily concerned with preserving China's customs revenue. After proposing, first, that each power not interfere with the vested interests of other powers within its sphere of influence, the notes then proposed, second, that only the Chinese government should collect customs duties, and only according to the Chinese treaty tariff, and, third, that no preferential harbor dues or railroad charges should benefit the subjects of a power having a sphere. It was not until Russia had begun to occupy Manchuria as a consequence of the Boxer Rising that Hay's supplementary notes of July 1900 raised the question of the integrity of China.

The Integrity of China. The Open Door began as a political, not a legal, doctrine. It was expressed in the form of policy statements and in bilateral treaties on many occasions after 1900, but it was not until 1922 that it was stated in a legal form binding on all parties. The doctrine itself underwent growth and expansion. The second set of notes of July 1900 was much more positive and supported Chinese "territorial and administrative entity," a phrase later supplanted by "territorial and administrative integrity." This reflected the fact that Russia had moved very rapidly into Manchuria, contrary to the interest of most of the powers. Thus by 1900 Hay had developed his doctrine actually to the point of attacking any extension of spheres of influence. The Anglo-Japanese alliance of 1902 introduced the phrase "equal opportunity." This was entirely in keeping with the British conception of the Open Door for trade. In later statements, however, "equal opportunity" was applied to "cultural" activities as well as commercial and was also made to embrace the idea of freedom of "movement." By 1938 American policy statements were regularly including the phrases "free competition" and "fair treatment."

In this way the Open Door doctrine developed two main tenets: the integrity of China, and the equal treatment of all foreigners there. Viewed cynically, the doctrine of China's integrity was a device to prevent other powers, for example, Russia, from taking over areas of China like Manchuria and excluding us from them. In the early 1900s John Hay felt he had "done the Chinks a great service," but as Michael Hunt has caustically demonstrated, the Americans actually disregarded China's interest and also made gross errors out of sheer "ignorance . . . misinformation and prejudice." Nevertheless the independence of China has appealed to Americans as a matter of political justice. Until recently it fitted the doctrine of the self-determination and sovereignty of weaker nations, which constituted one of our major political sentiments.

The nonrecognition doctrine of Secretary Byran in 1915 and Secretary Stimson in 1931, by which we refused to recognize any Japanese impairment of China's integrity, was a corollary of the integrity idea itself. As a doctrine, nonrecognition proved as unavailing as our other invocations of righteousness. In the later stages of Japan's aggression during the 1930s, Secretary Hull emphasized another aspect of the same idea, nonintervention. This became one of the chief moral thunderbolts he hurled so unavailingly at the Japanese. In 1949 the People's Republic, unaware of any benefit from it, closed the Open Door decisively, yet a certain residue from it remains in our thinking.

After World War I the United States sought to carry out its policy toward China through collective action, in marked contrast to Latin America where our Monroe Doctrine forbade a collective approach by the United States and European powers. It also contrasted with our European policy, in which we stayed out of the League of Nations and so in effect left Europe's problems to the British and French. Only in the Far East did we take the lead in action through the concert of powers—by the Washington Conference of 1921–22, particularly in the Nine Power Treaty concerning China. This was a codification of the Open Door doctrine in expanded form. In 1928 collective action was buttressed on paper by the Kellogg-Briand Pact outlawing war. The United States also joined collective action against Japan, to no avail, by associating an American representative with the League of Nations commission which fruitlessly investigated Japan's seizure of Manchuria in 1931. During the 1930s the foreign policy of Stimson and Hull generally followed the line of collective or at least parallel action as the best hope of mobilizing diplomatic pressure to stop Japan, a second-best and ineffective alternative at a time of isolationism.

After World War II the United Nations became another vehicle for collective action against aggression and we joined with it actively to repel the North Korean attack on the Republic of Korea in June 1950 and the Chinese intervention which followed. But our Vietnam venture in the 1960s, except for help from client states like South Korea, failed to secure much collective support. Vietnam indeed raised basic questions about our aims in East Asia.

The Nature of the American Interest. The American commercial interest in China has had a large admixture of imagination and hope. Paul Varg has described "the myth of the China market." Actually our financial investments in China and Japan in the 1930s were about equal. American investments in China, chiefly direct investments, were less than a quarter of a billion United States dollars, while our investments in Japan, chiefly in Japanese bonds, were also something less than a quarter of a billion. In fact, our entire investment in the Far East was only 5 or 6 percent of the total American investment abroad. Moreover, our financial investment in China was a very small part indeed of the total foreign stake in China, a good deal less than one tenth.

If we turn to foreign trade the figures are no more encouraging to the theory of economic determinism as the sole source of our policy. In the 1930s Japan took between 8 and 9 percent of our total foreign trade, while China accounted for less than half that amount (even counting Manchuria as still part of China). Japan's large foreign trade was conducted one third with the United States, while of all our Far Eastern trade two fifths was with Japan and only about one fifth was with China. Our missionary investment in China represented about 40 million dollars in terms of money but obviously a great deal more in terms of sentiment. However we approach the problem, dollars and cents, even in the minds of businessmen, have not been an all-compelling factor in our China policy.

The operation of sentiment rather than dollar diplomacy in the State Department has been documented by Dorothy Borg's study of the period 1925–28. She makes it plain that Secretary Kellogg based his China policy on a "simple almost instinctive reaction" typical of the general American attitude toward China in the 1920s. He wished to get rid of the unequal treaties and make China fully independent as soon as possible. He wanted to remain neutral among factions within China and refused to be obsessed by the Bolshevik menace there. He steadfastly refused to apply sanctions after the incident in which Americans were attacked at Nanking in 1927. On the other hand he was equally determined to deal only with a Chinese government that represented a unified country. He did not want to facilitate in any way a division of China into two parts. When the vigor of the anti-foreign feeling in China in 1925 caught the treaty powers as well as the missionaries by surprise, the Shanghai business community became convinced very soon that this Chinese anti-foreignism was a Moscow plot. Many voices were raised advocating intervention to save China from Soviet domination. Secretary Kellogg and his chief assistant, Nelson Johnson, refused to be stampeded by this hysteria.

Aid to China was by custom a private matter for the attention of the missionary profession, the public organs concerned with famine or flood relief, agencies like the Rockefeller Foundation interested in educational and medical development, and other groups and individuals. By the remission of part of the Boxer indemnity in 1908, the remainder in 1924, and similar gestures, the United States government began to take a hand in the process of helping China remake herself.

In 1934 Washington inaugurated, primarily for domestic reasons, a silver purchase program which soon began to dislocate and depress the Chinese economy. It led to vast amounts of silver being smuggled out of China, which had to leave the silver standard and adopt a managed paper currency in 1935. Subsequently, however, the Treasury under Secretary Morgenthau was able to make the silver purchase program of direct though unpublicized aid to the Nationalist government by paying it gold or US dollars for some 500 million ounces of silver. In 1937–39, for example, we paid 184 million dollars on this account.

With World War II government aid to China became the dominant form of American assistance. Beginning with loans in the months before Pearl Harbor and the clandestine development of Colonel C. L. Chennault's "Flying Tigers" (American Volunteer Group) as an air force in Burma and Yunnan, we embarked in 1942 upon a continuing government program of financial, material, and technical assistance.

This was a milestone, if not indeed a gravemarker, in our relations with the Chinese people. Before this, American philanthropy had been from person to person, group to group, small-scale but persistent, maintaining institutions or helping movements but never supporting governments. Now our aid was official as well as massive. It could go only to the recognized government of the country, which was well aware of its right to be the sole channel. Unfortunately our ally the Nationalist government was by 1942 already well advanced in that process of decline noted in a previous chapter. Our help could not remake its inner nature but served merely to make it less dependent on domestic opinion and more inclined eventually to rely upon its new American-made armaments. In fighting Japan we had no recourse, in conscience or in reality, but to support the government of Chiang Kai-shek. But our half-billion-dollar morale booster of early 1942, for example, was given with no strings attached. We never learned exactly who used it for what purposes. No country aid program was set up by treaty, calling for bilateral actions in planned phases. From the beginning of our wartime alliance, American officials found themselves dealing with an ineffective administration, too debilitated by its domestic problems to respond to foreign stimuli. Trying to aid it, we became entangled in its decline and fall.

America's Contribution and the Fate of Liberalism

The first half of the twentieth century saw the maximum American influence in China. Though only a portion of the general foreign invasion, this influence was pervasive yet sometimes ephemeral. Its needs appraisal.

While all nations find more in common from year to year —in worldwide problems if not in their solutions—American travelers to China today are struck by the great contrasts in the Chinese and American ways of life. How could we ever have been a model for China's regeneration? What did we in fact contribute? (Significantly, we have seldom asked what China gave us; for we assumed we knew the modern way for all mankind. That America should learn from China is a quite recent thought.)

Anyone who tries to defend the record of American activity in China gets into a two-front war—against the overstrident denunciations of Chinese revolutionists and against the criticisms of his own conscience. Who can defend or excuse any chunk of events? History is by nature a mix of good, bad, and moot. My object here is only to suggest that we need to study the record and find out what in fact happened. We can argue about it later. Even so, too much happened that is still beyond our ken. What follows are a few examples, and that is all.

One of the most spectacular and constructive examples of American private aid was the Rockefeller Foundation investment in the Peking Union Medical College from 1915 to 1947: to get started, it took over a missionary medical college in Peking and invested $9.8 million in a new site and buildings, dedicated in 1921. From 1924 to 1943 some 313 Chinese doctors of medicine and almost as many nurses were graduated while the foundation invested another $12 million in endowment and about the same amount in upkeep. The criticism that 300 doctors for the 450 million people of China were like a flea on an elephant missed the point: PUMC aimed throughout to produce specialists who could bring China the fruits of modern medical science. It was a research and training hospital, perhaps the best one east of Boston and west of San Francisco. There was a great variety of achievements, especially in parasitology, communicable diseases, and nutritional deficiencies so widespread in China. Major diseases like schistosomiasis, kala-azar, and hookworm were brought further under control. Drugs like ephedrine were developed from the ancient Chinese pharmacopaeia. Nursing by Chinese women, not men alone, was made a respectable profession. Out of 141 doctors graduated as of 1934, 95 percent were in teaching, research, or full-time hospital work, only 7 in private practice. PUMC, in short, did not reach the Chinese masses in public health work, but it trained a generation who could guide such work later.

American help was greatest in education, usually as part of the general foreign influence. In the absence of strong government, strong personalities emerged in private academic work. For example, Chang Po-ling of Tientsin with private Chinese support founded there in 1907 the Nankai Middle School. He visited Japan and the United States and got international as well as Chinese backing. By 1919 his school became Nankai University. By 1931 the Nankai Institute of

Economics, headed by American-trained economists, was pioneering in research on China's industrialization. Chang became a Christian. He responded to YMCA ideas but was above all a patriotic educator in the liberal arts, sponsoring the education of women as well as physical education, college sports, and dramatics. In the 1930s Nankai University, its boys and girls middle schools, experimental primary school, and graduate schools had over 3000 students, almost all from urban origins. In 1937 Japan bombed Nankai first of all, but its work continued in Chungking and Kunming.

Western missionary education was supported by Protestant constituencies mainly in the United States, Britain, and Canada. Christian educators had set up some 200 schools in different parts of China, out of which grew small institutions of higher education that by degrees merged and developed into the Christian colleges.* These institutions represented the cooperation of twenty-one Protestant societies and a dozen American universities. In 1936–37 their faculties totaled 652 persons including 466 Chinese, their student bodies, 6424. Chinese sources including tuition fees provided more than half their total income. Missionaries of the Catholic church had more converts but fewer institutions of higher education, their leading universities being Fu-jen at Peiping and Aurora at Shanghai. Western missionary education was on a small scale but of wide influence.

Its problems may be seen in the case of the leading Christian college, Yenching University, studied by Philip West. The group that created this institution on its attractive campus outside Peking began as a Christian fellowship partly of

---

* In the 1930s they were Cheeloo at Tsinan in Shantung, Yenching outside Peiping, St. John's at Shanghai, Lingnan near Canton, a trio of institutions at Hangchow, Soochow, and Shanghai, West China Union University at Chengtu in Szechwan, Nanking University and Ginling College for Women at Nanking, two institutions at Foochow, and a group of colleges forming Central China University at Wuhan.

American missionary and partly of Chinese Christian educators. The Americans saw faith in Jesus as the dynamic for China's salvation. They did not challenge the institution of private property or the current political order or least of all the individualism implicit in the Yenching motto, "Freedom through truth for service." Their Chinese counterparts had all found in Christianity the way to "serve the people" and help save China. In the early 1920s the radical nationalists' anti-Christian movement strained but did not break this Yenching partnership. After 1928 the university operated under two constitutions, one in English for the board of trustees in New York, who controlled the budget, and one in Chinese for the board of managers in China, who abided by Nanking government regulations. Straddling this gap between American financing and Chinese politics, Yenching educated the new middle class but also many who became leaders of the Communist movement.

During the decade of uneasy peace from 1927 to 1937, leading government institutions like Peking University and Tsing Hua University at Peiping achieved standards of scholarship in many fields superior to those of the Christian colleges. The fine new buildings, broad campuses, and thousands of students in these government universities dwarfed the missionary institutions. Their staffs belonged to a generation trained abroad. (By 1953, in the estimate of Y. C. Wang, at least 36,000 Chinese had studied in the United States.) The faculty of the wartime Southwest Associated University created at Kunming by the cooperation of Peita, Tsing Hua, and Nankai universities had more than 170 professors, out of 200 in all, who had received advanced training abroad. Of this 170, more than 100 had taken doctoral degrees in the United States.

When the Kuomintang came to power at Nanking in 1928 it established a European-type national research academy (Academia Sinica), which soon had a dozen institutes in various disciplines. Academic funding was also available from the American Boxer indemnity funds, which set up in 1924 the China Foundation for the Promotion of Education and Culture. Thus the republican era saw a joint use of private, foreign, and Chinese government support for developments in many fields. The palace at Peking was made into a national museum. With American help the new National Library of Peiping set new standards of scientific technique and stimulated the development of other libraries. The new scholarship at Yenching and elsewhere began to produce critical editions and indexes to classical sources, and monographs with specific footnote references—both indexes and footnotes being modern additions to a scholarly tradition based on verbatim memory of the classics.

Academic development required enormous persistence in the midst of many obstacles. Archaeology, for example, originally was sponsored by the Ministry of Industries' Geological Survey of China set up in 1916 to map the country and survey its natural resources including those in paleontology. Dr. A. Grabau, formerly geologist of New York State, became the Survey's adviser. In the 1920s archaeological field work was inaugurated as a new scientific discipline by archaeologists invited from half a dozen Western countries. The existence of Peking Man at the Chou-k'ou-tien site near Peking was first identified from a single tooth by a Canadian (Davidson Black). The Painted Pottery was first found by a Swede (J. G. Andersson). Such foreigners trained a new generation of Chinese scientists. A Harvard graduate, Dr. Li Chi, who became chief of the epochal Shang dynasty excavations at Anyang 1928–37, has quoted Fu Ssu-nien of Academia Sinica (who had been a student leader on May 4, 1919): "What was deficient in Chinese traditional education was the artificial division between body and mind." China's archaeologists, in short, had to be scholars who worked with their hands.

Liberals in Shanghai, 1933. From left, the American journalist Agnes
Smedley, George Bernard Shaw, Madame Sun Yat-sen (Soong
Ch'ing-ling), Ts'ai Yüan-p'ei, then head of Academia Sinica, and
Lu Hsün. Shaw was visiting China. The others had been founders of
the short-lived China League for Civil Rights.

They created a new discipline in China, the fruits of which
now astound the world. (In the mid-1970s magnificent Chinese exhibits in Japan, Western Europe, and North America
displayed dazzling works of art recently excavated from tombs
of the First Emperor of the Ch'in, and of the Han, T'ang, and
other periods, in bronze, sculpture, ceramics, textiles, tomb
paintings and even literary texts, accurately located and dated
for almost the first time.)

Against this background one can understand why the old traditions and the Western example produced liberal individuals in modern China, but no liberal movement. Liberalism could not become institutionalized. Those in power did not accept the civil liberties and basic freedoms of speech and person, habeas corpus and jury trial, in short the supremacy of law—to which Americans are all too unconsciously accustomed. Inclusion of such guaranties in constitutions and law codes was but a first step on a long hard road. Similarly there was no strong middle class of the Western type. Private property, like the individual, had little legal protection against an unconstrained officialdom. Liberals in China generally lacked the security of private economic means which has sustained the Western liberal movement. Lacking the defenses of law and property, the Chinese liberal found an uncertain security in the superior social status accorded the scholar. The fate of liberalism in China was therefore closely bound up with the fate of education. After 1937 education was attacked both from within and from without, by the traditional dominance of officials over scholars and by the Japanese war that destroyed the Nanking regime.

Yet these outer circumstances were not the only impediment. Within itself Western liberalism was not well defined or distinct from the pluralistic culture in which it flourished. It had no political doctrine and method exportable to warlord China. The proof appeared early on, when John Dewey of Columbia University, America's foremost philosopher of pragmatism and teacher of many young Chinese academic leaders, reached Shanghai on April 30, 1919, and for two years (until July 1921) lectured widely at Chinese centers of learning. Dewey traveled in eleven provinces, and like Bertrand Russell during his shorter stay (October 1920–July 1921) offered the best that the Western democracies had to offer. With what result? Barry Keenan concludes that "Deweyan experimentalism . . . offered no strategy his followers could use to affect political power." He assumed education must remain separate from politics and must reform it indirectly, but this could not be done in the uncontrolled environment of warlord China.

The contribution and in the end the failure of the American liberal approach to Republican China's salvation was epitomized in the career of Hu Shih (1891–1962), who served as the principal translator for the lectures of his teacher, John Dewey. True to pragmatism, he opposed sweeping solutions by abstract "isms." He avoided politics and revolution but undertook to free China from her dead past by critically reappraising it. As Jerome Grieder has said, Hu stood for "moderation, tolerance, intellectual freedom, individual liberty and the rule of law and reason . . . Much of what he strove to accomplish was what we ourselves might have hoped to see done." This approach did not strike at the Chinese people's central problems.

In the 1930s, the new liberalism, centered in Peiping, came under increasing pressure from the new bureaucracy at Nanking. KMT agents were planted in the universities. Students who criticized the government were seized by police squads raiding their dormitories at dawn, and carted off to prison. Teachers and editors were intimidated. After 1937 the Japanese bombings and the spectacular scorched-earth policy of the Chinese resistance were hardly more disastrous than the undermining of liberal institutions and ideas which the war facilitated. The fine beginnings of the preceding decade came under the wartime pressures of inflation and domination by political authorities.

When war came patriotic faculties and student bodies moved inland with the government. Institutions in Nanking and Wuhan took much of their equipment directly up the Yangtze. The Academia Sinica transported its unrivaled sinological library via Indochina to a village on the Yangtze in Szechwan. But the universities in Peiping suffered badly. Peita and Tsing Hua, moved in 1937 to a campus at Changsha which was soon bombed by the Japanese, necessitating a further removal by truck and on foot through the mountains to Kunming. There the French railway from Indochina formed the only real link with the outer world during the first years of war, like the Burma Road at a later date. Students and faculties survived mainly because the government rice allowances gave them something to eat. They had to sell or pawn books, clothes, and furniture in order to keep alive.

The KMT had always considered education to be a tool of the state. The political thinking of students was intimidated increasingly through the Kuomintang Youth Corps founded in 1938. Branches of the corps within every student body made it their business to exalt the official ideology and denounce deviant thought. Mass education was meanwhile discountenanced. As one example take the experience of Dr. T'ao Hsing-chih (Heng-chi Tao). After studying at the University of Illinois and with John Dewey at Columbia, T'ao had gone into rural education in China and helped develop the "little teacher" movement whereby schoolchildren became teachers to other illiterates. This literacy movement turned into a chain reaction, particularly during the united front of 1937–38 when the government was at Wuhan. Evidently it seemed like political dynamite. The KMT suppressed it.

Chapter 13

United States Policy and the Nationalist Defeat

The years 1912 and 1949 marked two phases of China's political metamorphosis. In the nineteenth century the Manchu dynasty had been forced to give the treaty powers a privileged role within its East Asian empire, but as the Chinese people awakened to national life, the alien monarchy was dissolved in 1912. In its absence the treaty powers' position grew more prominent while the national revolution gathered strength only gradually. After Japan's aggression began in 1931, the Western powers proved useful against it until 1945, by which time the United States had become involved in supporting the established government. When it collapsed in 1949, Western participation in Chinese life collapsed with it, and the unequal treaty century in China came to an end amid widespread recrimination.

Thus the American government's position in China, inherited from Britain, was built up in response to Japan's invasion. But as World War II progressed after December 7, 1941, China became a theater of supreme frustration. Chiang Kai-shek failed to get a coordinated allied strategy centered on himself. Britain failed to hold Singapore or the Burma Road. Joseph W. Stilwell, one of the ablest American generals, had hardly arrived to be Chiang's "chief of staff "when he took on the hopeless task of defending Burma. Burma fell in early

1942, and Stilwell then set himself the grueling three-year task of reopening a land route to China across the North Burma jungle. Yet even after it and its accompanying pipeline were opened in early 1945, the pioneer Hump airlift still carried more tonnage. Again, our Twentieth Bomber Command got five big airfields built near Chengtu in Szechwan, of rock crushed by Chinese corvée labor. Supplying their B-29s took more Hump tonnage in 1944 than was allocated to the Chinese armies. But they had hardly begun to bomb Japan before their base was shifted to the Marianas, supplied by sea and nearer Tokyo. Entering the war as the prospective allied base for defeating Japan, Free China found that job done by naval and air power at sea and herself cut off, a low-priority sideshow. The American aim became merely to keep Free China in the war. The result was not defeat but neither was it victory.

Chinese nationalism continued to suffer frustration after Japan's defeat. Well before Pearl Harbor, in May 1941, we had offered to abandon extraterritoriality as soon as peace should come in China. A new Sino-American treaty on equal terms was signed January 11, 1943. But within five months another agreement was made, freeing American troops in China (60,000 by 1945) from Chinese criminal jurisdiction. American bases, supply and transport services, radio networks, airlines, and army post offices were soon operating on Chinese soil in greater volume and with greater license than Southwest China had ever seen under the unequal treaties. At war's end Shanghai streets for many months were filled with GI's and roistering sailors far beyond the memory of treaty port days. This ill suited China's new great power status. China's new-found sovereignty took on a quizzical character. Right-wing chauvinists, Communists, and patriotic liberals could unite in inveighing against GI incidents connected with wine, women, and jeeps.

Americans in China in World War II. *Above:* Airfield. *Below:* Main street. From *All in Line* (Duell, Sloane and Pierce). © 1944, Saul Steinberg. Originally in *The New Yorker.*

American Aid and Mediation

From late 1943 American diplomats began to glimpse the inherent danger in KMT-CCP rivalry—"civil war at some undetermined date," which might hamstring the war effort and eventually let Russia back the Communists. The Americans aimed therefore to avert civil war by encouraging a political settlement, which Chiang Kai-shek advocated as early as September 1943, and to strengthen the Nationalist government position, partly by building up its armies, partly by getting it to reform itself. Armies were built up but reform proved impossible, for reasons already indicated. The idea of a political settlement, however, was accepted by all parties, at least verbally. KMT-CCP negotiations had been resumed early in 1943.

American policy proceeded on three levels. First, on the international stage we tried to make China a great power in form if not in substance. She was permanently excluded from the high command of the war at the British-American conference at Quebec in August 1943 but was included along with the Soviet Union in the Moscow Declaration of great-power principles in October. The British-American-Chinese Cairo Declaration of December 1943 promised to return to China all territories lost to Japan, and Roosevelt at the Teheran Conference stood firm for China's great power status on the future United Nations Security Council. But this conferring of great power status on the Nationalist government was an American accomplishment, not Chinese or, least of all British or Soviet. It was seen at the time as a fine and friendly gesture toward a great and deserving people. History, however, may view it with disillusion as a doctrinaire effort at trans-Pacific masterminding of Chinese history, trying with words from abroad to strengthen a regime already in decline at home.

Second, our military effort produced a modernized Nationalist army and air force. Stilwell's faith in the Chinese common soldier set in motion a program in India and China, with a thousand American instructors and advisers, to train and equip thirty-nine divisions.

Third, we tried to heal the KMT-CCP breach. The U.S. Army's single-minded concern for defeating Japan led it to question the efficacy of having 200 to 400 thousand Nationalist troops blockade the Communist area. In June 1944 Vice President Wallace visited Chungking to suggest that Nationalist and Communist forces both fight Japan rather than watch each other. He got Chiang to let an American military observer mission stay in Yenan, where Western journalists had already been admitted in May. This opened an interesting window on the Communist scene but it remained apparent that Chungking and Yenan were each more concerned about the other than about Japan. Japanese forces meanwhile by late 1944 had pushed south through the Hunan rice bowl and west from Canton to seize the major Sino-American air base at Kweilin. During this crisis Chiang had held out against Stilwell's appointment to overall command in China, and forced his recall in October; he also held out against the projected arming and use of Communist forces in a unified Chinese war effort. Unity and reform both remained remote hopes, but our new ambassador, Patrick J. Hurley, with more bravado than finesse, continued to encourage a Nationalist-Communist rapprochement.

At Yalta in February 1945 Roosevelt tried to secure Stalin's future support of the Nationalist government at the price of Russia's recovery of the tsarist position in northeast Asia. This was made known to Chiang, whose concurrence we had promised to obtain, only in June, and ratified in a Sino-Soviet treaty only as Japan surrendered, on August 14. By that date Russia was already in possession of Manchuria. The United States countered by sending 53,000 marines into Tientsin to inhibit a partition of China into a Communist north backed by the USSR and a Nationalist south backed by the USA. Behind all the infinitely detailed complexities of this story looms a basic fact: the Soviet Union and the Chinese Communists had the military capability to expand into Manchuria and parts of North China, respectively, and they could hardly have been controlled merely by a token show of force. Soon the Communists were further strengthened with surrendered Japanese arms which they got through Soviet connivance in Manchuria.

With the end of World War II, American logistic power tried to unify China under Chiang by a sea and air lift of half a million Nationalist troops back to the coastal areas and then into Manchuria. Communist forces raced overland to supplant Japanese garrisons, which were ordered to fight them off and surrender only to the forces of the recognized Nationalist government. The United States then repatriated 1,200,000 enemy troops to Japan, winding up World War II in China just in time for the beginning of the long foreseen civil war.

Against this background President Truman sent his wartime commander, George C. Marshall, to Chungking in December 1945. His first months there were a hopeful chapter of American diplomacy. His aim was to mediate a political settlement of the burgeoning civil war. The only statesman-like alternative to internecine warfare was to get the Chinese Communists into the political and military framework of a constitutional regime, in a position similar to that of Communist parties in Western Europe. The two contending parties would both be represented in a reorganized coalition government under Chiang; their armies would be merged and reduced, whereupon American economic aid would be forthcoming. In January 1946 the Political Consultative Conference in Chungking reached a political agreement. A cease-fire order was issued by both armies. In February a military merger was agreed to. Meanwhile an unprecedented tripartite agency, the Executive Headquarters, was set up to superintend the quelling of a subcontinental civil war. American planes took jeeps, radios, supplies, and truce teams, composed usually of an American colonel with Nationalist and Communist generals, to far-flung inaccessible spots where fighting was in progress. Fighting practically stopped.

This breathtaking achievement was a personal tribute to General Marshall. It involved a strenuous effort to remain neutral in China's internal political process, and simultaneously to uphold the supremacy of the recognized government without being used by it. The truce collapsed principally in Manchuria, which still remained beyond the effective cease-fire limits. Behind the renewal of civil war in 1946 lay an intransigent Nationalist confidence in their superior armament, a shrewd Communist calculation of the Nationalists' actual vulnerability. While Stalin showed little confidence in the Chinese Communists' being soon victorious over the Nationalists, the onset of his Cold War with the West gave them stimulus and opportunity to bid for power.

Might the American mediation, after all, have been successful? The Chinese people wanted peace, the United States felt it had enormous prestige and power to bring to bear upon the scene, the Communists stood to gain from the agreements, the KMT was heavily dependent upon us. Our problem was how to get a party dictatorship to pursue democratic reforms in order to head off a revolution. Actually we had a divided objective: to press the KMT leaders into reform which would diminish their autocratic power and facilitate internal peace; at the same time to strengthen the KMT-controlled regime as a step toward political stability in East Asia. We became involved in continuing to build up the KMT dictatorship materially at the same time that we tried to get it to tear itself down politically. But Chiang and his generals preferred to do things their way, with their new arms.

After General Marshall became secretary of state in 1947 and we checked Communist expansion with the Greek-Turkish aid program, some felt that we should have "saved" China in the same way. China was roughly forty-five times bigger than Greece in territory and eighty-five times in population. From our bitter experience in Vietnam we now know that to have treated China like Greece would have required millions of American troops and billions of dollars and even so would have been a failure. General Marshall, of all people, best knew the magnitude of such a task. We had no alternative after 1947 but to abstain from intervention in the Chinese civil war. Whether we should have given greater aid to the Nationalists in this period was later much disputed. Responsible American generals said there was no lack of arms. Many disputants overlooked the severe limitations of our capacity to affect the outcome by means of material aid from outside.

The outcome in 1949 showed not that Soviet aid had been greater than American (the reverse was true), but that the Chinese Communists had been able to mobilize and utilize the potentialities of revolution while the Nationalists had not. The Communist victory also showed that over a period of thirty years the American example had not contributed to the organization of political power in China as effectively as the Soviet example. We had no Comintern. More important than our lack of a conspiratorial revolutionary apparatus was the more general lack of any philosophy or method for forced-draft economic development and political collectivism.

The Nationalist Debacle

From 1946 to 1949 China saw one of the big wars of modern times. Nationalist forces totaled at the beginning about three million men, the Communists about one million. United States aid to the Nationalist government from 1941 to 1949 totaled six billion dollars in credits, goods, and equipment. By sheer weight of arms Nationalist forces spread out to major cities and, when eventually permitted by Russia, into Manchuria. An infinitude of factors undid them: the military under Chiang were out of civilian control, their postwar American-style reorganization heightened the confusion, the sessile Whampoa clique discriminated against provincial commanders and armies, particularly those of Kwangsi. Their strategic doctrine was to hold strong positions defensively, their instinct was to hoard supplies and wait for others to move first, their field tactics were sometimes masterminded by the Generalissimo from a great distance. Corruption, demoralization, and desertion steadily depleted the Nationalist armies. The Communists pursued opposite tactics, maneuvering in the countryside, recruiting among the populace, destroying railroads, avoiding unfavorable terms of battle. They took over the remainder of North China by triggering rebellion in the villages. A remarkable reporter, Jack Belden, observed this brutal struggle: the poor organized against the privileged, battered wives against domineering men, youth against the old order. The Communist forces grew in numbers and armament, both from the Japanese Manchurian stocks and from Nationalist defections, sales, and surrenders. By June 1948 they were roughly equal in numbers of men, rifles, and cannon. Late in 1947 they had cut off the Manchurian garrisons. In October 1948 they forced their surrender—a third of a million men. This set the stage for a showdown.

The balance of power had not shifted only at the front, where the Communists steadily built up their stock of American guns and supplies. The Nationalist cause had also been degutted in the rear, in its city bases, by an economic collapse indexed by inflation.

Bombing by an enemy, like flood, fire, earthquake, or other disasters of nature, though destructive, tends to increase public morale and community effort in the face of a common danger. Hyperinflation, on the other hand, impoverishes and demoralizes each salaried individual as it gradually destroys the regime's fiscal capacity and public confidence in it. Life under hyperinflation is a slow strangulation. Salaries and wages never keep up. Furniture, books, and clothing go for food. Gradual malnutrition produces skin diseases, stomach ailments, tuberculosis. The whole society sickens, and the responsibility is put on those in power. Nationalist military collapse when it came was headlined in America, the ten-year hyperinflation which preceded it was not.

Free China's price level had risen only moderately in 1937–39. The Nationalist currency still circulated over the whole country; Japanese puppet note issues began at Peking only in 1938 and at Nanking only in 1939. Thereafter the Japanese mounted a campaign to undermine Free China's price stability, and meanwhile Chungking steadily increased its expenditures, with income lagging far behind outlay. In 1941, when revenues provided only 15 percent of expenditures, the central government finally took over the land tax in kind. Income from it and from government monopolies and indirect taxes still provided, temporarily, only 30 percent of the budget. Government taxes, domestic loans, gold sales, and bond drives proved ineffective in mopping up the public's excess purchasing power. The situation steadily deteriorated, prices doubling every few months or weeks. In September 1945 the volume of note issue was 465 times that of July 1937.

The end of World War II gave a brief respite as the Nationalist currency spread back over all China, but large government expenditures continued. Counting on its military superiority to end the civil war quickly, Nanking let its foreign exchange reserve be gradually reduced to pay for consumer imports and industrial raw materials. Foreign exchange was at first not seriously rationed nor imports restricted, and so capital fled the country.

In order to break the vicious circle a "currency reform" in August 1948 demonetized the old currency and replaced it by the "gold yuan." At the same time price ceilings were set and enforced by police methods, and private holdings of specie and foreign currencies were forcibly converted to finance the civil war. Thus the few resources remaining to the most anti-Communist element, the urban upper middle class, were tied to the "gold yuan"; when it collapsed in late 1948 (prices finally rose 85,000 times in six months), the last remnant of civilian support for the Nationalist cause went with it.

The great two-month battle of the Huai-Hai was fought in the old Nien area of the Huai River basin, south of the Lunghai Railway, 100 miles or so north of Nanking. Generalissimo Chiang against the best advice of his staff committed some 50 divisions, out of 200 still remaining, to form a strong point on the plains around Hsuchow. He himself from Nanking directed their tactical movements down to the division level in battle. The Communists, however, not only controlled the villages but by reactivating the railways as they advanced were able to deploy large forces. One veteran, Teng Hsiao-p'ing, led a mobilization of two million peasant laborers who could transport supplies or dig tank traps as required. By mid-November, four Nationalist army groups, about 340,000 men, had been quickly cut off and encircled on the plain. A relief force of 120,000 troops, including the best American-trained divisions, was similarly blocked and encircled south of there. When the Hsuchow armies broke out to effect a junction, taking along their American trucks and cannon and the armored corps of tanks, this "mobile fortress" was blocked in turn by deep trenches and soon ripped by American-made Nationalist-surrendered heavy artillery. By late December the 130,000 surviving Nationalist forces, out of 66 divisions committed, were squeezed into 6 square miles, surrounded by 300,000 troops of the People's Liberation Army. They learned that Nanking proposed to destroy their treasured heavy equipment "by air bombardment—*in situ*," as Edmund Clubb (our last consul general in Peiping) puts it; they surrendered on January 10, 1949. Of 550,000 Nationalists lost, the Communists claimed 327,000 surrendered.

Typical of the entire Nationalist fiasco were Chiang Kai-shek's unwise decision to fight on the Hsuchow plain instead of the Huai River and his refusal to give command to the Kwangsi general, Pai Ch'ung-hsi, an able tactician who knew the terrain. Jealous noncooperation among the Whampoa commanders, nonuse of Nanking's monopoly of the air, inability to bring their American-made firepower to bear upon the enemy, every aspect of this great defeat underlines the old adage that armament alone cannot bring victory. Tientsin and Peking surrendered in January 1949. In April the Communists crossed the Yangtze, in May they entered Shanghai, in October Canton, in November Chungking.

The Nationalist debacle had been not only military but also economic, political, and moral. The chaos, disorders, and dangers of 1948–49 turned city dwellers irrevocably against the Nationalist government and therefore against American aid to it. Having backed that government increasingly since 1937, we could not in the Chinese view divest ourselves of responsibility for its evils even though our aid had been well-intended, often critical of those selfsame evils, and consequently limited in scope and amount. Our top generals opposed Chiang's strategy, to no avail.

Our worst disaster, however, came from the widening gulf between Chinese and American public feeling—in the post-

The problem of distribution in the 1940s. The well-nourished woman sits in front of a grain shop; the beggar boy has come from a famine area.

war years when ineptitude and corruption were thoroughly discrediting the Kuomintang in China, we were experiencing intensified alarm over Soviet expansionist aims and methods, particularly over the duplicity and ruthlessness of the Communist movement. As the experiences of daily life continued to diverge in China and America, communism seemed increasingly to be the only way out for the one people and the mortal enemy of the other.

The "Loss of China" in America

For a decade the American public had idealized Free China; now increasingly the combination of the atomic age, espionage, and the Cold War had intensified their fear of communism. To have Free China become Communist seemed a national disaster. Like the Great Depression, it became political ammunition against the party in office. The Republicans used it in the 1948 campaign. Soon the Hiss espionage case, the Fuchs atomic spy case, the fear of spies and conspiracies, capped by a major war against Communist China in Korea, among other complex factors, took the lid off the McCarthy era. The American public underwent an anti-Communist hysteria in which the "loss of China" was only one small aspect.

The open season on China specialists in 1951–52 has had pervasive repercussions on American thinking about China ever since. It was facilitated by several circumstances. The American corps of China specialists both in and outside the government had been a small group in the 1930s. Most of them knew one another professionally as Foreign Service officers, scholars, or journalists. They had nearly all been "associated" with one another, if only at social or professional gatherings. If one assumed that American aid was a determining factor in China's domestic affairs, that the Nationalists could have lost their military superiority only through treachery, that American policy makers had been anti-Chiang and therefore pro-Communist, and that Communist conspiracy could be detected through a man's associations (a series of untrue nonsequiturs accepted by many during the McCarthy era), then it became a public duty (and a rich opportunity) to investigate.

The motives for pursuing investigations were quite various. They ranged from the conscientious concern of officers responsible for our security to the shrewd calculations of political opportunists. In the background was a mood of anti-intellectualism and insecurity in a nation of whodunit readers suddenly fascinated by the morbid thought that almost anybody who seemed innocent of conspiracy might therefore be guilty of it. Along with the congressional investigations of the time came intensified security screenings in the executive branch and industry which still continue, in a defensive imitation of totalitarianism. (The defensiveness fitted the overly pessimistic thesis that the American liberal tradition had lost its creative capacity at home, in addition to being nonexportable to Asia.)

Among China specialists the opportunity to find guilt by association was enhanced by fortuitous circumstance. The Institute of Pacific Relations (IPR) since 1925 had pursued a program of research and publication punctuated biennially by private conferences of scholars, diplomats, and businessmen. This international organization was composed of member bodies, like the Royal Institute of International Affairs in London, in eleven countries concerned with the Pacific area. The IPR had produced some 1200 publications—books, pamphlets, reports—many of high scholarly value. While avoiding expressions of opinion itself, it had also sought contact with persons of many views and its records had been preserved. The files of the international secretariat and of the American IPR were replete with references to China specialists high and low, as well as some Communists, pro-Communists, and numerous foreigners. By seizing and exploiting these files a senatorial subcommittee was able to make frequent headlines for almost a year, up to the eve of the Republican convention of 1952.

The committee's report claimed in sweeping terms to show an IPR conspiracy to influence State Department policy makers under Democratic administrations in favor of the Chinese Communists. The fourteen volumes of hearings disregarded almost entirely the IPR's conferences and publications and concentrated on dubious contacts and questionable or pro-Communist utterances, whether or not actually connected with the IPR. My personal view is that the investigation got the truth of the matter thoroughly mixed up with hearsay, evidence out of context, and guilt by association.* If this had been combined with executive powers and police measures, it might have resembled a totalitarian purge trial. It was based on the necessary legislators' right of investigation, but exploited the great American tradition of playing cops and robbers and dirty politics.

The only action resulting from the IPR hearings was the indictment of one of Senator Joseph McCarthy's numerous targets, Owen Lattimore, for perjury allegedly committed during a record-breaking twelve days of public questioning. A federal court threw out this indictment in 1955.

These hearings and those on General MacArthur's recall from his command in Korea were only the visible top of the iceberg. They were paralleled by secret security investigations of Foreign Service officers and other government employees on a wide and continuing scale. The China specialists were generally transferred to other areas, some were dismissed, and some resigned. John S. Service was cleared six times in succession by the State Department Loyalty Board but was eventually dismissed at the request of the Loyalty Review Board.

---

* I was a trustee of the American Institute of Pacific Relations from 1946 until its demise a decade later. In Washington I was "identified" as a Communist (by L. Budenz) and as part of a "hard inner core" of an alleged pro-Communist conspiracy. In Peking I was cited as an "imperialist spy" and "the number-one cultural secret-agent of American imperialism," et cetera. Critics of earlier editions of this book in Taipei, the USSR, and elsewhere have called it variously an apology for American imperialism and for Chinese Maoism.

In June 1957 as a result of a Supreme Court order he was reinstated.

To an observer outside the government, the chief results of all these China policy investigations seems to have been security consciousness and conformity. Very little if any communism, espionage, or treachery was uncovered but everyone was intimidated. Fearfulness and conformity handicapped our official thinking for a long time afterward. Stanley Bachrack has shown how the Committee of One Million against the Admission of Communist China to the United Nations served as "an insider-type lobby" headed by congressmen and using their offices for the next eighteen years from 1953 to 1971. The China Lobby had a long career.

My own impression is that the American people responded to the Cold War and the Chinese Communist victory more fearfully than creatively. The chief significance of Joseph McCarthy was that he was tolerated for so long by those Americans who approved his stated aims but not his methods and yet out of fear were willing to countenance his methods. Fear was compounded by ignorance. After 1949 the score or more of American press correspondents formerly in China were excluded. The gigantic upheavals among the Chinese people, the metamorphosis of Chinese society, remained almost unknown in America. Meantime our hostility toward the People's Republic was encouraged by our close ties with its residual enemy.

Our Ally Taiwan

Our frontier of contact with the Chinese people from 1949 to 1972 was Formosa, as the Europeans named it, or Taiwan, as it is called in both Chinese and Japanese. It is about 250 miles long and 60 to 80 miles wide, with a good many peaks over 10,000 feet in the mountain spine on the east and only about a quarter of the area cultivable, mainly on the west. Chinese immigration became important only in the Ming period. The Dutch and Spanish both maintained trading settlements in the seventeenth century, and the island was the last Ming refuge against the Manchu conquerors. Nineteenth-century Western trade never became important, but four treaty ports were opened after 1860, and when Taiwan was detached from Fukien to become a separate province in 1885 many modern improvements were made before the Japanese takeover after the Sino-Japanese war in 1895.

Japanese colonialism established order, created some material progress, and eventually became less harsh. No real political life was encouraged, although by the 1930s the regime had moved toward local self-government with a limited franchise. The Japanese land policy checked absentee landlordism and encouraged farmers' associations for agricultural improvement, as well as public health services. With a single-minded interest in increasing production, the Japanese regime got about half the children into elementary schools and established a fairly high level of literacy, although fewer than a hundred students a year reached the university level.

The very small top class of modern-trained Taiwanese leaders of Chinese background which had been permitted to develop under the Japanese was decimated by the Nationalist massacres of March 1947, carried out to suppress complaints against the corruption of the Nationalist postwar takeover. Several thousand leading Taiwanese were killed—an inauspicious beginning for the remnant of the Nationalist government that moved to Taiwan in 1949. The American attitude until 1950 was to refuse responsibility for the island, but to continue economic aid without military aid, as part of our attempted disengagement from China. The North Korean aggression of 1950 led to our Seventh Fleet patrolling the Formosa Strait, to keep the island out of the war and protected from mainland attack. In 1954 we signed an alliance and mutual security treaty. An American military mission assisted in the application of our aid program, and the Nationalist forces of half a million or so eventually combatted superannuation by conscripting Taiwanese. Meanwhile the Nationalist government in exile remained superimposed upon the Taiwan provincial government which it dominated. Kuomintang reform efforts were accompanied by control measures, facilitated by a continued state of war with the mainland and martial law.

Economically, the island's earlier reliance on sugar and rice production for the Japanese market had to be followed by a considerable reorientation to achieve greater self-sufficiency and to push industrialization in the face of rapid population increase. The three million of 1905 had approached seven million by 1940; with an influx of two million or more from the mainland, the total by 1958 was about eleven million, and by 1978 seventeen million. Development proceeded within a general framework of government domination or monopolies in industry. American assistance of some two billion dollars fostered growth until the mid-1960s, with such success that industrialization then continued apace without our aid, and attracted increasing amounts of Japanese investment. The Nationalist armed forces, one of the world's heaviest per capita burdens, received continued American military aid, though in diminishing amounts. Abroad, the Republic of China at Taipei with American help year after year kept its seat in the United Nations Security Council and as of 1970 maintained more embassies abroad than the People's Republic at Peking.

One creative instance of Chinese-American collaboration was the Joint Commission on Rural Reconstruction, set up by our China Aid Act of 1948. When it began operations on the mainland in October 1948, the Joint Commission aimed to increase the food supply and raise the farmers' standard of living mainly through technological assistance. Agricultural specialists had often argued that, since land redistribution could not increase acreage, it bore little promise of increasing productivity as compared with the many improvements possible in seeds, breeding, tools, farming techniques, elimination of plant and animal diseases, and the like. As the program got started in South China and on Taiwan, it stressed development of irrigation through dike-building but left unsolved the problem of farmer organization as a means to mobilize local resources and secure credit to finance improvements. Experience soon led the Joint Commission to turn to the actual problem of land tenure reform, specifically the reduction of rent to the statutory 37.5 percent of the crop and at the same time the extension of contracts to more than one year as a safeguard against landlord extortion. Thus an American type of farm-extension approach, beginning with technology, soon found in practice that landlord-tenant relations were an essential aspect of a rural reform program in Asia.

Once confined to operations on Taiwan, the Joint Commission secured the backing of the provincial government and was able to build on the Japanese structure of farmer's associations. It carried through a general rent reduction and eventually a program for each farmer to own his own land. All this was combined with practical demonstrations, publications, producers' and credit cooperatives, and rural handicraft development. As an institution the Joint Commission also avoided the problems of official relations between two governments by having a single administrative echelon and by using established agencies rather than building up its own apparatus. It set an example of great interest to developing countries.

Taiwan during the Cold War had two faces. Looking backward, it claimed that there was only one China, no two Chinas (Peking agreed), that the civil war was not over, and the KMT would still somehow save the Chinese people from communism. Looking forward, however, Taiwan joined the industrial trading world and made good use of Japanese and American technology, trade, investment, and cultural contact. Building on these advantages, a skilled Chinese leadership guided industrialization for export rather in the Japanese style. Living standards rose above the mainland level. Ties with the United States multiplied.

Chapter 14

The People's Republic: Establishing the New Order

The Chinese revolution since 1949 has been the greatest in history, measured either by the number of people involved or by the extent and rapidity of the changes made. To the outside world it has also been the least known event of modern times. Frenzies of joyful enthusiasm and vengeful hatred, of organized effort and self-sacrifice, depths of terror and exhaustion, prolonged frustration, ardent self-discipline, new hope and pride, have been experienced among a population rising from 600 to 1000 millions. Yet this colossal drama until 1972 was only visible from a distance, by Peking diplomats, Hong Kong journalists, a few travelers. All broadcasts and publications were from the regime, but it largely stopped publishing statistics in the 1960s and professional or academic journals for a decade after 1966. The private voices were mainly those of refugees. Foreigners reading even the controlled Chinese press have numbered only a few thousand around the world. Never have such large events among so many been observed and studied by so few.

Ignorance fosters speculation and prejudice. The Cold War of the 1950s between pro-Communist expansionism and anti-Communist expansionism colored everyone's thinking about China. Today anyone who feels himself quite free from bias (in the sense of having a woefully incomplete view) is obviously a fool. There are, however, different ways of being biased about the Chinese revolution. At the extreme points on a spectrum, one can simply enthuse over Mao's inspirational message for mankind, or one can abjectly fear its police-state authoritarianism. Our real need is to understand the experience of the Chinese people, come what may. This means sympathizing but evaluating, comprehending but criticizing, trying to see the reality. Different observers may still see different truths in the same event there; nevertheless we must consciously seek the "truth" because the reality accessible to us consists of particular facts; the generalizations we supply ourselves, and they need constant scrutiny. Man is a moralizing animal, to be sure, but instant morality is too easy, subjective, value-laden, and culture-bound.

Our effort to comprehend China's metamorphosis, so far away and difficult to observe, must begin with certain assumptions. First, Chinese governments over the centuries, struggling to maintain a unified state and a uniform culture over a vast and diverse subcontinent, became skilled at imposing central controls and large-scale bureaucratic administration; the Chinese Communists inherited this great tradition of unified government from Peking. Like scholar-officials trained to apply Confucian principles with local initiative on behalf of the emperor, party members could act effectively for the CCP in far places roughly in proportion as they were trained in Marxism-Leninism and the thought of Mao Tse-tung.

Second, the ingredients of the central power that arose after 1949 had accumulated over several decades—not only in the twenty-eight-year experience of the Chinese Communist Party before its achievement of power but also in the experience of the whole Chinese people. The long era of warlordism and the Nationalist revolution, followed by the eight years of Japanese invasion and the four years of civil war, had produced a nationwide craving for central authority, firm leadership, peace and order. The forms and methods of a new order had also accumulated: the Leninist system of party dictatorship used by both parties; the organization of student youth, developed ever since the pioneer days of the Chinese YMCA and the Reform Movement of the 1890s; the techniques of material improvement in the village—famine relief, public health measures, fly-swatting, well-digging, tree-planting, crop improvement, the whole program of rural reconstruction, tracing back to nineteenth-century missionary beginnings and the mass education movement. Meanwhile, inspiring the use of these new methods was the spirit of devotion to country above all—including, for example, the ideals of citizenship espoused by Liang Ch'i-ch'ao, the welfare of "the people" invoked by Sun Yat-sen, the national unity at one time embodied in Chiang Kai-shek.

Of the several streams flowing into China's revolutionary melting pot, most outside observers have stressed the Marxist-Leninist and Soviet influences on ideology, organization, and policy, and this demands constant attention. But equally important behind these overt phenomena is the Chinese folk tradition, the largely unexplored and un-Confucian ways of life ingrained among the common people. This local, often illiterate tradition of folklore and custom is more various than that of the old Chinese ruling class. It underlies revolutionary developments like the cult of Mao and its fanaticism.

Such perspectives may suggest that the new regime in Peking was less monolithic than we assumed it was and less purely a product of Marxism-Leninism than it claimed to be. Its achievement was less to invent all the parts of the new order than to put them together, under an unprecedented degree of central direction made possible by Communist theory and practice. The result, in any case, was something quite new in Chinese experience.

Below we look first at the ideas and mechanisms by which

the Chinese Communist Party built up its control over the Chinese state and people, and second at its effort to remake them. Though the two processes went hand in hand, remaking depended on first controlling.

Political Control

The military takeover occupied a year and a half, from the fall of Shenyang (Mukden) on November 1, 1948, and of Peking and Tientsin in January 1949, until the occupation of all the mainland by May 1950. The Chinese People's Republic was proclaimed in the midst of this process on October 1, 1949. The takeover left in office most local administrators. On the surface the Communist cadres gave it a festive air, dancing the *yang-ko* in the streets, proclaiming peace and liberation. The troops generally behaved scrupulously. It was a hopeful honeymoon period, devoted to military mopping-up, economic recovery, and political organization.

Coalition Government. The policy for this period, laid down by Mao in January and confirmed by the CCP Central Committee in March 1949, amounted to a platform of getting rid of the KMT, supplanting it with a coalition government, and reforming China's armies, foreign relations, and economic system. In order to mobilize a broad basis of support, the coalition government should be organized by a new People's Political Consultative Conference, reminiscent in name but not in membership of the multi-party conference at the time of General Marshall's mediation.

This line was developed in Mao's statement of July 1, 1949, "On the people's democratic dictatorship." Echoing Lenin's phrase the "democratic dictatorship of workers and peasants," Mao propounded the quite un-Leninist thesis that the new government should be a democratic coalition under Communist leadership at the same time that it was a dictatorship directed against the reactionary classes or "enemies of the people." Thus the "people's democratic dictatorship" would attempt in united-front style to line up the broadest possible support for the regime and at the same time eliminate its foes within the Chinese world. The "people" were defined as composed of four classes: proletariat, peasantry, petty bourgeoisie, national bourgeoisie. For the peasantry there was a prospect of maintaining, at least temporarily, private property in land, and for the bourgeoisie, a sector of privately owned industry. This carried out the original idea of the New Democracy.

Since any individual could be transferred by a stroke of the pen to the category of reactionaries or enemies of the people, this framework was completely flexible as a basis for sifting out dissident members of the population. The power of class imputation remained with the Communist party, and a reformed "reactionary" could be declared by it to be a member of the "people." Leaving this mechanism at first in the background, Mao Tse-tung called upon his countrymen, in this moment of hope and general relief, to take the first step on a 10,000 mile march, to wipe out domestic and repulse foreign enemies and to remake Chinese society, without help from abroad except that of the Soviet Union, using the means at hand but learning from all quarters.

After several months' preparation, the Preparatory Committee of the People's Political Consultative Conference was set up at Peking in June 1949, nominally representing twenty-three parties or groups. The PPCC itself was convened in September for ten days, with 662 delegates. It passed the Common Program, a general statement of aims of the new coalition government, which, however, failed to mention class struggle, and the Organic Law of the Central People's Government, which made the working class the leader of the republic. Since the CCP was the vanguard which represents the working class, this meant that the government was to be its administrative arm. The new administration was given complete executive, legislative, and judicial powers on a centralist basis. Some thirty ministries or similar agencies were set up, fifteen of them connected with economic affairs. In the top committee, thirty-one out of fifty-six seats were occupied by Communists. Chou En-lai became premier (and remained so until his death in 1976).

This powerful autocratic administration by Communist desire left eight minor parties in existence, though without much following, and gave posts of prominence to non-Communists in order to carry out the idea of coalition government, that the talents of all the people must be used in building the new society. It was essential to use the training and ability of that major part of the upper class which had never been Communist. Liberal intellectuals were therefore given scope for their talents and placed in high position, interlarded in the new ministries with party members who lacked their abilities but were more disciplined. (One is reminded of barbarian conquerors' use of Chinese administrators.) The larger part of the Western-returned scholars, including those educated in the United States, appear to have been in this category. As patriots, they were devoted to their country's future. Long since estranged from the Kuomintang, they saw no alternative. The Communist party also had long since developed its united-front methods for manipulating and utilizing liberal intellectuals.

The Party, Government, and Army Structures. The Communists, like the Kuomintang, set up a tripod of power—party, government, and army, each forming a separate echelon but all three tied together by the leadership. The party grew to 2.7 million members by 1947, to 6.1 million by 1953, to fourteen million by 1959, to seventeen million by 1961. The

Central Committee included ninety-four members and ninety-three alternate members, as of 1962, but power was exercised by its Political Bureau of nineteen members and six alternates (who might participate in discussions but not vote), and ultimately by this bureau's Standing Committee of seven persons. Below the Central Committee the party structure descended through roughly eight levels, the principal ones being six regional bureaus; 28 provincial or equivalent committees; 258 special district committees; 2200 county *(hsien)* or similar committees; some 26,000 commune committees after 1958; and more than one million branch committees in the villages, factories, schools, and so on. These myriad committees exercised the party's powers of leadership, supervision, patronage, and control.

The party structure was paralleled by the government structure that its members interpenetrated. Communist government reached far below the old KMT level. People's Representative Congresses, like Russian soviets, were set up in a hierarchy at the three main levels of administrative villages (after 1958 communes), counties, and provinces, all under the National People's Congress at Peking, which was first convened in 1954. These government congresses met annually to approve budgets and elect councils, which met once or twice a month to do their part in administration. This structure provided an arena for popular participation in "democratic centralism" but had little power in a Western legal sense. The local government structure also included for coordination and supervisory purposes a "district" level between administrative village (or commune) and county, and a "special district" level between county and province.

In 1954 the new government constitution (to be distinguished from the new party constitution of 1956) diminished the role of non-Communists and strengthened that of the premier. Chou En-lai now headed a State Council which included as many as sixteen vice premiers and the heads of some seventy ministries or similar bodies. A. Doak Barnett, John W. Lewis, Franz Schurmann, and others have studied how this government was controlled by the party and operated in tandem with it. In brief, the administration was divided into major functional systems which handled all over the country certain major government functions. The major systems concerned political and legal (internal) affairs; propaganda and education (cultural matters) ; agriculture, forestry, and water conservancy (rural work) ; industry and communications; finance and trade. These various lines of administration were pursued in a vertical structure of agencies stretching down from the capital through the various territorial levels of the administrative hierarchy. Each of these systems was supervised both by an office of the State Council and by an office of the party Central Committee. There was a direct flow of instructions from the top down and of reports from the bottom up, but this "vertical rule" extending downward through lower-level branch agencies was balanced by "dual rule" when such branch agencies were also coordinated through committees operating laterally at a given level in the hierarchy. The specialties of foreign affairs and military affairs were both handled by functional systems, and the term was applied also to united front work by the party among the people and to the programs of party work among youth and among women.

In all operations the party set the policy and the government agencies carried it out. The party not only issued directives from the top, it also had its members in most of the key administrative posts within the government hierarchy; and its regional, provincial, and local party committees could supervise as they coordinated action at the various levels. Within each government agency party members had their own organization in committees and branches, and the leading party members formed a top group or "party fraction."

The People's Liberation Army (PLA), the third leg of the new tripod of power, had been a party army from its inception. Mao Tse-tung headed the Military Council that controlled it, but as William Whitson's analysis makes plain, Mao's concept of "people's war," stressing small-unit operations among a fully mobilized populace, had guided the CCP military only in times of greatest adversity—in Kiangsi in 1931 and North China in 1942–44. Most of the time the military professionals like Yeh Chien-ying, P'eng Te-huai, Lin Piao, and Teng Hsiao-p'ing, influenced by, if not actually trained in, the Soviet style, had preferred mobile warfare by regular troops. Their interest in professional training committed them to being "expert" first of all and "red" secondarily; but the potential militarism of an officers corps was checked by the military leaders both being party members and frequently becoming civil administrators. The six administrative regions into which China was divided during the years 1949–54 in effect grouped together the provinces which the original five field armies had taken over: thus the First Field Army was in the Northwest, the Second Field Army in the Southwest, the Third in the Eastern Region, the Fourth in the Central-South Region, and the Fifth or North China Field Army around Peking. The tendency of these army organizations to develop loyalty networks had been somewhat countered by their units being scrambled and commanders shuffled about in the course of twenty years fighting. (In 1961 the setting up of six regional party bureaus was to be accompanied by the division of military command under thirteen regional headquarters.)

The Mass Organizations. Parallel to the structures of party, army, and government, there were the new nationwide mass organizations. These organizations had originated during the KMT-CCP collaboration of the 1920s, but the Kuomintang had let them wither away after its rise to power at Nanking. The All-China Federation of Trade Unions had been founded in 1922; in 1956 it claimed a membership of over 13 million. In 1949 there was created a full panoply of parallel bodies: an All-China Federation of Democratic Women (76 million members in 1953); of Democratic Youth (34 million in 1957); of Cooperative Workers, that is, peasants in cooperatives (162 million in 1956); and of Literature and Art, under the prolific writer Kuo Mo-jo, to mobilize intellectuals. In addition there were an All-China Students' Federation (4 million in 1955), a children's Young Pioneer corps (30 million in 1957), and many comparable bodies more specialized in nature, dealing with science, art and learning, welfare activities, or international relations—for example, the Sino-Soviet Friendship Association (68 million members in 1953) and similar associations for Sino-Indian and Sino-Burmese friendship. Finally in 1953 was established the All-China Association of Industry and Commerce, for the national bourgeoisie, who at that time still existed.

Mass organizations reached the individual in his professional or social role, among his peers, in ways that the government could not. Each was controlled from the top by "democratic centralism" though authority was nominally vested in a national congress meeting at long intervals. Party members of course predominated in key posts and through them reached out to mobilize the general public. Each organization had broadly defined purposes and programs and an extensive administrative apparatus. Something like half the adult Chinese population were thus brought into one or another action group and involved in its program of meetings, study, and agitation.

The mass organizations developed big training programs with schools and indoctrination centers and served as recruiting agencies for talented and activist personnel. Their welfare and cultural work included such things as labor insurance, leave and pension systems, literacy classes, maternity hospitals and midwife training, or recreational activities, accompanied by a large output of books, magazines, and pamphlets circulated through libraries. Their members could also be used in the security system or in nationwide campaigns like that against reactionaries. All this had its ultimate effect through the local units of organization, the neighborhood (street) committees and small groups at places of work.

The mass organizations performed primarily political functions as quasi-government agencies, bridging the immemorial gap between populace and officialdom. In James Townsend's phrase, they "politicized an apolitical population" as one part of the apparatus which applied the concept of the "mass line": that the CCP leadership must be guided by constant contact with the worker-peasant masses, first securing from the party workers full and accurate reports as to the masses' problems and opinions, then issuing policy directives to meet these problems, and finally getting the masses to adopt the policies as their own and carry them out. The mass organizations received government aid and even representation in the People's Congresses. In actuality, their main function was to indoctrinate. Working directly with the populace through meetings and demonstrations as well as propagandizing through mass media, they were able to manipulate the climate of opinion. Local police stations also used the street committees, whose duty it was to promote not only welfare measures but also mutual surveillance and denunciation among neighbors and within families. When coordinated in each locality, this whole apparatus could bring to bear upon every individual a pervasive and overwhelming public pressure.

The mechanism to increase this pressure was the campaign or movement. Campaigns might appear to start spontaneously, but they developed only as the Central Committee of the party decreed. Campaigns quickly set in motion the enormous new apparatus of party, state, and mass organizations and directed its hammer blows against one target after another among the various classes and their institutions. The campaign method of revolutionary development, encouraging the cadres to attack certain heterodox ideas or undesired activities, could develop a high momentum and easily overshoot the mark, achieving "excesses." Each campaign might therefore give rise to another to check, redirect, or supersede the previous one. One of the earliest, for the Elimination of Counterrevolutionaries, ran from late February through the rest of 1951 as a reign of terror in the cities. It was characterized by mass arrests and mass executions sometimes even reported in the press—for example, 293 in Shanghai on April 30, 32 on May 6, 208 on May 31.

Law and Security. Standing behind this whole apparatus were secret services within the party and army and under the Ministry of Public Security, which also oversaw the local police and public security forces. Local street committees or residents' committees and their mediation officers were encouraged to dispose informally of conflicts arising among individuals from day to day. Also at the local level the police stations handled cases or if necessary passed them on to the hierarchy of "people's courts," also an arm of the central administration, which were headed by the Supreme People's Court and the Supreme People's Procuracy. As Jerome A. Cohen has made plain, serious criminal cases normally came to trial only after the accused had been thoroughly interrogated, without benefit of counsel, had fully confessed, and had denounced any others concerned in the crime with which he had been charged. Since law expressed the revolutionary policy of the party, it remained largely uncodified and changeable. This uncertainty of the law for both judges and accused was, to be sure, reminiscent of the traditional Chinese system. Justice was still weighted on the side of the state, in effect personal and particular, to be secured by applying universal principles to the circumstances discerned in each case, with a minimum of procedure. Litigation was disesteemed, legislation unimportant. Codes remained unpublished, but norms of conduct were of course made known through political indoctrination.

Economic Reconstruction

The intensive program of political organization to set up the apparatus sketched above was carried on concomitantly with a vigorous economic program. Early in 1949 Mao announced a "shift to the cities" as the focus of effort, reaffirming the primacy of the urban proletariat in a party which was now about 90 percent of peasant origin. The CCP had inherited three economic sectors: the circular-flow subsistence economy of the countryside, the separately based, foreign-trade-and-industry economy of the treaty ports, and finally Manchuria as a heavy industry base created by the Japanese in an undeveloped area. The problem was to organize these three economies into one.

The first industrial objective set in 1949 was to get production back to its prewar level within about three years. Japan's industrial build-up in Manchuria had been reduced in 1945 by Russian removal of more than half the capital equipment, with an estimated replacement value of at least two billion American dollars. In China proper, railroads had been torn up by civil war, urban labor demoralized by hyperinflation. After the Communist victory it took some time to convince the city worker that Liberation had brought him first of all the opportunity to work harder. Wartime blockades between city and country had increased rural self-sufficiency; market crops like cotton had to be revived. Meanwhile inflation was still a major problem. Military operations were still continuing in 1949–50 and some 9 million persons were on government rations or payrolls (including minor Nationalist administrative and military personnel who had been taken over). The substitution of a new "people's currency" for the Nationalist banknotes, even at favorable rates, left the regime still obliged to expand its note issue steadily to meet a budget deficit of perhaps 75 percent. Shanghai prices rose 70 times in nine months, from May 1949 to February 1950. All this demanded strenuous measures.

The first move toward quelling the inflation was to get the budget more or less balanced by increasing revenue, first in the countryside by collecting agricultural taxes in kind, then in the cities through devices like a sales tax on each major commodity and business taxes set by "democratic appraisal" of trade associations to meet quotas previously set by government. The result of the sales and business taxation was to squeeze money out of the more monetized sector of the economy. Second, the entire fiscal administration was reorganized and rationalized to give the central government control over formerly local taxes, to eliminate private banks' handling of official funds, and generally to reduce expenditures, licit and illicit. The regime gradually made the collection process more efficient, controlling it for the first time directly down to the village level. Through the banks the government got control of money and credit. It also set up six government trading corporations to dominate prices in major consumer commodities.

One device for restoring confidence was to express wages, salaries, bank deposits, some government payments, and bond issues in terms of commodity units (commodity basket values), defined in quantities of goods of daily use rather than in monetary prices. A typical unit might be composed of 6 catties (8 lbs.) of rice, 1½ catties of flour, 16 catties of coal, and 4 feet of white shirting. As prices rose, the commodity-based unit would rise accordingly in money terms. Paid in this unit, one could save by making bank deposits or buying bonds in similar units; either way, one was protected against further inflation. Thus by a variety of methods designed to achieve a balance between the supply of goods and the flow of money income, the inflation was conquered by mid-1950, an impressive achievement.

Another achievement of the first year was an extensive re-opening of railway track, to get most of China's 13,500 miles back into operation. Economic recovery was aided by three good harvests in 1950, 1951, and 1952. By 1952, the pre-1949 peaks of production had been equaled or surpassed in pig iron, cement, steel, and oil (all very modest in China), and in coal, electric power, flour, and cotton cloth, but production was still short of the pre-1949 peak in some consumer goods such as sugar. Most important, by 1952 the three sectors of the old economy had been given greater national unity than ever before. Railway track had expanded to 15,000 and high-ways to 75,000 miles. A centralized banking system and single uniform currency now covered the country. Budgeting could be attempted realistically for the first time.

Peking's long-term economic aim was to mobilize China's resources and reallocate them for purposes of industrialization. This required a gradual extension of government control over all segments of the economy. Private enterprise was permitted to continue in form but in fact it was brought increasingly under state control through numerous devices—taxation and capital levies, rationing of credit, competition by state enterprise, demands of labor unions—so that businessmen practically became bureaucrats. By controlling credit and raw materials and monopolizing key commodities, the state could now dominate production and commerce, in addition to its outright control of most heavy industry, railways, and foreign trade. The other requirement was a traditional one brought up-to-date—control of the surplus product of the land.

Land Reform. In the history of Chinese communism there had been several shifts of land policy, exemplified by the severity of the Kiangsi period, when many landlords were exterminated, and the moderation of the Yenan period, when they were guaranteed a sizable rent. As Communist power expanded after 1946, land reform had proceeded on a piecemeal and often violent basis, sometimes with more peasant violence than the party claimed to have desired.

The nationwide land reform, begun in mid-1950 and completed by late 1952 or early 1953, was not merely economic but also social and political in aim. A work team of cadres coming to a village first identified out-and-out enemies, if necessary got them out of the way, and then explained the desirability of land reform to the poor peasantry in particular, who would theoretically be the main beneficiaries. By this means active elements were selected who had the motivation and the capacity to lead the forthcoming movement. After this preparation a period of "class struggle" was inaugurated. In a series of "struggle meetings" the accumulated grievances of the populace could be brought forth in "speaking bitterness" or "settling accounts." Hatred could be fanned into mob violence in public "trials." Unpopular landlords or "local despots" chosen for public denunciation were either killed, expelled, or brought to confess and reform, while the entire community by taking violent measures committed themselves to the new order. When combined with the urban campaign against counterrevolutionaries, this added up to millions of people killed in the three years from 1949 to the end of 1952—sober estimates vary between two million (Maurice Meisner) and five (Jacques Guillermaz).

The next phase was to create peasants' associations which by a process of community assent could work out the definition of class status for each individual as landlord, rich peasant, poor peasant, or farm laborer and could carry on the classification, confiscation, and redistribution of landholdings. The resulting "equalization of land tenure" was in the old tradition of peasant rebellions. Through Communist direction of this process, the activists were usually favored, the well-to-do reduced, and the remnants of the landlord gentry wiped out either in person or in status, while the party representatives established their authority over the village. The tiller now had title to his land, at least for the moment.

This New Democracy phase of private ownership had been advertised in 1950 to last for a "rather long time," but in fact it lasted no longer for the farmer than it had for the capitalist. To supplant the old order the Communist regime moved without delay toward the construction of the new collectivist agrarian system, beginning with a first stage of cooperatives.

Cooperation could achieve greater efficiency: six donkeys could go to market with one donkey driver, not six. One housewife at a time could cook for several families. Since there were fewer draft animals than households, their use could be shared. Joint savings could buy a pump or a tool no individual could afford. In particular, handicraft cooperatives could use scattered local materials and unemployed farm labor in the off season to increase the production of consumer goods with rather little state investment. As larger units of operation, they could create a division of labor, with specialization. With organization might come literacy, health, technology, and higher productivity. Rural supply and marketing cooperatives meanwhile promoted exchange between farm and factory, handling state purchases and making available a wider variety of manufactures than the villages had seen before.

In agriculture the reform program for increased production, as it was termed, moved gradually from north to south through a series of planned phases, first setting up temporary, usually seasonal, small-scale mutual aid teams, then larger permanent ones, and then agricultural producers' cooperatives. In the cooperatives the peasants began to cultivate in common and share a common product in proportion to their pooled contributions of land, equipment, and labor. The cooperatives were still posited on private ownership of land and voluntary cooperation for mutual benefit. However, the goal began to shift. The regime had heretofore argued that land redistribution in itself, by eliminating landlordism (though without much increase of acreage), would release the peasantry's "productive energy." Now it was admitted that only eventual collectivization could effect the increase in agricultural product necessary to pay for industrialization. The effort was to lead the inveterately property-conscious peasant, through propaganda, practice, and steady pressure, to become (as René Dumont put it) "a socialist without knowing it."

Social Reorganization

China's traditional ancestor reverence, family-clan cohesiveness, and filial piety had long been eroding. Communist "liberation" furthered the process. By the new marriage law of May 1, 1950, women were given full equality with men in rights of marriage, divorce, and property ownership. This liberation from family tyranny struck a body blow at the ancient extended family and clan. In the various campaigns of the 1950s, children were commended for denouncing their parents, thus spectacularly reversing the ancient stress on filial piety as the highest virtue. Extended family ties were disparaged as feudal and romantic love as bourgeois. The new state with its ubiquitous branches tried to displace the Chinese patrilineal family system, leaving the nuclear family as the norm and leaving the individual shorn of family support, at the mercy of the authorities.

The totalitarian mobilization of the populace was made easier in late 1950 by the Korean War (see p. 386). Reports of China's early victories and later of alleged germ warfare by the United States provided a useful sanction for intensifying anti-American sentiment and destroying the generally favorable Chinese image of America. War was also an opportunity to get rid of irreconcilables. A major campaign was mounted, to "Resist America, aid Korea," in addition to the one already mentioned to "eliminate counterrevolutionaries." Both called for patriotic spying on relatives and neighbors, public denunciation even of parents, and consignment of enemies of the people, reactionaries, and counterrevolutionaries to "reform through labor." Execution of such enemies, together with persons condemned by "people's courts" in the land reform, spread terror everywhere. The honeymoon was over. The regime destroyed the remnants of the KMT and the landlord gentry and benefited by extensive confiscations of property. It showed its claws and teeth, and the effect was not lost upon the populace, who became more amenable to discipline and direction.

The pressures and dangers of a war with the United States, whose power had bulked so large in the Chinese mind, were thus turned to purposes of social reorganization and industrial efficiency. The germ warfare hoax was also elaborately fabricated and publicized, with the approval of an international board of left-wing scientists and a mass of circumstantial evidence, to blacken the American name. Yet even here a subsidiary aim was also realized, since the germ warfare theme stimulated public health measures all over the country.

In this context of terror on the one hand and patriotism on the other, foreign missionaries were denounced as spies and jailed or expelled. A "three-self" movement was set going, for "self-government, self-support, and self-propagation" of the Christian church in China, free of the missionaries' alleged "cultural imperialism." Uncooperative church leaders were gradually eliminated from positions of leadership, and "national churches" free of foreign ties were finally set up to give Chinese Christians a religion subservient to the Communist state. In 1958, having cut off foreign support and having pressured Chinese Christian leaders to join, the three-self movement unified the worship of all denominations in each locality. A Chinese Catholic church was also created, independent of the Pope, who responded with excommunication. All these efforts tried to reverse China's Western orientation. Comparable programs of organization brought Muslims, Buddhists, and Taoists under control.

Ethnic minorities like Mongols, Uighur Turks, and Kazakhs, some 54 groups in all, totaled only 6 percent of the population but were strategically important because they inhabited 60 percent of the land area, including most of the frontier regions of Inner Asia. In particular, some four million Uighurs were a majority of the population in Sinkiang with its large mineral and oil reserves. Pursuing a Soviet-style policy of integration while encouraging "cultural autonomy" in language and customs, the PRC began, as June Dreyer says, by "doing good and making friends" in order to secure local cooperation in revolutionary changes.

In general, the mechanisms for mobilizing public pressure against designated types of individuals were used more and more plainly for refashioning China's social structure. A new height in this effort came with the Three-anti and Five-anti movements of 1951–52. These were organized very thoroughly and proceeded through well-defined phases with standardized methods.

The Three-anti campaign was directed against officialdom, in the government, in state industries, and in the party. The movement was anti-corruption, anti-waste, and anti-bureaucratism—plainly an attempt to weed out and invigorate the vast administrative apparatus inherited from the Kuomintang and rapidly added to since 1949. The Three-anti movement permitted replacement of administrative personnel by new blood, as fast as it could be developed for the purpose, and brought the enlarged bureaucracy more thoroughly under central control by keeping the bureaucrat insecure in his new power. Like many major drives, it began in Manchuria, the most advanced area under the new regime. Special committees and an apparatus were soon formed to promote the movement countrywide with spectacular denunciations, public "trials," and great publicity.

The Five-anti movement, which ran until June 1952, was a similarly well organized and concerted attack on merchants and manufacturers, the bourgeoisie in general. Nominally it was against bribery, tax evasion, theft of state assets, cheating in labor or materials, and stealing of state economic intelligence. Employees were inspired to accuse employers, customers accused shopowners, and there was a general screening of all persons in urban trade and industry. As in all campaigns, the public were mobilized, committees established, and appearances created of great popular initiative, righteous anger, and enthusiasm for the triumph of virtue. Confessions, apologies, and the reform or elimination of culprits by suicide, execution, or labor camp followed. But it is evident that one immediate aim in this anti-middle class program was financial. Large sums were squeezed out of the business class, probably worth between one and two billion United States dollars. From this time the "national bourgeoisie," those small-scale businessmen and industrialists not allied with foreigners, existed on sufferance: those who remained in business were thereafter thoroughly amenable to the continued pressure for socialization of private enterprise. (Eventually they were all expropriated and in January 1956 dutifully celebrated, with firecrackers and dancing, their own demise as a social class.)

All these manipulations of the body politic got rid of numerous enemies of the regime. Forced labor camps were the natural result, built both on the Soviet model and on the ancient corvée tradition of China. Muscle power had always been the country's chief natural resource. The modern use of labor armies of four million persons on one project of public works, like the much-publicized Huai River dikes and dams, was no great innovation except for its increased scope and the edifying moral exhortation which accompanied it. Whether the millions of Chinese who now performed forced labor on short rations were more numerous than the millions who had normally starved while farming every year, no one could say. The difference was that the grinding down and slow extinction of life through prolonged and ill-equipped labor, always a part of the Chinese scene whether planned or purely circumstantial, was now well organized.

Pre-Communist China was premodern and particularistic in many ways—in the neglect of punctuality, the lack of civic consciousness and public neatness, in putting family before community and personal interests before national, in all those attitudes and habits that the futile New Life Movement had condemned in 1935. In the old days, everyone haggled over prices, took note of manners, and treated every situation ad hoc and every person according to the circumstances if not on his merits. All this was quite contrary to the efficient impersonality of modern, universalistic market relations. This premodern character of Chinese society, its "medieval" traits, had fascinated foreigners and humiliated patriots for a century. The Confucian scholars who sought a panacea in gunboats, then technology, and finally in the reform of institutions had now been succeeded by revolutionists who condemned old ways as "feudal" and sought to remake their cosmos by applying the allegedly universal, abstract principles of a new Marxist-Leninist "science" of society. With reforming zeal their Leninist party, once thoroughly in control, applied itself to remaking not only the economy and social order but also the individual.

Thought Reform. The Communist achievement in organization, among a people so recently famous for their lack of it, depended upon the inspiring, coercing, or manipulating of individual personalities. Building upon methods used in Yenan to Leninize the party (as well as to convert Japanese war prisoners), Liu Shao-ch'i and other organizers developed empirical procedures to deal with every type of enemy or supporter. When American prisoners of war in Korea "confessed" to germ warfare and collaborated with their Chinese captors, they were responding to techniques developed through use with Chinese of all sorts, including party members. As a result of these methods capitalists and rich peasants smilingly gave their property to the state, professors scathingly denounced their Western bourgeois education, secondary school students devotedly gave their lives to party work.

These diverse phenomena represented the real Communist effort at revolution, to change Chinese thinking and behavior. Though very diverse, thought reform generally had certain common features: control of the environment, both of the person physically and of the information available to him (this was now true of the whole country); the stimuli both of idealism and of terror, intermixed; and a grim psychological experience, undergone with guidance through successive phases and intensified by the manipulation of one's sense of guilt and shame. The Chinese slang term "brainwashing" imparted perhaps too much mystery to a process faintly visible elsewhere in religious crusades of the past, only now more thoroughly organized. Modern psychologists can explain how privation, prolonged insecurity, and tension, combined with extended fatigue and repetitive indoctrination, can shatter the individual's sense of inner identity and create pressures from which the only escape for many is submission to authority and acceptance at least temporarily of new attitudes and concepts. This coercing of the human mind, quite different in degree from the mild voluntary form of American advertising methods, is still only partially understood and exploited. Spread over the world it would create the ultimate crisis of individualism. Perhaps it is not surprising that in China, where the practical art of human relations has been more fully developed than anywhere else, these psychological methods should be so advanced.

For the Chinese student class, from whom the CCP had to get its cadres, this intellectual-emotional reconditioning was carried out in the big revolutionary colleges set up through the reorganization and expansion of the educational system. Thousands of trainees went through indoctrination courses of several months' duration. A center of this type containing 4000 students might be subdivided into classes of one or two hundred and then into study groups of six to ten persons. A psychiatrist who analyzed the process, Robert Lifton, divided a typical six-month thought reform into three stages—first, group identification, a period of togetherness and considerable freedom and enthusiasm. During this stage major Marxist-Leninist-Maoist concepts were studied and discussed mainly in small groups. A free exchange of views, with a high esprit de corps, led the trainee to expose himself and engage wholeheartedly in a "thought mobilization."

The second phase was one of induced emotional conflict within each individual. The daily schedule continued to be physically exhausting. The milieu, carefully controlled, now seemed to close in. The individual submitted his first summary of his own life and thought. As criticism and self-criticism intensified, the dangers of being rejected became apparent. The evils within the old individual were now attacked, not merely the old society in the abstract, and the student strove to dig up his failings and correct them. Group pressures were focused by experienced leaders so that each individual became heavily involved emotionally, under assault. He might struggle with himself and be "struggled with" by his group-mates over an excess of subjectivism or objectivism, of opportunism or dogmatism, bureaucratism or individual heroism, and so forth. The individual who attempted to hold back and resist the process took a psychological beating. Each participant was completely alone, isolated within himself like all his fellows. Under this pressure, similar to that used against prisoners, the individual soon felt guilt (he had sinned and should be punished) and also a sense of shame (he had lost face and self-esteem), which created intense humiliation. In attacking himself, he was thus prepared for confession and self-condemnation, feeling as though he were mentally ill and needed a cure.

The third phase was that of submission and rebirth. When his final thought summary or confession was accepted by the group and the authorities, the individual was likely to feel exhilarated, cleansed, a new person. This months-long process was on a larger scale a sort of induced religious conversion, like those of our own revival meetings, but with added elements of pressure and psychotherapy. The individual had been manipulated, the wellsprings of his own nature had put him under pressure, and the relief from this self-induced tension was associated with the external authority of the party, on whom he should henceforth be dependent. For the party's aim was not only to control disciplined activists but also to improve their performance by changing their idea of themselves, their goals and values. They renounced family and father and accepted the party and the revolution in their place.

This process was most successful with malleable young minds. In the case of older intellectuals, particularly returned students from the West, criticism, self-criticism, and confession could only be an overlay of their formative experience. Many statements by Peking professors were pro forma. They denounced the corrupting influence of the bourgeois West and their former subjection to it, possibly with some sense of guilt at having been seduced or alienated from their native culture. But the net effect of their self-criticism was less to change these individuals than to align them properly in the public eye as supporters of the new order. Thus the one class who might represent a Western non-Communist influence neutralized themselves and presented no model for youth.

Communism and Confucianism. Few who have lived in China will assume that a revolution, however irresistible, can quickly remake the immovable Middle Kingdom. Our schematic account of thought reform should not imply that it could easily remake the Chinese personality. However, the strategy was long term, to maintain a controlled environment of lip service if not love for the regime until the new socialist generation could take over.

Out of the Chinese inheritance, moreover, authoritarian traditions could be invoked for modern purposes. Thus Confucianism in one of its aspects has a certain resonance with Marxism—not an identity, only a partial overlap. This point of resonance was in the unity of theory and practice. The Bolshevik emphasis on putting theory into revolutionary practice contended that theory was no good in itself but must be applied in activity, as part of an effort not only to understand the world but to change it. Marxism as a "science of history" when put into practice must become an ethic, a personal philosophy animating one's entire thought and conduct. Self-criticism was a necessary part of discipline for this purpose. It was also a Communist doctrine that Marxist-Leninist theory should be applied according to the content of each national background, blending Communist ideas with the local tradition. As Mao said, "We must unify appropriately the general truth of Marxism with the concrete practice of the Chinese revolution."

Communist self-criticism was reminiscent of the Confucian doctrine of self-cultivation in the form associated particularly with the sixteenth-century philosopher Wang Yang-ming (1472–1529). Wang attacked the dualism of knowledge and action. In Wang's view, as David Nivison puts it, "To know is to know how and to know that one ought." The completely sincere man must express his moral perceptions in equally moral conduct. Wang and others therefore urged self-cultivation as a process by which the true philosopher can bring his thought and conduct into consonance, so that knowledge is realized in action and action contributes to knowledge. This idea was echoed in Sun Yat-sen's "Knowledge is difficult, action is easy" and later by Chiang Kai-shek.

While Confucian self-cultivation was not a group affair, it stressed the moral improvability of human nature, the ancient Chinese belief that through proper ethical instruction and exhortation, man can be made into a more social being. Individual self-cultivation and group self-criticism have something in common. Thought reform at Yenan made use of traditional Chinese terminology and invoked Confucian sanctions. The good Communist, according to Liu Shao-ch'i, must discipline himself through self-cultivation, through "watching himself when alone," so as to become flexibly and resourcefully obedient to the party's leadership. Through greater consciousness of the historical influences playing upon him, it was argued, he might indeed achieve a certain feeling of freedom within the confines of the historical process. Thus where Confucianism instilled loyalty to family, father, and emperor, Maoism now diverted it to the people, the party, and the leader. The classics were quoted for this purpose.

Criticism, Literary and Political. In thought reform, the Chinese literary world was obliged to follow Mao Tse-tung's dictum on literature and art of 1942, that they are political tools in the class struggle and thoroughly subordinate to politics. The full force of meetings, denunciations, and special publications was assembled to attack Hu Shih as the symbol of "decadent American bourgeois pragmatism." One campaign was against his interpretation of the famous eighteenth-century novel *The Dream of the Red Chamber* as an autobiographical work. Communists preferred to see in it the inner collapse of China's feudal society, thus salvaging this fascinating book from China's heritage as belonging to "the people," like other selected heroes, poets, and cultural inheritances. The campaign simultaneously discredited Western-type literary criticism based on historical research, as part of the attack upon Chinese liberalism and its foreign allies.

But the Communist party's creative writers still tended occasionally to be critics, the same as in the Soviet Union. Some who had gained fame attacking the evils of the old order now criticized imperfections in the new, particularly the Central Committee's claim through its literary commissar, Chou Yang, to be the final arbiter of artistic excellence. A rebellious disciple of Lu Hsün named Hu Feng was pilloried for this in a nationwide campaign. Eventually his denunciators, like Ting Ling, were also denounced and purged by Chou Yang (who was himself to be purged in 1966.)

Just as thought reform and other campaigns winnowed the population, separating out potential enemies and recruits, so the great corpus of China's historical inheritance had to be reappraised in Marxist-Leninist terms and integrated into the new state-and-culture. "Applying the universal principles of Marxism-Leninism to the concrete realities of China" was a never-ending process. Most of China's glorious past, for example, had to be put by definition within the Marxian period of "feudalism." Precisely when "capitalism" had begun in China was disputed; but since 1840, it was argued, foreign "capitalist imperialism," allied with domestic "feudal reaction," had checked and distorted China's "normal" capitalist development. Such formulas, imposed upon academic learning for political purposes, raised some new questions and absorbed scholarly attention.

The Korean War and Soviet Aid

Having early in 1949 proclaimed his policy of "leaning to one side" against "capitalist imperialism," Mao Tse-tung spent nine weeks of hard bargaining in Moscow (December 1949–February 1950). Finally he signed a thirty-year Sino-Soviet alliance treaty against aggression by Japan or any power (meaning the United States) joined with Japan. Soviet power thenceforth provided a shield behind which the Chinese Communists could pursue their domestic revolution, get rid of the last vestiges of imperialist rights and privileges, and reassert China's control over border areas.

It is unlikely that Peking expected to join in the Soviet-armed North Korean aggression of June 1950 against South Korea. Instead, the CCP evidently hoped to seize Taiwan from the Nationalists, but this was prevented when President Truman ordered the American Seventh Fleet to stop invasion either way across the Taiwan Strait. As the Korean War developed, China's chief strategic concern was for the security of her principal industrial base inherited from the Japanese in south Manchuria.

Under the well-prepared North Korean assault, the outnumbered Korean-American forces initially were forced southward and made a stand in a rectangular fifty-by-fifty-mile perimeter around Pusan in the extreme southeast. General Douglas MacArthur as UN commander soon demonstrated the offensive power of modern military technology with a massive amphibious landing September 15 on the west coast at Inchon, the port for Seoul. This was a gamble that succeeded brilliantly and was soon followed by recovery of Seoul and destruction of the North Korean invasion.

The war entered a new phase when United States forces crossed the 38th parallel in early October and pushed north toward the Yalu. They now expanded their aim from repulse of the northern invasion to an ill-advised effort to reunite Korea by force. This military purpose, stemming from MacArthur's victory and acquiesced in by Washington, disregarded China's strategic need for a buffer state, so as to avoid having a declared enemy lodged on the frontier of her northeast industrial base. China issued several clear warnings of intervention which the Americans discounted. In mid-October massively organized Chinese Communist "volunteers," units of Lin Piao's Fourth Field Army, secretly began to cross the Yalu into North Korea. Marching long distances through the mountains by night, lying hidden from air reconnaissance by day, they waited until by late November they totaled 300,000 or more. Meanwhile the two main American thrusts toward the Yalu were under separate commands, divided by fifty miles of "impassable" mountains. Unexpected Chinese flank attacks suddenly forced the American motorized columns into a costly retreat of 275 miles in the winter cold, all the way south of Seoul. Thus Stalin's disaster in the defeat of the North Koreans was salvaged by the Chinese intervention. But China's attempt in her turn to use her vast resources of manpower to unify Korea by force was now contained by United Nations firepower that eventually produced a stalemate on about the 38th parallel.

Truce talks began in July 1951 and dragged on at the border post of Panmunjom for two years. During this period fighting continued and the Chinese forces in Korea were built up with heavy Soviet weapons and an air force. The 142,000 casualties suffered by the United States made the Korean War the fourth largest in American history up to that time. (South Korean casualties were estimated at 300,000, North Korean at roughly 520,000, and Chinese at perhaps 900,000.) An armistice was finally signed July 27, 1953; in 1978 it was still in effect, with a closed border across the peninsula.

The People's Liberation Army also invaded Tibet in October 1950 and reasserted Chinese control in a year-long campaign of "liberation" and subjugation. Despite their cost, these campaigns built up China's military power. Afterward, military modernization used Soviet models and assistance. In 1955 compulsory military service began to draw on the five or six million young men reaching the age of eighteen each year, to create an enormous reservoir of manpower. A professional officer corps was created with Soviet-style ranks, uniforms, and differential pay at the top level of a regular army of about 2.6 million men. But jet planes and their fuel, for example, still had to be procured from the USSR.

From the start, Soviet aid came only at a price. In 1950 Sino-Soviet "joint-stock" companies were set up, on the model used in Eastern Europe, for the development of mining in Sinkiang and similar purposes potentially beneficial to the

USSR. However, after the death of Stalin in March 1953 these companies were liquidated. Similarly the Soviets gradually gave up their special position in Manchuria, ending joint control of the main railway in early 1953 and withdrawing from the Port Arthur naval base in 1955.

In industrialization the Soviet example and expertise were at first the Chinese Communists' greatest inspiration. Thousands of Chinese trainees went to the USSR, and as many as ten thousand Russian technicians at a time came armed with blueprints to help renovate or build the 211 old and new projects that led the industrial program (125 more projects were added in 1958–59). Starting in 1950, the Soviet Union loaned China $60 million a year in economic aid for five years, to be repaid by Chinese exports of raw materials. China's prewar pattern of foreign trade was reversed, flowing to the Soviet bloc instead of to the West and Japan. A second loan in 1954 provided $26 million a year for five years, though by that time such a sum would hardly cover the repayments due the USSR on the first loan. China received essential help in technology, unknown amounts of military hardware, and capital equipment but went into debt accordingly.

Though the limitations of the Soviet example were not at first apparent to Peking, China's capacity to follow the Stalinist Russian industrial model was inhibited by certain specific conditions. China had extensive coal and iron ore reserves, and other mineral and oil resources greater than had been realized, but utilizing them would require a costly investment in power and transport. As Alexander Eckstein has shown, China at her level of industrial development in the early 1950s was actually closer to the Russia of 1900 than to the Soviet Union of 1928 when the five-year plans began the Soviet industrialization. Russia in 1900 already had a higher per capita production of pig iron, steel, and cotton goods, and more railroad track per square mile, than China in 1952—and only one quarter the rural population density. By 1928 Russia had a much more extensive rail network and her production of coal, iron, steel, power, textile products, and the like in per capita terms was far greater than China's in 1952. Again, Russia had a far larger corps of modern-educated technical and professional manpower and a more developed education system. The Soviet model of industrialization, which stressed heavy industry at the expense of the peasant, was thus not really suited to China's situation. Yet the CCP at first was determined to stress heavy industry even more than the Soviets had.

Viewed against the population increase and the balance between population and food resources in the two countries, China's prospects of emulating Russia grew perceptibly dimmer. The superabundance of people (estimated by the census of 1953 at 583 million and increasing about 12 to 14 million yearly), together with the comparative lack of new land for cultivation, meant that China's population must press upon the food supply even more than Russia's had. Even though the centralized Chinese state might build up a superstructure of heavy industry and military power, it would remain a colossus weak in the stomach, vulnerable to natural calamity.

Mao and his colleagues were loath to accept any limits on their hopes. Consequently the ineradicable limitations in China's material resources, combined with the CCP's success in consolidating its power and mobilizing the country's human resources, set the stage by the late-1950s for one of the great national efforts and frustrations of history.

Chapter 15

The Struggle for Socialist Transformation

The revolutionary process within the People's Republic can best be understood as two revolutions, one economic, the other social, that have sometimes worked together and sometimes at cross purposes. The struggle for economic growth —building heavy industry, light consumer goods industries, scientific agriculture, and all that goes with them—has been generally intelligible to us from our own or at least from the Soviet experience. But the social transformation is far from American ways and hard to grasp.

The social revolution has tried to make peasants into citizens, to bring the rural masses into a modern life of technology in production and activism in local politics. But this has required getting rid of the old China's most durable achievement, the ruling class tradition. To a reader of the preceding chapters we need hardly reiterate that China's rural populace was inured to a perpetual symbiosis with the privileged few whose education and connections gave them access to landlord property and official prerogatives. Ruling class status and all its trappings were posited on the classical dictum that muscle workers naturally are governed by brain workers. Since the ruling class had generally governed the countryside from the cities, the CCP problem after taking power was how to reach the village to revolutionize it. If it could not, the villagers would retain the ancient ideas that sanctioned the ruling class—for example, that education qualifies one to govern others—and thus the old village would remain ready to accept a new ruling class.

The Maoist social revolution, to remake the society by remaking the people, thus became a semi-controlled process of struggle, between ideas, behavior patterns, and the interests of classes, regions, and individuals. While much of this struggle was carried on face to face in meetings large and small—five-hour reports by party secretaries, abashed self-criticisms in study groups—it was also reflected in reams of print. A small but able corps of Western specialists has followed this Chinese output and analyzed the course of events. This brief chapter, though built upon their work (see Suggested Reading), can only begin to represent its range and insight. From such studies we can know little of personal lives in China—the hopes and woes of individuals, who loved whom, and whatever happened to old Wang and Chang after they were publicly humiliated—but we get nevertheless an impression of the issues and anxieties in public life and of the meagerness of private life among political activists.

One striking feature of the revolution has been the continued fusion of morality and politics, such that a policy mistake is a moral crime, on the ancient (Confucian) assumption that conduct is character made manifest, that theory and practice should be one, and whoever acted with good intent but bad results was in the wrong. This unitary system has worked in the People's Republic as under imperial Confucianism because moral-ideological authority and political power have been combined at the top—first in the party Central Committee and then in the great leader, Mao himself.

Theory and practice, thought and behavior, in this Chinese view interpenetrate and interreact, and ideology is constantly shifting in its application to events. It is a complex structure.

Class struggle is the basic assumption, class status therefore a basic criterion. Contradictions are the stuff of dialectical conflict: contradictions of socialism against imperialism in the outer world, of the needs of industry against agriculture within China, of "proletarian" against "bourgeois" tendencies within oneself, and so on in endless profusion and in all aspects of life. Contradictions when perceived lead to struggle, eventual polarization, and resolution in a new unity, or so it is hoped. But in fact one struggle generally led only to another on slightly different terms, without any end to the process, which Mao aptly called "continuing revolution," a way of life. What a contrast with the old Chinese ideal of harmony! In this prolonged effort the economic and social revolutions were at first pursued in unison. They split apart only gradually.

Collectivization of Agriculture

The practical completion of land reform by the end of 1952, together with the tightening of controls over the urban and industrial sector of the economy, put Peking by 1953 in a position to plan joint programs for industrialization and for the collectivization of agriculture. Catching up with the West materially would require a harsh regimentation of economic effort over a prolonged period. The process would lead to urbanization: Shanghai, for example, instead of withering away as first proposed, was already approaching seven million. The swelling cities would increase their demand for agricultural products. Industrialization would also necessitate imports of Soviet-bloc capital goods, which could be paid for only by exporting, again, agricultural products. To extract more from the farm economy (by buying cheap and selling dear) the state needed a squeezing mechanism in the form of true collectives. These might lower incentives among agricultural workers, but they seemed the only sure way to enforce savings and check the incipient revival of a "rich peasant" class based on private landowning. Collectives were also the most efficient means for putting underemployed off-season farmers, including women, to work at public projects like afforestation or handicraft sidelines and for spreading modern agronomic technology.

Collectivization required what Alexander Eckstein has called "high-pressure gradualism," using coercion short of violence and manifold forms of persuasion on the farming populace. The initial decision to move toward collectivization, announced in December 1953 after some intra-party debate, had got results much faster than anticipated. Fifteen percent of the farm land and farming families were in agricultural producers' cooperatives (which were already called "semi-socialist collectives") by mid-1955, with many reports of 10 percent or even higher increases in production. Mao Tse-tung spent several weeks touring the major provinces, testing local sentiment. Encouraged by a bumper harvest, the CCP Central Committee, though apparently not without misgivings and objections, accepted his startling proposal for accelerated collectivization, with the final elimination of the rich peasant, the merchant speculator, land rent, and all capitalistic tendencies in rural life. This bold plan, pushed by eager cadres, again went faster than expected—within a year, by mid-1956, nine tenths of the peasantry (some 110 out of 120 million families) were reported to have joined agricultural producers' cooperatives. They were quickly asked to move on to the higher level of socialized agriculture by giving up their shares in the cooperatives and becoming wage laborers on full collective farms.

With the traditional Chinese genius for applying central blueprints by a creative adaptation to local circumstances, the new advanced cooperatives varied widely in size, say from

100 to 250 families whose houses and private garden plots occupied say 2 to 5 percent of the land and who divided among themselves say 60 to 70 percent of their common product. The resulting 700,000 or so new farming units with the best will in the world would need a long shakedown period. The peasants' motivation was all-important. How had this stupendous selling job been accomplished?

The experienced French agronomist René Dumont, who visited forty-three villages in late 1955, pointed to a number of factors. Unlike the disastrous Soviet collectivization of 1929–32, the process in China did not lead directly to state ownership of the land but to ownership by the individual cooperatives, which formally bought the land from the peasant owners. Cooperatives were not too different from the villages with which villagers were already identified. They now promised to be, as Jacques Guillermaz remarks, "a kind of mutual insurance policy" guaranteed by the state. Right off, combining scattered fragments of small family holdings into big fields was obviously a net gain in more efficient land use. Moreover, collectivization was gradual. The process moved from temporary mutual aid teams by successive stages to permanent full-scale cooperatives, from small groups to large ones. Most important, the program at its successive stages had evidently produced results enough to obviate resistance —at least very little was reported. A sufficient proportion of China's peasantry saw no alternative but to have faith in Chairman Mao and the party. The terror of land reform and the celebrated burning of landlords' title deeds were still fresh in memory even though the New Democracy had now run its course in only five years. Unlike Lenin, Mao had begun with the villages, and all anti-Communist leadership had been eliminated. Even so, there had been opposition both on the land and within the party, where leaders like Liu Shao-ch'i held to the orthodox Marxist-Leninist view that mechaniza-

插秧

晨雨麥秋潤午風槐
夏涼溪南與溪北笑
歌插新秧擲不停
手左右無亂行我教
插秧馬代勞民莫忘

Manpower agriculture. Transplanting rice seedlings. (From an early eighteenth-century work praising the emperor's patronage of agriculture.) *Right:* Harvesting by hand, 1963.

tion (changing the material means of production) should precede collectivization (changing the relations of production).

In the new structure, state farms (3300 at the end of 1955) served only as pilot operations to meet technical problems of the region, absorbing graduates of some twenty-six agricultural colleges. Mechanized agriculture, except on the new lands of Manchuria, remained for the distant future. Instead of the machine tractor stations of the Soviet Union, the center of the Chinese rural program remained the cooperatives. One or two to a village, they became the new focus of village life, undertaking the local public works and welfare activities which under the empire had been the province of gentry leadership. Where the former Confucian degree holders of the big families—a conservative-minded and often exploitative elite —had traditionally taken the initiative to repair temples and bridges or maintain schools and charities, it was now the local cooperative or collective farm chairman, usually an enthusiastic party appointee, who initiated projects for reforestation, combatting erosion, care of the aged, or improving the village dispensary. While the directives came down from above, the actual measures must be worked out at this level—introduction of pumps or new plows, literacy classes, campaign meetings.

At this level also the ambitious twelve-year rural plan for 1956–67 set forth bright promises: to see cultural amenities introduced (radios, libraries, movie theaters), the multitude of diseases and all flood and drought eliminated, forests widely planted, labor fully employed. Mainly by full employment (never achieved in the past), the plan hopefully envisioned 400 man-days of work applied annually to every hectare of land, doubling production in South China, increasing it by half nationally. Equally ambitious was the long-term plan to control the Yellow River by a "staircase" of forty-six dams on the main stream, plus hydropower and multi-purpose projects, so as to irrigate much of North China.

For the farm boy just learning to read, this confident vision was undoubtedly inspiring. For doubters and dissenters there was plainly announced "reform through labor." Meantime food was rationed and quotas were set for compulsory delivery of commercial crops.

The First Five-Year Plan

Preparation for a Soviet-type forced-draft industrial development had gone forward with the nationalization of banking, industry, and trade, with the state buying shares in enterprises to make them joint state-private concerns, and with campaigns to exhaust the entrepreneur and make him in effect a state employee. The first five-year plan for 1953–57 was not finally published until two and a half years had elapsed for testing it, training technicians, and building up statistical services. In July 1955, it was heralded as inaugurating the "transition to socialism," which had formally superseded the New Democracy as of 1953. Among 1600 major projects in all fields, some 700 would be in industry (including 156 announced in 1953–54 to be commenced with Soviet aid). Of 6000 minor projects, 2300 would be industrial. The new plants would make tractors, trucks, generators, ships, the materials and equipment for heavy industry. University graduates would be one third engineers, produced at the rate of 20,000 a year.

The conflict between the development of agriculture and industry, and the consequent subordination of the former, was apparent in the first five-year plan targets announced in 1955; steel to be tripled, power and cement doubled, machine tools more than tripled, but cotton goods to be increased by less than one half and food grains by less than one fifth. In other words, industry could grow only as the farmer kept his consumption down. Collectivization had put him in a box; through price manipulation in favor of industry, his product could be taken from him indirectly as well as by outright collection of crops and taxes. Consumer goods would be manufactured to exchange for rural products. But just as man had been cheaper than armament in Chinese warfare, so in her agricultural development China would have to stress capital-cheap, labor-intensive projects like flood control dikes and irrigation ditches. Pigs could be multiplied to provide both food and manure, but artifical fertilizer, for example, was to be limited. Meanwhile capital investment was to be concentrated in heavy industry, which would receive seven or eight times the investment in light, consumer-goods industry.

The Maoist enthusiasts who now dominated the CCP Central Committee beat down the "rightist conservatism" of their policy opponents by calling for a "leap forward" in which the people's productive energies would be psychologically liberated and incentive devices such as emulation campaigns among competing workers' groups would achieve "quantity, speed, quality, and economy" of production all at once. This forced-draft industrialization eventually channeled something like 30 percent of the Chinese people's gross national product through the government, which used it approximately one fourth for defense, one fourth for administration and social services, and one half for investment. China's industrial growth in this period seemed rapid and substantial—as of 1957, the fastest of any underdeveloped Asian country.

The railroad network was extended to the northwest, to Outer Mongolia so as to connect with the trans-Siberian in 1956 and to Turkestan, in order to reach Russian Central Asia (though the final connection was not made). These lines, accompanied by migration, opened up the arid northwest for mineral exploitation and also had political-strategic importance, strengthening the revived Chinese grip on Inner Mongolia and Sinkiang.

China's economic dependence on Russia meanwhile had led to the reversal of her foreign trade pattern. Formerly Japan and the West had taken her soybeans, tung oil, and other farm products, and the Communist-bloc area took hardly 2 percent of the total. Now China's trade was mainly with the latter and stressed capital goods imports.

The Struggles with Intellectuals and with Cadres

"Socialist construction" required the mobilization of all the nation's energies, including those of the thin stratum of about 100,000 technical, professional, and academic "higher intellectuals" who had been mainly Western-oriented. The party heads believed, optimistically, that their leadership and doctrines had by this time re-educated, "spiritually transformed," and won allegiance from this group; but they were evidently concerned that the new party apparatus with its host of young cadres had stifled intellectual life and tyrannized over the older intellectuals. Campaigns were therefore mounted in 1956–57 to manipulate these two strategic elements, intellectuals and cadres.

The party early in 1956 initiated a campaign among the urban intellectuals in order to ensure their fullest contribution to the tasks of socialist transformation. This was to be achieved by improving the intellectuals' working conditions, giving them more access to foreign publications, more free time, more scope for initiative, and at the same time getting them to "remold" themselves ideologically and qualify in large numbers for party membership. A campaign for freer criticism of the cadres and bureaucracy was also begun in May 1956 under the classical slogan "Let a hundred flowers bloom together, let the hundred schools of thought contend." This was not a clarion call for free speech. Criticism must not overstep the implicitly assumed limits of complete devotion to the party's final authority. This would be in the imperial censor's tradition of "loyal remonstrance," not like a "loyal opposition" in the West, which could attack a regime's policies while remaining loyal to the state.

It is a neat trick to foster intellectual vitality within a framework of uncritical loyalty. In the aftermath of the Hungarian rising of October–November 1956 and Russia's suppression of it, which coincided with signs of discontent in China, Mao in February 1957 announced within the party his doctrine of contradictions—some "antagonistic" as between the regime and its "enemies" abroad or at home, and some "nonantagonistic," normal and arguable, as between the bureaucracy and "the people." Within this framework he evidently hoped that a continuing "struggle" over the execution of policy, using his method of "unity-criticism-unity," could be healthily pursued and yet contained. As in the ideological reform movement of the Yenan period, this dialectical process would call forth criticism and then would meet it, letting extreme views emerge to be dealt with through open argument, in order to discover faults and correct them and also to discover faultfinders and reform them. (Any of "the people" who seemed hypercritical and disloyal could be classed as "enemies" to be coerced.) Mao estimated in March that among five million or so higher and ordinary intellectuals perhaps 1 to 3 percent were hostile to Marxism, while most simply needed education in it. He was soon to be disillusioned.

A movement announced in April 1957 for rectification of the party's working style finally triggered an explosion of the intellectuals' accumulated hundred flowers of criticism. A year's repeated invitations at last released a surprising torrent of publicly expressed dissatisfaction, on the part of intellec-

The Struggle for Socialist Transformation

tuals and the professionally trained elite, with the CCP's totalitarian system, its ideas, aims, and methods. This widespread and basic criticism surprised and startled the party in May 1957. After five weeks it was stopped.

Meanwhile the party's Central Committee had faced the even more serious problem of controlling the enormous apparatus of cadres that executed its policies. The twin drives in agriculture and industry had achieved spectacular results. Yet this vast "surging tide of socialism" had entailed a struggle not only against material conditions but also against recalcitrant personalities and human nature under the guidance and urging of the party cadres.

The rapid growth of this apparatus of activists was indexed by the rise in party membership—from 4.4 million in 1949 to 17 million in 1961. In addition, there were the Young Communist League (about 25 million in 1959) and the Young Pioneers (about 50 million in 1962). This multitude was needed to do the party's work yet it was largely unseasoned and inexperienced. Four fifths of the party members probably lacked a high school education. Young cadres fresh from their indoctrination, though given the prestige of learning and a code of leadership through self-sacrifice, might easily fall into the evils of "blind optimism," "dogmatism," and "commandism," or of "conservatism," "empiricism," and "blind opportunism," instead of manipulating the peasantry through discussion, logic, and persuasion. Cadres could be stimulated by Mao's ideological pronouncements and the party line more easily than they could be restrained and given wisdom, or saved from the corruption and false reporting that had inveterately characterized peasant-official relations in the past. Agricultural collectivization had in fact proceeded unevenly, with considerable friction on the spot and overoptimistic reporting to superiors. The Eighth Party Congress, meeting in September 1956, had found that the peasantry had been widely misled by the cadres' false promises. Industrial projects had similarly been over-ambitious. The masses had actually suffered a lowering of their standard of living.

Roused by the dangers of excessive "commandism" and of being "out of touch with the masses," an evil that also seemed to be exemplified in the Hungarian revolt, the CCP inaugurated in April 1957 the above-cited great ideological campaign for "Rectification" of the party cadres' working style, parallel to the Hundred Flowers campaign to induce criticism from the intellectuals.

Thus by mid-1957 the CCP found both intellectuals and cadres out of proper control. Its answer was a big Anti-Rightist campaign targeted at both groups which in the rest of 1957 forced many ex-liberals and minor party members out of public life and purged many thousands of cadres. The erstwhile critics including many writers were harshly attacked, obliged to recant publicly and condemn one another. The United Front seemed at an end. Finally great numbers of people were subjected to a big campaign for "downward transfer" *(hsia-fang)* to move teachers, students, and city cadres and functionaries into the countryside so that by manual labor among the villagers they would avoid "separation from the masses" and could also help agricultural production and reduce urban unemployment. Thomas Bernstein concludes that in the period 1957–66 about 1.2 million urban youth were actually resettled in the countryside (whereas in 1968–75 the total resettled rose to about 12 million).

But it proved easier to discipline the small number of intellectuals than to curb the overenthusiasm of the millions of cadres—or indeed to remain uninfected by it. The fanaticism of the revolution soon rose to a new height and the top leadership fell victim to its own enthusiasm. This climate of feeling was inspired partly by the apparent success of communism worldwide.

The Struggle for Socialist Transformation

China in the World Scene

Revolution at home had been accompanied by a militant attitude toward the outside world, and CCP thinking became fixed upon the universalistic theme of "American imperialism" as the enemy and China's "liberation" as the model for all colonial and semi-colonial peoples. Circumstance imposed upon Peking the traditional aim of strong dynasties: to dominate contiguous areas in defense of the Middle Kingdom. But this practical aim of conventional power politics was seen as part of a great worldwide struggle of the progressive "socialist camp" against the reactionary "imperialist camp." In these terms China's newly heightened nationalism found expression in a broader universalism, in which People's China relied upon the Soviet Union as its "elder brother." In this spirit, Peking during the 1950s utilized both coercion and persuasion in foreign policy, as on the home front.

The first phase, 1950 to 1954, began belligerently in an interaction with American belligerence, which was triggered specifically by the Soviet-backed North Korean invasion of South Korea in June 1950. As we have noted, this precipitated the American-backed United Nations defense of South Korea and a resumption of American military-naval support of the Nationalist government on Taiwan. Soon after Chinese troops intervened in Korea and entered Tibet (see p. 000), Chinese military support aided the Viet Minh in Indochina. But after two years of negotiation, the Korean armistice was signed in July 1953; and after the defeat of the French at Dien Bien Phu, France's withdrawal from Indochina was agreed upon, with China participating as a great power, at Geneva in July 1954.

This expansion of Peking's influence, however, was paralleled by an expansion of American commitments. On this front of the Cold War, both sides sought security through militant action. In September 1954 a joint defense system, the Southeast Asia Treaty Organization (SEATO), was created by the United States to include Britain, France, Australia, New Zealand, the Philippines, Thailand, and Pakistan. Washington also signed defensive alliances with Seoul (October 1953) and Taipei (December 1954). Thus, by the time the Communist-Nationalist confrontation over the offshore island of Quemoy in Amoy harbor led to a crisis in early 1955, China's activity concerning four contiguous areas was matched by an American led and financed anti-Communist effort at "containment."

After the militancy of these early years came a phase of greater reliance on diplomatic persuasion. At the Geneva conference of April–July 1954, Chou En-lai joined the foreign ministers of the other powers in an effort to create stability in Indochina as France withdrew. In negotiating at this time with India and Burma, Chou enunciated five principles of "peaceful coexistence." These also formed his main theme at the conference held in April 1955 at Bandung in western Java by leaders of twenty-nine Asian and African states. In tune with the "Bandung spirit," the American and Chinese ambassadors at Warsaw began in August 1955 to hold periodic talks.

Yet this "soft" line soon yielded to a "hard" one. Imperialism seemed to be on the defensive after Russia launched the first intercontinental ballistic missile (ICBM) in August 1957 and its first satellite, "Sputnik," orbited the earth in October. In November Mao went to Moscow, leaving China for the second time, to attend a conference of twelve Communist parties and celebrate the fortieth anniversary of the Bolshevik revolution. Mao's seniority was evident but so also was the divergence within the socialist camp between European and Chinese trends and problems. Declaring that "the east wind prevails over the west wind," he called for a new belligerency in Cold War relations.

The Struggle for Socialist Transformation

This soon became evident in the Taiwan Straits, where the American build-up of Nationalist military power had been resumed in 1951. The Nationalists increasingly harassed the mainland by espionage, reconnaissance and leaflet-dropping flights, and commando raids. They also strengthened the fortification of "the front" on Quemoy, committing to it a third of the Nationalist forces. Eventually, Communist bombardment in August–September 1958 created a second Quemoy crisis, which subsided but left Quemoy a bone of contention, still held by the Nationalists as a recognized part of the mainland.

Another area of renewed belligerency was Tibet, whose people were pressed toward a socialist revolution that would amount to sinicization. A rising at Lhasa in March 1959, when the Dalai Lama fled to India, led to harsh repression by the Chinese and to Tibetan charges of genocide. During the following summer Sino-Indian friction increased on both ends of the Himalayan frontier. It finally erupted in hostilities in October 1962. China got control of the strategic route between Tibet and Sinkiang through the Aksai-Chin region and shattered the Indian dream of peaceful coexistence. Intensified efforts were now made to absorb the Tibetans into the Chinese state as a minority nationality in an Autonomous Region, like the Inner Mongolian Autonomous Region founded in 1947 and the Sinkiang Uighur Autonomous Region founded in 1955. Accordingly Han (Chinese) settlers as well as troops and officials were sent into Tibet, while Tibetans were taken into the People's Liberation Army and their old social groupings broken up. Tibet ceased to be a buffer state.

Similarly Chinese had expanded into the thinly populated border regions of northern Manchuria, Inner Mongolia, Kansu, Ch'ing-hai, Sinkiang, and even Hainan Island. Settlers, prisoners, and volunteers brought in to cultivate virgin lands or develop mineral resources tended to dominate the local minority peoples. The vast area once ruled by the Ch'ing dynasty as a multi-racial empire was now largely occupied by the new Chinese nation.

To the south, North Vietnam continued its tradition of local independence of Chinese rule while imitating Chinese institutions. North Vietnam's attack on South Vietnam after 1959, first supporting guerrilla warfare, sabotage, and terrorism, then sending in troops, made full use of CCP techniques and assistance. This application of Chinese methods capitalized on the long-established gulf between city and countryside, between the urban upper class and the peasant village, where a new and tighter Vietnamese social and political order could be based on nationalist feeling and Communist doctrine. All this struggle in the late 1950s on China's frontiers seemed to be winning the day. It encouraged in these years an even greater effort on the domestic scene.

The Great Leap Forward

The Third Plenum of the Central Committee (elected at the Eighth Party Congress of 1956) met in September–October 1957 and faced a crucial problem. The completion of "socialist transformation" had given the new state-and-party apparatus an effective control over the economy, and party committees at all levels now made economic decisions. Mass mobilization to pressure businessmen or rich peasants was no longer necessary, and mass organizations had begun to atrophy. But, as Ezra Vogel puts it, "the appetite of Communist leaders for control over the economy had been greater than their knowledge, experience, and judgment." Red tape had grown faster than production. Collectivization had not actually increased the agricultural product received by the regime, which faced a dire problem of agricultural stagnation.

The Struggle for Socialist Transformation

During 1952–57 rural population had increased by about 9 percent while the city population grew about 30 percent, but the government grain collection hardly grew at all, and meanwhile China had to begin repaying Soviet loans out of agricultural products. The Soviet model of taxing agriculture to build industry faced a dead end. Moreover, urbanization, having outstripped industrialization, produced urban unemployment, which was added to the underemployment in the populous countryside. The first five-year plan had got results as expected but to go ahead with more of same, the second five-year plan, would invite disaster. In retrospect we can see that the only real solution both for the food supply and for rural employment was the technological transformation of agriculture, symbolized, for example, by the production of chemical fertilizer. But this was not the solution attempted in 1958.

The development strategy of the Great Leap Forward was the sort of thing guerrilla warriors could put together. They had learned how to mount campaigns and mobilize the populace to attain specific social objectives, much like capturing positions in warfare—indeed military terminology was commonly used. The whole apparatus of campaign mechanisms was now directed to an economic transformation, the simultaneous development of agriculture and industry, a strategy of dualism or, as Mao said, "Walking on two legs," to achieve development in the modern industrial sector and the rural agricultural sector as two distinct though related processes. Mass mobilization would make use of rural labor never before fully employed: first, to use labor intensively for irrigation and flood control works and land reclamation; second, to raise agricultural productivity per unit of land by using more hands to plant, weed, and cultivate; and third, to expand small-scale industry locally with materials and equipment at hand in order to produce consumer goods and equipment for the farmers. It was hoped that there would be no increase of rural consumption above the current, more or less subsistence level, and that rural development would not need much help from the modern industrial sector but on the contrary could provide a surplus to it through taxes and requisitions.

Meanwhile the modern industrial sector of the economy would put its product into exports for securing capital goods from abroad or into investment in further plant construction, thus permitting the modern sector's expansion. (One cannot help being reminded of the contrast between the treaty port and rural sectors of China's economy in the imperialist era.) The CCP effort was to take advantage of China's rural backwardness and manpower surplus by realizing the Maoist faith that ideological incentives could get economic results, that a new spirit could unlock hitherto untapped sources of human energy without the use of material incentives.

This utopian reliance on the exhortations of the Chairman was combined with institutional reform reminiscent of the old statecraft tradition. The effort was made easier in 1958 because collectivization of agriculture had proceeded so successfully in the preceding years, whereas the professional experts and economists, like other intellectuals, had suffered downgrading as a result of the Hundred Flowers campaign and the Anti-Rightist movement that followed. The new stress on the mass line envisioned the unleashing of productive energies simply through mass mobilization. For this purpose there was a general decentralization of economic management in late 1957. Many enterprises and even monetary controls were decentralized down to the local level. The central statistical bureau was broken up and localized together with functions of economic planning. This was the context in which the over-ambitious targets of the Great Leap were formulated in each locality, not by economists but by cadres inspired by emulation who were contemptuous of experts but intensely loyal to the cause.

The result was a mighty paroxysm of round-the-clock labor. The face of the country was changed with new roads, factories, cities, dikes, dams, lakes, afforestation, and new cultivation, for which the 650 millions of China had been mobilized in nationwide efforts of unparalleled intensity and magnitude. The feat most publicized abroad was the campaign begun in July 1958 to produce steel from small "backyard" iron smelters without special guidance or equipment. Some thirty to fifty thousand smelting furnaces were reported set up by the end of July, 190,000 in August, 700,000 by the end of September, a million in October, with 100 million people engaged in this "battle for steel." Unfortunately the product of all this effort proved largely unusable, though many people had indeed confronted the practical problems of metallurgy. Thus the Great Leap brought small-scale industry into the countryside, applying technology and mobilizing manpower as never before, but the immediate results were chaotic and uneconomic.

The state statistical bureau claimed that in 1958 production of food crops and cotton had nearly doubled in one year, and on this basis the Central Committee set ambitious targets for 1959 to increase again by 50 percent. The shortages in 1958 and 1959 were blamed on transport bottlenecks due to an unprecedentedly large harvest. The leadership became a captive of its own claims. In fact 1958 was a good crop year and production rose perhaps 10 or 15 percent, while experimental plots also got very high increases. But since the statistical bureau had been decentralized, it could not check on estimates reported.

The incredible crop figures that the Central Committee[*] trumpeted abroad had to be humiliatingly withdrawn in the late summer of 1959. The next years saw poor harvests due to bad weather. Food shortages continued and rationing also. Given an annual population growth of between 1.5 and 2.5 percent and a decline in food production in the five years after 1958, one can only conclude that the food supply suffered by as much as 20 percent in the year of greatest stringency, 1960–61. Given a normal intake of only about 2000 or 2200 calories a day per person, this drop was disastrous. The substitution of sweet potatoes for rice and a shortage of animal products were both evident. After 1961 the reintroduction of private plots and subsequent good harvests helped the situation. But since fertilizer production is capital-intensive, it could not solve the food problem. By 1962 chemical fertilizer production was only around two million tons, a bare beginning.

The Communes

The commune was an integral part of the Great Leap, based on the mass line idea of the release of the "spontaneous initiative of the masses." This mass mobilization was also accompanied by decentralized economic management. A typical commune was formed by amalgamating a number of agricultural producers cooperatives of the higher stage, that is, collective farms. Some communes were as large as districts (*ch'ü*), while smaller communes with a membership of four to five thousand households, say 20,000 people, were roughly coinci-

---

[*] Thus the CCP claims and hopes for grain production were announced as follows: production in 1957, 185 million metric tons; production in 1958 (as claimed in December 1958 and April 1959), 357 million tons; forecast (in December 1958) for 1959, 525 million tons; revised claim for 1958 (as of August 1959), 250 million tons.

dent with the administrative village *(hsiang).* The commune included local government functions, both military and security, as well as local trade, finance, taxation, accounting, statistics, and planning, all under party control. It was divided into production brigades, which were made up of production teams that more or less corresponded to the old agricultural producers cooperatives, perhaps half a village. Private plots were taken over, as well as private possessions down to the level of pots and pans, chairs and tables. Many peasants for a time ate in large mess halls. All labor was to be controlled. Everyone was to work twenty-eight days of the month, while children went into day nurseries. This would bring large-scale efficiency to the village and get all its labor, including the womanpower, into full employment. This grandiose concept was pursued like a military campaign with great fanfare and utopian fervor—for example, by trying to set up a free supply of food and other necessities "according to need." The result, it was hoped, would be agricultural cities with the peasants proletarianized and uprooted from their own land. This would give better control of manpower, change the peasants' attitudes, and call forth their initiative to create a self-sufficient local society, including their own militia forces for defense.

This revolution collapsed from general overwork and exhaustion, the damaging of incentives and the incapacities of management. The egalitarian wage system, paying each according to his needs, lowered productivity. So did shifting labor about like military platoons within the commune. China's intensive hand-gardening agriculture could not be organized on the big scale of the Russian kolkhoz, especially in the absence of mechanization.

In December 1958 the Central Committee, at its Sixth Plenum in Wuhan, had to transfer the center of decision making from the commune back down to the level of the production brigade as the basic unit for accounting, taxing, and distributing income. The free supply system was de-emphasized and wages were paid again according to labor done and work points acquired. As the agricultural crisis worsened in 1960, the commune was further decentralized and the production team with an average membership of about twenty to forty households that could work together became the basic unit. Private garden plots were reintroduced and mess halls given up. By 1962 the number of communes, as they were reduced in size, rose from about 24,000 to 74,0000, roughly the same as the old number of rural market areas.

China's original land reform had avoided the destructive evils of the Soviet collectivization because the CCP proceeded slowly, by stages and with persuasion. Yet in the end they ran into the problem of incentives just the same, and they faced agricultural stagnation. But when they began to innovate through decentralization, mass mobilization, and communes, they also met failure. Their economic recession and industrial standstill after 1960 were greater than any that had occurred in the better-off Soviet economy at any time. The decade of the 1950s had benefited from one-time economies of rehabilitation and from Soviet aid and credits. The early 1960s suffered from adverse weather and withdrawal of Soviet technicians and aid.

After overleaping itself in 1958–60, with "politics in command" and the party almost merged with the government, China underwent several years of serious economic dislocation. Gross national product declined by perhaps one third in 1960. Malnutrition was widespread and some starvation occurred. The people were exhausted and apathetic. Transportation broke down. Industry stagnated, as in a severe economic depression. Many plants closed, and statistics were no longer published. The regime acknowledged that agriculture, short-changed for a decade, must now receive top priority. Though nature was blamed, it became apparent that Mao and the CCP, using their political power, had made economic errors on a truly gigantic scale. As Mao said in a post-mortem of 1959, "Coal and iron cannot walk by themselves; they need vehicles . . . This I did not foresee . . . I concentrated mainly on the revolution . . . I understand nothing about industrial planning." In the result the cadres were demoralized, the people disillusioned.

The mounting extremism of the Chinese revolution during the late 1950s, the feverish tendency to accelerate campaigns and revise targets upward, is reminiscent of other great social upheavals. Many, including the Soviets, have attributed this tendency to the wilfulness of Mao as a revolutionary romantic, a proud and imperious Chinese seeking a Chinese road to socialism. Further study may suggest that his personality was not unique but rather representative. In any case extremism was continually encouraged by Mao and the Central Committee in the faith that the masses would respond to a Marxist-Leninist leadership that knew how to unleash the latent "productive forces" of the society and free the "creative capacity" of the Chinese working class that had previously, it was believed, been held in check by domestic and foreign exploiting classes.

Seldom has faith been frustrated on so vast a scale. By the 1960s the Chinese people had learned how to coexist with the CCP regime, as they had with autocracies in the past, but the initial enthusiasm of the revolution had been spent. Meanwhile the party leaders, who had risen to power through their "love for the masses" and "to serve the people," found themselves in the position of new rulers in hard times, feared and distrusted accordingly, up against intractable problems and less united in their own counsels.

In 1960–62 Liu Shao-ch'i and the other Peking leaders took vigorous action to revive production. They restored central planning of industry, financial incentives (bonuses and prizes) for workers, and private plots and markets for farmers. Their retreat from socialism was less drastic than Lenin's New Economic Policy of 1921. But it fostered greater income differentiation in both industry and agriculture, more elitism and bureaucratization. By 1962 Mao and his supporters saw a trend toward a revival of capitalism, a revisionist "bourgeois restoration."

Chapter 16
The Second Revolution

The fifteen years from 1962 until Mao's death in September 1976 are the era in China's modern history that we can least understand, not only because it is too soon for definitive studies but also because the events seem so bizarre and confusing to us outside observers. (They confused people in China too.)

Mao and His Opponents

After 1966 the long-touted unity of CCP leadership was riven by a "power struggle," but when the world press tried to use this theme to make sense of things, they often became still murkier. For Mao s deviousness, or skill, was such that old colleagues in the Politbureau who later became the top targets of his second revolution had joined him as early as September 1962 and frequently thereafter in denouncing "revisionist ideas" and "opportunist ideological tendencies in the Party," thus unwittingly digging their own graves. Mao's motives, complex as usual, have been thought by some to focus on ensuring his own "revolutionary immortality" (in the psychiatrist Robert Lifton's phrase) through finding successors committed to his vision. He was against occupational specialization and distrusted intellectuals; he was anti-urban and anti-bureaucratic—all attitudes typical of the common people in the villages. His visionary deviation from the Stalinist model of industrialization in the Great Leap and communes of 1958 had resulted in disaster, and after 1958 he stayed out of administration; by 1962 China's economy was recovering. Yet Mao now believed the revolution was endangered by a "struggle between two lines"—either a conventional development of state industry and elitist bureaucratism or another attempt to achieve an egalitarian socialism, Chinese-style.

The Two Approaches to China's Revolution. In the historical background, first of all, were the two views of revolution inherent in the European origins of Marxism. As Benjamin Schwartz has remarked, one stems from Rousseau and views history as a moral drama and revolution as a moral crusade to achieve the reign of virtue. The other stems from the Physiocrats and sees the progress of the arts, especially technological development in material terms, as the agent of revolution enabling new forces of production to create new classes to lead the way. Pursuing these cognate themes, Mao could stress the moral pursuit of egalitarian justice and proletarian virtues, while Liu Shao-ch'i, Teng Hsiao-p'ing, and their colleagues could stress the need of planning and material progress.

In modern China this latter strain of "scientific Marxism" had been espoused, for example, by Ch'en Tu-hsiu. It assumed that a society's "superstructure" of political, social, and cultural life reflects its material base, the relations of production (as between capitalist and laborer or landlord and tenant); and these must be changed before the superstructure can be changed. In contrast, the voluntarism (willfulness, not "volunteering") and populism espoused by Li Ta-chao asserted that the will of the masses, once energized, could con-

The Second Revolution

quer all. In Mao's background one can also see the anarchist view that had appealed to so many Chinese idealists early in the century, to abolish all government and all capitalism, and create a free society based on mutual cooperation.*

Mao also got sustenance from a certain degree of convergence between Rousseauism and the moral self-cultivation urged in the Chinese classics, particularly in the *Mencius*—the idea that all men are potentially good and only need teaching to realize their potentialities, and that leadership must be taken by an ethical elite whose moral superiority can transcend their environment and transform the populace. This residual strain in Confucianism fostered the supreme role of a sage hero, whereas the Soviet-trained Liu Shao-ch'i and his colleagues omitted in the new CCP constitution of 1956 the "thought of Mao" and opposed a cult of Mao's personality. Stuart Schram has noted how Comrade Liu, writing on the party and stressing its equal discipline for all, could declare that "Comrade Mao Tse-tung is the leader of the whole party but he, too, obeys the party"; in contrast Mao could ask quite early in praising Stalin, "If we did not have a Stalin, who would give the orders?"

The dualism of these inherent alternatives was evidenced in the contrast between Mao, the chief rebel, and Liu, the chief organizer. Liu Shao-ch'i was also from Hunan. He had worked with Mao first in 1922 and very closely from 1943. His first success had been in organizing in cities, in KMT- or Japanese-occupied areas. At Yenan he became chief of the CCP organization and in 1959 chief of state. Lowell Dittmer, using Harold Lasswell's terms, has classed the quiet, colorless Liu as a "compulsive" type, bent on impersonal uniformity

---

* Anarchists hoped to create a society where "there are no landowners, no capitalists, no parasites, no leaders, no officials, no deputies, no family heads, no armies, no prisons, no police, no courts of justice, no law, no religion, no marriage." Chinese anarchist manifesto, July 1914, quoted by Olga Lang.

and institutional order, and the kinetic Mao as a "dramatizing" type, broader in scope, tolerant of diversity, innovative, seeking response. The contrast can be suggested under several rubrics, beginning with policy versus operations and vision versus implementation. *Leader versus commissar.* Mao was the distant, charismatic leader, a symbol of paternal compassion, whereas the party commissars under Liu Shao-ch'i had to exercise local power and demand discipline. Mao stood above his colleagues, a figure apart. *The mass line versus party building.* Mao stood for struggle. He wanted the cadres to serve the people, guide their liberation, stir them up and respond to their stirrings in the spirit of the mass line. Liu and the other party builders preferred to keep struggle in its proper place, subordinate to party unity, and stressed the training of cadres and party members to be a new elite that could guide China's transformation. *Village versus city.* After 1949, Mao's concerns harked back to his peasant background and the simple existence of the Yenan era. He disdained city life, distrusted its evils, thought rather of the peasant mass, whose vast energies, once liberated, could be harnessed to move mountains. His ideal was the omnicompetent man of the soil, a combined farmer, craftsman, and militia soldier in a self-sufficient countryside. Practical organizers in the Central Committee, in contrast, saw the need of talent and skills for industrialization, the importance therefore of the urban elite of educated and professional people, the necessity of technical education to produce specialists who could contribute to a modern state. *Voluntarism versus planning.* Most of Mao's contemporaries, confronting enormous tasks, favored the systematic effort of Five-Year Plans, the steady accumulation of investment capital and building up of industry, as inescapable needs. Mao was less concerned with economics than with politics because he believed that with the correct attitude and determination, man could overcome all obstacles. This reliance on the will, voluntarism, was an article of Mao's personal faith, confirmed by his experience. It led him to favor local initiative versus central control, the people versus bureaucratism, the peasantry versus any revival of a ruling class, and in the most general terms politics versus economics. The most publicized of all these contrasts was that of *Red versus expert,* the politically trained versus the professionally trained. Invoking this slogan, doctrinaire activists harried the old intellectuals left over from before 1949 and condemned their foreign learning.

These different paths to China's future had not always been mutually exclusive but had been advocated as cognate principles in many Central Committee pronouncements. Roderick MacFarquhar has pinpointed the tug-of-war in 1956–57 between Mao's optimistic hope of enlisting even intellectuals and rich peasants in support of CCP aims and the concern of Liu and other organizers to preserve the power of the party. Mao saw the underlying issue as "the relationship of party and people." He believed it was the party's being in power that "led cadres to behave in bureaucratic ways." But in the 1950s he still agreed with the politburo that "the leading position of the CCP in state and society was sacrosanct." Unity was preserved. Commissars like Liu Shao-ch'i backed the utopianism of the distinctly Maoist Great Leap. But its failure precipitated a hardening of attitudes over the pace of change, the degree of effort, and also its direction. After the Wuhan Plenum of December 1958, when Mao "voluntarily" gave up his position as chief of state to Liu Shao-ch'i, debate continued, but the CCP leadership now confronted the questions that come to every revolution: When are its gains to be consolidated? When should change give way to stability? Alternatively, how can the revolutionary spirit be kept alive? This was the problem of revisionism, whether to revise the goals of the movement, a dilemma which the Soviet Union had also faced. This made the impact of Soviet revisionism on Chinese politics all the greater.

The Sino-Soviet Split

During the Cold War of the late 1940s and early 1950s, "monolithic international Communism" seemed to be unified by a single dominant ideology as well as by the final authority of Stalin. So strong was this appearance that the burden of proof was on those who doubted it. For several years after the death of Stalin in 1953, the facade of unity was maintained as an obvious asset in the general Communist cause.

The Sino-Soviet split developed on several levels at once. The Chinese and Russian peoples were separate nations with different histories, self-images, needs, and goals. Memory made them suspicious each of the other: the Mongol horde of the thirteenth century had enslaved South Russia, tsarist imperialists had encroached on Manchuria, Mongolia, and Turkestan. Behind the facade of Communist rhetoric, history provided few bonds of mutual admiration or successful cooperation. Their recent collaboration, chiefly in the form of Soviet aid paid for by China, had followed the desires of their leaders, who could as easily disrupt it. Just as the ideology of Communist revolution had been the original bond, so it became the point of fracture.

Mao knew no foreign languages. By the time he acquired a Marxist concept it had often been a bit sinicized in the mere process of translation. Moreover, Mao had begun with revolutionary action; he acquired ideology as he went along. It is customary to say he applied or adapted Marxism-Leninism to "the concrete realities of China." One can also say the concrete realities of his experience dictated what ideology he found useful.

On the verbal level Mao's homely exhortations are studded with Chinese proverb and metaphor, both classical and colloquial. He castigates neutralists who would "sit on top of a mountain to watch the tigers fight" as well as supercilious cadres who think arguing with peasants is like "playing music to a cow." No one who has skirted a pit of nightsoil covered with maggots can fail to understand Mao's abhorrence of what he calls "the deep, stinking cesspool of Chinese reaction." To quote Confucius' sage advice, "think twice," does not necessarily promote Confucianism, but it helps to fit communism into the Chinese landscape.

On the level of theory, Mao continued to warp and bend Communist doctrine to fit it to local needs. Stalin had asserted that the Soviet experience which reached socialism through the "dictatorship of the proletariat" offered the only path to socialism, which must be followed by the people's democracies of eastern Europe and presumably by all others. But the CCP after 1949 set up a "people's democratic dictatorship" and claimed that a mere "hegemony of the proletariat" at the head of a united front and a coalition government representing the whole "people," a combination of all "revolutionary classes," could lead China to socialism and moreover could do it by a gradual, persuasive, nonviolent transformation, quite unlike the abrupt and violent change postulated by Lenin and Stalin.

After Stalin's death in 1953, N. S. Khrushchev became (until 1964) the principal Soviet leader. His denunciation of Stalin's multiple crimes at the Soviet party's Twentieth Congress in February 1956, the beginning of Soviet "de-Stalinization," surprised and embarrassed the CCP at a time when it was still invoking Stalin's name. To be sure, the Twentieth Congress doctrine of "many paths to socialism" gave ground to the Maoist as well as the Titoist modifications of Marxism-Leninism and also accepted Peking's claim to be the model for Asia to follow; Sino-Soviet ideological solidarity was preserved, but only at the price of concessions which cut the ground from under Marxist-Leninist doctrine. From this time forward, the split widened, at first below the surface and by 1963 in full public polemics. The CCP had asserted both its organizational and its ideological autonomy. Peking like Moscow was now an autonomous center of doctrinal authority. International communism was no longer monolithic, and under the pull of national interests, friction, if not rupture, was inevitable.

On the personal plane, though Mao could acknowledge Stalin's seniority, Khrushchev should now by rights acknowledge Mao's. But Khrushchev was on the crest of the Soviet success in launching the first sputnik and did not approach Mao as an inferior. On the contrary, he denounced and ridiculed the Great Leap and the communes, with which Mao claimed to be surpassing Moscow, as left deviations, dangerous fanaticism. In return, Soviet "revisionism" under Khrushchev seemed to Peking an opportunist deviation, a sellout to capitalism. Although Moscow had promised Peking nuclear weapons assistance in 1957, it was subsequently stopped. As relations grew worse, the whole force of Soviet technicians with their blueprints were suddenly withdrawn from China in August 1960. All this provided concrete grievances.

National interests soon came into conflict on the world's longest frontier. The two multi-racial states governed Turkic minorities in Central Asia, and nomadic peoples like the Kazakhs and Kirghiz, who lived on both sides of the border and might support whichever side catered to their interests. In the 1960s a lively fear of Chinese fanaticism and expansion grew up in the Soviet Union, and by 1969 armed border clashes arose both along the Amur in the northeast and in Central Asia.

Viewed historically, the Soviet paramountcy in China's foreign affairs during the 1950s may be compared with earlier decades of foreign influence—for example, of the British after 1860, the Japanese after 1900, or the Americans in the 1940s. Many outside peoples have had their day in aiding the transformation of the Middle Kingdom, but none permanently. All have been cast off.

As the Sino-Soviet split widened, Peking sought to capture the leadership of the Communist world revolution, exporting cultural missions, exhibitions, and militant propaganda, giving aid to new nations and supporting "national liberation movements," especially in Asia and Africa. Mao's policy formulation for this period was stated in a speech of Lin Piao, in September 1965 on "People's Wars of Liberation." Expanding China's experience to the world scene, Lin pictured the Chinese model of revolution applied to the underdeveloped two thirds of mankind against the industrialized imperialist powers. The metaphor was to "surround the cities from the countryside," but its concrete practicality was not assessed. It was not a Hitlerite blueprint for conquest. The advocacy of self-reliance for all people's revolutions meant that China could point the way and offer aid but not itself achieve the world revolution by its own expansion. (One is reminded of the ancient theory of tributary relations: China was a model which other countries should follow but on their own initiative.)

This do-it-yourself prescription for world revolution was issued at a time of setback in Peking's foreign relations. In February 1965, the United States began continuous bombing of North Vietnam; this aggression on China's doorstep was accompanied by promises not to invade North Vietnam on the ground; and Peking suffered the humiliation of impotence, unable to protect a neighboring ally. The effort to organize an Afro-Asian conference excluding the Soviet Union failed in June. And in October, an abortive coup in Indonesia was followed by the slaughter of the pro-Peking Indonesian Communist Party. These and other failures abroad turned China inward.

The Growth of Bureaucratic Evils

Behind the civil strife of the late 1960s were deep strains and stresses. The first was the gap between China's poverty and the expectations of her citizens, newly active in politics. To destroy the old order, the CCP had roused a whirlwind and now had to ride it. Where the Kuomintang had been a small, superficial regime, not active in China's million villages, the CCP had asserted its authority down to the very rice roots. Shortages before, in the old free market economy, had been no one's fault. Now they reflected poor planning.

Having taken on this staggering burden, the CCP had built enormous structures of administration. Once established, local committee secretaries and various administrators of collective units had tended to become increasingly occupied with paper work, less concerned with common labor, closer to being an upper class, a new local elite like the gentry of old. Careerists and familists reappeared, seeking to use the "back door" *(hou men)* to secure connections and privileges, better education for their children, private property. The work point system was corrupted by insiders, bonuses were paid to some and not others, piece work was creeping into the village labor system. Just as the factory proletariat sought special privileges, so farmers wanted larger private plots, free markets, and output quotas based on the family household—family farming again. The revolutionary spirit was evaporating in the countryside.

Among a people still only half literate, whose ancestors for 3000 years had looked up to a ruling class that had special skills and prerogatives of education and status, government was still going to be by an elite. "Liberation" of the common peasant, making him a citizen, had not diminished but greatly intensified the competition for elite status. In place of the million or so gentry degree holders of the imperial era, there were now on the order of a hundred million active members of mass organizations, aware of politics, and many millions of able youth anxious to rise in the world, seeking education, jobs, and official status.

The CCP dilemma, common in developing countries, was that expectations could be created so much faster than they could be realized. The new party-government-army power structure was an elite organization, intensely status- and security-conscious, controlled from the top downward. Once its ranks filled up, the upper incumbents became more cautious and less revolutionary while the lower levels felt boxed in and frustrated.

The axiom that revolutionaries supplant an *ancien régime* only to inherit its evils was evidenced in the wide gap between the cadres and the Chinese public. Within this new cadre ruling class were many gradations—first of all, between the "local cadres" in communes or collectives and the "state cadres" paid by the government, party, or mass organizations. Instead of the eighteen grades of officialdom under the Empire, the People s Republic had twenty-four salary grades in urban areas and twenty-six in rural areas. The top salary was about nine times that of the bottom. Since these ratings carried with them prerogatives and privileges, they constituted a ladder of success and prestige. By the time this system was standardized in 1956 a distinct pecking order had emerged: at the top were cadres from the Long March period of the mid-1930s, then those from the Yenan decade 1936–45. Lower down were the "liberation war cadres" who joined the party after 1945, and the "uprising cadres" who joined at the end of the civil war in 1948–49.

A revolution of youth. *Left:* Chou En-lai about 1924 with his wife, Teng Ying-ch'ao. *Right:* Chou En-lai, Chu Te, Mao Tse-tung, and Liu Shao-Ch'i with delegates of the New Democratic Youth League, Peking, early 1957.

Cadre Life. Of a thousand cadres assigned to a typical Peking ministry studied by A. Doak Barnett, about a third were party members, organized in a complex structure of small groups under branches at all levels of the ministry. The personnel bureau worked closely and secretly with the ministry's party committee. This party structure was responsible for the thought and behavior, loyalty and discipline, of all party members, who were set apart from nonparty members and deeply involved in the "party life" of constant meetings, criticism and self-criticism, reporting on subordinates, and trying to maintain a good record in the secret files of the personnel, control, and supervisory offices. Nonparty members, while less strenuously occupied, were also involved in small study groups that met regularly for political discussion, as well as in mass organizations such as their labor union or women's association or the Young Communist League. Party branches met every Friday evening and might be given classi-

fied materials to study, not to be discussed with nonparty members. Every Saturday afternoon saw compulsory, directed reading and discussion by all party and nonparty personnel in the ministry, in study groups of ten to twenty persons at levels appropriate to their educational background.

To enter the party, one had to submit a long personal history with the endorsement of two party members. The party might secretly appoint a member to get to know the applicant unobtrusively. A worthy applicant might then have to argue for his admission before a special party meeting in order to become a candidate member. A candidate might go through this application procedure two or three times before winning acceptance, not unlike the repeated efforts of scholars to pass the examinations in the old days.

Whether in the party or not, a cadre's personal dossier was almost more important than himself. He never saw it, but he knew that it contained his own statement of his personal history and background, his experience and ideological views, and all his family and other associations. At the end of every year and every campaign, the cadre wrote a personal summary of all his activities and ideas. This was scrutinized and criticized in a group meeting, the group leader added his own assessment together with that of the group, and all this went into the secret dossier. Dubious individuals would be systematically investigated, and in campaigns, of course, a vulnerable individual might become a target. Where the ancient examination system had made for self-indoctrination, the Communist system made for self-intimidation. Even the most able man's career could be torpedoed by his class background; for he could never get rid of a "bourgeois taint."

The ministry was periodically convulsed by campaigns and since these might threaten anyone's career, anxiety gripped the community. Quite aside from the specific evils attacked by a campaign, the eventual selection of certain human targets for systematic denunciation and public humiliation was sufficient to remind all observers that, but for the grace of the party, they too might be pilloried. These unnerving public spectacles strikingly reaffirmed the party's authority. Typically they moved individuals who felt threatened to denounce their pilloried colleagues with unusual vehemence, an activity which could not increase any individual's self-respect.

The privileges of cadres, in addition to their prestige and power vis-à-vis the masses, included a degree of financial security, free medical care, low-rent housing, cheap food, and better schooling for their children. But staying in one place was not among these privileges; and a husband and wife might be transferred to different cities. The worst fate was to be "transferred downward" to the countryside, a program developed in 1957 with multiple aims—to build up local leadership, to educate cadres or punish them through farm labor, or to reduce central government personnel and city populations.

Graham Peck, describing the Chinese public's disenchantment with the Kuomintang in the 1940s, wrote of "that secret smile" he saw among those who passively let the status quo collapse. As a researcher in Hong Kong, Michel Oksenberg analyzed how campaigns, the engines of social change, could lose their efficacy in the 1960s. Cadres learned how to go through the proper forms. In criticism sessions an ambitious activist would speak early but not go beyond the limits set by the leader. A trouble avoider would speak in the middle of the session, offering the minimum expected comments. A friend determined to be a "sympathetic critic" of the person under fire would probably speak toward the end of the session and mix in some favorable comments. But cadres learned to avoid close friendships lest they involve subsequent denunciations in intimate detail. In addition to coping with small-group criticism, an activist learned how to ride out campaigns, feigning a progressive enthusiasm in the mobilization phase, anticipating the campaign's next stage, and becoming properly prudent and self-critical in the consolidation phase. The party establishment, in short, had learned how to protect itself against Mao's methods of "permanent revolution," and was thereby losing its capacity really to mobilize the people.

Mao Revives the Revolution: The Socialist Education Movement

With economic recovery evident in 1962, Mao and the Central Committee in September reasserted the primacy of class struggle, even within the party. In the next two years they inaugurated comprehensive programs along many lines, under the name of the Socialist Education Movement. On the whole this movement failed to secure the hoped-for responses from various sectors of the people, but it laid out basic aims and methods that later became the stuff of the Cultural Revolution.

The Cult of Mao. This cult centered on the thought of Mao Tse-tung expressed in a few of his more homiletic writings ("Serve the People"; "In Memory of Norman Bethune," the Canadian surgeon who sacrificed himself for the Eighth Route Army; and "The Foolish Old Man Who Moved the Mountain," who did it by persistence, he and his descendants).

Imitation of the army. "Learn from the PLA" in total dedication, ideological purity, personal unselfishness, and similar traits. The army was to tutor the masses.

Manual labor. Cadres, teachers, students, white collar workers, and the whole party must learn to join the peasant masses in manual work, forever ending the gulf between brain and muscle power.

Education for all. It should be simplified: reduce book learning and combine it with productive work and practical skills.

Revival of collectivism. The poor and middle peasants should be mobilized to regenerate the collectivist spirit: "In agriculture learn from Tachai," a Shansi brigade of exemplary austerity and self-reliance.

A proletarian culture. In the arts and academia a new political didacticism began to supplant the old culture, hitherto rather little changed by the revolution.

These and similar themes of 1963–65 turned out to be blueprints for a second great revolution. But they had to get their striking power from the organized faith and fanaticism of a millenarian Second Coming pictured as class struggle against "bourgeois revisionism" within the establishment as well as among the masses. The charisma of Mao Tse-tung and his inner vision were the essential catalyst for this great effort. The evils that he sought to overcome were not the product of social relationships and objective conditions, but rather a taint in the human personality. As Benjamin Schwartz put it, " 'bourgeoisie' and 'proletariat' have been transmuted in the Maoist universe into something like two pervasive fluids, one noxious and the other beneficial, which can find their lodgments anywhere. The source of the proletarian truth resides in no group or even organization but in the thought of Mao Tse-tung."

The thirty years of Mao's leadership after 1935 had seen success on a scale to warp even the finest judgment. To be at the top in Chinese politics, where tenure is unlimited, commonly gives the power holder a self-image of identity with "China," which the monolithic power structure in fact demands. We can imagine that a hundred Sons of Heaven whispered somewhere behind Mao's back, and the repeated success of his style of militant struggle made it a habit. In short, his unassailable position confirmed the correctness of his ideas and impulses. The personal dominance of Mao Tse-tung was steadily built up by the needs of the movement he headed and he took the lead in formulating and balancing the party's policy alternatives—for example, in the Ten Great Relationships between heavy and light industry, coastal and inland development, growth and defense, center and regions, and so on. Yet within the spectrum of alternatives he was repeatedly the protagonist of the all-out left line as against the prudential counsels of party managers and economic developers—a titanic utopian in their midst.

The issue of what Mao called revisionism arose from the fact that too many party members had lost faith in Mao's romantic, Heaven-storming approach to China's problems. Experienced party bureaucrats like Liu Shao-ch'i and the secretary general, Teng Hsiao-p'ing, opposed the Maoists' fanaticism, zealotry, and purism because they would only hinder economic recovery. Wrestling with practical problems, the bureaucrats dragged their feet in the Socialist Education movement. Richard Baum has pointed out the contrasts between it and the subsequent Cultural Revolution—contrasts between the use of elite work teams under party control as against mass organizations under their own steam, between a reform-from-above targeted on local cadres as against a revolution-from-below aimed at top party leaders. In short, Mao by 1965 was ready to accuse his closest colleagues of a "conspiracy" aiming at a "capitalist restoration." Disillusioned with the party, he had already turned to the army.

Repoliticizing the Army. The military equivalent of government and party bureaucratism had appeared in the Soviet-type professional officer corps, established in February 1955. Ranks and uniforms, differential pay, the many regulations and new military academies, all diminished comradely relations between officers and men. Persuasion gave way to punishment. The professional officers challenged the political commissar system and attacked "politics in command." Against the PLA tradition of dual command they favored the Soviet principle of unity of command. As a result party committees in the armed forces declined until by 1960 one third of all companies had no party committee. Party membership also declined.

But after Defense Minister P'eng Te-huai was ousted in September 1959, for criticizing the Great Leap and having had contact with the Soviets, he was succeeded by General Lin Piao, who now worked closely with Mao. A quarter of a million new party members were recruited into the armed forces in short order, and company party committees were re-established. New military manuals and regulations were issued to combat the indiscriminate borrowing of foreign, that is, Soviet methods. The army problem of "red versus expert" was met by reimposing the more pervasive political apparatus which had been diluted by the Soviet model. Within the army a separate echelon of party members now had its own organization at successive levels down to the company and the squad, and its members were in positions of leadership. Indoctrination and surveillance were both part of this institutional structure. For example, an army squad of nine was typically divided into three teams of three each. The three men in such a team were responsible for each other, and the leader was probably connected with the party. They were to watch each other both in combat and out. Indoctrination gave an authoritative interpretation of events. All these measures maintained troop morale. There was little stress on rank and less corporal punishment or abuse. The political officers in the army, down to the company level, kept this system functioning and prevented the formation of groups of like-minded dissidents. Criticism and self-criticism were part of a system to repress undesirable thoughts as well as deviant behavior. The army was thoroughly indoctrinated, so well that by 1964 it was possible to launch a nationwide emulation campaign to "learn from the experience of the PLA in political and ideological work." Meanwhile the economic administration was increasingly staffed with political and military personnel borrowed from the PLA.

By May 1965 it was possible again to abolish military ranks, with no distinction in mode of dress, uniform, or insignia. Meanwhile from among the six million youths reaching the age of eighteen every year, some 750,000 were being inducted into the army. The doctrine of man's superiority over weapons was revived, and P'eng Te-huai was attacked in retrospect for his bourgeois thinking. Thus the PLA in the fall of 1965 provided the base of strength from which Mao was able to move toward his Great Revolution for a Proletarian Culture. In doing so he even used the PLA newspaper as his organ.

The Cultural Revolution

The cultural revolution was a supercampaign that ran roughly from May 1966 to April 1969. But it was more a happening than a controlled program. As Mao moved against outspoken critics in the fall of 1965, he evidently found more party support for them than he had foreseen. As with the "hundred flowers" criticisms of 1957, opposition proved surprisingly widespread, but this time it was within the party. Mao responded with a vast new effort to mobilize support from outside the party. The public scene was soon filled with mass meetings, parades, and propaganda displays exalting Mao as "the red sun in our hearts." Tremendous excitement, even hysteria, among millions of youth led to exhaustion, apathy, and further surges of effort. Out of it all came a purge of the party by the leader. But where Stalin had purged the CPSU from within, secretly and using the party apparatus, Mao purged the CCP from without, publicly and using mass organizations, such as the Red Guard youth. Where Stalin used his secret police and killed millions of people, Mao relied on the PLA and used methods of public humiliation. Violence erupted chiefly as civil strife in competitions for local power.

Mao's campaign, like a guerrilla operation, followed a rhythm of attack and pause, destruction and consolidation. His first move was to assure his control of the mass media at the center by attacking cultural and educational commissars and the Peking Party Committee. His eventual targets, Liu Shao-ch'i, the chief of state, and Teng Hsiao-p'ing, the secretary general of the party, cooperated in this phase by sending out campaign teams, which Mao later accused of impeding his efforts. In August 1966 he gained ground by packing the membership of the Eleventh Plenum of the Central Committee. He had already gone outside the party apparatus to field groups of teenagers as Red Guards, calling upon them to "sweep aside all monsters" and in a big-character poster in his own hand to "bombard the headquarters." They were to "learn revolution by making revolution." Also outside party channels, he had set up a nationwide Cultural Revolution organization headed by a special committee that included his wife. In the fall of 1966 with logistic support from the PLA, some thirteen million Red Guards came to Peking for a succession of nine mass rallies and then dispersed over the country to carry out their own "Long Marches" and to attack the "four olds" (old ideology, thought, habits, and customs). These were found first among the educated upper class, who were also attacked for possessing foreign books or clothing or even foreign-style haircuts. An urban reign of terror ensued. Homes and offices were invaded. Victims were harassed, beaten, and sometimes killed. Many committed suicide.

In January 1967, Mao escalated the revolution still further to attack the party structure itself, inciting the "revolutionary masses" to seize power from below as in the Paris Commune of 1870. Though Chou En-lai and other moderates had succeeded at first in keeping the Red Guards out of the factories and the countryside below the county level, the Cultural Revolution in its final phase was spread among workers in industry and also into rural districts. Its agents were young and zealous, often mere boys and girls, equipped with the little red booklet *Quotations from Chairman Mao Tse-tung*. The cult of Mao dominated the media and grew to the point of mass hysteria among youthful demonstrators.

Working with only a minority faction of the CCP but from his unassailable position as the "Great Helmsman" backed by the PLA, Mao thus precipitated an unprecedented degree of struggle, indeed a sort of urban guerrilla warfare, first of dissident groups against individuals in power who were "taking the capitalist road" and second between groups. Party power holders were attacked piecemeal and had no way to organize among themselves. As in all campaigns, there was a call for local initiative and a great build-up of ad hoc organizations and their membership. The process of struggle was by no means controlled or predetermined except as the Maoists could excite it, damp it down, or redirect it. The party establishment was thoroughly shaken up, if not shattered, but the results outside it were mixed. Many industrial workers and farmers resented the intrusion of student youth and opposed their radical aims. Increasingly, the PLA had to be called upon to intervene in support of the revolutionaries.

To take the place of the old structure of authority, Mao eventually called for "revolutionary committees" at all the levels of government to consist of a "three-way alliance" of, first, representatives of the Red Guards and "revolutionary rebels" (that is, mature workers and cadres), who were now all together called "revolutionary masses," and who would be new blood; second, representatives of the People's Liberation Army; and third, party cadres who had been adequately revolutionized. But the party establishment fought back bitterly in one place after another by fielding their own Red Guards and executing what Mao denounced as "false power seizures," proclaiming their loyalty to him but defeating his forces and keeping their own grip on power. These defensive actions and the rebels' seizure of arms soon produced pitched battles between armed groups. But even after major officials had been denounced and jailed, fighting continued between the more radical and more conservative groupings of organizations. The CCP as such ceased to function. After a new phase of violent attacks by the "revolutionary masses" in the summer of 1967, civil strife had reached a point where the army had to be called in more and more to restore order. Meanwhile, Mao and Lin reorganized nearly half the local military commands and held training classes for senior officers.

By January 1968 revolutionary committees had been set up in all the twenty-nine provinces and major cities, but an effective core of party members, skilled in administration, had not been built up within them. It was easier to bring together army officers and zealous newcomers than it was to create effective administrations. By the summer of 1968, renewed attacks on senior personnel led to further violence and still more authority being given to the PLA. The attack on the party had given civil power to the army.

In the midst of all this frenzied turmoil, the universities and schools had remained closed while intellectuals and experts were being attacked and students revolutionized in factional fighting. Rebellious protest through armed factionalism had come in large part from graduates dissatisfied with the jobs, particularly in the countryside, to which they had been assigned; and from discharged soldiers and casual workers who lacked the skills to support themselves adequately. Their job opportunities had fallen behind their hopes. But the "political revivalism" of the Cultural Revolution, to use Ezra Vogel's phrase, could not solve the basic problems of economic and political growth. In the fall of 1968, millions of student youth including erstwhile Red Guards were sent down to communes. With them went many urban cadres, as the opportunity was seized to reduce the government bureaucracy and drive unemployed city dwellers out to the countryside.

In October 1968 Mao again packed the Twelfth Plenum of the Central Committee, and "China's Khrushchev," Liu Shao-ch'i, was finally read out of the party. The Ninth Party Congress met eight years late in April 1969. It was prepared for in many meetings throughout the provinces, while proposed membership lists were screened at the center. The 1500 selected delegates elected a new Central Committee, whereupon this new committee itself elected the Politburo and its standing committee of five, among whom Chou En-lai, still premier, was the only nonzealot. The new party constitution named Lin Piao to be Mao's successor, while the new Central Committee of 279 full and alternate members had a preponderance of military personnel, and only 53 members left over from the previous committee. In effect, Mao had eliminated all his opponents, many of the old guard. In their place the Cultural Revolution had transferred power to the military as the one portion of the party structure who had their own basis of loyalty.

The Aftermath. The Cultural Revolution produced factionalism, a hatred of group against group, that shattered party unity from top to bottom. This splintering of loyalties within the organization fostered radical extremism and indeed left a group of doctrinal zealots including Mao's wife, Chiang Ch'ing, in control of the arts, the media, and education. In order to ensure China's proletarian future, they tried to restrict higher education to young people of worker-peasant background, nominated by their work units and approved by the party, who had had two years practical experience after middle school. Universities found them often inadequately prepared. Meanwhile Chiang Ch'ing and her colleagues tried to produce a new "proletarian" culture for the Chinese people, but the eight authorized dramas and other products of their efforts suffered from sterility. Based partly on Shanghai and on younger elements active since 1965, the radicals continued Mao's moral crusade against self-seeking materialism in order to "serve the people" with true socialist dedication. Its witch-hunting approach was evident in the slogan "the bourgeoisie are within the Communist party." The more pragmatic wing, composed of the great majority of administrators in office, remained concerned about material incentives to inspire economic production and technical skills to aid China's material progress. For a time in Chairman Mao's last years "radicals" dominated the media while "pragmatists" ran the administration.

After 1969 major efforts went into rebuilding the party and reviving production. Most cadres targeted in the Cultural Revolution were rehabilitated. But Lin Piao, minister of national defense and number two in the hierarchy, long touted as Mao's "closest comrade-in-arms" and designated successor, not only headed a powerful military faction but evidently remained committed to the radicalism of the Cultural Revolution, after Mao seems to have moved tactically beyond it. Lin soon found himself opposed by a Mao-Chou combination, isolated and on the way out. On September 13, 1971, he was killed in a plane crash in the Mongolian People's Republic. Almost two years later it was officially explained to China and the world that Lin Piao had plotted to kill Mao, been discovered, and died in flight.

After the fall of Lin Piao the role of the military in government was reduced and the party reconstructed. The Tenth Party Congress met in August 1973 with 1200 or more delegates representing 28 million party members. It was held in secret and lasted only four days. Younger faces that had appeared in the leadership to represent the protagonists of the Cultural Revolution were balanced by the reappearance of party veterans. The new Central Committee was more broadly based. In 1973–74 a study campaign was mounted to "criticize Lin Piao and Confucius" in order to expose their reactionary views, despite the 2500 years that separated them historically. In January 1975 the Fourth National People's Congress convened in Peking briefly with 2800 delegates to adopt a new state constitution which put the government more explicitly under the CCP as a proletarian dictatorship.

Chou En-lai in Peking 1973.

The congress strove to symbolize the resoration of party unity in preparation for the change of leadership, for both Chou En-lai as prime minister and Mao Tse-tung as party chairman were by this time seriously ill.

After seven years in obscurity, the one-time secretary general of the party, Teng Hsiao-p'ing, who had been denounced as the number two "capitalist-roader" and target of the Cultural Revolution, was rehabilitated in 1973 and soon restored to power. He evidently helped diminish the military role in government. By 1975 he was a party vice-chairman and a member of the politburo, as well as army chief of staff and senior vice-premier of government. When Chou En-lai died on January 8, 1976, Teng was acting premier—a blunt little man intent on getting results. But Mao outlived Chou, and in April the enormous outpouring of popular bereavement at Chou En-lai's death, expressed in a great pile of wreaths and eulogies in the T'ien-an men square, was forcefully suppressed while the Politburo dismissed Teng from all his posts and made the relatively unknown Hua Kuo-feng acting premier. Following the terribly destructive Tangshan earthquake of August 1976, Mao Tse-tung died on September 9. Hua was soon made party chairman in his place, and almost immediately the four Cultural Revolution protagonists at the top of the Central Committee, including Mao's widow, Chiang Ch'ing, were arrested and out of power. Their control over the media, the Peking radio and the *People's Daily* came to an end, and they were systematically denounced as anti-party renegades, while Teng Hsiao-p'ing reappeared in power at the top.

Subsequently this "Gang of Four" were denounced for having stressed ideological purity over production, sabotaged industry, and fomented anti-examination, anti-teacher, and anti-intellectual attitudes in education. But when leaders spoke privately of "ten lost years" they implied that Chairman Mao in his last decade had given way to a sectarian fanaticism that smacked of folk religion more than modern development. The upheaval of the late 1960s was in the cities and in the establishment more than in the countryside, but the anti-intellectual fanaticism of the millions who marched for Mao and denounced his enemies reminds one of a peasant movement, descended from the long tradition of China's millenarian folk sects even though Marxified in terminology, in short, a popular cult of Mao for the salvation of the Chinese people. It stood for Mao Tse-tung's continuing moral revolution to liberate the common people and change their motivation, to combat the ancient evils of bourgeois selfishness, bureaucratism, and special privilege, and to give opportunity especially to the frustrated younger generations of party activists. This was the cause of social revolution. If suppressed, it could lie dormant, ready to rise again.

Against it stood the competing practical demands of modern development, stated in terms more easily intelligible to outsiders—how to keep food supply ahead of population growth, how best to use China's newly discovered and very extensive oil reserves such as those on the Hopei-Shantung coast and offshore, how to balance the desires for self-sufficiency and for foreign technology and capital, and a host of similar problems. Behind them all lay the question of how to reconcile the patriotic desire to make China a great power with the Maoist drive to serve the people. Policy makers faced a constant choice between investing in the power of the state and investing in the welfare of the Chinese masses.

The Eleventh Party Congress of August 1977, representing 35 million party members, and the Fifth National People's Congress of March 1978 finally confirmed the revival of party control and the primacy of economic growth. Revolutionary committees, though retained in the countryside, were replaced in universities and factories by single presidents and plant managers. Competitive examinations were again the criteria for college entrance. Scholars and specialists felt a great sense of relief as the regime committed itself to science and technology. Artists and writers came back from the countryside, the traditional Peking opera was revived, new archaeological finds amazed the world, and cultural life entered a new course. Without any explicit de-Maoification, the Cultural Revolution was declared at an end. The united front was revived at least in form by stressing the representational role of the Chinese People's Political Consultative Conference. China turned outward again.

Mao Tse-tung's Monument. The death of Chou En-lai and

The archaeological revolution. Terracotta warrior being excavated in 1976 from ːear tomb of First Emperor of the Ch'in (d. 210 B.C.), part of an army of ːnprecedented life-size figures.

Mao Tse -tung in 1976 marked the passing of the revolutionary generation that had turned to Marxism-Leninism as the salvation of China fifty-five years before. The achievements of the movement they led are still largely beyond present-day capacity to appraise: for example, the people of China have doubled in numbers and become a nation; they have created enormous new structures of government and industry. China has undergone tremendous ups and downs. During the active lifetime of this generation, the Nationalist revolution to unify China against foreign imperialism (1923–28), the efforts of the Nanking government in modernization (1928–37), and the destructiveness of Japan's invasion (1937–45), all set the stage for the Communists' build-up of a new order at Yenan (1936–46), their victory in civil war (1947–49), and the subsequent remaking of China under the People's Republic. Mao and Chou from 1949 to 1976 were successors to the traditional Son of Heaven and his chief minister at the top of state and society. (Chou En-lai held the world record of 48 years continuous service on his party's politburo.) But they functioned as revolutionaries intent on social change. Their achievement was that of a whole people, prepared by long years of disaster to mobilize their collective energies in a great national regeneration.

For those who traveled through Chinese provinces before 1949 it is only necessary to go into the countryside today: the achievements of the great revolution strike one on every side—a people renewed, a land remade. Granted that travelers today see untypical examples like the Tachai Brigade or the Red Flag Canal, the fact remains that these are live models for all China to emulate in spirit if not in detail. The evidence of regeneration is countrywide and overwhelming. Public health and medical services are brought to the village by a million or more paramedic "barefoot doctors," aided by Chinese innovations like acupuncture anaesthesia and abortion by suction. Primary schooling is widely available along with practical technology.

Rural mechanization got its first great impetus during the Great Leap Forward of 1958–59 and again during the Cultural Revolution in 1968–69. Labor-intensive programs for land reclamation, leveling of fields, soil improvement, water-capture, -storage, and -control, interplanting and multi-cropping had paved the way. Mechanization had begun with electric pumps to move water (two fifths of the arable land was said to be irrigated in 1973). Today this small-scale industrialization of the countryside is on a do-it-yourself basis. China's heavy industry in major centers like Shanghai, Wuhan, or Tientsin seeks the large-scale economies so beloved of classical economists whether Western or Soviet. But the million villages are still generally beyond the reach of easy transport by road, rail, or water and lack marketing networks and purchasing power adequate for an American-style distribution system. Instead, their production of foodstuffs, clothing, agricultural machinery, cement, bricks, fertilizer, steel, and hydropower meets local needs in a dual economy. It uses the manpower and natural resources—coal, limestone, iron ore, water, grains, fibers—on the site where they are. Long-distance transport is not needed. Outside financing is avoided. Central direction is minimal. The benefits are enormous: the rural small-scale industries can respond flexibly to local needs. They achieve full employment by using slack time and female labor, which can also be available for harvesting. They spread technological skills among the people and thereby facilitate local repair and maintenance. They reduce the intellectual-social gap between city and countryside and create a degree of self-sufficiency and self-reliance that, when combined with the enormous people's militia organization, helps both the national defense and the chances of democratic self-government.

These ideals, which inspired the pioneer Industrial Co-operative (Indusco) movement during World War II, can be very practically pursued. For instance, agricultural mechanization usually begins with equipment for rice milling, grain threshing, and cotton spinning because such machines are so much more efficient that they free manpower to produce more raw materials to be processed. The rural flour and cloth so produced may be coarse but they are adequate and far more abundant. Urban factory products are kept out by their high transport costs and by "administrative tariff barriers": as the Rural Small-Scale Industry Delegation of American specialists led by Dwight Perkins reported for 1975, prices are "set to give relatively large profits to inefficient producers of low technology goods." In short, rural industry is helped to get started at levels reminiscent of earlier generations in the industrialized West or Japan, but it grows fast and its standards rise.

Watching skilled workers make molds in a Honan iron foundry, one remembers that cast iron was in fact invented in this region in ancient times, many centuries before it was known in Europe. The capacity to make machinery, already so widespread in rural China, has implications for the future. For example, the light, two-wheeled diesel tractor seen on so many Chinese roads was designed so that its five horsepower could be used for pumping water or threshing grain or tilling fields or hauling vehicles. By 1973 half a million of these multi-purpose machines were being assembled in several score centers supplied from local networks of parts producers. Modifications were made regionally to meet local conditions, the one major requirement being that every locality involved should have a workshop repair and maintenance capacity. This kind of growth can rapidly build up. In 1975 the delegation above quoted heard of 2800 cement plants, 1100 nitrogenous fertilizer plants, 50,000 hydropower installations. This rural industrialization bears the stamp of Chairman Mao, as opposed to his more conventional-minded opponents. Tarnished or not, his monument is in the countryside.

Chapter 17

Perspectives:
China and Ourselves

The first century of contact between America and China had great significance for both peoples. But it ended in the final dissolution of the old order—both of traditional Chinese civilization and of the unequal treaty system which had ushered it into contact with the modern world. Our traditional China policy and the attitudes which underlay it were bankrupted and in fact reversed by the rise of the People's Republic.

Where before 1949 we had supported the Open Door for trade, for twenty years thereafter we embargoed American relations with the mainland. Where we had formerly defended China's administrative and territorial integrity, after 1949 we impaired it by our steadfast support of Taiwan in a continuing state of civil war. Only one thing was not reversed: we were still uninvited intruders in the Chinese scene, though now on the periphery. As Robert Oxnam says, our relations had been "grossly asymmetrical."

To say that this record of unbalanced relations between the Chinese and American peoples was all our fault would be as purblind as to say it was all their fault. It is time for us to get beyond making righteous moral judgments and seek at all costs a realistic perspective, for now all peoples are in trouble together.

Yet the first step toward a realistic perspective is surely to recognize that it was the West that invaded China, not China the West; and the chief lesson the Chinese learned from the Western invasion (as from all earlier invasions of China) was that China had to become strong in self-defense, which today implies nationalism, a mobilized populace.

In short, if we acknowledge that the West brought modern ways to China, we must accept the great Chinese revolution of the twentieth century as something we helped to start. In the end the Chinese Communist Party undertook to carry out in fact a whole host of changes that foreign administrators and missionaries, as well as patriotic reformers and revolutionaries, had advocated and attempted with increasing vigor for a century past.

Unfortunately for us, a proud people when weak do not enjoy receiving help. The American attitude toward China during the century of the unequal treaties was consciously acquisitive but also benevolent, seeking to give as well as get. We were proud of our record, indeed a bit patronizing toward the imperialist powers of lesser virtue. At the same time many Americans, like other Westerners, fell in love with their upper-class experience of Chinese culture, its aesthetic subtleties, its warmth of personal friendships. It became *their* China with the possessiveness so well exemplified by writers from Florence Ayscough to Simon Leys.

Inevitably, however, the Chinese experience of Sino-American relations was different from the American experience. We found our contact with China adventurous, exhilarating, rewarding in material or spiritual terms. Americans who did not like it could avoid it. China, on the other hand, found this contact forced upon her. It was a foreign invasion, humiliating, disruptive, and in the end catastrophic. The Western menace to the traditional Chinese way of life often seemed in the nineteenth century every bit as dire, evil, and ominous as the totalitarian Nazi and Stalinist threats to the American way in the 1940s. The Chinese, behind their polite exterior, did not fully share our national enthusiasm for Sino-American friendship.

Out of the mix of past Sino-American relations, Chinese today can stress American imperialism where we see mainly our philanthropy, exploitation where we see American aid to the Chinese people; and of course both views will be true and documentable as far as they go. But a conscientious observer, even an unconscionable realist, cannot rest content with the view of one side alone. In order to survive together in mankind's uncertain future, Americans and Chinese will have to find some common ground in their understanding of their common history, as to how they dealt with each other in times past.

As we continue to construct our image of Sino-American relations, we can be sure of one thing: our thinking will tend to favor our side. This will be so even if, with moral feelings of guilt, we righteously denounce our past sins. I mean that to decry the evil influence of American imperialism on China may still be a very American thing to do; for example, it may self-importantly exaggerate the extent of the American influence on China. For as we abandon the American nostalgia for that treaty port China that is no more, we must increasingly recognize the extreme self-sufficiency of Chinese life and our own incapacity to change it.

Our China Policy and the Wars in Korea and Vietnam

On December 7, 1941, the Japanese hit us at Pearl Harbor because we would not acquiesce in their attempted conquest of China and the rest of East Asia. After Japan's defeat in 1945 we refused to recognize the Chinese Communists' victory in the Chinese civil war. In June 1950 under United

China and Ourselves

Nations auspices we defended South Korea against North Korea's invasion. Each time we felt ourselves the champions of freedom against tyranny.

However, the war in Korea became a Chinese-American war and ended in a stalemate. After the Korean armistice of 1953, which is still in force, we allied with Taiwan in 1954 and supported France in Indochina. From 1960 we gave increasing aid to South Vietnam and from 1965 intervened against North Vietnam with half a million troops, the last of which were withdrawn in another stalemate in 1973. We had been at war in East Asia half the time since 1941. Was all this fighting on the other side of the Pacific simply a support of freedom against tyranny? Or were its causes not so simple?

Viewed historically, the American intervention in Vietnam in the 1960s was an incident of gunboat diplomacy writ large: from outside we hoped by superior firepower to shape the domestic polity of an Asian people.

North Vietnam was part of the Chinese empire before Julius Caesar conquered Gaul. A country as old as France, it won its independence of Chinese rule a thousand years ago. But, as with Korea, its culture and institutions remained a variant of the Chinese model, using Chinese characters, the Confucian classics and family system, and the Chinese forms of bureaucratic government. Vietnam was known to the West by its Chinese name, Annam ("the pacified south"), but it was absorbed by force into French Indochina by the 1880s and neither American merchants nor missionaries had much contact with it. Vietnam was historically part of the Chinese culture area, and modern Vietnamese patriots followed the Chinese example in both their reform efforts, dating from the 1890s, and their revolutionary efforts from the 1920s. But the United States regarded Vietnam as part of France. After World War II, during which the French had surrendered to Japan in Indochina, we supported their effort to make Vietnam a colony again. It failed in 1954. The American public knew little more of the area than its name, but we then became gradually involved in a power politics intervention to save South Vietnam from communism by using our superior resources and firepower.

Since no informed American can think of Vietnam without shame, it is essential that we try to understand the mainsprings of our intervention there. It is not enough to assert the platitudes of original sin (that great powers still have a propensity to use their arms) or imperialism (that the United States, thanks to modern technology, is the most expansive power of all time). We are still far from a specific understanding of our conduct in Vietnam; but it is indubitably linked to our earlier experience in East Asia and especially in China.

In the background, first of all, is our aversion to the domination of East Asia by a hostile power, whether the militarist Japan of the 1940s or the assumed international Communist monolith of the Cold War era. This sentiment echoes the aversion felt by Britain, as a maritime trading power, to the continental expansion of the Russian colossus in the nineteenth century.

Unfortunately our experience in East Asia to 1940 had been long on rhetoric and short on political experience. We sent our black ships to Japan with Perry in 1853–54 and to Korea in 1871, but never fought a war. Others successfully applied pressure upon rulers—for instance, those of China, Japan, Vietnam, Siam, and Burma—in the mid-nineteenth century. But we Americans did not go in for power politics.

Only in 1941 did we really enter upon the few decades of our strategic hegemony in the Western Pacific and face the hard choices of how to use our power. But after World War II, we decided very wisely not to intervene with troops in the KMT-CCP civil war. Yet our interests suffered from its outcome. Where China had formerly seemed condemned by fate to a quaint if sometimes exasperating backwardness in all things economic, political, and social, we now faced a strong People's Republic in a developing country. Nationalism, though long retarded, had achieved maturity. Our thinking, in conservative America, could not keep pace with China's revolution. The first reaction of many Americans, suddenly confronted by a China strong, chauvinist, and anti-Western (instead of weak and pro-American) was to seize upon international communism as the explanation and attribute our reverse to Kremlin plots and State Department treachery.

The Chinese Communist rise to power in 1949 called into question our own view of ourselves and our place in the world process. Insofar as the missionary conversion and general uplift of the Chinese people had expressed our conviction that we led the march of human progress, our self-confidence was dealt a grievous blow. One fourth of mankind in China spurned not only Christianity but also the supremacy of law, the ideals of individualism, the multi-party election process, civil liberties, indeed, our entire political order and its concepts of freedom and security through due process. We felt our basic values directly menaced. *If* the Chinese people willingly chose communism, it could be concluded that a majority of mankind was not going our way—at least, not for the present.

One consolation in this crisis, therefore, was to think that the new Chinese Communist dictatorship did not represent the interests of a large enough proportion of the Chinese people, that it maintained itself only by force and manipulation, that, in fine, it was too evil to last, and in any case must be opposed as a matter of principle and duty. This ideological stance of the Cold War seemed thoroughly justified by the bitter European experience under totalitarianism.

We therefore set ourselves at least to "contain" the expansion of the Sino-Soviet monolith outside its borders, and this we did in the Korean War, in our alliance with Taiwan, and by supporting the French in Indochina until 1954 and South Vietnam after that date.

Yet a policy of containment could not be the same in East Asia as in Europe. There, containment as a policy to check the Soviet Union could stress the industrial recovery and political health of the Western European democracies that joined us in the NATO military alliance. In East Asia too we fostered industrial recovery in Japan and development in South Korea and Taiwan, but the military power had to be supplied more purely from the United States and, as it turned out, it had to be used in actual warfare, as in South Korea.

Future research should show that we intervened in Vietnam in the 1960s partly because we had *not* intervened in China in the late 1940s but *had* intervened in Korea in 1950. The "loss" of China had been used against the Democratic administration in American politics, whereas the Korean War had been accepted as an unavoidable defense of collective security and occupied Japan.

Our intervention in the 1960s to support South Vietnam was cast in the same moral framework as in Korea—to repel aggression and support self-determination. However, the circumstances proved to be different: the north had a firmer claim to embody the people's nationalism; our technologically advanced firepower proved immensely destructive, but the more things and people we destroyed materially, the more we inspired patriotic resistance. We discovered, moreover, that communism was not really monolithic, that Vietnamese national interests differed from Chinese national interests, as well as Chinese from Soviet. We had intervened in still another civil war, against another national revolution, not the Chinese revolution, much less a movement led from Moscow.

Curiously, the Chinese People's Republic under Mao Tse-tung's leadership had not proved to be very expansive. It withdrew its forces from Korea, put up with the Chinese Nationalist "front" on Quemoy, fought with Indian forces in 1962 only to assert boundary claims, and did not intervene against us in Vietnam.

What were we to conclude from all this?—that our "containment" of China had successfully prevented its expansion? or that the Chinese revolution was destined to expand, as Mao claimed, only by example (and in fact only in parts of the Chinese culture area)? Is it possible that we did not really understand what we were dealing with?

This, I think, will be the verdict. Historians like Michael Hunt and Alexander Woodside among others have shown the ignorance and ineptitude of our policy thinking over the years. To coexist now and survive, we have to seek a new understanding both of Asian realities and of our own aggressiveness.

New Perspectives of the 1970s

President Nixon's trip to Peking in February 1972 was a dramatic turn away from Cold War confrontation onto the long road of Sino-American understanding. The Nixon-Mao handshake had been due ever since the open Sino-Soviet split of 1960, for great power triangles naturally tend to become equilateral. Each party must deal with the other two if only to prevent their combining. Peking and Washington, each a rival of Moscow, could not afford to remain estranged, letting the Soviets enjoy the inside or middle position of greater contact, knowledge, and room to maneuver. Yet it took the Americans and Chinese twelve years to get together. This length of time was a tribute to the fact that only Richard Nixon could safely reverse the anti-Communist stance on which his political career had so largely been based.

Sino-American rapprochement had been made possible by the exhaustion of two major efforts: the American war effort in Vietnam and Mao's revolution to establish a proletarian culture in China. In Washington after 1968, the Nixon administration's gradual withdrawal of troops from Vietnam was accompanied by an effort to normalize relations with China. In Peking meanwhile, the decline of the Cultural Revolution in 1969 was followed by a domestic normalization evidenced in the gradual reappearance of many intellectuals and bureaucrats, chastened or subdued perhaps by farm work in May 7 cadre schools but nevertheless back in the establishment. The fall from power of Lin Piao and other generals in September 1971, thinning out the top leadership, marked a general decline in the prominence of the military. Thus, as the United States tried to pull back militarily from the Asian continent, China turned outward again in more normal diplomatic activity. After two decades of hostility they now felt they had more problems in common than there were dividing them.

Having decided to seek the normalization of Chinese-American relations, the Nixon administration early in 1969 began a series of unilateral steps to relax the bans on American contact and trade with China. Each of these small moves, like using "Peking" instead of "Peiping," served as a signal. Parallel to these public and symbolic acts, Nixon conveyed secretly through third parties his desire for contact. After two years of silence, Peking responded in April 1971 by inviting the American table tennis team, then competing in Tokyo, to visit China and inaugurate "people's diplomacy." This was followed by Henry Kissinger's secret trip to Peking in July as the President's emissary and the surprise announcement of the projected Nixon visit. In October 1971 this trend eventuated in the admission of the People's Republic to the United Nations and the expulsion of the Nationalist Republic of China.

Resumption of a limited Washington-Peking contact after two decades of enmity unfroze the thinking of cold warriors, but the Peking summit, though it ushered in a new era and raised new hopes, also revived old problems that had lain dormant. One problem was how to stabilize the swings of American opinion and avoid the excesses of sentimental image-making. The American President used his foreign journeys to dominate the media in an election year, while the same media brought Chou En-lai before an interested American television public. One was reminded how in the late 1930s Chiang Kai-shek appeared on American magazine covers and in 1942 Madame Chiang addressed both houses of Congress, symbolizing China's heroic resistance to Japan's aggression; yet in the very next year disillusionment began to tarnish the overblown American image of Free China's nobility. Similarly the Nixon-Chou Shanghai communique in February 1972 envisaged normal relations, and in 1973 liaison offices at the ambassadorial level opened in Peking and Washington. Yet as trade and exchanges of delegations (mainly in technology and sports) began to flow both ways, the initial American wonder at the new China began to fade, while chagrin grew in Peking at the slowness of the American pursuit of normalization. This was due to several factors, beginning with the Watergate and succession problems in Washington and the succession struggle under way in Peking.

Most obvious was the problem of Taiwan, which had figured for so long in American party politics. The ambivalence of Taiwan's situation sprang from the fact that the people of Taiwan were ethnically and culturally Chinese, while the island's economic activity connected it indubitably with the international trading world in which Japan and the United States bulked so large. Taiwan's export economy, helped by its early development as a Japanese colony and later by American aid and Nationalist enterprise, had produced a foreign trade larger than that of the entire mainland. Although voted out of the United Nations in October 1971, the Republic of China on Taiwan seemed likely to continue for a long time to maintain active trading relations abroad and a strong military establishment at home. Chiang Kai-shek had remained adamantly opposed to any idea of independence of Taiwan from the mainland, but he had nevertheless created the fact of a separate government in a separate area. After Chiang died in 1975, his son and successor, Chiang Ching-kuo, could hardly reverse his father's course.

In thinking about Taiwan, we Americans can assert no single principle that overrides all others. First, self-determination depends on the size of the political unit to be self-determined. Peking, (like the Union side in the American Civil War) says the unit is the whole country. Taipei also says that Taiwan is part of China, a position we did "not challenge" in the Shanghai communique of 1972. Second, freedom of contact is a traditional American principle: we could not ourselves break off our economic and cultural relations with Taiwan, however the political relationship might be changed. Third, Taiwan historically is part of China's expansion overseas in migration, settlement, and trade, part of Maritime China, a growth largely independent of the mainland in politics.

In the short run we face problems of power politics—how not to abandon a small ally we have supported for 24 years by a mutual security treaty; how to update and get beyond a posture of supporting Taipei in a civil war it lost 29 years ago; how to develop useful relations with almost a billion people who now constitute a great power.

In the long term the principal fact confronting us is the nature and reality of Chinese nationalism. The idea of One

China or the unity of the Chinese realm goes back to the beginning of Chinese history. It cannot be expunged from the Chinese language or from the minds of Chinese people. This is not only an idea but a sentiment, a basic feeling habituated by millennia of conduct. It attaches the highest importance to Chinese civilization, which consists of all those people who live in the Chinese way. This is expressed in the ancient phrases, "all within the four seas" or "all under heaven" (*t'ien-hsia*, civilization, the Chinese realm). China's unity, in short, is an attribute of Chineseness itself. It springs from a sense of culturalism, something a good deal stronger than mere Western-style nationalism. Without it, there would be no People's Republic as a single state. It is this elemental political force which demands that Taiwan be considered part of the mainland because it is populated by members of the same Chinese people.

Once this basic concept is acknowledged, it can also be acknowledged in China and abroad that within the Chinese realm various degrees of autonomy have normally existed and that some degree of autonomy (local government) may well make sense for a region as different as Taiwan. After all, Taiwan is the only province of China completely surrounded by water, a hundred miles at sea, and therefore dependent upon sea lanes and naval power. The essence of regional autonomy is that an autonomous area may have its own local political order, but it must not be a threat to the sovereignty and ruling power of the central Chinese state. In particular, Taiwan cannot be autonomous in this sense if it continues in a posture of civil war as a rival claimant to rule the mainland. From 1972 American policy wisely acknowledged that the relationship of Taipei to Peking was a Chinese problem to be worked out between the Chinese parties involved, that the American military presence must sooner or later be withdrawn from the island, but that the American defense treaty of 1954 could not be summarily renounced until some sort of intra-China stability of Taiwan-mainland relations was in prospect. Happily in 1979 this finally seemed assured.

What we see here is a further step toward the accommodation of China's revolutionary nationalism, toward the liquidation of the maritime trading powers' intervention in China that began with the Canton trade, the Opium War, and the treaty system. Yet this revival of China's central power is not the only process at work. The outside world of trade, industry, and armament still grows and rivals China's growth, Taiwan is on the border between these two worlds, facing one way economically and the other way politically. Her future will intertwine with that of the People's Republic.

China Today in the Light of Her Past

Historians and social scientists have given us two images of China, one stressing present-day continuities with China's long past, the other stressing novel features of revolutionary change and innovation. We need to combine these two images. After all, continuity and discontinuity go together as the warp and weft of history. Consider how, in our own lives, every day is brand new to us, yet we live it as creatures of habit. China's great revolution is a similar blend of tradition and innovation. Looking first at certain continuities of form may help us see what is new in fact.

Echoes of the Dynastic Cycle. The decline and fall of the Ch'ing Empire and the rebellions of the nineteenth century had many classic features, which we need not recapitulate. In the interregnum which followed 1911, Yuan Shih-k'ai, Sun Yat-sen, Chiang Kai-shek, and Mao Tse-tung with increasing success strove to reunify the Middle Kingdom. The Kuomintang was the precursor of the Chinese Communist Party in seeking to train a new type of scholar-bureaucrat in a new ideology, so as to revive the functions once performed by the Confucian scholar-gentry and the classics.

Generalissimo Chiang sought to quell the warlords by his personal rectitude as well as by bigger armies and smarter politics. Like emperors of the T'ang and Sung, he traveled widely over the provinces on tours of inspection and performed ritual acts, climbed T'ai Shan, the sacred mountain, conducted sacrifices at the tombs of the Han Emperors near the Yellow River north of Loyang. Beginning his rule by the military conquest or hamstringing of his rivals, he proceeded in the 1930s to draw scholars into his civil administration while himself setting a moral example as the paternal head of the state. His strength lay in these traditional qualifications: courage and determination to retain power, ethical fervor and austerity that gave him personal prestige, loyalty to those who were loyal to him, ruthlessness and subtlety in balancing his rivals against one another. It was entirely in keeping with this ancient pattern that Chiang Kai-shek, a prisoner of the past, should seek to progress from the status of Hero to that of Sage, a transformation symbolized in 1943 when he became head of the National Central University at Chungking and published *China's Destiny* as a textbook.

Mao Tse-tung in his turn unified the country as a hero risen from the people, like the founders of the Han and Ming. He went them one better and swam the Yangtze to encourage his people to use and overcome nature. Mao's armies in the 1940s were not a scourge upon the peasantry but avenged their wrongs. He "won the hearts of the people" sufficiently to secure food and soldiers from territorial bases. He attracted college students to staff his administration. His ideology claimed the Mandate of History, if not of Heaven. Once in power, his regime surveyed, classified, and redistributed both the land and the populace. Rising to power with barbarian

help, he yet patronized Chinese culture and employed scholars to document the record of the previous regime and point
the lesson of its fall. He celebrated the revolution in classical
poetry, and his calligraphy adorned public places. His example mightily affected the peripheral states. In Peking in front
of the great palace built by the Ming Emperors of the fifteenth century he built a great square, whither came delegations from Southeast Asia and the Western Regions to watch
the great processions. Today Mao's body lies embalmed in
the center of the square.

In his gargantuan achievements from 1949 to 1976, Mao
depended at every turn upon the loyalty of his prime minister,
a man of upper-class origins and great personal charisma,
quick, astute, and indefatigable, who never seemed to oppose
his leader's policies but always strove to carry them out while
keeping China's central administration and foreign policy
under control. If Mao's imperious will was that of a dragon
upon the throne, unpredictable and violently demanding,
Chou En-lai's selfless and sympathetic handling of personnel
both Chinese and foreign was in the great tradition of sophisticated statecraft. At his death he seemed more beloved by
the people.

The reader can continue for himself to recognize echoes of
the past in China today. C. P. Fitzgerald, for example, summarized the traditional Chinese social concepts as embracing
a single authority coterminous with civilization, a balanced
economy basically managed by the state, an orthodox doctrine
which harmonizes and guides all forms of human activity,
including the selection of intellectuals for state service. As
of 1952 he suggested that these concepts, destroyed during
modern times in their traditional forms, had found expression
again under communism. Yet at the time of writing he foresaw the New Democracy persisting for some time and collectivization remaining afar off. Events have now outstripped

the historian's precedents. Institutional changes have broken the cadence, and the differences between past and present are as great as the similarities.

Values have changed as well as institutions. The K'ang-hsi Emperor never watched the calisthenics of 10,000 selected maidens wearing shorts, nor commended sons for denouncing their fathers. He did no physical jerks to the noon radio. His succession was provided for in the bedchamber where he begat thirty-five sons, and was fought out among them, within a family, not a party. K'ang-hsi wooed the scholars, who had nowhere else to turn, but they had only to criticize the classics textually, not themselves in every act and thought. He paid no honors to peasants who exceeded norms nor to the idea of progress or the dialectic, though he would have acknowledged the sequence of *yang* and *yin*.

Since the patterns of the past cannot be entirely expunged, they remain curiously intertwined with new motifs. Peking has created a Marxist-Leninist-Maoist ideological orthodoxy as vigorous as Confucianism used to be; but it believes in progress toward a future millennium, not cyclical repetition descending from a golden age. Dynastic absolutism has been replaced by party dictatorship, the Son of Heaven by the party chairman, the imperial family-clan council by the central executive committee, the scholar elite by a party elite, tax-gatherers by cadres in the countryside, Confucian classics by Communist classics, written examination by group discussion, scholarly self-cultivation by guilt-ridden self-criticism. Merchants continue to be disesteemed, being undoubtedly bourgeois, but soldiers are now glorified. The sages are class-analyzed and re-evaluated. Labor and army heroes are the new models to emulate. Women do not aspire to lily feet but approach their romantic nadir, functional interchangeability with men. Responsibility for good conduct is still mutually shared among family and neighborhood groups, but now this ancient automatic check on deviance is extended to include the neighbors' thoughts. The *pao-chia* is replaced by the street committee. Villages still are mobilized for public works, but the state philosophy of seeking harmony with nature has given way to the industrial urge to conquer nature. Government used to be thinly spread out and superficial and the peasant passive, a subpolitical animal. Today the government penetrates every hut, and peasants are people, unless they misbehave.

Processes of Modernization. In trying to explain China's modern history, the chief alternative to the traditional Chinese pattern is, of course, a traditional Western one. Where the Chinese pattern was cyclical, the Western view of history is based on the idea of linear progress (the two can be combined in a spiral). The expansion of the Atlantic community underlies this Western pattern. Since the Marxist-Leninist scheme was drawn up mainly with the expansion of Europe in mind, much of China's modern history, seen as a product of this expansion, can be fitted into the categories of the Communist interpretation. When we apply the Western view, certain phases may be distinguished, even though they overlap in time.

Phase One: Collapse. The traditional Chinese state, being incompatible with and weaker than the modern world, is attacked and mortally wounded. Over a period of a century, from the 1840s to the 1940s, the old order is progressively destroyed as a result of contact with the West. The imperial military system is discredited by Western firepower. The emperor's prestige is dimmed by successful foreign aggression against the peripheral vassal states and eventually within spheres of influence in China proper. Efforts at self-defense on the part of the Confucian scholar-administrators—such as by adoption of Western arms, technology, and industry—prove unavailing because the agrarian-bureaucratic society of China cannot modernize as rapidly as the Western nations are modernizing. China's old order is out of date, maladjusted, and unable to respond adequately and in time. Efforts to reform the administration while retaining its Confucian values are attempted, but they are foredoomed to failure.

Phase Two: New Beginnings. During this process of decline, new dynamic elements of modernity are absorbed into the traditional Chinese society and begin to work their transformation. One of these is the Western type of nationalism—loyalty to state and country as sovereign symbols in an international order of similar nations. This undermines the old faith in the Confucian relationships under the emperor. Naturally, the new nationalism has behind it a large backlog of ethnocentrism and xenophobia, suspicion of foreigners and devotion to things Chinese. The transformation from a sinocentric culturalism to a more modern nationalism requires the destruction of the alien Manchu dynasty and leads eventually to a Chinese cultural nationalism more solid than Western nationalism, for it is coterminous with the entire culture, not merely with the state.

Another new element is the apotheosis of science and technology, what D. W. Y. Kwok terms "scientism," as a new focus of belief in place of the Confucian order. It justifies the idea of economic development, particularly under official supervision and leadership. Economic growth has, of course, been a fact even before the early Western trade entered into China's domestic universe of commerce. China's great increase in population since the eighteenth century has been a permanent and not a cyclical change. The ingress of foreign transport in the form of coastal and river steamships, followed by railroads, mines, and textile mills, all demonstrate the growth capacities of modern industrialization based on science and technology. The early reformers themselves attempt to achieve economic development under the banner of the traditional idea of strengthening the state. In the process, a new type of scholar, the scientific technician, emerges, and more specialized administrators are required to guide the multiform types of industrial effort.

Modern technology also fosters militarization, beginning with gentry leadership of regional forces and then provincial arsenals that mass-produce modern arms. The new officer class is technically trained, and patriotic youths flock to it. In the 1930s resistance to Japan's aggression is led by a generalissimo, while his chief adversary survives as a strategist of guerrilla warfare.

By the 1930s there develops the concept of rural reconstruction, the application of modern technology to the agrarian economy, a part of the worldwide effort at rural development. While the Nanking government achieves relatively little in this regard, during its period of rule the concept takes firm shape among Chinese patriots. As in so many other lines of growth, the Western missionaries' interest in village reconstruction points the way to a new China in which missionaries will have no part.

Other new elements from abroad which affect the Chinese social order in the early part of this century are Christianity and Western liberalism—a body of concepts and practices from which China makes a rather fastidious but nonetheless important selection. For example, the freedom of the individual from family controls goes hand in hand with the denial of the authority of the sages in intellectual matters and of the Son of Heaven in politics. In some degree we may speak of the influx of the ideals of the French Revolution, flowing into China a century afterward and undermining the old order before the subsequent wave of Marxism. Startling upsets and reversals of values now occur, often helped by Christian missionary teachings. Youth is honored over age, or at least youth is able to acquire the prestige of scholarship which age formerly monopolized. Egalitarianism likewise extols the common man, and the paternalistic Confucian concern for the populace is converted into the cult of the people, who now supplant Heaven's mandate as the source of legitimacy. In this welter of changes, women as individuals are freed from the severe inequalities of their former status and their quiet but rapid emancipation is one of the greatest unrecorded revolutions of the century. Under the general banner of liberalism, democracy, laissez-faire, and humanitarianism, there emerge new values and new social groups, which have yet to be integrated into a new order.

Phase Three: Rebirth. Looking back over the last century, one can see the emergence of those new forces, methods, ideals, and social classes which served as raw material for the Nationalist and the Communist organizers in turn. Patriotic youth are ready to sacrifice themselves to wipe out China's past humiliations and build a new nation. New classes of factory workers and treaty port merchant capitalists have been created by economic growth. New social groups—emancipated women, soldiers possessed of a new social status, peasants ready to participate in political life, students ready to join a party—are now in being. The very multiplicity of these new elements creates a great need for a new unity under the banner of nationalism and industrialism.

If one follows this Western-type pattern of unilinear social change in modern China, one may imperceptibly work one's historical interpretation around to the dubious conclusion that Chinese communism represents an inevitable phase of China's "modernization." This would be just as simpleminded as to conclude that it is merely another in a long succession of dynasties. Neither view seems to me adequate.

In actual fact, of course, historical trends seldom develop in straight lines and Mao Tse-tung's achievement depends on at least two particular circumstances among others: first, that Japan attacked and destroyed the more modern area of Kuomintang China; second, that Chiang Kai-shek, indomitable and uninstructible, developed in his long years on the mainland no rural reconstruction program such as was later achieved on Taiwan. Meanwhile the positive force in the rise of the People's Republic was not simply the one man, Mao, whom we use to symbolize the event, but rather the devotion and organizing capacity of a whole generation of patriots who served mainly in the Chinese Community Party. Their work, snowballing from 1921 to 1949 and into the 1970s, has been a tremendous feat of organization. Only the inheritors of China's political tradition, one may argue, could have done it. Foreign models and foreign activities in China, whether Japanese, Western, or Soviet, could serve only as stimuli, not as substance. To say that the new order under the PRC is the latest phase of China's response to the outside world would omit the heart of the matter, which is the Chinese people's great mass, inertial momentum, and native genius for creating their own culture.

The first edition of this book in 1948, at the onset of the Cold War, concluded that "the disintegration of the old order in China leaves that country open to reorganization under the dominant influence" of either the USSR or the United States as superpowers. What nonsense! China has gone her own way.

Problems of the New Order

The alternatives in China, the banks within which the flow of events must find its channel, are narrower than we can

Liberation and industry. Women's unloading team, Lanchow Oil Refinery, 1974.

easily imagine. The pressure of numbers, new to us, is an old experience in China. Bureaucratic organization, at which we chafe, was invented there. The new order will inevitably retain many police-state features, but in our present ignorance of life among the masses, we should be slow to characterize it over all.

As the revolutionary generation leaves the scene, one of the first problems confronting China's new leaders is a widespread craving for relaxation and stability. We outsiders can hardly appreciate how fast things have changed in modern China. The past century has seen more drastic transformations than any other country has ever experienced, beginning with five major rebellions and five wars involving every world power within the seventy years *before* World War I. The Chinese had a prouder and more distinctive tradition, responded more slowly to its collapse, suffered the humiliations of backwardness longer than any other major people. We in America have moved fast, from the horse, buggy, and kerosene lamp to television, jets, and missiles, but we have not scrapped and rebuilt in the same short time our system of government and foreign relations, our language and the contents of our learning, our whole society. We have not felt the same proud urge to catch up, nor tried to do it in great leaps. This frenetic pressure for change makes one wonder if Mao Tse-tung will not figure in history like his favorite character, the First Emperor of the Ch'in, or the founder of the Sui, men who created a new order by violent activity during a brief span of despotism and were followed respectively by the long-lived regimes of Han and T'ang.

We should now expect the Chinese revolution to slow down and consolidate its new order. As it does so, we can conclude with Maurice Meisner that "the post-Maoist era will be marked by the permanence of bureaucracy and its dominance over society." The test will therefore be the durability of

Mao's slogan "Serve the people." This is another way of saying that bureaucratic government has a constant problem of probity and morale.

Compounding this problem is the extraordinary size of the Chinese polity. Never before have a billion people lived under one regime. The secret of this feat, and whether it can persist, are not clear to us. Certainly a degree of decentralized regionalism is essential to it, together with an equilibrium between regional material interests and central ideological interests, presumably balancing regional profit and central prestige. Similarly the unity of the party and of the army must both be sustained within a framework of civilian party dominance over the military. Such formulas touch upon the overall mystery, the accumulated Chinese capacity for large-scale organization, something worth studying. Equally extraordinary in this enormous polity is the peculiarly Chinese reliance upon ethics more than law, upon moral consensus more than judicial procedure. In Western terms we might say that an element of religious faith lent strength to the Maoist leadership, so that the law codes could remain unpublished.

But every system has its weak point, and even with the new build-up of legal procedures and constitutional constraints upon authority, the ancient evils of bureaucratism still lie in wait for Peking's mammoth administration at any time its morale declines. Precedent is not encouraging. The constant CCP effort never to be "out of touch with the masses" bespeaks a historical tradition that modern governments must still overcome—the fact that the imperial mandarinate could be a world unto itself, superimposed as it was on the local elite of gentry notables who managed local affairs. As a result officials were so far above commoners as to be a law unto themselves. Their role was to manipulate the people, not to represent them, and so their administration was personal, according to the officials' character and sense of responsibility. If they became self-seeking, their personal relations within the government lent themselves to collusion and corruption. These could be organized the more thoroughly because the old society did not rely primarily on its legal institutions. Officials could remain moral family pillars while they connived at defrauding the emperor. The emperor's only ultimate safeguard was to ensure that they kept a correct attitude. Even today, Mao Tse-tung's successors must still rely less on laws and procedures than on moral exhortation and personal example. Bureaucrats with the wrong style can defeat their ends and destroy their power.

To stave off a decline in morale, CCP methods for keeping officials incorrupt are far more intensive than anything the old China ever devised. Yet the sense of hierarchy persists, and office means perquisites. Note how fallen power holders, from Teng Hsiao-p'ing (he played bridge!) to Chiang Ch'ing and her silk bedsheets, have been retrospectively accused of morally debased self-indulgence in special privileges, made all the easier by the regular provision of limousines, circuit hostels, orderlies, and special planes, special food shops, and special schools for the hierarchy. The cadre class inevitably tends to perpetuate itself as did the mandarinate.

The temptation to corrupt dealing is ever present under communism just as it was under imperial Confucianism; for one rises in China's crowded society with even more attention to personal relationships than we are accustomed to. For example, if a village boy can make it from the ubiquitous local militia into army service, it is his best way to see the world, his quickest channel for upward mobility. He is likely to return from army service with education and party membership and so join what Victor Nee calls the "old boy network of demobilized PLA soldiers," who form part of the local elite, almost like a new gentry. Austerity and self-sacrifice among such an elite are fragile qualities—especially when kinship still remains one basis of social organization in the village, and the new measures of collectivism, as William Parish remarks, "have given peasants a new sense of collective unity" so that they may "not support all government goals." "Corruption," in short, seldom a simple thing, may be sanctioned by local loyalties against the state's interest.

Even with the best social and political motives among populace and bureaucrats, China also faces serious economic problems In agriculture, the population/food supply balance remains precarious. Population increases more easily than crop acreage. China's agriculture now faces diminishing returns. The arduous creation of new soil to till, the use of new-found oil to power farm machinery and transport, and the increase of irrigation and chemical fertilizers to boost crop production are valiant but limited bases for China's food supply. Pressure of numbers is still the most grievous part of China's inheritance. Every year, crop failures wait somewhere around the corner. Food imports must continue from abroad. Energy use in America could be reduced more readily than food intake in China.

In industry during the past quarter-century, central planning and control of state enterprises' profits for reinvestment helped China's industrial output increase as much as 10 percent a year, doubling every seven years. For this purpose producers' goods were imported at first from the socialist bloc ($6.5 billion worth of machinery between 1952 and 1973) in the face of the Western embargo on such shipments until 1960. In fact from 1949 to 1973 the machine-building industry grew 20 percent a year, as did the output of iron and steel and, after 1965, oil production. China became the world's largest producer of machine tools. By the mid-1970s her industrial production was comparable to that of Japan in 1960. But as Nicholas Lardy points out, this high rate of investment in industry was possible because productivity increased more rapidly than wages, which rose only 30 to 40 percent during twenty-five years. The decline of revolutionary fervor has now required wage increases, greater material incentives, to obviate labor unrest and even strikes.

In foreign trade, where the Maoist policy of self-reliance has been revised, the problem is how to import massive foreign technology and not suffer a foreign trade deficit. The eight-year trade agreement with Japan in 1978 was one attempted remedy, along with the Sino-Japanese treaty of peace and friendship. Other spectacular remedies proposed were the sending of thousands of Chinese students abroad, mainly for scientific training, and the borrowing of large foreign loans.

Yet despite these and many other problems, the economic record of the People's Republic has been a remarkable success story. For example, China has significantly outperformed the Indian economy. From 1952 to 1976 the Chinese economy grew on the average 6 or 7 percent a year, two or three times the growth rate per capita in India, even though India received some $13 billion worth of foreign aid and loans whereas China received Soviet loans of hardly more than $1 billion and meanwhile put out some $7 billion of economic aid to other countries.

China's foreign policy has tried to lead the developing countries of the "third world" in opposition to the alleged domination or "hegemony" of the two "superpowers" (USA and USSR). As a model of foreign aid in Africa, China completed in 1975 the building of the Tanzania-Zambia railway. Meanwhile China's satellites circled the earth, her nuclear tests slowly continued, a large coastal defense navy took shape—a great power was in the making. Yet her foreign policy still tried to apply revolutionary united front tactics to the world scene, identifying the USSR as the "major contradiction" and so conciliating the USA as a minor enemy.

This policy aimed not so much to represent long-term national interests as to manipulate foreign powers tactically, as when Japan was asked to subscribe to an "anti-hegemony" (that is, anti-Soviet) treaty clause and Americans were earnestly enjoined to prepare for an "inevitable" war with the Soviets.

In our future relations we face a continuing kaleidoscope of Sino-American cultural conflict-and-harmony—enough to ensure our continued fascination with China. We must expect our two peoples to coexist with differing values, one extolling civil liberties and the other self-sacrifice, one denouncing the police state and the other individualism. Donald Munro concludes that "there is no place in the Maoist conception of the self for either a private realm of beliefs or for unique and innate inner forces that determine individuality." China is really different.

Yet we have reached a time of new beginnings in which mutual respect is possible. Post-Vietnam America may be less arrogantly righteous. China after Mao may remain less ideologically embattled. As Michel Oksenberg suggests, we have "responded ineffectively to Chinese nationalism because we have assumed that Chinese nationalism is similar to ours," whereas in fact the Chinese state and society are differently constructed, with a greater sense of hierarchic order, to be sure, but also with a greater intensity of interpersonal relations and a greater stress on conscious morality of conduct.

In short, our American way is not the only way, nor even the majority way for man's and woman's future. Our recourse to legislation, contracts, legal rights, and litigation is meeting limitations. China offers alternatives. Time may favor China, for the explosive growth to which we are accustomed cannot indefinitely continue; the American individualist may face more future adjustment than his Chinese counterpart. The thousands of Americans who visit China every year in the new tourism are beginning to realize that the old China's central function as a cultural model for other peoples is being revived in a new style of concern for man in nature (ecology) and for man in society (community life).

But the dilemma of the two revolutions, technological and social, will not go away. Chou En-lai's vision of modernizing agriculture, industry, technology, and defense must be pursued to create a modern state. Yet education and public health must also grow to serve the people's welfare on a scale never seen in the world before. Can large amounts of foreign technology be imported without alienating the urban technicians from the rural masses?

Our China relations will now demand more and more understanding on our part, not less. American policy in 1979—working out normalization with Peking while maintaining special relations with the people of Taiwan—far from removing us from Chinese politics, brings us back onto their periphery. One has to get acquainted with Chinese life to realize how very complex it is.

Suggested Reading

Suggested Reading

China still is a journalist's dream and a statistician's nightmare, with more human drama and fewer verifiable facts per square mile than anywhere else in the world. For the American reader it is essential to penetrate the past and get a long-run view of China's recent transformation. As successful revolutionaries the PRC leaders have interpreted Chinese history in rather black and white terms. This has stimulated historians by raising new issues but has led to more compiling of documents than encouragement of scholarship. Outside historians are thus left to tell their foreign readers about the Chinese people's experience as best they can.

Research in libraries and observation in the field are both indispensable in the study of another society, but I believe the latter has a special value in the case of China. The present volume probably owes as much to seven years spent in various parts of China as it does to forty years devoted to study of books. This is because the ways of an alien land have to be experienced to be understood or even believed. Western writers of each generation, whether philosophers of the eighteenth-century Enlightenment or exemplars of the treaty port mind, have viewed Chinese civilization with a large degree of subjectivity. I doubt that social scientists can entirely avoid doing so today, for the final portrait that one makes of an entire culture or society is a work of art, not of measurement.

The only recourse in this situation is for the reader to become

Suggested Reading

in part a student, comparing one book with another, and in part a statesman, remembering that life is never quite encompassed in print, least of all Chinese life.

The world is seeing multiple explosions in population, technology, and learning, with problems multiplying faster than solutions. In this frenetic expansion, Chinese studies have not been left behind. So much has been published in the 1970s that this bibliography has again increased in length, even though I have omitted many works cited in the first three editions, as well as works not in English. Specifically excluded are articles (some are more important than many books), picture books (some of which are superb), many selections of translated materials and compilations of reading, travel accounts (unless the travelers were exceptionally qualified or experienced), and works of sinology that assume a knowledge of Chinese. The flow of academic publication from the PRC almost ceased in the latter half of the 1960s during the Cultural Revolution and has only recently resumed. While we try harder to understand the Chinese people, they hardly try to explain themselves.

Since this bibliography has grown by following the contours of publication rather than the Dewey decimal system, you will find philosophy under 2.3 and thought under 3.5, history under 2 and 4, and humanities and social sciences under 3.

Sections 1 through 4 below indicate major studies or recent works on various aspects of China—traditional and modern. The aim here is not to list all important works, which would take a volume, but to note certain outstanding landmarks and then add recent works, which naturally refer to earlier ones. On the problem of maintaining an informed and critical view of the Chinese People's Republic and American policy, see sections 5 and 6.

Except in the case of university presses, unless otherwise noted, publishers are in New York. UP means University Press. The habitats of UP, such as Cambridge, London, New York, Melbourne for the Cambridge UP, are not fully given nor is the fact that the Princeton UP is at Princeton, NJ, the Yale UP at New Haven, Conn., etc., etc. Since the knowledge explosion has been accompanied by a tidal wave of reprinting, the reader is warned that publishers when they reprint a work may update its title page, on the specious grounds that the date of reprinting deserves such recognition.

After drafting this *tour de force* I got very helpful further suggestions from Jeffrey Kinkley.

Names of authors in the following pages are in the index.

1. GENERAL WORKS OF REFERENCE

1.1 *Bibliographies.* In general the most recent bibliographies should be the most useful. Chun-shu Chang, *Premodern China: A Bibliographical Introduction* (Ann Arbor: U. of Mich., Center for Chinese Studies, 1971), tells you where to go for what. Andrew J. Nathan, *Modern China, 1840-1972: An Introduction to Sources and Research Aids* (Ann Arbor: U. of Mich., Center for Chinese Studies, 1973), includes Chinese works as well as Western. The monumental G. William Skinner et al., *Modern Chinese Society: An Analytical Bibliography* (Stanford UP, 1973), 3 vols., is highly organized for sociological analysis; volume I is in Western languages, volumes II and III, Chinese and Japanese. The most comprehensive work, also arranged by topics, is Tung-li Yuan, *China in Western Literature* (Far Eastern Publications, Yale U., 1958), which lists 18,000 books and pamphlets published between 1921 and 1957 in English, French, and German. The most comprehensive listing of current publications is the annual *Bibliography of Asian Studies,* ed. the Knowledge Availability Systems Center, U. of Pittsburgh, for the Association for Asian Studies. More specialized bibliographies are under topics below.

1.2 *Geography.* The informative first-hand description based on extensive travel in the 1920s and 30s by George B. Cressey, *Land of the 500 Million* (McGraw-Hill, 1955), is out of date, but no one can update it by travel today. For a successor see T. R. Tregear, *A Geography of China* (Chicago: Aldine, 1965). Most informative on recent developments is Theodore Shabad, *China's Changing Map: National and Regional Development, 1949-71* (Praeger, 2nd ed., 1972 [1956]). Note also Joseph B. R. Whitney, *China: Area, Administration and Nation Building* (Dept. of Geography, U. of Chicago, 1969).

1. General Works of Reference

For historical maps consult the new edition, edited by Norton Ginsburg, of Albert Herrmann, *An Historical Atlas of China* (Chicago: Aldine, 1966; based on *Historical and Commercial Atlas of China,* Harvard-Yenching Institute, 1935). P. J. M. Geelan and D. C. Twitchett, eds., *The Times Atlas of China* (London: Times Books, 1974) now provide the best detailed maps of the provinces, some 30 cities, and geo-economic features like climate and communication. This landmark in cartography supersedes everything else including the Central Intelligence Agency's *Communist China Administrative Atlas* (Washington, D.C., 1969). Note also Chiao-min Hsieh, *Atlas of China* (McGraw-Hill, 1973). The latest Chinese atlas is entitled ZHONGHUA RENMIN GONGHEGUO FEN SHENG DILUJI (HANYU PINYINBAN*),* using the *pinyin* transcription and with boundaries as in the 1971 edition (Peking: New China Bookstore, 1977). Jack F. Williams, *China in Maps, 1890-1960: A Selective and Annotated Cartobibliography* (East Lansing: Mich. State U., Asian Studies Center, 1974), lists modern maps of China made by seven different nations, with a history of the subject and some 130 charts showing area maps made by each survey.

1.3 *Historical Surveys.* For comparative chronology note that William L. Langer, *An Encyclopedia of World History,* 5th ed. (through 1970, Abrams, 1972), has been updated and combined with 2000 illustrations in a mammoth *New Illustrated Encyclopedia of World History* (Abrams, 1975), 2 vols.

General works often come out of teaching experience in major universities. From Michigan, Charles O. Hucker, *China's Imperial Past: An Introduction to Chinese History and Culture* (Stanford UP, 1975) is the most recent survey to 1850, well organized and well based in scholarship. The marvelously condensed paperback of this, Charles O. Hucker, *China to 1850: A Short History* (Stanford UP, 1978) puts the most in the least— certainly the most value per ounce in the China field. From Columbia, Wm. Theodore de Bary, Wing-tsit Chan, and Burton Watson, comps., *Sources of Chinese Tradition* (Columbia UP, 1960), offer 950 pages of carefully selected translations with interpretive comments on the whole sweep of philosophical, religious, and political ideas from Confucius to communism. Also from Columbia, John Meskill, ed., with the assistance of J. Mason Gentzler, *An Introduction to Chinese Civilization* (Lexington, Mass.: D. C. Heath, 1973), combines a historical narrative by the editor with essays by eight others on major aspects. From Berkeley, Wolfram Eberhard, *A History of China* (U. of Calif. Press, 1950, 4th ed., 1977), rather idiosyncratically stresses the non-Chinese peoples in Chinese social history. From Harvard, the two volumes by Edwin O. Reischauer and John K. Fairbank, *East Asia: The Great Tradition* (Boston: Houghton Mifflin, 1960), and John K. Fairbank, Edwin O. Reischauer, and Albert M. Craig, *East Asia: The Modern Transformation* (Boston: Houghton Mifflin, 1965), have been condensed into *East Asia: Tradition and Transformation* (1973, new impression, 1978); and also divided to make *China: Tradition and Transformation* (1978). One of the best surveys in brief compass is still L. Carrington Goodrich, *A Short History of the Chinese People* (Harper, 3rd ed., 1959), especially on the growth of China's material culture and foreign contacts. C. P. Fitzgerald, *China: A Short Cultural History* (Praeger, 3rd ed., 1961), contains well-informed essays. From Cambridge, Michael Loewe, *Imperial China: The Historical Background to the Modern Age* (Praeger, 1966), offers interesting analytic notes by a classicist. From Oxford, Mark Elvin, *The Pattern of the Chinese Past* (Stanford UP, 1973) pursues controversial socioeconomic themes. From Paris, Jacques Gernet, *Le monde chinois* (Paris: Armand Colin, 1972), is being translated for an English edition (London: Dawson, 1979). Werner Eichhorn, *Chinese Civilization: An Introduction* (Praeger paperback, 1969, trans. from German ed. of 1964), combines an intimate use of the record with a concern for the life of the people. Raymond Dawson, ed., *The Legacy of China* (Oxford: Clarendon, 1964), contains survey chapters by experts on thought, religion, literature, art, science, government, and the like. David C. Buxbaum and Frederick W. Mote, eds., *Transition and Permanence: Chinese History and Culture: A Festschrift in Honor of Hsiao Kung-ch'üan* (Hong Kong, printed by Cathay Press, 1972), honors a leading professor at Seattle with 18 articles on intellectual and institutional history, criticism, and poetics. For surveys of modern history see sections 4.1 and 5.3.

1.4 *Fine Arts*. This is a world that cannot be dealt with here. There is a wealth of handsomely illustrated volumes from several continents, too many to list. For expert surveys aimed at the general reader see Laurence C. S. Sickman and Alexander Soper, *The Art and Architecture of China* (Harmondsworth, England: Penguin, 3rd rev. ed. 1971); and Michael Sullivan, *The Arts of China* (U. of Calif. Press, rev. ed., 1977), both with summary bibliographies. Note also James Cahill, *Chinese Painting* (Geneva: Skira, 1977), and Sherman E. Lee, *A History of Far Eastern Art* (Englewood Cliffs: Prentice Hall, rev. ed., 1974), a textbook including Japan and India. William Watson, *Style in the Arts of China* (Baltimore: Penguin, 1974), is a broad analytic work. For a massive compilation of books and articles, with 8954 entries, see Harrie A. Vanderstappen, ed., *The T. L. Yuan Bibliography of Western Writings on Chinese Art and Archaeology* (London: Mansell, 1975), one of many bibliographical memorials to China's leading wartime librarian.

On the neglected subject of architecture, Andrew Boyd, *Chinese Architecture and Town Planning: 1500 B.C.–A.D. 1911* (U. of Chicago Press, 1962).

1.5 *Technology*. Our view of China's contribution to world science and technology, traditionally confined to paper, printing, the compass, gunpowder, and similar great inventions, has been revolutionized by the work of Joseph Needham and his collaborators, Wang Ling, Lu Gwei-djen and others, who are producing a multi-tomed, seven-volume series, *Science and Civilisation in China* (Cambridge UP): vol. I, *Introductory Orientations* (1954); vol. II, *History of Scientific Thought* (1956); vol. III, *Mathematics and the Sciences of the Heavens and the Earth* (1959); vol. IV, *Physics and Physical Technology*, pt. 1, *Physics* (1962); vol. IV, pt. 2, *Mechanical Engineering* (1965); vol. IV, pt. 3, *Civil Engineering and Nautics* (1971); vol. V, *Chemistry and Chemical Technology*, pt. 2, *Spagyrical Discovery and Invention: Magisteries of Gold and Immortality* (1974); pt. 3, *Spagyrical Discovery and Invention: Historical Survey from Cinnabar Elixirs to Synthetic Insulin* (1976); pt. 4, *Spagyrical Discovery and Invention: Apparatus, Theories and Gifts* (1979). Volumes I and II have been condensed in Colin A. Ronan, *The Shorter Science and Civilisation in China,* vol. I (1978). Selections of incidental papers and addresses have also been published, for example, Joseph Needham, *Clerks and Craftsmen in China and the West* (Cambridge UP, 1970); Joseph Needham, *The Grand Titration: Science and Society in East and West* (U. of Toronto Press, 1969), reprints eight pieces that parallel the larger series of volumes. Nathan Sivin has published *Chinese Alchemy: Preliminary Studies* (Harvard UP, 1968) and also Shigeru Nakayama and Nathan Sivin, eds., *Chinese Science: Explorations of an Ancient Tradition* (MIT Press, 1973), a symposium including Needham, A. C. Graham, and several Japanese specialists. A major Chinese encyclopedia of technology by Sung Ying-hsing compiled in 1638 has been translated by E-tu Zen Sun and Shiou-chuan Sun, *T'ien-kung k'ai-wu, Chinese Technology in the Seventeenth Century* (Penn. State UP, 1966). For a bibliography of 944 items up to 1972 with indications of contents, mainly on recent times, see Genevieve C. Dean, *Science and Technology in the Development of Modern China: An Annotated Bibliography* (London: Mansell Information Publishing, 1974), an item in the research aids series of the East Asian Institute at Columbia.

On the early technical developments that produced inscriptions, writing, paper, and eventually the Chinese book, see Tsuen-hsuin Tsien, *Written on Bamboo and Silk: The Beginnings of Chinese Books and Inscriptions* (U. of Chicago Press, 1962). A classic monograph is by Thomas Francis Carter, *The Invention of Printing in China and Its Spread Westward,* revised and updated by L. Carrington Goodrich (Ronald Press, 2nd ed., 1955 [1925]). On calligraphic technique, Chiang Yee, *Chinese Calligraphy* (Harvard UP, 3rd ed., rev., 1973; London, 1954); and T. C. Lai, *Chinese Calligraphy: An Introduction* (Seattle: U. of Wash. Press, 1973). On painting, Alison Stilwell Cameron, *Chinese Painting Techniques* (Tokyo: Tuttle, 1968).

As part of China's erotic technology, note Howard S. Levy, *Chinese Footbinding: The History of a Curious Erotic Custom* (Walton Rawls, 1966). On traditional medicine, the basic analysis is Manfred Porkert, *The Theoretical Foundations of Chinese*

Medicine: Systems of Correspondence (MIT Press, 1974). See also Pierre Huard and Ming Wong, *Chinese Medicine,* trans. from the French (McGraw-Hill, 1968), illustrated; and Heinrich Wallnoefer and Anna von Rottauscher, *Chinese Folk Medicine* (Crown, 1965). See also section 5.15.

On the neglected subject of military history and technology see Frank A. Kierman, Jr., and John K. Fairbank, eds., *Chinese Ways in Warfare* (Harvard UP, 1974), developed from a 1969 conference. For the still pertinent classic text on warfare see Samuel B. Griffith, *Sun Tzu: The Art of War* (Oxord UP, 1963).

1.6 *Biographical Dictionaries.* American sinology has produced a notable series of volumes spanning 1368 to 1965: L. Carrington Goodrich and Chaoying Fang, eds., *Dictionary of Ming Biography, 1368–1644* (Columbia UP, 1976), 2 vols. A. W. Hummel, ed., *Eminent Chinese of the Ch'ing Period, 1644–1912* (Washington, D.C.: Government Printing Office, 1943, 1944), 2 vols. Howard L. Boorman and Richard C. Howard, eds., *Biographical Dictionary of Republican China* (Columbia UP, 1967-71), 4 vols. Donald Klein and Anne B. Clark, *Biographic Dictionary of Chinese Communism 1921–1965* (Harvard UP, 1971), 2 vols.

2. CHINA'S TRADITIONAL CIVILIZATION

2.1 *Archaeological Origins.* Hundreds of excavations in recent decades have recast the picture of prehistoric times. The authoritative summary of this archaeological revolution is Kwang-chih Chang, *The Archaeology of Ancient China* (Yale UP, 1963, 2nd ed., rev. 1977). Note also K. C. Chang, *Early Chinese Civilization: Anthropological Perspectives* (Harvard UP, 1972), a set of pioneering essays. Impressions of visiting archaeologists in 1975 including K. C. Chang and David N. Keightley are recorded in W. W. Howells and Patricia Jones Tsuchitani, eds., *Paleoanthropology in the People's Republic of China: A Trip Report of the American Paleoanthropology Delegation* (Washington, D.C.: National Academy of Sciences, 1977, Comittee on Scholarly Communication with the People's Republic of China, report no. 4). The new evidence is also reflected in a thematic survey, Ping-ti Ho, *The Cradle of the East: An Inquiry into the Indigenous*

Origins of Techniques and Ideas of Neolithic and Early Historic China, 5000–1000 B.C. (U. of Chicago Press, 1976). Meanwhile the history of the birth of modern Chinese archaelogy in the 1920s and 1930s is recorded by a pioneer leader, Li Chi, *Anyang* (Seattle: U. of Wash. Press, 1977). The excitement of the early finds was well captured in a book now outdated, Herrlee G. Creel, *The Birth of China: A Survey of the Formative Period of Chinese Civilization* (London: Cape, 1936; New York: Frederick Ungar, 1964). Dr. Li's lectures, *The Beginnings of Chinese Civilization* (Seattle: U. of Wash. Press, 1957) are still pertinent, as are also the survey volumes by Cheng Te-k'un, *Archaeology in China,* vol. I, *Prehistoric China* (Cambridge, England: Heffer, 1959); vol. II, *Shang China;* vol. III, *Chou China* (U. of Toronto Press, 1960, 1963). William Watson, *China before the Han Dynasty* (Praeger, 1961), is a graphic survey of archaeological finds with 77 photographs and many drawings.

2.2 *The Classics.* These are above all works of literature. For an introduction see Wm. Theodore de Bary and Ainslie T. Embree, eds., *A Guide to Oriental Classics* (Columbia UP, 2nd ed., 1975), pp. 143-216, on "classics of the Chinese tradition," which lists complete and partial translations of the *Four Books* with secondary readings and discussion topics; and does the same for other early philosophers, Chu Hsi and Wang Yang-ming, Chinese Buddhist texts, four major novels, and Chinese poetry.

The *Five Classics* are considered with bibliography in another valuable vademecum by Jordan D. Paper, *Guide to Chinese Prose* (Boston: G. K. Hall, 1973), which discusses 142 items of classics, history, philosophy, belles lettres, short stories, novels and twentieth-century literature. In sections 3.1-3 below the attempt is mainly to update, not repeat (much less summarize), what these two guidebooks have to offer.

2.3 *Chinese Philosophy.* See Wing-tsit Chan, *An Outline and an Annotated Bibliography of Chinese Philosophy* (rev. and expanded ed., Yale U. Far Eastern Publications, 1969). The leading general survey is the translation by Derk Bodde of Fung Yu-lan, *A History of Chinese Philosophy* (vol. I, Peiping: H. Vetch, 1937; reissued together with the publication of vol. II,

2. Traditional Civilization

Princeton UP, 1952). Fung Yu-lan, *A Short History of Chinese Philosophy* (Macmillan, 1948), though edited by Derk Bodde, is a separate study. The greatest of the sages is restudied in detail by H. G. Creel, *Confucius: The Man and the Myth* (John Day, 1949). See also his nontechnical survey, *Chinese Thought from Confucius to Mao Tse-tung* (U. of Chicago Press, 1953). Basic texts of neo-Confucianism have been translated by Wing-tsit Chan, *Reflections on Things at Hand: The Neo-Confucian Anthology compiled by Chu Hsi and Lü Tsu-ch'ien* (Columbia UP, 1967); and *Instructions for Practical Living and Other Neo-Confucian Writings by Wang Yang-ming* (Columbia UP, 1963). Most recent are Tu Wei-ming, *Neo-Confucian Thought in Action: Wang Yang-ming's Youth, 1472–1509* (U. of Calif. Press, 1976), and Julia Ching, *To Acquire Wisdom: The Way of Wang Yang-ming* (Columbia UP, 1976). Note also Chung-ying Cheng, trans., *Tai Chen's "Inquiry into Goodness"* (Honolulu: East-West Center Press, 1971).

A fascinating, fresh account of Taoism is presented in Holmes Welch, *The Parting of the Way: Lao Tzu and the Taoist Movement* (Boston: Beacon Press, 1957). The Legalist-administrative tradition is given a new underpinning in articles by Herrlee G. Creel, *What is Taoism? and Other Studies in Chinese Cultural History* (U. of Chicago Press, 1970). Note also his *Shen Pu-hai: A Chinese Philosopher of the Fourth Century B.C.* (U. of Chicago Press, 1975). A recent study of classical values is by Donald J. Munro, *The Concept of Man in Early China* (Stanford UP, 1969), part of a trilogy; see also Vitaly A. Rubin, *Individual and State in Ancient China: Essays on Four Chinese Philosophers,* trans. and intro. by Stephen I. Levine (Columbia UP, 1976). See section 3.5, Chinese Thought. ("Thought," used generally by non-philosophers, seems to include "Philosophy" within wider, less formal, boundaries.) There is a *Journal of Chinese Philosophy* (Boston, 1973–).

2.4 *Dynastic Histories and Historiography.* This vast and complex field has been systematically surveyed in a multilingual *tour de force* by Endymion Wilkinson, *The History of Imperial China: A Research Guide* (Harvard UP, 1973 and reprints dated 1974 and 1975), which describes how the main bodies of Chinese historical literature developed and have been appraised, translated, indexed, and otherwise dealt with by scholars worldwide. Less replete with Chinese and Japanese titles and still informative is the brief introduction to the craft of Chinese history writing by Charles S. Gardner, *Chinese Traditional Historiography* (Harvard UP, 1938, reprinted with additions by L. S. Yang, 1961). A notable series of articles by leading scholars is in W. G. Beasley and E. B. Pulleyblank, eds., *Historians of China and Japan* (Oxford UP, 1961). Two works by Burton Watson bring us close to the great pioneer historian Ssu-ma Ch'ien, *Records of the Grand Historian of China* (Columbia UP, 1961), 2 vols., a translation of the *Shih-chi,* and *Ssu-ma Ch'ien: Grand Historian of China* (Columbia UP, 1958). A recent addition to the remarkable corpus of translations by Burton Watson is *Courtier and Commoner in Ancient China. Selections from the "History of the Former Han" by Pan Ku* (Columbia UP, 1977).

2.5 *Studies of Early History.* From Paris, Jacques Gernet, *Ancient China from the Beginnings to the Empire* (U. of Calif. Press, 1968), provides a quick introduction. Herrlee G. Creel, *The Origins of Statescraft in China,* vol. I, *The Western Chou Empire* (U. of Chicago Press, 1970) opens a new door to the Legalist-administrative tradition. The political institutions of the Warring States period are analyzed by Richard L. Walker, *The Multi-State System of Ancient China* (Hamden: Shoe String Press, 1953). Cho-yun Hsü, *Ancient China in Transition: An Analysis of Social Mobility, 722–222 B.C.* (Stanford UP, 1965), deals with the social history of this period in general. On the problem of ancient China's social structure, see also Derk Bodde's chapter "Feudalism in China" in Rushton Coulborn, ed., *Feudalism in History* (Princeton UP, 1956). A recent monograph, based on a PRC publication of 1973, is Li Yu-ning, ed., *Shang Yang's Reforms and State Control in China* (White Plains: M. E. Sharpe, 1977). On the Ch'in unification, Derk Bodde, *China's First Unifier: A Study of the Ch'in Dynasty as Seen in the Life of Li Ssu 280?–208 B.C.* (Leiden: Brill, 1938), has been reprinted with a new foreword (Hong Kong UP, 1967). A notable monograph on the Han economy is by Ying-shih Yü, *Trade and Expansion in Han China: A Study in the Structure of Sino-Barbarian Economic Relations* (U. of Calif. Press, 1967). Michael Loewe, *Crisis and Conflict in Han China, 104 B.C. to A.D. 9* (London: Allen and Unwin, 1974) is a political history of cases and crises. On the political transition from Early to Later Han, Hans Bielenstein has studied *The Restoration of the Han Dynasty* (Stockholm: Museum of Far Eastern Antiquities, vol. I, 1954; vol. II, 1959). On law see A. F. P. Hulsewe, *Remnants of Han Law* (Leiden: Brill, 1955). Chi-yun Chen, *Hsün Yüeh, A.D. 148–209: The Life and Reflections of an Early Medieval Confucian* (Cambridge UP, 1975), is on the transition at the end of the Han. Derk Bodde, *Festivals in Classical China: New Year and Other Annual Observations during the Han Dynasty 206 B.C.–A.D. 200* (Princeton UP, 1975), provides useful data.

2.6 *The Middle Period.* So strong was the hold of the Chinese classical tradition that until 1950 relatively few monographic studies had appeared on the long period from A.D. 220 to 1644. This lack is now being rapidly made up. Edwin O. Reischauer, *Ennin's Diary: The Record of a Pilgrimage to China in Search of the Law* (Ronald Press, 1955), translates a unique first-person account of T'ang China. The companion volume, *Ennin's Travels in T'ang China* (Ronald Press, 1955), is an absorbing summary and commentary, rounding out this ninth-century Marco Polo's picture of China at the apex of world civilization. Arthur F. Wright and Denis Twitchett, eds., *Perspectives on the T'ang* (Yale UP, 1973) is a major symposium developed from a conference. Volumes III and IV of *The Cambridge History of China* edited by Denis Twitchett will concern *Sui and T'ang 589–906.* Other recent monographs on successive periods include Arthur F. Wright, *The Sui Dynasty: The Unification of China, A.D. 581–617* (Knopf, 1978); Howard J. Wechsler, *Mirror to the Son of Heaven: Wei Cheng at the Court of T'ang T'ai-tsung* (Yale UP, 1974), introductory to the period; Edwin G. Pulleyblank, *The Background of the Rebellion of An Lu-shan* (Oxford UP, 1955); Denis C. Twitchett, *Financial Administration under the T'ang Dynasty* (Cambridge UP, 1963, 2nd ed., 1970); Wang

2. Traditional Civilization

Gungwu, *The Structure of Power in North China during the Five Dynasties* (Kuala Lumpur: U. of Malaya Press, 1963), dealing with the interregnum between T'ang and Sung: Liu I-ch'ing with commentary by Liu Chün, *Shih-shuo hsin-yü: A New Account of "Tales of the World,"* trans. and intro. by Richard B. Mather (U. of Minnesota Press, 1976); E. A. Kracke, Jr., *Civil Service in Early Sung China, 960–1067* (Harvard UP, 1953); James T. C. Liu, *Reform in Sung China: Wang An-shih (1021–1086) and His New Policies* (Harvard UP, 1959); John Winthrop Haeger, ed., *Crisis and Prosperity in Sung China* (U. of Arizona Press, 1975), eight articles from a 1971 conference; Brian E. McKnight, *Village and Bureaucracy in Southern Sung China* (U. of Chicago Press, 1971) on local administration; and Herbert Franz Schurmann, *Economic Structure of the Yuan Dynasty* (Harvard UP, 1956).

One of the most vivid re-creations of Chinese life in an earlier age is H. M. Wright's translation from the French of Jacques Gernet, *Daily Life in China on the Eve of the Mongol Invasion, 1250–1276* (Macmillan, 1962; Stanford paperback, 1970). Edward H. Schafer, *The Golden Peaches of Samarkand: A Study of T'ang Exotics* (U. of Calif. Press, 1963), is actually a mine of information on the material culture of the period. See also his *The Vermilion Bird: T'ang Images of the South* (U. of Calif. Press, 1967); and *Pacing the Void: T'ang Approaches to the Stars* (U. of Calif. Press, 1978). Lien-sheng Yang, *Studies in Chinese Institutional History* (Harvard UP, 1961), reprints nine articles by this leading institutional sinologist, from the *Harvard Journal of Asiatic Studies*. See also his *Money and Credit in China: A Short History* (Harvard UP, 1952). John L. Bishop, ed., *Studies of Governmental Institutions in Chinese History* (Harvard UP, 1968), reprints half a dozen major articles from the *Harvard Journal of Asiatic Studies*.

2.7 *Sino-Barbarian Relations.* For an introductory survey coming down to recent times see Morris Rossabi, *China and Inner Asia: From 1368 to the Present Day* (Pica Press, 1975). Study of Chinese border relations with Manchuria, Mongolia, and Sinkiang have been illumined and greatly stimulated by Owen Lattimore, *Inner Asian Frontiers of China* (American Geographical Society, 2nd ed., 1951 [1940]), which builds on the author's earlier publications and field experience — for example, his *Manchuria: Cradle of Conflict* (Macmillan, 1932). See his *Studies in Frontier History: Collected Papers, 1928–1958* (Oxford UP, 1962). Wolfram Eberhard, *Conquerors and Rulers: Social Forces in Medieval China* (Leiden: Brill, 2nd ed., 1965), pursues the same themes historically, differing with certain views of K. A. Wittfogel. For data on the regime of the Khitan Mongols, see K. A. Wittfogel and Feng Chia-sheng, *History of Chinese Society: Liao 907–1125* (Philadelphia: American Philosophical Society, 1949). On the tribute system as the vehicle of China's early modern foreign relations, see J. K. Fairbank, ed., *The Chinese World Order: Traditional China's Foreign Relations* (Harvard UP, 1968). J. V. G. Mills, *Ma Huan: Ying-yai sheng-lan, "The Overall Survey of the Ocean's Shores" (1433)* (Cambridge UP, 1970), translates a primary record of China's overseas trade and the Cheng Ho expeditions, with a 65 page introduction.

The most thorough work on the Mongols in history has been done in Europe, particularly in France. On the Mongol conquests in Central Asia, see V. V. Barthold, *Turkestan down to the Mongol Invasion,* trans. H. A. R. Gibb (London: Luzac, 2nd ed., 1958). A detailed study of the Mongols' trans-Asian imperial structure is given in George Vernadsky, *The Mongols and Russia* (Yale UP, 1953). Among many studies that have appeared, one of the most readable and authoritative is the English translation (from the French edition of 1944), by Denis Sinor and Marian MacKellar, of René Grousset, *Conqueror of the World: The Life of Chingis-Khan* (Toronto: Clarke, Irwin, 1967), which Sinor has updated on points of scholarship to 1965. Notable recent studies include Jing-shen Tao, *The Jurchen in Twelfth-Century China: A Study of Sinicization* (Seattle: U. of Wash. Press, 1977); and John W. Dardess, *Conquerors and Confucians: Aspects of Political Change in Late Yuan China* (Columbia UP, 1973).

2.8 *Marco Polo and Others.* This is a field in itself. Polo's better-known precursors and contemporaries are recorded in Christopher Dawson, *The Mongol Mission: Narratives and Letters of the Franciscan Missionaries in Mongolia and China in the*

Thirteenth and Fourteenth Centuries (Sheed and Ward, 1955). Leonardo Olschki, *Marco Polo's Asia: An Introduction to His "Description of the World" called "Il milione"* (U. of Calif. Press, 1960), has worked out a fascinating topical analysis of the content of Polo's great account. For the authoritative English translation, see A. C. Moule and P. Pelliot *Marco Polo: The Description of the World* (London: Routledge, 1938), 2 vols. Of the many popular versions, several are in paperback. Henry Hart, *Venetian Adventurer* (Stanford UP, 1942; Bantam, 1956), is a readable biography.

2.9 *Ming and Early Ch'ing.* This early modern era is now under intensive study. Many works of institutional history are noted in other sections. Graphic details are provided by a leading Japanese scholar, Ichisada Miyazaki, translated by Conrad Schirokauer, *China's Examination Hell: The Civil Service Examinations of Imperial China* (Weatherhill, 1976). Edward L. Farmer, *Early Ming Government: The Evolution of Dual Capitals* (Harvard UP, 1976) deals with Nanking and Peking. On Ming administration, see Charles O. Hucker, *The Traditional Chinese State in Ming Times, 1368–1644* (U. of Arizona Press, 1961); and Charles O. Hucker, ed., *Chinese Government in Ming Times: Seven Studies* (Columbia UP, 1969), a symposium volume. Aspects of dynastic decline are dealt with by Kwan-Wai So, *Japanese Piracy in Ming China during the 16th Century* (East Lansing: Mich. State UP, 1975); and James Bunyan Parsons, *The Peasant Rebellions of the Late Ming Dynasty* (U. of Arizona Press, 1970).

On the early Ch'ing there are now several studies of the major rulers, led by a best-seller in the emperor's own words, Jonathan D. Spence, *Kang-hsi, Emperor of China* (Knopf, 1974). Also Jonathan D. Spence, *Ts'ao Yin and the K'ang-hsi Emperor: Bondservant and Master* (Yale UP, 1966); Robert B. Oxnam, *Ruling from Horseback: Manchu Politics in the Oboi Regency, 1661–1669* (U. of Chicago Press, 1975); Lawrence D. Kessler, *K'ang-hsi and the Consolidation of Ch'ing Rule, 1661–1684* (U. of Chicago Press, 1976); Pei Huang, *Autocracy at Work: A Study of the Yung-cheng Period, 1723–1735* (Indiana UP, 1974); and Harold L. Kahn, *Monarchy in the Emperor's Eyes: Image and*

3. Culture and Society

Reality in the Ch'ien-lung Reign (Harvard UP, 1971). Aspects of local administration are analyzed by John R. Watt, *The District Magistrate in Late Imperial China* (Columbia UP, 1972); and in the conference volume, Frederic Wakeman, Jr., ed., *Conflict and Control in Late Imperial China* (U. of Calif. Press, 1975). The fiscal basis of dynastic power is illuminated by Preston M. Torbert, *The Ch'ing Imperial Household Department: A Study of its Organization and Principal Functions, 1662–1796* (Harvard UP, 1978). The misery and vicissitudes of ordinary life are portrayed in Jonathan D. Spence, *The Death of Woman Wang* (Viking, 1978).

A new view of literacy among the Chinese people is suggested by Evelyn S. Rawski, *Education and Popular Literacy in Ch'ing China* (U. of Mich. Press, 1978).

On one facet of the Ch'ing empire, see L. Petech, *China and Tibet in the Early 18th Century: History of the Establishment of the Chinese Protectorate in Tibet* (Leiden: Brill, 1950). Ch'ing activities concerning Inner Asia are detailed by Joseph Fletcher in John K. Fairbank, ed., *The Cambridge History of China*, vol. X, *Late Ch'ing, 1800–1911, Part 1* (Cambridge UP, 1978).

Economic history of the Ming and early Ch'ing has been stimulated by several monographic studies: Evelyn Sakakida Rawski, *Agricultural Change and the Peasant Economy of South China* (Harvard UP, 1972); Ray Huang, *Taxation and Governmental Finance in Sixteenth-century Ming China* (Cambridge UP, 1974); Yeh-chien Wang, *Land Taxation in Imperial China, 1750–1911* (Harvard UP, 1974); and Han-sheng Chuan and Richard A. Kraus, *Mid-Ch'ing Rice Markets and Trade: An Essay in Price History* (Harvard UP, 1975).

3. CHINESE CULTURE AND SOCIETY

3.1 *Literature in General.* This area is exploding in a barrage of publications. For an introduction to the different genres with lists of translations and studies, see James Robert Hightower, *Topics in Chinese Literature: Outlines and Bibliographies* (Harvard UP, 1953, 4th printing, 1966). For a recent reference work, see Jaroslav Prusek, general ed., Zbigniew Slupski, volume ed., *Dictionary of Oriental Literatures,* vol. I, *East Asia* (Basic Books, 1974), with a dozen contributors. Note the guidance for the general reader from W. T. de Bary, *A Guide to Oriental Classics,* and Jordan D. Paper, *Guide to Chinese Prose,* cited in section 2.2 above; and a briefer companion volume, Roger B. Bailey, *Guide to Chinese Poetry and Drama* (Boston: G. K. Hall, 1973). One excellent starting point is Liu Wu-chi, *An Introduction to Chinese Literature* (Indiana UP, 1966); see also Ch'en Shou-yi, *Chinese Literature: A Historical Introduction* (Ronald Press, 1961). Jaroslav Prusek, *Chinese History and Literature* (Prague: Academia, 1970), presents the studies of a leading European sinologist.

Among a number of surveys and anthologies, note Cyril Birch, comp. and ed., Donald Keene, assoc. ed., *Anthology of Chinese Literature,* vol. I, *From Early Times to the Fourteenth Century* (Grove Press, 1965), and Cyril Birch, ed. and intro., *Anthology of Chinese Literature,* vol. II, *From the Fourteenth Century to the Present Day* (Grove Press, 1972); William McNaughton, ed., *Chinese Literature: An Anthology from the Earliest Times to the Present Day* (Rutland: Tuttle, 1974); H. C. Chang, ed. and trans., *Chinese Literature,* vol. I, *Popular Fiction and Drama,* vol. II, *Nature Poetry* (Columbia UP, 1973, 1977); and Y. M. Ma and Joseph S. M. Lau, eds., *Traditional Chinese Stories: Themes and Variations* (Columbia UP, 1978).

There has also been a notable growth in the area of literary criticism, mainly through collections of essays by specialists: Andrew H. Plaks, ed., *Chinese Narrative: Critical and Theoretical Essays* (Princeton UP, 1977); Adele Austin Rickett, ed., *Chinese Approaches to Literature from Confucius to Liang Ch'i-ch'ao* (Princeton UP, 1978); William H. Nienhausen, Jr., ed., *Critical Essays on Chinese Literature* (UP of Hawaii, 1976); and Cyril Birch, ed., *Studies in Chinese Literary Genres* (U. of Calif. Press, 1974).

For comparison with traditional Chinese theories of literature and the arts, one may consult James J. Y. Liu, *Chinese Theories of Literature* (U. of Chicago Press, 1975); Vincent Yu-chung Shih, trans. with intro., *"The Literary Mind and the Carving of Dra-*

3. Culture and Society

gons" by *Liu Hsieh: A Study of Thought and Pattern in Chinese Literature* (Columbia UP, 1959), on the greatest single Chinese work of literary criticism; and David E. Pollard, *A Chinese Look at Literature: The Literary Values of Chou Tso-jen in Relation to the Tradition* (U. of Calif. Press, 1973).

3.2 *Poetry.* For a clear and concrete introduction see James J. Y. Liu, *The Art of Chinese Poetry* (U. of Chicago Press, 1962); and Julia C. Lin, *Modern Chinese Poetry: An Introduction* (Seattle: U. of Wash. Press, 1972). On the ancient northern and southern anthologies, see Ching-hsien Wang, *The Bell and the Drum: Shih Ching as Formulaic Poetry in an Oral Tradition* (U. of Calif. Press, 1974); and David Hawkes, *Ch'u Tz'u, the Songs of the South: An Ancient Anthology* (Oxford: Clarendon, 1959). In the great tradition are Burton Watson, *Chinese Lyricism: Shih Poetry from the Second to the Twelfth Century with Translations* (Columbia UP, 1971); A. C. Graham, *Poems of the Late T'ang* (Baltimore: Penguin, 1965); Hans H. Frankel, *The Flowering Plum and the Palace Lady: Interpretations of Chinese Poetry* (Yale UP, 1976) translating and interpreting 106 Chinese poems under themes and styles; and Wai-lim Yip, ed. and trans., *Chinese Poetry: Major Modes and Genres* (U. of Calif. Press, 1976). Note also for the general reader David Hawkes, *A Little Primer of Tu Fu* (Oxford: Clarendon, 1967). The most recent anthology is Wu-chi Liu and Irving Yucheng Lo, eds., *Sunflower Splendor: Three Thousand Years of Chinese Poetry* (Indiana UP, 1975), a comprehensive selection with translations by some fifty different translators, organized by chronological periods, with notes on poets and poems.

Poets through their works lend themselves to biographical treatment, and a notable series of studies has resulted: Arthur Waley, *The Poetry and Career of Li Po, 701–762 A.D.* (London: Allen and Unwin, 1950); Arthur Waley, *The Life and Times of Po Chü-i, 772–846* (London: Allen and Unwin, 1949); Lin Yutang, *The Gay Genius: The Life and Times of Su Tungpo, 1036–1101* (London: Heinemann, 1948); F. W. Mote, *The Poet Kao Ch'i, 1336–1374* (Princeton UP, 1962), which re-creates the atmosphere of the founding of the Ming dynasty; and Arthur Waley, *Yuan*

3. Culture and Society

Mei, Eighteenth-Century Chinese Poet (London: Allen and Unwin, 1956; Grove Press, reprint.)

3.3 *The Novel.* One neglected shortcut to understanding China is the corpus of novels that in late imperial times provided the well-known type-characters and incidents of everyday literate conversation. Best known abroad perhaps are Pearl Buck's rather free translation of *Shui-hu chuan* entitled *All Men are Brothers* (John Day, 1933, 2 vols.; Grove Press, 1957); and Bernard Miall, trans. from German of Franz Kuhn, *Chin P'ing Mei: The Adventurous History of Hsi Men and His Six Wives* (London: John Lane, 1939; Putnam, 1940; reprint Capricorn, 1962). Other translations of these and other novels are described in the Paper and de Bary guidebooks cited in 2.2. For a recent addition, note Anthony C. Yu, trans. and ed., *The Journey to the West,* vol. I (U. of Chicago Press, 1977). *Hung Lou Meng* or *Dream of the Red Chamber* is now being translated in a thorough, not condensed, rendition by David Hawkes, trans., *The Story of the Stone: A Chinese Novel by Cao Xueqin,* in 5 vols.: vol. I, *The Golden Days,* vol. II, *The Crab-Flower Club* (Harmondsworth, England: Penguin, 1973, 1977). Study of *Hung Lou Meng* continues apace, often in the style of Western literary criticism: Andrew H. Plaks, *Archetype and Allegory in "The Dream of the Red Chamber"* (Princeton UP, 1976); and Lucien Miller, *Masks of Fiction in "Dream of the Red Chamber"* (U. of Arizona Press, 1975). See also Jeanne Knoerle, S.P., *"The Dream of the Red Chamber": A Critical Study* (Indiana UP, 1972).

For a most interesting introduction to the six major vernacular novels, see C. T. Hsia, *The Classic Chinese Novel: A Critical Introduction* (Columbia UP, 1968). Note also W. L. Idema, *Chinese Vernacular Fiction* (Leiden: Brill, 1974) on origins and early development; and Patrick D. Hanan, *The Chinese Short Story: Studies in Dating, Authorship and Composition* (Harvard UP, 1973).

Social historians are just beginning to tap the very extensive corpus of late Ch'ing fiction as reflecting social problems and conflicts of values. One such novel, translated by Harold Shadick, is *The Travels of Lao Ts'an* by Liu T'ieh-yün (Cornell UP,

3. Culture and Society

1952). Among many translations by Yang Hsien-yi and Gladys Yang published by the Foreign Languages Press in Peking is Wu Ching-tzu (1701–1754), *The Scholars* (1957), a translation of *Ju-lin wai-shih.* Other examples are Li Ju-chen, *Flowers in the Mirror,* trans. Lin Tai-yi (U. of Calif. Press, 1965); and an abridgement of Wu Wo-yao, *Bizarre Happenings Eyewitnessed over Two Decades* published as Shih Shun Liu, *Vignettes from the Late Ch'ing* (Chinese U. of Hong Kong, 1978).

Another field of growth is in vernacular literature apart from and often preceding the novel: Arthur Waley, ed. and trans. *Ballads and Stories from Tun-huang: An Anthology* (Macmillan, 1960); Cyril Birch, *Stories from a Ming Collection: The Art of the Chinese Story-teller* (London: Bodley Head, 1958); and Li Li-ch'en, trans., *Master Tung's Western Chamber Romance (Tung Hsi-hsiang chu-kung tiao): A Chinese Chantefable* (Cambridge UP, 1976).

3.4 *The Drama.* On the drama see A. C. Scott, *The Classical Theatre of China* (Barnes and Noble, 1957); and A. C. Scott, *Traditional Chinese Plays* (U. of Wisc. Press, 1967, 1969), 2 vols. Recent publications include Chung-wen Shih, *The Golden Age of Chinese Drama: Yüan Tsa-chü* (Princeton UP, 1976); George A. Hayden, *Crime and Punishment in Medieval Chinese Drama: Three Judge Pao Plays* (Harvard UP, 1978); William Dolby, trans., *Eight Chinese Plays, from the Thirteenth Century to the Present Day* (Columbia UP, 1978); Colin P. Mackerras, *The Rise of the Peking Opera, 1770–1870: Social Aspects of the Theatre in Manchu China* (Oxford: Clarendon, 1972), a topical treatment from many angles; Ch'en Shih-hsiang and Harold Acton with the collaboration of Cyril Birch, trans., *K'ung Shang-jen: The Peach Blossom Fan (T'ao-hua-shan)* (U. of Calif. Press, 1976); and Colin P. Mackerras, *The Chinese Theatre in Modern Times: From 1840 to the Present* (U. of Mass. Press, 1975).

3.5 *Chinese Thought.* Under the sponsorship of a committee of the Association for Asian Studies, a series of research conference symposia presented a wide range of some fifty-seven articles by specialists from several countries: Arthur F. Wright, ed., *Studies in Chinese Thought* (U. of Chicago Press, 1953); J. K.

3. Culture and Society

Fairbank, ed., *Chinese Thought and Institutions* (U. of Chicago Press, 1957); David S. Nivison and A. F. Wright, eds., *Confucianism in Action* (Stanford UP, 1959); A. F. Wright, ed., *The Confucian Persuasion* (Stanford UP, 1960); and A. F. Wright and D. C. Twitchett, eds., *Confucian Personalities* (Stanford UP, 1962). A. F. Wright, ed. and introd., *Confucianism and Chinese Civilization* (Atheneum paperback, 1964), is a selection from the last three of these volumes on Chinese thought. Further symposia have appeared under the sponsorship of the American Council of Learned Societies' Committee on Studies of Chinese Civilization; these are by Wm. Theodore de Bary and the Conference on Ming Thought, *Self and Society in Ming Thought* (Columbia UP, 1970); and Wm. Theodore deBary and the Conference on Seventeenth Century Chinese Thought, *The Unfolding of Neo-Confucianism* (Columbia UP, 1975). Wolfgang Bauer, *China and the Search for Happiness: Recurring Themes in Four Thousand Years of Chinese Cultural History* (The Seabury Press, 1976), is a sophisticated discussion of concepts, folklore and cosmology. Thomas A. Metzger, *Escape from Predicament: Neo-Confucianism and China's Evolving Political Culture* (Columbia UP, 1977) analyzes the Confucian moral experience in meaningful terms. A major historian is studied by David S. Nivison, *The Life and Thought of Chang Hsueh-ch'eng (1738–1801)* (Stanford UP, 1966).

3.6 *Religion.* For an interesting survey of the vast subject of Buddhism in China, see Arthur F. Wright, *Buddhism in Chinese History* (Stanford UP, 1959); for a longer monograph, E. Zürcher, *The Buddhist Conquest of China: The Spread and Adaptation of Buddhism in Early Medieval China* (Leiden: Brill, 1959), 2 vols.; for a general account, Kenneth Ch'en, *Buddhism in China: A Historical Survey* (Princeton UP, 1964); also Kenneth K. S. Ch'en, *The Chinese Transformation of Buddhism* (Princeton UP, 1973); and for a graphic eyewitness description of monastic life in recent times, Holmes Welch, *The Practice of Chinese Buddhism, 1900–1950* (Harvard UP, 1967). For a basic text see Leon Hurvitz, *Scriptures of the Lotus Blossom of the Fine Dharma (The Lotus Sūtra)*, trans. from the Chinese of Kumārajīva (Columbia UP, 1976). On one aspect of Buddhism now in vogue, a

3. Culture and Society

convenient popular collection is *The Essentials of Zen Buddhism: Selected from the Writings of Daisetz T. Suzuki,* ed. Bernard Phillips (Dutton, 1962).

On religion in general, the most recent guide is Laurence G. Thompson, *Studies of Chinese Religion: A Comprehensive and Classified Bibliography of Publications in English, French and German through 1970* (Encino, Calif.: Dickenson Publishing Co., 1976), including general studies and Chinese religion exclusive of Buddhism as well as Chinese Buddhism, under 65 categories, very comprehensive. For studies of folk sects and modern conditions, see sections 4.6 and 4.18.

3.7 *Social Structure.* Chinese ways have been more often described than analyzed. A great impetus came from the German sociologist Max Weber, whose pioneer work on China has been largely translated by Hans Gerth as *The Religion of China: Confucianism and Taoism* (Glencoe: The Free Press, 1951). Note that the paperback edition (Macmillan, 1964) has an invaluable thirty-page introduction by C. K. Yang (Yang Ch'ing-k'un) who puts Weber's work in context and evaluates his contribution, including its unavoidable shortcomings. Another broad impetus through a neo-Marxist approach has come from Karl A. Wittfogel, *Oriental Despotism: A Comparative Study of Total Power* (Yale UP, 1957). For an iconoclastic analysis of one main European view of the East, see Lawrence Krader, *The Asiatic Mode of Production: Sources, Development and Critique in the Writings of Karl Marx* (Assen, the Netherlands: VanGorcum, 1975). The brilliant early study of 1922 in the French tradition of E. Durkheim, by Marcel Granet, has been reprinted with annotations by the late Maurice Freedman, *The Religion of the Chinese People* (Harper and Row, 1975). For historical studies of social structure and bureaucracy, see Etienne Balazs, *Chinese Civilization and Bureaucracy* (Yale UP, 1964), which brings together trenchant essays by a leading European scholar, brilliantly translated. Nearly everyone, of course, touches on this subject in some fashion. For statistical research on the gentry class, in the sense of degree holders, see Chung-li Chang, *The Chinese Gentry, Studies on Their Role in Nineteenth-Century Chinese Society*

(Seattle: U. of Wash. Press, 1955). This analysis has been further developed and modified by Ping-ti Ho, *The Ladder of Success in Imperial China, Aspects of Social Mobility* (Columbia UP, 1962). Leon E. Stover, *The Cultural Ecology of Chinese Civilization: Peasants and Elites in the Last of the Agrarian States* (Pica Press, 1974) is tendentious and provocative.

Two recent collections in this field are *The Study of Chinese Society: Essays by Maurice Freedman,* intro. by G. William Skinner (Stanford UP, 1979); and Arthur P. Wolf, ed., *Studies in Chinese Society,* selected from the seven-volume series Studies in Chinese Society (Stanford UP, 1978).

3.8 *Village Community and Family.* These have seldom been studied by foreign-style field work since 1949 but are studied under the PRC more diffusely and less nominally in many works cited in sections 5.6, 5.7, 5.14 and elsewhere below. Village studies were just getting started in the 1940s following the work of a few pioneers. One of the earliest was the American missionary, Arthur H. Smith, whose *Chinese Characteristics* (2nd ed., Fleming H. Revell, 1894) and *Village Life in China: A Study in Sociology* (London: Oliphant, Anderson, and Ferrier, 1899) were very influential, even in Japan. Sidney D. Gamble, *North China Villages: Social, Political and Economic Activities before 1933* (U. of Calif. Press, 1963), describes leadership and other functions in eleven villages out of 100 or so visited by university students. Among social anthropologists, one creative modern writer was Hsiao-t'ung Fei, whose works in English include *Peasant Life in China: A Field Study of Country Life in the Yangtze Valley* (Dutton, 1939); and with Chih-i Chang, *Earthbound China: A Study of Rural Economy in Yunnan* (U. of Chicago Press, 1945). A volume of Fei's essays, *China's Gentry* (U. of Chicago Press, 1953), was published after his absorption into the new order in Peking.

For work on the family and clan (or lineage) by a leader in this field, see Maurice Freedman, *Chinese Lineage and Society: Fukien and Kwangtung* (London: Athlone, 1966). Note also Hui-chen Wang Liu, *The Traditional Chinese Clan Rules* (Locust Valley, N.Y.: Augustin, 1959). The family system at work in a village may be seen in a number of case studies: Martin Yang,

3. Culture and Society

A Chinese Village: Taitou, Shantung Province (Columbia UP, 1945); Lin Yüeh-hua, *The Golden Wing: A Sociological Study of Chinese Familism* (London: Kegan Paul, Trench, Trubner, 1948); Francis L. K. Hsu, *Under the Ancestors' Shadow: Chinese Culture and Personality* (Columbia UP, 1948); Sidney D. Gamble, *Ting Hsien, a North China Rural Community* (Institute of Pacific Relations, 1954; reissued, Stanford UP, 1968); Morton H. Fried, *Fabric of Chinese Society: A Study of the Social Life of a Chinese County Seat* (Praeger, 1953); and Margery Wolf, *The House of Lim, A Study of a Chinese Farm Family* (Appleton-Century-Crofts, 1968). An early theoretical work is by Marion J. Levy, *The Family Revolution in Modern China* (Harvard UP, 1949; Atheneum paperback, 1968). Recent work is represented in Maurice Freedman, ed., *Family and Kinship in Chinese Society* (Stanford UP, 1970), papers by ten specialists from an SSRC conference of 1966. See also I. C. Jarvie, ed., *Hong Kong: A Society in Transition. Contributions to the Study of Hong Kong Society* (London: Routledge and Kegan Paul, 1969), fourteen sociological studies, with photos.

For historical perspective, Patricia Ebrey, *The Aristocratic Families of Early Imperial China: A Case Study of the Po-ling Ts'ui Family* (Cambridge UP, 1977); and Hilary J. Beattie, *Land and Lineage in China: A Study of T'ung-ch'eng County, Anhwei, in the Ming and Ch'ing Dynasties* (Cambridge UP, 1978).

3.9 *Rural Economy.* Another vital stimulus, leading toward the study of "local systems," has come from G. William Skinner's three-part article, "Marketing and Social Structure in Rural China," *Journal of Asian Studies* (1964–65). The incidence of landlordism at the end of the Ch'ing period has been illuminated by Yuji Muramatsu, "A Documentary Study of Chinese Landlordism in the Late Ch'ing and the Early Republican Kiangnan," *Bulletin of the School of Oriental and African Studies,* U. of London, vol. 29, pt. 3, (1966). Endymion Wilkinson, trans., Jing Su and Luo Lun, *Landlord and Labor in Late Imperial China: Case Studies from Shandong* (Harvard UP, 1978), makes available an important piece of research from the People's Republic. R. H. Tawney, *Land and Labor in China* (Harcourt, Brace, 1932),

3. Culture and Society

is still a classic analysis of the farm economy about 1930, by a leading specialist on late medieval Europe. A recent analysis is Jack M. Potter, *Capitalism and the Chinese Peasant. Social and Economic Change in a Hong Kong Village* (U. of Calif. Press, 1968), which questions whether foreign economic influence was as disastrous as many like Fei Hsiao-t'ung once assumed. Modern Japanese as well as Chinese studies of the North China farm economy, village and market, are appraised by Ramon H. Myers, *The Chinese Peasant Economy. Agricultural Development in Hopei and Shantung, 1890–1949* (Harvard UP, 1970). James D. Clarkson, *The Cultural Ecology of a Chinese Village, Cameron Highlands, Malaysia* (Dept. of Geography, U. of Chicago, 1968), gives a detailed picture of Chinese agriculture and care in land management. See also section 5.14 below.

3.10 *Population.* The enigma of population growth is attacked by Ping-ti Ho, *Studies on the Population of China, 1368–1953* (Harvard UP, 1959); also by Irene B. Taeuber and Wang Nai-chi, "Population Reports in the Ch'ing Dynasty," *Journal of Asian Studies,* 29 (1959–60), 403-417. An arresting historical analysis of the growth of people and food supply is in Dwight H. Perkins, with the assistance of Yeh-chien Wang and others, *Agricultural Development in China, 1368–1968* (Chicago: Aldine, 1969). Here we may also note the path-breaking survey, K. C. Chang, ed., *Food in Chinese Culture: Anthropological and Historical Perspectives* (Yale UP, 1977), arranged by periods, with ten contributors. See also section 5.16.

3.11 *Law and Administration.* T'ung-tsu Ch'ü, *Law and Society in Traditional China* (The Hague: Mouton, 1961), provides vivid details of the uses of law to regulate the social order. Wallace Johnson, ed. and trans. *The T'ang Code,* vol. I, *General Principles* (Princeton UP, 1978), makes a basic document available. Sybille van der Sprenkel, *Legal Institutions in Machu China: A Sociological Analysis* (London: Athlone, 1962), surveys the traditional means of conflict resolution. Derk Bodde and Clarence Morris, *Law in Imperial China, Exemplified by 190 Ch'ing Dynasty Cases* (Harvard UP, 1967) describes the operation of the imperial legal system and its chraracteristics, with illus-

3. Culture and Society

trative cases. The most concrete study of one of China's primary administrative institutions is by Charles O. Hucker, *The Censorial System of Ming China* (Stanford UP, 1966). T'ung-tsu Ch'ü, *Local Government in China under the Ch'ing* (Harvard UP 1962; Stanford UP paperback, 1969), is a classic analysis of what goes on inside a hsien magistrate's yamen. Kung-chuan Hsiao, *Rural China: Imperial Control in the Nineteenth Century* (Seattle: U. of Wash, Press, 1960), describes the whole range of control mechanisms and policies. On the Manchus' control and use of their homeland, see Robert H. G. Lee, *The Manchurian Frontier in Ch'ing History* (Harvard UP, 1970).

A recent study of central administration is by Silas H. L. Wu, *Communication and Imperial Control in China. Evolution of the Palace Memorial System, 1693–1735* (Harvard UP, 1970). Thomas Metzger, *The Internal Organization of Ch'ing Bureaucracy: Legal, Normative and Communications Aspects* (Harvard UP, 1973) offers radically new insights and approaches to this whole field. See also David C. Buxbaum, ed., *Chinese Family Law and Social Change in Historical and Comparative Perspective* (Seattle: U. of Wash. Press, 1977), a symposium. For a guide to materials and their use in research on the Ch'ing administration, see John K. Fairbank, *Ch'ing Documents: An Introductory Syllabus* (Harvard UP, 3rd ed. with index added, 1970), 2 vols. For work of Jerome A. Cohen and others on the recent period see 5.19.

3.12 *Urbanization*. This is another area stimulated by G. W. Skinner and an SSRC committee. Paul Wheatley, *The Pivot of the Four Quarters: A Preliminary Enquiry into the Origins and Character of the Ancient Chinese City* (Edinburgh UP, 1971), is a wide-ranging classical approach. Gilbert Rozman, *Urban Networks in Ch'ing China and Tokugawa Japan* (Princeton UP, 1973) uses modern methods of quantification. G. William Skinner, ed., *The City in late Imperial China* (Stanford UP, 1977) is an exemplary symposium that maps out broad areas for further research. Mark Elvin and G. William Skinner, eds., *The Chinese City between Two Worlds* (Stanford UP, 1974), results from a conference on the modern period. For the third volume in this series see under 5.13. The most recent monograph is by David D. Buck, *Urban Change in China: Politics and Development in Tsinan, Shantung, 1890–1949* (U. of Wisc. Press, 1978). Ross Terrill, *Flowers on an Iron Tree: Five Cities of China* (Boston: Little, Brown, 1975), has interesting on-the-spot vignettes of Shanghai, Dairen, Hangchow, Wuhan, Peking.

4. MODERN CHINA TO 1949

4.1 *General Accounts.* The chief recent survey is by Immanuel C. Y. Hsu, *The Rise of Modern China* (Oxford UP, 1970, 2nd ed., 1975). On modern East Asia, in addition to items cited in 1.3 above, there are a number of substantial and interesting works: Marius B. Jansen, *Japan and China: From War to Peace 1894–1972* (Chicago: Rand McNally, 1975), by one of the few Sino-Japanese specialists; George E. Taylor and Franz H. Michael, *The Far East in the Modern World* (Holt, 1956, rev. ed., 1964); Paul Clyde and Burton Beers, *The Far East: A History of Western Impacts and Eastern Responses, 1830–1975,* (Prentice-Hall, 6th ed., 1975, descended from a text first published by Paul Clyde in 1948 and steadily developed ever since).

Modern China to 1911 is dealt with in two volumes of *The Cambridge History of China:* vol. X, John K. Fairbank, ed., *Late Ch'ing, 1800–1911, Part 1*; and vol. XI, John K. Fairbank and Kwang-Ching Liu, eds., *Late Ch'ing, 1800–1911, Part 2*; and in a very readable volume from Paris by Jean Chesneaux, Marianne Bastid, and Marie-Claire Bergère, <u>China from the Opium Wars to the 1911 Revolution</u> (Pantheon, 1976).

The theme of rebellion and revolution is especially pursued in several survey studies: Albert Feuerwerker, *Rebellion in Nineteenth-Century China* (Ann Arbor: U. of Mich., Center for Chinese Studies, 1975); Jean Chesneaux, *Peasant Revolts in China, 1840–1949* (Norton, 1973), popular and illustrated; Jean Chesneaux, ed., *Popular Movements and Secret Societies in China, 1840–1950* (Stanford UP, 1972); Michael Gasster, *China's Struggle to Modernize* (Knopf, 1972); Victor Nee and James Peck, eds., *China's Uninterrupted Revolution from 1840 to the Present*

(Pantheon, Random House, 1975); Frederic Wakeman, Jr., *The Fall of Imperial China* (The Free Press, 1975).

Selected readings are provided in a volume of translations with commentary by Ssu-yü Teng and John K. Fairbank, *China's Response to the West: A Documentary Survey, 1839–1923* (Harvard UP, 1954; Atheneum paperback, 1963, 1965); and in Franz Schurmann and Orville Schell, *The China Reader,* vol. I, *Imperial China,* vol. II, *Republican China,* and vol III, *Communist China* (Random House, 1967), a selection mainly of extracts from observers and historians. A fourth volume, *People's China,* comp. David Milton, Nancy Milton, and Franz Schurmann, has now been added (Random House, 1974), 4 vols. For an ingenious and entrancing sequence of excerpts from some 280 first-person narratives during a century and a half, from all sides, see Roger Pelissier, *The Awakening of China, 1793–1949* (G. P. Putnam's Sons, 1967; trans. from French ed., *La Chine entre en scene,* 1963). H. F. MacNair, *Modern Chinese History: Selected Readings* (Shanghai: Commercial Press, 1923; reprinted Taipei, 1957; Paragon reprint, 1967), dates from an earlier era; its documentation parallels the basic survey, mainly from the British record, by Hosea Ballou Morse, *The International Relations of the Chinese Empire* (London: Longmans Green, 1910, 1918; reprinted in Taipei), 3 vols.

For the Republican period, a very useful survey is by O. Edmund Clubb, *20th Century China* (Columbia UP, 1964, 3rd ed., 1978).

4.2 *Early European Contact.* For a general survey of European expansion, see John H. Parry, *The Age of Reconnaissance* (Cleveland: World Publishing Co., 1963). A small paperback of extracts from some two-score authors, selected by Joseph R. Levenson, ed., *European Expansion and the Counter-Example of Asia, 1300–1600* (Prentice-Hall, 1967), conveys very well the extraordinary vitality and intellectual enthusiasm of the editor. The Portuguese pioneers in China have been illumined in a series of notable studies by C. R. Boxer, including, on Macao, *Fidalgos in the Far East, 1550–1770* (The Hague: Nijhoff, 1948); and C. R. Boxer, ed., *South China in the Sixteenth Century* (London:

Hakluyt Society, 1953), three narratives of adventures in 1550–1575. John E. Wills, Jr., *Pepper, Guns and Parleys: The Dutch East India Company and China, 1662–1681* (Harvard UP, 1974), shows the potentialities of the Dutch archives when combined with Chinese records. Frances V. Moulder, *Japan, China and the Modern Economy: Toward a Reinterpretation of East Asian Development ca. 1600 to ca. 1918* (Cambridge UP, 1977), is a broad but brief and theoretical work. More substantial is K. N. Chaudhuri, *The Trading World of Asia and the English East India Company, 1600–1760* (Cambridge UP, 1978).

Like Marco Polo, the Jesuit pioneers at Peking form an entire field in themselves. Their own record has been newly appraised in a well-informed study by George H. Dunne, S.J., *Generation of Giants: The Story of the Jesuits in China in the Last Decades of the Ming Dynasty* (U. of Notre Dame Press, 1962). For a somewhat different view see Columba Cary-Elwes, O.S.B., *China and the Cross: Studies in Missionary History* (Longmans Green, 1957). For a popularly written account of Matteo Ricci, see Vincent Cronin, *The Wise Man from the West* (London: Rupert-Hart-Davis, 1955). For a version of his own account, see Louis J. Gallagher, S.J., trans., *China in the Sixteenth Century: The Journals of Matthew Ricci, 1583–1610* (Random House, 1953). A recent analysis is by George L. Harris, "The Mission of Matteo Ricci, S.J. A Case Study of an Effort at Guided Culture Change in China in the Sixteenth Century," *Monumenta Serica*, Tokyo, 25 (1966). Donald W. Treadgold, *The West in Russia and China: Religious and Secular Thought in Modern Times*, vol. I, *Russia, 1472–1917*, vol. II, *China, 1582–1949* (Cambridge UP, 1973), in his China volume carries on from the Jesuits through the Protestant missionaries, Sun Yat-sen, K'ang Yu-wei et al. to the Chinese Communists, a real *tour de force!*

On the early Ch'ing contact with Russia, see Mark Mancall, *Russia and China: Their Diplomatic Relations to 1728* (Harvard UP, 1971); and Eric Widmer, *The Russian Ecclesiastical Mission in Peking during the Eighteenth Century* (Harvard UP, 1976).

4.3 *China in the Enlightenment.* A multi-volume review of western literature and art on China is being made by Donald

Lach, *Asia in the Making of Europe* (U. of Chicago Press, vol. I, *The Century of Discovery*, in 2 books, (1965); vol. II, *A Century of Wonder*, Book One: *The Visual Arts* (1970), Book Two: *The Literary Arts* (1978), Book Three: *The Scholarly Disciplines* (1978). These volumes deal with the sixteenth and seventeenth centuries, respectively. At present the broadest brief survey of the eighteenth century is still Adolf Reichwein, *China and Europe* (Knopf, 1925). The most trenchant researches are in French. Studies of chinoiserie are W. W. Appleton, *A Cycle of Cathay: The Chinese Vogue in England* (Columbia UP, 1951); and Hugh Honour, *Chinoiserie: The Vision of Cathay* (London: J. Murray, 1961). A general view of successive ages is in Raymond Dawson, *The Chinese Chameleon: An Analysis of European Conceptions of Chinese Civilization* (Oxford UP, 1967). The study of Sino-European intellectual relations in this period has been long delayed and is just beginning: see David E. Mungello, *Leibniz and Confucianism: The Search for Accord* (U. of Hawaii Press, 1977).

4.4 *The Canton Trade*. New light on the Chinese context of the early European trade comes from Sarasin Viraphol, *Tribute and Profit: Sino-Siamese Trade, 1652–1853* (Harvard UP, 1977), which details the role of tribute ships, the rice trade, and a great deal more in the growth of China's foreign trade. The major source on European participation is still H. B. Morse, *The Chronicles of the East India Company Trading to China* (Oxford UP, 1926–1929), 5 vols. The most recent and massive study is by Louis Dermigny, *La Chine et l'occident: Le commerce à Canton au XVIIIe siécie, 1719–1833* (Paris: S.E.V.P.E.N., 1964), 3 vols. and vol. IV album. For Chinese documentation in general, see Lo-shu Fu, *A Documentary Chronicle of Sino-Western Relations, 1644–1820* (U. of Arizona Press, 1966), 2 vols.; and in particular, J. L. Cranmer-Byng, "Lord Macartney's Embassy to Peking in 1793 from Official Chinese Documents," *Journal of Oriental Studies*, U. of Hong Kong, 4.1–2 (1957–58), 117–187. The classic, roseate account of Sino-foreign contact is by William C. Hunter, *The "Fan Kwae" at Canton before Treaty Days, 1825–44* (London, 1882; 2nd ed., Shanghai, 1911, reprinted 1949). See also Michael Greenberg, *British Trade and the Opening of China, 1800–42* (Cambridge UP, 1951).

4.5 *Opening Western Relations.* A new and graphic review by Peter Ward Fay, *The Opium War, 1840–1842* (Cambridge UP, 1975), opens up new angles of iniquity; and Jack Beeching, *The Opium Wars in China, 1834–1860* (London: Hutchison, 1975), retraces the vagaries of British opinion. On the Chinese side the major study of the first war's origins is by Hsin-pao Chang, *Commissioner Lin and the Opium War* (Harvard UP, 1964). For Chinese accounts, see Arthur Waley, *The Opium War through Chinese Eyes* (London: Allen and Unwin, 1958). For the social forces at work at Canton see Frederic Wakeman, Jr., *Strangers at the Gate: Social Disorder in South China, 1839–1861* (U. of Calif. Press, 1966). J. Y. Wong, *Yeh Ming-ch'en: Viceroy of Liang Kuang, 1852–8* (Cambridge UP, 1976) gives an inside and revisionist view of a Chinese governor general at work. For the British, American, and French efforts to set up the new system of treaty relations, see respectively John K. Fairbank, *Trade and Diplomacy on the China Coast: The Opening of the Treaty Ports, 1842–1854* (Harvard UP, 1953; Stanford UP paperback), 2 vols.; Earl Swisher, *China's Management of the American Barbarians: A Study of Sino-American Relations, 1841–1861, with Documents* (New Haven: Far Eastern Publications for the Far Eastern Association, 1951); and John F. Cady, *The Roots of French Imperialism in Eastern Asia* (Cornell UP, 1954, for the American Historical Association). For a study of the second war from the British side see Douglas Hurd, *The Arrow War: An Anglo-Chinese Confusion, 1856–1860* (Macmillan, 1967). The last word on Ward and Gordon defending Shanghai is Richard J. Smith, *Mercenaries and Mandarins: The Ever-Victorious Army in Nineteenth Century China* (KTO Press, 1978).

On a leading American missionary-diplomat, Edward V. Gulick, *Peter Parker and the Opening of China* (Harvard UP, 1973). China's first systematic look at the West is skillfully analyzed by Fred W. Drake, *China Charts the World: Hsu Chi-yü and His Geography of 1848* (Harvard UP, 1975). For the Ch'ing side of the military-constitutional crisis, see Masataka Banno, *China and the West, 1858–1861: The Origins of the Tsungli Yamen* (Harvard, 1964).

On the development of Hong Kong, see G. B. Endacott, *Government and People in Hong Kong, 1841–1962: A Constitutional History* (Hong Kong UP, 1964). The eventual scope of the treaty system may be traced in W. W. Willoughby, *Foreign Rights and Interests in China* (Johns Hopkins UP, 2nd ed., 1927 [1920]) 2 vols. The general British approach to treaty port life is popularly described by George Woodcock, *The British in the Far East* (London: Weidenfeld and Nicolson, 1969).

4.6 *Nineteenth-Century Rebellions.* An early classic on rebellion in China was by the British consul Thomas Taylor Meadows, *The Chinese and Their Rebellions* (London, 1856; Stanford: Academic Reprints, 1953). The place of peasant risings in Chinese history and current theory is analyzed by James P. Harrison, *The Communists and Chinese Peasant Rebellions: A Study in the Rewriting of Chinese History* (Atheneum, 1969). For a new look at the religious origins of risings, see Daniel L. Overmyer, *Folk Buddhist Religion: Dissenting Sects in Late Traditional China* (Harvard UP, 1976). The fiasco of 1813 is intimately detailed by Susan Naquin, *Millenarian Rebellion in China: The Eight Trigrams Uprising of 1813* (Yale UP, 1976). These two studies break new ground.

On the Taipings, the extensive literature is appraised by Ssu-yü Teng, *Historiography of the Taiping Rebellion* (Harvard UP, 1962). A strikingly detailed and comprehensive account is by a long-time leading specialist, Jen Yuwen, *The Taiping Revolutionary Movement* (Yale UP, 1973). The most basic study is by Franz Michael in collaboration with Chung-li Chang, *The Taiping Rebellion: History and Documents* in three volumes (Seattle: U. of Wash. Press): vol. I, *History* (1966); vols. II and III, *Documents and Comments* (1972). A key document is studied by C. A. Curwen, *Taiping Rebel: The Deposition of Li Hsiu-ch'eng* (Cambridge UP, 1977). See also Vincent Y. C. Shih, *The Taiping Ideology: Its Sources, Interpretations, and Influences* (Seattle: U. of Wash. Press, 1967). Foreign relations and a good deal more are wrapped up by S. Y. Teng, *The Taiping Rebellion and the Western Powers: A Comprehensive Survey* (Oxford UP, 1971). Taiping foreign relations are also studied in J. S. Gregory, *Great Britain and the Taipings* (Praeger, 1969).

On the Nien there are two works, Siang-tseh Chiang, *The Nien Rebellion* (Seattle: U. of Wash. Press, 1954); and S. Y. Teng, *The Nien Army and Their Guerrilla Warfare, 1851–1868* (The Hague: Mouton, 1961). On the Muslim rebellion in the Northwest, see Wen-djang Chu, *The Moslem Rebellion in Northwest China, 1862–1878: A Study of Government Minority Policy* (The Hague: Mouton, 1966). Less has been published on the rebellion in Southwest China. The social and institutional repercussions of all this disorder are masterfully analyzed in Philip A. Kuhn, *Rebellion and Its Enemies in Late Imperial China: Militarization and Social Structure, 1796–1864* (Harvard UP, 1970).

4.7 *Restoration and Self-Strengthening.* The major study of Ch'ing policy in the 1860's is by Mary Clabaugh Wright, *The Last Stand of Chinese Conservatism: The T'ung-chih Restoration, 1862–1872* (Stanford UP, 1957, also paperback). The interaction of restoration and westernization is surveyed in Kwang-Ching Liu, "Nineteenth-Century China: The Disintegration of the Old Order and the Impact of the West," in Ping-ti Ho and Tang Tsou, eds., *China's Heritage and the Communist Political System,* vol. I of *China in Crisis* (U. of Chicago Press, 1968, in two books). See also the same author's "Li Hung-chang in Chihli: The Emergence of a Policy, 1870–1875," in Albert Feuerwerker, Rhoads Murphey, and Mary C. Wright, eds., *Approaches to Modern Chinese History* (U. of Calif. Press, 1967), pp. 68–104; Stanley Spector, *Li Hung-chang and the Huai Army* (Seattle: U. of Wash. Press, 1964); and Kenneth E. Folsom, *Friends, Guests, and Colleagues: The Mu-fu System in the Late Ch'ing Period* (U. of Calif. Press, 1968). On the navy, John L. Rawlinson, *China's Struggle for Naval Development, 1839–1895* (Harvard UP, 1967). On the acquisition of Western technology, Knight Biggerstaff, *The Earliest Modern Government Schools in China* (Cornell UP, 1961); and Adrian Arthur Bennett, *John Fryer: The Introduction of Western Science and Technology into Nineteenth-Century China* (Harvard UP, 1967). On postal reform,

4. *Modern China to 1949*

Ying-wan Cheng, *Postal Communication in China and Its Modernization, 1860–1896* (Harvard UP, 1970). The latest appraisal of the Restoration is by Kwang-Ching Liu in *Cambridge History of China,* vols. X and XI.

4.8 *Economic Developments.* Major aspects of Sino-Western economic relations are researched in a symposium, Dwight H. Perkins, ed., *China's Modern Economy in Historical Perspective* (Stanford UP, 1975). Another valuable collection in this field is W. E. Willmott, ed., *Economic Organization in Chinese Society* (Stanford UP, 1972). On the "official-control and merchant-operation" system of development, the main study is by Albert Feuerwerker, *China's Early Industrialization: Sheng Hsuan-huai, (1844–1916) and Mandarin Enterprise* (Harvard UP, 1958). The same author's systematic study, *The Chinese Economy ca. 1870–1911* (Ann Arbor: Mich. Papers in Chinese Studies, no. 5, 1969), appears, slightly revised, in the *Cambridge History of China,* vol. XI. On traditional banking, Andrea Lee McElderry, *Shanghai Old-Style Banks (ch'ien-chuang), 1800–1935* (Ann Arbor: U. of Mich., Center for Chinese Studies, 1976). On enterprise generally see Kwang-Ching Liu, *Anglo-American Steamship Rivalry in China, 1862–1874* (Harvard UP, 1962); Edward Le Fevour, *Western Enterprise in Late Ch'ing China: A Selective Survey of Jardine, Matheson and Company's Operations, 1842–1895* (Harvard UP, 1968); and Wellington K. K. Chan, *Merchants, Mandarins, and Modern Enterprise in Late Ch'ing China* (Harvard UP, 1977). On the cotton industry in particlar, Kang Chao, *The Development of Cotton Textile Production in China* (Harvard UP, 1977). On the foreign activity in the chief modern mining enterprise, Ellsworth C. Carlson, *The Kaiping Mines, 1877–1912* (Harvard UP, 2nd ed., enlarged, 1971); in railway building, E-tu Zen Sun, *Chinese Railways and British Interests, 1898–1911* (Columbia UP, 1954); and in the salt revenue administration, S. A. M. Adshead, *The Modernization of the Chinese Salt Administration, 1900–1920* (Harvard UP, 1970).

The whole question of foreign investment and imperialist exploitation is discussed in Chi-ming Hou, *Foreign Investment and Economic Development in China, 1840–1937* (Harvard UP, 1965).

The comprador class is similarly researched by Yen-p'ing Hao, *The Comprador in Nineteenth Century China: Bridge between East and West* (Harvard UP, 1970). For a broad appraisal of the treaty ports' economic role in general see Rhoads Murphey, *The Outsiders: The Western Experience in India and China* (Ann Arbor: U. of Mich. Press, 1977). See also Paul A. Cohen, "Ch'ing China: Confrontation with the West, 1850–1900," in James B. Crowley, ed., *Modern East Asia: Essays in Interpretation* (Harcourt, Brace and World, 1970).

4.9 *Late Ch'ing Foreign Relations.* One inside view of the working of the treaty system is provided in Stanley F. Wright, *Hart and the Chinese Customs* (Belfast: Mullan, 1950); and Hart's role as foreign manager and advisor is glimpsed in J. K. Fairbank, K. F. Bruner, and E. M. Matheson, eds., *The I.G. in Peking: Letters of Robert Hart, Chinese Maritime Customs, 1868–1907* (Harvard UP, 1975), 2 vols. On the inauguration of diplomatic relations, see Immanuel C. Y. Hsü, *China's Entrance into the Family of Nations: The Diplomatic Phase, 1858–1880* (Harvard UP, 1960); the same author's *The Ili Crisis: A Study of Sino-Russian Diplomacy, 1871–1881* (Oxford: Clarendon, 1965); and Lloyd E. Eastman, *Throne and Mandarins: China's Search for a Policy during the Sino-French Controversy, 1880–1885* (Harvard UP, 1967).

Imperialist rivalry is most cogently surveyed in William L. Langer, *The Diplomacy of Imperialism* (Knopf, 2nd ed., 1950 [1935]), 2 vols. Recent background studies include R. K. I. Quested, *The Expansion of Russia in East Asia, 1857–1860* (Kuala Lumpur: U. of Malaya Press, 1968); Andrew Malozemoff, *Russian Far Eastern Policy, 1881–1904* (U. of Calif. Press, 1958); and Alastair Lamb, *Britain and Chinese Central Asia: The Road to Lhasa, 1767 to 1905* (London: Kegan Paul, 1960). On British policy, among many studies see Nathan A. Pelcovits, *Old China Hands and the Foreign Office* (American Institute of Pacific Relations, 1948; reprinted, Octagon, 1967). For a recent Chinese account of nineteenth-century imperialism in China see Hu Sheng, *Imperialism and Chinese Politics* (Peking: Foreign Languages Press, 1955; first published in Chinese, 1948). Three recent studies on 1900 are Chester C. Tan, *The Boxer Catastrophe* (Columbia UP, 1955); Victor Purcell, *The Boxer Uprising: A Background Study* (Cambridge UP, 1963); and a popular narrative, Peter Fleming, *The Seige at Peking* (Harper, 1959). On Manchuria see George Alexander Lensen, *The Russo-Chinese War* (Tallahassee: The Diplomatic Press, 1967). On Germany, John E. Schrecker, *Imperialism and Chinese Nationalism: Germany in Shantung* (Harvard UP, 1971).

4.10 *Christian Missions.* The basic factual survey is still that of Kenneth Scott Latourette, *A History of Christian Missions in China* (London: Society for Promoting Christian Knowledge, 1929; reprint Ch'eng-wen Publishing Co., Taipei, 1966). In briefer compass, missions in nineteenth-century China are surveyed in K. S. Latourette, *A History of the Expansion of Christianity,* vol. VI, *The Great Century in Northern Africa and Asia, A.D. 1800– A.D. 1914* (see chapter 5 "The Chinese Empire"). Study of Christian missions as part of China's institutional and intellectual history is just beginning. John K. Fairbank, ed., *The Missionary Enterprise in China and America* (Harvard UP, 1974) presents conference papers on several major problem areas. The literature at the Missionary Research Library (now part of the Union Theological Seminary library in New York) and elsewhere is surveyed by Jonathan T'ien-en Chao, *A Bibliography of the History of Christianity in China: A Preliminary Draft* (Waltham, Mass.: China Graduate School of Theology, preface dated 1970). One pathbreaking work on the anti-Christian movement is by Paul A. Cohen, *China and Christianity: The Missionary Movement and the Growth of Chinese Antiforeignism, 1860–1870* (Harvard UP, 1963). An exemplary and highly enjoyable study of personalities is by Irwin Hyatt, *Our Ordered Lives Confess: Three Nineteenth Century American Missionaries in East Shantung* (Harvard UP, 1976). Ellsworth C. Carlson, *The Foochow Missionaries, 1847–1880* (Harvard UP, 1974) follows the vicissitudes of a community. The role of missions in international relations is also just beginning to be investigated. Two recent studies are by Paul A. Varg, *Missionaries, Chinese and Diplomats: The American Protestant Missionary Movement in China, 1890–1952*

(Princeton UP, 1958) and Edmund S. Wehrle, *Britain, China, and Antimissionary Riots, 1891–1900* (U. of Minn. Press, 1966). Brief histories of most of the Christian colleges have been published by the United Board for Christian Higher Education in Asia, New York City. The best overall account is Jessie Gregory Lutz, *China and the Christian Colleges, 1850–1950* (Cornell UP, 1971). See also Reuben Holden, *Yale in China: The Mainland, 1901–1951* (New Haven: Yale in China Association, Inc., 1964). On the YMCA, see Shirley S. Garrett, *Social Reformers in Urban China: The Chinese Y.M.C.A., 1895–1962* (Harvard UP, 1970). Other facets of missionary activity are explored in a collection edited by Kwang-Ching Liu, *American Missionaries in China: Papers from Harvard Seminars* (Harvard UP, 1966). The vast literature on individuals, from Robert Morrison to Timothy Richard, is now being explored but Chinese Christian leaders and institutions are still generally neglected.

4.11 *Reform.* Background on the Western effort to stimulate reform is given in Jonathan Spence's fascinating bird's-eye view, *To Change China: Western Advisors to China, 1620–1960* (Boston: Little Brown, 1969). The sending of students abroad is canvassed broadly but with detailed data in Y. C. Wang, *Chinese Intellectuals and the West, 1872–1949* (U. of N. Carolina Press, 1966). On the conservative approach to reform, see William Ayers, *Chang Chih-tung and Educational Reform in China* (Harvard UP, 1971); and Daniel H. Bays, *China Enters the Twentieth Century: Chang Chih-tung and the Issues of a New Age, 1895–1909* (Ann Arbor: U. of Mich. Press, 1978). On the radical reformers, Kung-chuan Hsiao has analyzed the thought of K'ang Yu-wei in his magistral volume, *A Modern China and a New World: K'ang Yu-wei, Reformer and Utopian, 1858–1927* (Seattle: U. of Wash. Press, 1975). Lawrence G. Thompson has translated and summarized *Ta T'ung Shu: The One-World Philosophy of K'ang Yu-wei* (London: Allen and Unwin, 1958); Jung-pang Lo, *K'ang Yu-wei: A Biography and a Symposium* (U. of Arizona Press, 1967), gives a life history. On Kang's younger colleague see Joseph R. Levenson, *Liang Ch'i-ch'ao and the Mind of Modern China* (U. of Calif. Press paperback [Harvard UP, 1953]); Hao

4. Modern China to 1949

Chang, *Liang Ch'i-ch'ao and Cultural Transition in China, 1890– 1907* (Harvard UP, 1971); and Philip H. Huang, *Liang Ch'i-ch'ao and Modern Chinese Liberalism* (Seattle: U. of Wash. Press, 1972). The broad factual summary of the subject by Meribeth E. Cameron, *The Reform Movement in China, 1898–1912* (Stanford UP, 1931; reprinted, Octagon, 1963), though now out of date, can still be used. Note the sometimes tentative essays on numerous topics in Paul A. Cohen and John Schrecker, eds., *Reform in Nineteenth Century China* (Harvard UP, 1976).

The principal work on the late Ch'ing attempt to profit from Western thought is the study by Benjamin I. Schwartz, *In Search of Wealth and Power: Yen Fu and the West* (Harvard UP, 1964). See also Wolfgang Franke, *The Reform and Abolition of the Traditional Chinese Examination System* (Harvard UP, 1968 [1960]); and two studies of legal reform: Marinus J. Meijer, *The Introduction of Modern Criminal Law in China* (Batavia: De Unie, 1950), and M. H. van der Valk, *Conservatism in Modern Chinese Family Law* (Leiden: Brill, 1956). Leading figures are studied by Paul A. Cohen, *Between Tradition and Modernity: Wang T'ao and Reform in Late Ch'ing China* (Harvard UP, 1974); Samuel C. Chu, *Reformer in Modern China: Chang Chien, 1853–1926* (Columbia UP, 1965); and Roger V. DesForges, *Hsi- liang and the Chinese Revolution* (Yale UP, 1973).

4.12 *The Revolution of 1911.* The principal conspectus of the origins of the 1911 Revolution is by Mary Clabaugh Wright, ed. and intro., *China in Revolution: The First Phase, 1900–1913* (Yale UP, 1968). For indications of sources and problems, note Winston Hsieh, *Chinese Historiography on the Revolution of 1911* (Stanford: Hoover Institution Press, 1974). A number of monographs round out the picture, first on Sun Yat-sen: Harold Z. Schiffrin, *Sun Yat-sen and the Origins of the Chinese Revolu- tion* (U. of Calif. Press, 1968); Marius B. Jansen, *The Japanese and Sun Yat-sen* (Harvard UP, 1954); the early study by Lyon Sharman, *Sun Yat-sen, His Life and Its Meaning: A Critical Biography* (John Day, 1934; reissued, Stanford UP, 1968), on the many phases of Sun's career and the uses of him after his death, is now superseded by C. Martin Wilbur, *Sun Yat-sen: Frustrated*

Patriot (Columbia UP, 1976), which will probably be definitive for some time to come.

On other leaders and various regions of China see Chün-tu Hsüeh, *Huang Hsing and the Chinese Revolution* (Stanford UP, 1961); Mary Backus Rankin, *Early Chinese Revolutionaries: Radical Intellectuals in Shanghai and Chekiang, 1902–1911* (Harvard UP, 1971); Edward J. M. Rhoads, *China's Republican Revolution: The Case of Kwangtung, 1895–1913* (Harvard UP, 1975); and Joseph Esherick, *Reform and Revolution in China: The 1911 Revolution in Hunan and Hubei* (U. of Calif. Press, 1976). Social-intellectual movements are pursued by Michael Gasster, *Chinese Intellectuals and the Revolution of 1911: The Birth of Modern Chinese Radicalism* (Seattle: U. of Wash. Press, 1969); Martin Bernal, *Chinese Socialism to 1907* (Cornell UP, 1976); and Don C. Price, *Russia and the Roots of the Chinese Revolution, 1896–1911* (Harvard UP, 1974), a path-breaking study. Yen Ching Hwang, *The Overseas Chinese and the 1911 Revolution: With Special Reference to Singapore and Malaya* (Oxford UP, 1977), presents new documentation. For a review of problems, Ernest P. Young, "Nationalism, Reform, and Republican Revolution: China in the Early Twentieth Century," in James B. Crowley, ed., *Modern East Asia: Essays in Interpretation* (Harcourt, Brace and World, 1970). On one controversy precipitating the revolution, see En-han Lee, *China's Quest for Railway Autonomy, 1904–1911: A Study of the Chinese Railway-Rights Recovery Movement* (Singapore UP, 1977).

4.13 *The Warlord Era.* The rise of the military is traced by Ralph L. Powell, *The Rise of Chinese Military Power, 1895–1912* (Princeton UP, 1955); and Jerome Chen, *Yuan Shih-k'ai, 1859–1916* (Stanford UP, 1961). An outstanding study by Ernest P. Young, *The Presidency of Yuan Shih-k'ai: Liberalism and Dictatorship in Early Republican China* (Ann Arbor: U. of Mich. Press, 1977), analyzes the problems of Peking; and Edward Friedman, *Backward toward Revolution: The Chinese Revolutionary Party, 1914–1916* (U. of Calif. Press, 1974), the problems of the revolutionaries. On the warlord era proper (1916–1928), Andrew J. Nathan, *Peking Politics 1918–1923: Factionalism and the*

4. Modern China to 1949

Failure of Constitutionalism (U. of Calif. Press, 1976), studies the central government and its vicissitudes. See also Hsi-sheng Ch'i, *Warlord Politics in China, 1916–1928* (Stanford UP, 1976).

A number of volumes now look at specific leaders and areas: James E. Sheridan, *Chinese Warlord: The Career of Feng Yü-hsiang* (Stanford UP, 1966); Donald Gillin, *Warlord: Yen Hsi-shan in Shansi Province, 1911–1949* (Princeton UP, 1967); Robert A. Kapp, *Szechwan and the Chinese Republic: Provincial Militarism and Central Power, 1911–1938* (Yale UP, 1973); Angus W. McDonald, Jr., *The Urban Origins of Rural Revolution: Elites and the Masses in Hunan Province, China, 1911–1927* (U. of Calif. Press, 1978); Diana Lary, *Region and Nation: The Kwangsi Clique in Chinese Politics, 1925–1937* (Cambridge UP, 1974), a basic analysis of regionalism; J. C. S. Hall, *The Yunnan Provincial Faction 1928–1937* (Canberra: Australian National University, 1976); Gavan McCormack, *Chang Tso-lin in Northeast China, 1911–1928: China, Japan, and the Manchurian Idea* (Stanford UP, 1978). For a political analysis actually written some years ago, see Lucian W. Pye, *Warlord Politics: Conflict and Coalition in the Modernization of Republican China* (Praeger, 1971).

For an overview of the era in context, see James E. Sheridan, *China in Disintegration: The Republican Era in Chinese History, 1912–1949* (The Free Press, 1975).

4.14 *The Intellectual Revolution.* The major survey is that of Chow Tse-tsung, *The May Fourth Movement: Intellectual Revolution in Modern China* (Harvard UP, 1960); see also his *Research Guide to the May Fourth Movement* (Harvard UP, 1963); and Benjamin I. Schwartz, ed., *Reflections on the May Fourth Movement: A Symposium* (Harvard UP, 1972). Note the monograph by Joseph T. Chen, *The May Fourth Movement in Shanghai: The Making of a Social Movement in Modern China* (Leiden: Brill, 1971). Studies of intellectual leaders include William J. Duiker, *Ts'ai Yuan-p'ei: Educator of Modern China* (Penn. State UP, 1977); Laurence A. Schneider, *Ku Chieh-kang and China's New History: Nationalism and the Quest for Alternative Traditions* (U. of Calif. Press, 1971); Jerome B. Grieder,

Hu Shih and the Chinese Renaissance: Liberalism in the Chinese Revolution, 1917–1937 (Harvard UP, 1970); Charlotte Furth, *Ting Wen-chiang: Science and China's New Culture* (Harvard UP, 1970); and Guy S. Alitto, *The Last Confucian: Liang Shu-ming and the Chinese Dilemma of Modernity* (U. of Calif. Press, 1978). Note the volumes by D. W. Y. Kwok, *Scientism in Chinese Thought, 1900–1950* (Yale UP, 1965); Stephen N. Hay, *Asian Ideas of East and West: Tagore and His Critics in Japan, China, and India* (Harvard UP, 1970); and for still other aspects, Charlotte Furth, ed., *The Limits of Change: Essays on Conservative Alternatives in Republican China* (Harvard UP, 1976); and Lin Yü-sheng, *The Crisis of Chinese Consciousness: Radical Anti-traditionalism in the May Fourth Era* (U. of Wisc. Press, 1978). On the American input and its limitations, Barry Keenan, *The Dewey Experiment in China: Educational Reform and Political Power in the Early Republic* (Harvard UP, 1977); and Robert W. Clopton and Tsuin-chen Ou, trans. and ed., *John Dewey: Lectures in China, 1919–20* (Honolulu: East-West Center, 1973). O. Briere, S.J., *Fifty Years of Chinese Philosophy, 1898–1950* (Shanghai, 1949; London: Allen and Unwin, 1956; reprinted with new introduction and bibliography, Praeger, 1965), identifies movements of ideas and "systems" derived from oriental or occidental sources. On the leading founders of the Communist movement, see Maurice Meisner, *Li Ta-chao and the Origins of Chinese Marxism* (Harvard UP, 1967), a basic study; and Thomas C. Kuo, *Ch'en Tu-hsiu (1879–1942) and the Chinese Communist Movement* (South Orange, NJ: Seton Hall UP, 1975).

Analysis of this whole era has been greatly stimulated by the writings of Joseph R. Levenson, *Confucian China and Its Modern Fate*, vol. I, *The Problem of Intellectual Continuity*, vol. II, *The Problem of Monarchial Decay*, vol. III, *The Problem of Historical Significance* (U. of Calif. Press, 1958, 1964, 1965). For an illuminating application of Levensonian conceptions, see Ralph C. Croizier, *Traditional Medicine in Modern China: Science, Nationalism, and the Tensions of Cultural Change* (Harvard UP, 1968). John de Francis, *Nationalism and Language Reform in China* (Princeton UP, 1950), is still a basic work for this period.

4.15 *The Nationalist Revolution and Government.* On this era research is just getting started. Chiang Kai-shek is still almost unstudied. On the power politics of the 1920s see Akira Iriye, *After Imperialism: The Search for a New Order in the Far East, 1921–1931* (Harvard UP, 1965) and other items in section 6.5. A rather various collection of essays edited by Jack Gray is on *Modern China's Search for a Political Form* (Oxford UP, 1969). On the Kuomintang see George T. Yu, *Party Politics in Republican China: The Kuomintang, 1912–1924* (U. of Calif. Press, 1966); and William L. Tung, *The Political Institutions of Modern China* (The Hague: Nijhoff, 1964). The rise to power is chronicled by Donald A. Jordan, *The Northern Expedition: China's National Revolution of 1926–1928* (UP of Hawaii, 1976). The principal studies of the Nanking decade are by Hung-mao Tien, *Government and Politics in Kuomintang China, 1927–1937* (Stanford UP, 1972), well informed; and Lloyd E. Eastman, *The Abortive Revolution: China Under Nationalist Rule, 1927–1937* (Harvard UP, 1974), more iconoclastic. See also for fiscal and monetary aspects, Arthur N. Young, *China's Nation-Building Effort 1927–1937: The Financial and Economic Record* (Stanford: Hoover Institution Press, 1971); and for other aspects, Paul K. T. Sih, ed., *The Strenuous Decade: China's Nation-Building Efforts 1927–1937* (St. John's UP, 1970), a symposium by a score of sympathetic authors. A still useful, realistic and informed study of the Kuomintang in power is by Ch'ien Tuan-sheng, *The Government and Politics of China, 1912–1949* (Harvard UP, 1950; Stanford UP paperback, 1970). An uncritical collection of documents is reprinted in Milton J. T. Shieh, *The Kuomintang: Selected Historical Documents, 1894–1969* (St. John's UP, 1970). On the military under Chiang Kai-shek one of the few accounts is by F. F. Liu, *A Military History of Modern China, 1924–1949* (Princeton UP, 1956). On the student movement: John Israel, *Student Nationalism in China, 1927–1937* (Stanford UP, 1966); also John Israel and Donald W. Klein, *Rebels and Bureaucrats: China's December 9ers* (U. of Calif. Press, 1976), which traces later careers of participants in the 1935 movement. A monograph on a key event is Tien-wei Wu, *The Sian Incident: A Pivotal*

Point in Modern Chinese History (Ann Arbor: U. of Mich. Center for Chinese Studies, 1976).

Economic development under the Republic is analyzed by Albert Feuerwerker, *The Chinese Economy, 1912–1949* (Ann Arbor: Michigan Papers in Chinese Studies, no. 1, 1968), a chapter in the *Cambridge History of China*, vol. XI. A careful quantification made for the SSRC Committee on the Economy of China is by John K. Chang, *Industrial Development in Pre-Communist China* (Chicago: Aldine, 1969); see also Cheng Yu-kwei, *Foreign Trade and Industrial Development in China: An Historical and Intergrated Analysis through 1948* (Washington, D.C.: UP of Wash., 1956). On Nationalist economic policies in wartime see Chang Kia-ngau, *The Inflationary Spiral: The Experience in China, 1939–1950* (John Wiley, 1958); Chou Shun-hsin, *The Chinese Inflation, 1937–1949* (Columbia UP, 1963); and Arthur N. Young, *China's Wartime Finance and Inflation, 1937–1945* (Harvard UP, 1965).

4.16 *Modern Literature.* This is an area of rapid growth. For bibliography, Donald A. Gibbs and Yun-chen Li, with the assistance of Christopher C. Rand, *A Bibliography of Studies and Translations of Modern Chinese Literature, 1918–1942* (Harvard UP, 1975), arranged by authors. For surveys: C. T. Hsia, *A History of Modern Chinese Fiction, 1917–1957* (Yale UP, 1961); Tsi-an Hsia, *The Gate of Darkness: Studies on the Leftist Literary Movement in China* (Seattle: U. of Wash. Press, 1968); Merle Goldman, ed., *Modern Chinese Literature in the May Fourth Era* (Harvard UP, 1977), with sixteen contributors; and John Berninghausen and Ted Huters, eds., *Revolutionary Literature in China: An Anthology* (White Plains: M. E. Sharpe, 1976). Outstanding individual studies have also appeared: Bonnie S. McDougall, *The Introduction of Western Literary Theories into Modern China, 1919–1925* (Tokyo: Center for East Asian Cultural Studies, 1971): and Leo Ou-fan Lee, *The Romantic Generation of Chinese Writers* (Harvard UP, 1973). In the large and proliferating field of Lu Hsün studies, note William A. Lyell, Jr., *Lu Hsün's Vision of Reality* (U. of Calif. Press, 1976); and Patrick Hanan, "The Technique of Lu Hsün's Fiction," *Harvard Journal of Asiatic Studies* 34 (1974), 53-96. Harold R. Isaacs, ed., foreword by Lu Hsün, *Straw Sandals: Chinese Short Stories, 1918–1933* (MIT Press, 1974), presents some 25 translations first assembled in 1934.

On other authors, see: David Tod Roy, *Kuo Mo-jo: The Early Years* (Harvard UP, 1971); Olga Lang, *Pa Chin and His Writings: Chinese Youth between the Two Revolutions* (Harvard UP, 1967); Ranbir Vohra, *Lao She and the Chinese Revolution* (Harvard UP, 1974); also Zbigniew Slupski, *The Evolution of a Modern Chinese Writer: An Analysis of Lao She's Fiction with Biographical and Bibliographical Appendices* (Prague: Oriental Institute in Academia, 1966); Ernst Wolff, *Chou Tso-jen* (Boston: Twayne, 1971); Joseph S. M. Lau, *Ts'ao Yü* (Hong Kong UP, 1970); Bonnie S. McDougall, *Paths in Dreams: Selected Prose and Poetry of Ho Ch'i-fang* (St. Lucia: U. of Queensland Press, 1976); Howard Goldblatt, *Hsiao Hung* (Boston: Twayne, 1976); and finally Jaroslav Prusek, *Three Sketches of Chinese Literature* (Prague: Oriental Institute in Academia, 1969).

Among recent collections are Kai-yu Hsu, ed., *Twentieth Century Chinese Poetry: An Anthology* (Doubleday, 1963); C. T. Hsia and Joseph S. M. Lau, eds., *Twentieth-century Chinese Stories* (Columbia UP, 1971); and Joseph S. M. Lau and Timothy A. Ross, eds., *Chinese Stories from Taiwan, 1960–1970* (Columbia UP, 1976).

One distinguished achievement in this area is *Renditions: A Chinese-English Translations Magazine,* George Kao and Stephen C. Soong, eds., published by Center for Translation Projects, Chinese U. of Hong Kong, seven issues since 1973.

4.17 *The Japanese War.* Research on wartime Nationalist China is still meager. One of the few items is Lincoln Li, *The Japanese Army in North China, 1937–1941: Problems of Political and Economic Control* (Oxford UP, 1975). Two books deal with the Wang Ching-wei defection: John Hunter Boyle, *China and Japan at War, 1937–1945: The Politics of Collaboration* (Stanford UP, 1972); and Gerald E. Bunker, *The Peace Conspiracy: Wang Ching-wei and the China War, 1937–1941* (Harvard UP, 1972). Paul K. T. Sih, ed., *Nationalist China during the*

Sino-Japanese War, 1937–1945 (Hicksville, N.Y.: Exposition Press, 1977) presents papers and discussions of 22 panelists at a 1976 conference.

4.18 *Cultural and Religious Life under the Republic.* This area is largely untouched. The broadest, quick overview is by A. C. Scott, *Literature and the Arts in Twentieth Century China* (Doubleday Anchor, 1963), with a bibliography. For specialized surveys, see Michael Sullivan, *Chinese Art in the Twentieth Century* (London: Faber, 1959); Jay Leyda, *Dianying: An Account of Films and the Film Audience in China* (MIT Press, 1972); and Roger Pelissier, *Les bibliothèques en Chine pendant la première moitié de XXe siécle* (Paris: Mouton, 1971). Wartime cultural and technical contact is described in Wilma Fairbank, *America's Cultural Experiment in China, 1942–1949* (Washington, D.C.: Supt. of Documents, U.S. Government Printing Office, 1976), by an administrator of the State Department's Cultural Relations program both in Washington and in the American embassy. On public communication see Lee-Hsia Hsu Ting, *Government Control of the Press in Modern China, 1900–1949* (Harvard UP, 1974), an unhappy record.

On religion the main analysis is by C. K. Yang, *Religion in Chinese Society: A Study of Contemporary Social Functions of Religion and Some of their Historical Factors* (U. of Calif. Press, 1961). See also Wing-tsit Chan, *Religious Trends in Modern China* (Columbia UP, 1953); and Holmes Welch, *The Buddhist Revival in China* (Harvard UP, 1968). On mainland religion since 1949 see section 5.22. For studies in Taiwan see Arthur P. Wolf, ed., *Religion and Ritual in Chinese Society* (Stanford UP, 1974), with 15 contributors; Emily M. Ahern, *The Cult of the Dead in a Chinese Village* (Stanford UP, 1973); and David K. Jordan, *Gods, Ghosts, and Ancestors: The Folk Religion of a Taiwanese Village* (U. of Calif. Press, 1972). On Taoism note Michael Saso, *The Teachings of Taoist Master Chuang* (Yale UP, 1973); and Michael Saso and David W. Chappell, *Buddhist and Taoist Studies Number 1* (UP of Hawaii, 1977).

4.19 *Foreigners' Experiences.* Almost every foreigner who lives in China writes about it, sooner or later. Here are a very few examples from an enormous genre: Rodney Gilbert, *What's Wrong with China* (London: John Murray, 1926), expressing the Shanghai mind; Hugh Trevor-Roper, *Hermit of Peking: The Hidden Life of Sir Edmund Backhouse* (Knopf, 1977), sleuthing out a gifted imposter; Chester Ronning, *A Memoir of China in Revolution from the Boxer Rebellion to the People's Republic* (Pantheon, 1974), by a multi-purpose Canadian diplomat; Ida Pruitt, *A China Childhood* (San Francisco: Chinese Materials Center, 1978), a memoir of girlhood in Shantung; Ruth V. Hemenway, M.D., *A Memoir of Revolutionary China, 1924–1941,* ed. and intro. by Fred W. Drake (U. of Mass. Press, 1977), by a medical missionary in Fukien; Marc Kasanin, *China in the Twenties* (Moscow: Central Department of Oriental Literature, 1973), trans. from Russian, by an official of the Far Eastern Republic who was later on Blucher's staff; G. H. Gompertz, *China in Turmoil: Eye-witness, 1924–1948* (London: J. M. Dent & Sons, 1967), by a Hong Kong -born member of Jardine Matheson & Co.; William L. Tung, *Revolutionary China: A Personal Account, 1926–1949* (St. Martin's Press, 1973), from a long career ending as a Nationalist ambassador; John Leighton Stuart, *Fifty Years in China* (Random House, 1954), by the chief figure at Yenching University, later ambassador; Pearl S. Buck, *My Several Worlds* (John Day, 1954), an autobiography; Edgar Snow, *Journey to the Beginning* (Random House, 1958), illuminating reminiscences; Han Suyin, *Birdless Summer* (Putnam, 1968), part of a trilogy, passionately patriotic; and Willis Airey, *A Learner in China: A Life of Rewi Alley* (Christchurch, New Zealand: Caxton Press and Monthly Review Society, 1970), about the New Zealander who led Indusco, the Chinese Industrial Cooperatives.

5. THE PEOPLE'S REPUBLIC

5.1 *Reference Works.* The research explosion is nowhere better demonstrated than in the major guide to materials for research on mainland China since 1949 and on Taiwan since 1945, Peter Berton and Eugene Wu, *Contemporary China: A Research Guide* (Stanford: Hoover Institution, 1967), which describes some 2200 items up through 1963 in Chinese, Japanese, English, and Russian; but these items include only bibliographies, reference works, documents, serials, and dissertations, and exclude most secondary works. For educators generally, Arlene Posner and Arne J. DeKeijzer, eds., *China: A Resource and Curriculum Guide,* 2nd ed., rev. (U. of Chicago Press, 1976 [1972, 1973]), has sections on curriculum units, audiovisual materials, books (especially paperbacks) under fourteen categories (periodicals, and so on) — very helpful. Systematic coverage of data is provided by Donald P. Whitaker and Rinn-Sup Shinn, with five others, *Area Handbook for the People's Republic of China* (Washington, DC: American University, 1972, for sale by the Superintendent of Documents, U.S. Government Printing Office). More specialized, James C. F. Wang, *The Cultural Revolution in China: An Annotated Bibliography* (Garland Publishing, 1976), has nine topical sections with 364 annotated items. The latest compendium is Harold C. Hinton, ed., *The People's Republic of China: A Handbook* (Boulder: Westview Press, 1978).

Translations of the *Selected Works of Mao Tse-tung,* which were first published in Chinese in 4 volumes (Peking: People's Publishing Co., 1951, 1952, 1953, 1960), were published in English in 5 volumes (International Publishers, 1954–1962). The Chinese vol. V (Peking: published in English by the Foreign Languages Press, 1977) contains writings and speeches from September 1949 to November 1957. For English translations of the little red book, *Mao Chu-hsi yü-lu,* see *Quotations from Chairman Mao Tse-tung* (Peking: Foreign Languages Press, 1966; reprinted, Bantam, 1967).

5.2 *Periodicals.* The most substantial series of translations comes from the United States Consulate General, Hong Kong: *Survey of the China Mainland Press* (since November 1973, *Survey of People's Republic of China Press*), *Selections from China Mainland Magazines, Current Background;* and from the Joint Publications Research Service, Washington, D.C. Also from Hong Kong are publications of the Union Research Institute; as well as *China News Analysis* and *Current Scene.* The leading academic journal is *The China Quarterly* (London, 1960–), which is of course more specialized than the quarterly *Journal of Asian Stu-*

dies (Ann Arbor, Mich.). For revisionist criticism see also *The Bulletin of Concerned Asian Scholars* (Charlemont, Mass., 1969–); *Modern China: An International Quarterly* (Beverley Hills, Calif., January 1975–); *Contemporary China* (Columbia U., East Asian Inst., quarterly, 1976–). Among weeklies note especially the *Far Eastern Economic Review* (Hong Kong). The main outflow of books from the mainland in English is from the Foreign Languages Press, Peking. The chief Peking periodicals in English are *Peking Review* (successor to *People's China*), *China Reconstructs, China Pictorial,* and *Chinese Literature. Chinese Studies in History* (White Plains) contains unabridged translations of articles mainly from five PRC publications.

5.3 *Histories and Surveys.* Outstanding in this category are two works: Maurice Meisner, *Mao's China: A History of the People's Republic* (The Free Press, 1977), a well-informed narrative evaluation from the viewpoint of the revolutionaries' socialist ideology aided by a critical grasp of European Marxism; and James Pinckney Harrison, *The Long March to Power: A History of the Chinese Communist Party, 1921–1972* (Praeger, 1972), a judicious summary taking account of the extensive research done on this subject. Jacques Guillermaz, *The Chinese Communist Party in Power, 1949–1976* (Boulder: Westview Press, 1976 [French ed., 1972]) is by a leading French specialist with special attention to foreign relations. Several surveys stress political history: John Bryan Starr, *Ideology and Culture: An Introduction to the Dialectic of Contemporary Chinese Politics* (Harper & Row, 1973); Harold C. Hinton, *An Introduction to Chinese Politics* (Praeger, 1973); and James R. Townsend, *Politics in China* (Boston: Little Brown, 1974). On the domestic structure see Peter S. H. Tang and Joan M. Maloney, *Communist China: The Domestic Scene, 1949–1967* (Seton Hall UP, 1967). Michel Oksenberg, ed., *China's Developmental Experience* (Praeger, 1973), contains interpretive articles by leading scholars. Franz Michael, *Mao and the Perpetual Revolution* (Woodbury, N.Y.: Barron's Educational Series, 1977), is a well-informed and critical summary account.

5.4 *Early History of the CCP to 1936.* Here there is already a vast literature. Beginning with surveys, Jacques Guillermaz, *A History of the Chinese Communist Party, 1921–1949* (Random House, 1972), a judicious, skeptical, and well-documented account, by a former French military attaché in China; Warren Kuo, *Analytical History of the Chinese Communist Party* (Taipei: Institute of International Relations, vols. I and II, 1968, vol. III, 1970), by a leading researcher in Taiwan, comes up to July 1939. For a history by an early CCP leader, Chang Kuo-t'ao, *The Rise of the Chinese Communist Party 1921–1927: The Autobiography of Chang Kuo-t'ao,* vol. I, *1921–1927,* vol. II, *1928–1938* (UP of Kansas, 1971–72); 2 vols. On the Soviet intervention and its complications, see C. Martin Wilbur and Julie Lien-ying Howe, *Documents on Communism, Nationalism, and Soviet Advisors in China, 1918–1927* (Columbia UP, 1956); Allen S. Whiting, *Soviet Policies in China, 1917–1924* (Columbia UP, 1954); Peter S. H. Tang, *Russian and Soviet Policy in Manchuria and Outer Mongolia, 1911–1931* (Durham: Duke UP, 1959); Xenia J. Eudin and Robert C. North, *Soviet Russia and the East, 1920–1927* (Stanford UP for the Hoover Library, 1957), with documents; and Conrad Brandt, *Stalin's Failure in China, 1924–1927* (Harvard UP, 1958). This subject has now been put together by Sow-theng Leong, *Sino-Soviet Diplomatic Relations, 1917–1926* (Canberra: Australian National University, 1976).

Two special studies are Jean Chesneaux, trans. H. M. Wright, *The Chinese Labor Movement, 1919–1927* (Stanford UP, 1968); and Harold Isaacs, *The Tragedy of the Chinese Revolution* (Stanford UP, rev. ed., 1951 [1938]). On the early development of the party line Arif Dirlik, *Revolution and History: The Origins of Marxist Historiography in China, 1919–1937* (U. of Calif. Press, 1978). See also Conrad Brandt, Benjamin Schwartz, and John K. Fairbank, *A Documentary History of Chinese Communism* (Atheneum paperback, 1966 [Harvard UP, 1952]). On the later Soviet relationship, Charles B. McLane, *Soviet Policy and the Chinese Communists, 1931–1946* (Columbia UP, 1958). On the beginnings in Kwangtung, Roy Hofheinz, Jr., *The Broken Wave: The Chinese Communist Peasant Movement, 1922–1928* (Harvard UP, 1977); and in Kiangsi, a remarkable series of monographs: Derek J. Waller, *The Kiangsi Soviet Republic: Mao and the National Congresses of 1931 and 1934* (U. of Calif., Center for Chinese Studies, 1973); Ilpyong J. Kim, *The Politics of Chinese Communism: Kiangsi under the Soviets* (U. of Calif. Press, 1973); Trygve Lötveit, *Chinese Communism, 1931–1934: Experience in Civil Government* (Lund, Sweden: Studentlitteratur, 1973); Shanti Swarup, *A Study of the Chinese Communist Movement, 1927–1934* (Oxford: Clarendon, 1966); Richard C. Thornton, *The Comintern and the Chinese Communists, 1928–1931* (Seattle: U. of Wash. Press, 1969); John E. Rue, *Mao Tse-tung in Opposition, 1927–1935* (Stanford UP, 1966); Tso-liang Hsiao, *The Land Revolution in China, 1930–1933: A Study of Documents* (Seattle: U. of Wash. Press, 1969); and Tetsuya Kataoka, *Resistance and Revolution in China: The Communists and The Second United Front* (U. of Calif. Press, 1974). These studies may have wrapped up the subject until new evidence appears.

5.5 *The Yenan Period and the Civil War.* On the rise of Mao and Maoism: the classic account, by Mao himself, is in Edgar Snow, *Red Star over China* (Random House, 1938; 1st rev. and enlarged edition, Grove Press, 1968; Bantam, 1978). Lively, full-length biographies are by Stuart Schram, *Mao Tse-tung* (Simon and Schuster, 1966); and Jerome Ch'en, *Mao and the Chinese Revolution* (Oxford UP, 1967). Studies are by Robert C. North, *Kuomintang and Chinese Communist Elites* (Stanford UP, 2nd ed., 1963 [1952]); and Edgar Snow, *Random Notes on Red China, 1936–1945* (Harvard UP, 1957, 2nd printing, 1968). On the surgeon-hero of the Border Region, Ted Allan and Sydney Gordon, *The Scalpel, The Sword: The Story of Dr. Norman Bethune* (Boston: Little Brown, 1952, rev. ed., 1971); and Roderick Stewart, *Bethune* (Don Mills, Ontario: PaperJacks (1973) 1975), on his career worldwide based on more than 100 interviews. For ideological perspective: Donald M. Lowe, *The Function of "China" in Marx, Lenin, and Mao* (U. of Calif. Press, 1966); and H. Carrère d'Encausse and Stuart R. Schram, *Marxism and Asia: An Introduction with Readings* (London: Allen Lane, The Penguin Press, 1969). On the Yenan era in general; Mark Selden, *The Yenan Way in Revolutionary China* (Harvard UP, 1971); Boyd Compton, trans., *Mao's China: Party Reform Documents, 1942–44* (Seattle: U. of Wash. Press, 1952); and Peter Schram, *Guerrilla Economy: The Development of the Shensi-Kansu-Ninghsia Border Region, 1937–1945* (State U. of New York Press, 1976).

The Chinese Communist rise to power is analyzed in Benjamin I. Schwartz, *Chinese Communism and the Rise of Mao* (Harvard UP, 1951); Chalmers A. Johnson, *Peasant Nationalism and Communist Power: The Emergence of Revolutionary China, 1937–1945* (Stanford UP, 1962); Lyman P. Van Slyke, *Enemies and Friends: The United Front in Chinese Communist History* (Stanford UP, 1967); and Suzanne Pepper, *Civil War in China: The Political Struggle, 1945–1949* (U. of Calif. Press, 1978). Two remarkable on-the-scene reports from this period of struggle are by Jack Belden, intro. by Owen Lattimore, *China Shakes the World* (Harper, 1949, Monthly Review Press, 1970); and William Hinton, *Fanshen: A Documentary of Revolution in a Chinese Village* (Monthly Review Press, 1966). Biographies of principal leaders include Agnes Smedley, *The Great Road: The Life and Times of Chu Teh* (Monthly Review Press, 1956) by an American radical who knew the Red Army leaders personally; Nym Wales (Helen Foster Snow), *The Chinese Communists: Sketches and Autobiographies of the Old Guard*, book I, *Red Dust*, book II, *Autobiographical Profiles and Biographical Sketches* (Westport, Conn.: Greenwood, 1972), from a visit to Yenan; and Kai-yu Hsu, *Chou En-lai: China's Gray Eminence* (Doubleday, 1968), based on Taipei archives as well as 46 informants. A Doak Barnett, *China on the Eve of Communist Takeover* (Praeger, 1963), reprints 23 field reports from the Nationalist area in 1947–49.

5.6 *Visitors' Impressions of the PRC, 1949–71.* The two extremes in this contemporary literature, works by enthusiasts for the ideals of a new day, and by horrified victims of revolutionary coercion, confront the reader with unresolved anomalies. The literature is enormous and only a few samples can be listed here: Derk Bodde, *Peking Diary: A Year of Revolution* (H. Schuman, 1950), by a leading American sinologist who was in Peking before and after the takeover; and Lynn and Amos Landman, *Profile of Red China* (Simon and Schuster, 1951), by two American correspondents, mainly in Shanghai, reflect the initial sense of relief and the mixed impressions of the honeymoon period. Liu Shawtong, *Out of Red China* (Duell, Sloane and Pearce, 1953), and Maria Yen, *The Umbrella Garden: A Picture of Student Life in Red China* (Macmillan, 1954), are two of the disillusioned writings by intellectuals who came out. Works by Protestant and Catholic missionaries exemplify a large body of such writings: Quentin K. Y. Huang, *Now I Can Tell: The Story of a Christian Bishop under Communist Persecution* (Morehouse-Gorham Co., 1954), by the Anglican bishop of Yunnan-Kweichow; John W. Clifford, S.J., *In the Presence of My Enemies* (W. W. Norton, 1963), jailed in Shanghai; Harold W. Rigney, *Four Years in a Red Hell: The Story of Father Rigney* (Chicago: Regnery, 1956), bitterly hostile. Allyn and Adele Rickett, *Prisoners of Liberation* (Cameron Associates, 1957), based on a similarly long incarceration, is comparatively sympathetic; Anthony Grey, *Hostage in Peking* (Garden City: Doubleday, 1971), is by the Reuters correspondent detained in his house for 26 months 1967–69.

Reports of later visitors vary not only according to the visitor but according to the year of the visit. Authors and publishers may conspire to hide how long the author was actually in China and whether he ever got off the standard route. The most valuable observers are those who saw China before 1949 and have a before-and-after perspective. Pre-eminent among them is Mao's biographer (in *Red Star over China,* 1937) Edgar Snow, who returned for an extensive look in 1960 and wrote an absorbing account, *The Other Side of the River: Red China Today* (Random House, n.d., copyright 1961, 1962). Out of the copious flow of first-person accounts, the following stem from the most immediate contact: Isabel and David Crook, *Revolution in a Chinese Village: Ten Mile Inn* (London: Routledge and Kegan Paul, 1959), a reconstruction of a village history from the Japanese invasion to Communist liberation by two teachers of English in Peking. Isabel and David Crook, *The First Years of Yangyi Commune* (London: Routledge and Kegan Paul, 1966), based on summer visits in 1959 and 1960. Mu Fu-sheng, *The Wilting of the Hundred Flowers: The Chinese Intelligentsia under Mao* (Praeger, 1962), by a scholar who after twelve years abroad returned to China in the late 1950s, but came out a year later. Jacques Marcuse, *The Peking Papers: Leaves from the Notebook of a China Correspondent* (Dutton, 1967), the new China as seen in 1962–1964 by a long-time French correspondent who had been resident in Peking in the 1930s and 1940s. Stuart and Roma Gelder, *Memories for a Chinese Granddaughter* (Stein and Day, 1968), by a British journalist who was in China in the 1940s and again in 1960 and 1966. Another before-and-after visitor with the perspective of a historian was C. P. Fitzgerald, *Flood Tide in China* (London: Cresset Press, 1958), by a resident of Peking in the early 1930s, after his return to China again in 1956.

Other travelers of special competence include Dick Wilson, *Anatomy of China: An Introduction to One Quarter of Mankind* (Weybright and Talley, 1968; first published in England in 1966 as *A Quarter of Mankind: An Anatomy of China Today*), by a former editor of the *Far Eastern Economic Review*, Hong Kong, 1958–1964, who visited the mainland in 1964; Jan Myrdal, *Report from a Chinese Village* (Pantheon Books, 1965), translated from Swedish ed. of 1963, based on a month in a village in the Yenan area in 1962; Jan Myrdal and Gun Kessle, *China: The Revolution Continued* (Pantheon, 1970), based on two weeks in 1969 in the same village seen in 1962; K. S. Karol, *China: The Other Communism* (Hill and Wang, 1967; trans. from French ed. of 1966), by an observer acquainted with the Soviet system; K. S. Karol, *The Second Chinese Revolution* (Hill and Wang, 1973), based on a return trip in 1971; Klaus Mehnert, *Peking and Moscow* (Putnam's 1963, trans. from German ed. of 1962), by a German who spent some five years each in Russia and in China; and Klaus Mehnert, *China Returns* (E. P. Dutton, 1972; trans. from the German), based on a trip in 1971; Ross Terrill, *800,000,000: The Real China* (Boston: Little Brown, 1972), very perceptive, by an Australian scholar, after two visits. In contrast with the evaluative efforts of teachers and journalists, note also the writings of a long-time resident who simply loves the

5. The People's Republic

Chinese people, Rewi Alley, *Travels in China, 1966–71* (Peking: New World Press, 1973).

5.7 *Socio-Political Organization and Leadership.* This and the following sections try to pigeonhole a mounting corpus of books written about China from the outside. Since many deal with several subjects, they can be pigeonholed only arbitrarily. A revolution is not a flock of pigeons. I have omitted many studies in favor of later ones, although for scholarly purposes they may not have been superseded at all.

First, on the party and its roles, John W. Lewis, *Leadership in Communist China* (Cornell UP, 1963); John W. Lewis, ed., *Party Leadership and Revolutionary Power in China* (Cambridge UP, 1970), a dozen papers from a 1968 conference; A. Doak Barnett, with a contribution by Ezra Vogel, *Cadres, Bureaucracy, and Political Power in Communist China* (Columbia UP, 1967), like so many other works, based partly on Hong Kong interviews; Robert A. Scalapino, ed., *Elites in the People's Republic of China* (Seattle: U. of Wash. Press, 1972), with 14 contributors, in the Joint Committee on Contemporary China series of Studies in Chinese Government and Politics. Most recent is Paul Wong, *China's Higher Leadership in the Socialist Transition* (The Free Press, 1976), on organizational networks, functional systems, elites, leadership, mobility, etc.

On the theme of integration, see Alan P. L. Liu, *Communications and National Integration in Communist China* (U. of Calif. Press, 1971); and Dorothy J. Solinger, *Regional Government and Political Integration in Southwest China, 1949–1954: A Case Study* (U. of Calif. Press, 1977), which examines the great administrative regions and one in particular.

On mass mobilization, James R. Townsend, *Political Participation in Communist China* (U. of Calif. Press, 1968); Gordon Bennett, *Yundong: Mass Campaigns in Chinese Communist Leadership* (Center for Chinese Studies, U. of Calif., 1976), with a typology of the kinds of movements; and Charles P. Cell, *Revolution at Work: Mobilization Campaigns in China* (Academic Press, 1977). Another symposium, A. Doak Barnett, ed., *Chinese Communist Politics in Action* (Seattle: U. of Wash. Press, 1969) presents 11 papers from a conference on "microsocietal study of the Chinese political system."

All these works are guided by the use of social science concepts, which are applied broadly across the board in Franz Schurmann, *Ideology and Organization in Communist China* (U. of Calif. Press, 1966). On the other hand Ezra Vogel, *Canton under Communism: Programs and Politics in a Provincial Capital, 1949–1968* (Harvard UP, 1969) uses the data of this one area to exemplify the main phases and problems in the revolutionary process generally—a most successful study. C. K. Yang (Yang Ch'ing-k'un), *A Chinese Village in Early Communist Transition* (MIT Press, 1959), is on a village near Canton. Finally, the problems of law and order, leadership and bureaucracy, and modern urban ills are canvassed in a conference volume, John Wilson Lewis, ed., *The City in Communist China* (Stanford UP, 1971).

On the family, C. K. Yang, *The Chinese Family in the Communist Revolution* (MIT Press, 1959), benefits from experience in China before and after 1949. Sidney L. Greenblatt, ed. and intro., *The People of Taihang: An Anthology of Family Histories* (White Plains: International Arts and Sciences Press, 1976), is actually a selection of 17 didactic "speak-bitterness" stories of pre-Liberation suffering that use "history" to point a moral lesson. James L. Watson, *Emigration and the Chinese Lineage: The Mans in Hong Kong and London* (U. of Calif. Press, 1975), studies the causes and results of emigration. On family life see Ruth Sidel, *Families of Fengsheng: Urban Life in China* (Baltimore: Penguin Books, 1974); and Martin King Whyte and William Parish, Jr., *Village and Family in Contemporary China* (U. of Chicago Press, 1978), a major study.

On the psychological motivation of individuals in groups, labor camps, and elsewhere, several significant studies are now available: Lynn T. White, III, *Careers in Shanghai: The Social Guidance of Personal Energies in a Developing Chinese City, 1949–1966* (U. of Calif. Press, 1978); Thomas P. Bernstein, *Up to the Mountains and Down to the Villages: The Transfer of Youth from Urban to Rural China* (Yale UP, 1977), a basic study of the enormous programs for sending city youths to the country-side; Martin King Whyte, *Small Groups and Political Rituals in China* (U. of Calif. Press, 1974), a pioneer study; David M. Raddock, *Political Behavior of Adolescents in China: The Cultural Revolution in Kwangchow* (U. of Arizona Press, for the Association for Asian Studies, 1977), based on interviews with 35 young Cantonese; Tung Chi-ping and Humphrey Evans, *The Thought Revolution* (New York: Coward-McCann, 1966), a personal account; Amy Auerbacher Wilson, Sidney Leonard Greenblatt, Richard Whittingham Wilson, eds., *Deviance and Social Control in Chinese Society* (Praeger, 1977), 10 contributions from a 1975 conference; and Paul J. Hiniker, *Revolutionary Ideology and Chinese Reality: Dissonance under Mao,* intro. by Ithiel de Sola Pool (Beverley Hills: SAGE Publications, 1977), a psychological study. For a sociological analysis in terms of conflict theory, see Alan P. Liu, *Political Culture and Group Conflict in Communist China* (Santa Barbara: Clio Books, 1976).

5.8 *Mao and His Thought.* An early and influential study is Stuart Schram, *The Political Thought of Mao Tse-tung* (Praeger, 1963). Li Jui, *The Early Revolutionary Activities of Comrade Mao Tse-tung,* trans. from Chinese, intro. by Stuart R. Schram in 34 pp. (White Plains: M. E. Sharpe, 1977) is a pedestrian political biography of 1957, since repudiated but the only thing of its kind. Stuart R. Schram, ed. and intro., *Chairman Mao Talks to the People: Talks and Letters, 1956–1971* (Pantheon, 1974; English edition: *Chairman Mao Unrehearsed*), brings together materials mainly from Red Guard publications of the late 1960s. Jerome Ch'en ed., *Mao Papers: Anthology and Bibliography* (Oxford UP, 1970), likewise makes available letters and talks with a chronological list of Mao's works 1917–68. Another of Mao's writings derived from the Red Guard publication *Long Live the Thought of Mao Tse-tung* (1967, 1969) is Mao's *A Critique of Soviet Economics,* trans. by Moss Roberts, annot. by Richard Levy, intro. by James Peck (Monthly Review Press, 1977). Similarly revealing is a study of PRC treatment of Ch'in Shih-huang-ti, by Li Yu-ning, ed., *The First Emperor of China: The Politics of Historiography* (White Plains: M. E.

5. The People's Republic

Sharpe, 1975), using re-evaluations published in China in 1972.

Benjamin Schwartz, *Communism and China: Ideology in Flux* (Harvard UP, 1968), collects the trenchant essays of a major scholar. Albert Feuerwerker, ed., *History in Communist China* (MIT Press, 1968), has a dozen Western historians analyzing CCP treatment of various eras and aspects, from a 1964 conference. Frederic Wakeman, Jr., *History and Will: Philosophical Perspectives of Mao Tse-tung's Thought* (U. of Calif. Press, 1973), studies what Mao studied, stressing the Germanic background. Chalmers Johnson, ed., *Ideology and Politics in Contemporary China* (U. of Wash. Press, 1973), presents ten conference papers by leading scholars—a major collection. See also James Chieh Hsiung, ed., *The Logic of "Maoism": Critiques and Explication* (Praeger, 1974), eight various papers from a 1973 panel; and James Chieh Hsiung, *Ideology and Practice: The Evolution of Chinese Communism* (Praeger, 1970).

On the psychological context of Mao's leadership, bold but influential analyses are by Lucian W. Pye, *The Spirit of Chinese Politics: A Psychocultural Study of the Authority Crisis in Political Development* (MIT Press, 1968); and Richard H. Solomon, *Mao's Revolution and the Chinese Political Culture* (U. of Calif. Press, 1971); see also Lucian W. Pye, *Mao Tse-tung: The Man in the Leader* (Basic Books, 1976). Robert J. Lifton, *Revolutionary Immortality: Mao Tse-tung and the Chinese Cultural Revolution* (Random House, 1968), by a psychiatrist, has a different approach. For ancillary approaches, see Willis Barnstone, trans., intro., and notes, in collaboration with Ko Ching-po, *The Poems of Mao Tse-tung* (Harper and Row, 1972); and Endymion Wilkinson, trans., *The People's Comic Book* (Doubleday, 1973), cartoons with translated captions reflecting Communist views. Han Suyin, *Wind in the Tower: Mao Tse-tung and the Chinese Revolution, 1949–1975* (Boston: Little Brown, 1976), is a panegyric, continuing her earlier biographical account, *The Morning Deluge: Mao Tse-tung and the Chinese Revolution, 1893–1954* (Boston: Little Brown, 1972). Dick Wilson, ed., *Mao Tse-tung in the Scales of History: A Preliminary Assessment Organized by the China Quarterly* (Cambridge UP, 1977), has 11 highly quali-

5. The People's Republic

fied contributors who deal with Mao as philosopher, Marxist, political leader, soldier, teacher, economist, patriot, statesman, and Chinese innovator. Mao's ideas of course figure prominently in most of the following sections, too.

5.9 *The Cultural Revolution: Politics, 1962–76.* For background, Roderick MacFarquhar, *The Origins of the Cultural Revolution,* vol. I, *Contradictions among the People, 1956–1957* (Columbia UP, 1974), a highly skilled textual analysis. For the 1960s, two studies based on Hong Kong lay out the framework of amazing and spectacular events: Stanley Karnow, *Mao and China: From Revolution to Revolution* (Viking, 1972), by a principal correspondent; and Edward Rice, *Mao's Way* (U. of Calif. Press, 1972), by the American consul-general at the time. More academic surveys include Jürgen Domes, *The Internal Politics of China, 1949–1972* (Praeger, 1973), concise and comprehensive, by a major German specialist. Richard Baum, *Prelude to Revolution: Mao, the Party, and the Peasant Question, 1962–66* (Columbia UP, 1975), traces the antecedents from which the Cultural Revolution emerged. See also Hong Yung Lee, *The Politics of the Chinese Cultural Revolution: A Case Study* (U. of Calif. Press, 1978); and Byung-joon Ahn, *Chinese Politics and the Cultural Revolution: Dynamics of Policy Processes* (Seattle: U. of Wash. Press, 1976). Thomas W. Robinson, ed., *The Cultural Revolution in China* (U. of Calif. Press, 1971), a symposium, goes up to early 1968. Parris H. Chang, *Power and Policy in China* (Penn. State UP, 1975), researches pluralistic decision making in five cases 1955 to 1965. Lowell Dittmer, *Liu Shao-ch'i and the Chinese Cultural Revolution: The Politics of Mass Criticism* (U. of Calif. Press, 1974), traces Liu's career in comparison with Mao's in theory and style.

Among first-hand reports, of which there are a great many, note David Milton and Nancy Dall Milton, *The Wind Will Not Subside: Years in Revolutionary China, 1964–1969* (Pantheon, 1976); Gordon A. Bennett and Ronald N. Montaperto, *Red Guard: The Political Biograpry of Dai Hsiao-ai* (Garden City: Anchor, 1972); Ken Ling, trans. Miriam London and Ta-ling Lee, *The Revenge of Heaven: Journal of a Young Chinese*

(G. P. Putnam's Sons, 1972); and Jack Chen, *A Year in Upper Felicity: Life in a Chinese Village during the Cultural Revolution,* illus. by author (Collier Macmillan, 1973). Jack Chen, *Inside the Cultural Revolution* (Macmillan, 1975), is a broad survey. These works run a considerable gamut from enthusiasm to disillusion. Most knowingly unenthusiastic is Simon Leys (Pierre Ryckmans), *The Chairman's New Clothes: Mao and the Cultural Revolution,* trans. from French ed. 1972 (St. Martin's Press, 1977), a diary of the Cultural Revolution with vigorous comments and appended documents; and especially Simon Leys, *Chinese Shadows,* trans. from French ed. 1974 (Viking Press, 1977), vividly excoriating the anti-intellectualism and vulgarity of the Chiang Ch'ing era in art and letters. On the career of Mao's wife the chief work is Roxane Witke, *Comrade Chiang Ch'ing* (Boston: Little Brown, 1977). On the political struggles of 1969–74 see Jürgen Domes, *China After the Cultural Revolution: Politics between Two Party Congresses,* with a contribution by Marie-Luise Näth, trans. from German ed. 1975, (U. of Calif. Press, 1977). For the sensitive insights of a recent visitor, Orville Schell, *In the People's Republic* (Random House, 1977), impressions from travel, factory, and farm. Alain Peyrefitte, *The Chinese: Portrait of a People,* trans. from French ed., 1973 (Bobbs-Merrill, 1977), is a top-level French visitor's illustrated and judicious panorama, one of the most widely read of this genre.

5.10 *The Military.* The principal work, a small encyclopedia including biographies, major battles, and theory is by William W. Whitson, *The Chinese High Command: A History of Communist Military Politics, 1927–72* (Praeger, 1972). On the literature, see Edward J. M. Rhoads, *The Chinese Red Army, 1927–1963: An Annotated Bibliography* (Harvard UP, 1964). Three studies are outstanding: Samuel B. Griffith, II, *The Chinese People's Liberation Army* (McGraw-Hill, 1967), a general historical and topical account; John Gittings, *The Role of the Chinese Army* (Oxford UP, 1967), an analytic history of its growth and relation to the regime; and Harvey W. Nelsen, *The Chinese Military System: An Organizational Study of the Chinese People's Liberation Army* (Boulder: Westview Press, 1977), a structural and political analysis done at the consulate general in Hong Kong and attaché's office in Taipei. Ying-mao Kau, *The People's Liberation Army and China's Nation-building* (White Plains: International Arts and Sciences Press, 1973), is a collection of 32 documents with a 57-page introduction. Of narrower scope are the case study by Alexander L. George, *The Chinese Communist Army in Action: The Korean War and Its Aftermath* (Columbia UP, 1967); and Richard M. Buschel, *Communist Chinese Air Power* (Praeger, 1968), a full and technical account. Michael Elliott-Bateman, *Defeat in the East: The Mark of Mao Tse-tung on War* (Oxford UP, 1967), is a theoretical work. Samuel B. Griffith, trans. *Mao Tse-tung on Guerrilla Warfare* (Praeger, 1961; also published with a work of Che Guevara and a foreword of Liddell Hart, London; Cassell, 1962), is Mao's essay on *Yu Chi Chan* of 1937. Stuart R. Schram, trans., and intro., *Mao Tse-tung: Basic Tactics* (Praeger, 1966), reproduces Mao's lectures of 1938, a different work from the foregoing.

5.11 *The Economy in General.* The best starting point is the final analysis completed by a leader in this field, the late Alexander Eckstein, *China's Economic Revolution* (Cambridge UP, 1977); see also Alexander Eckstein, *China's Economic Development: The Interplay of Scarcity and Ideology* (Ann Arbor: U. of Mich. Press, 1975), a useful collection of articles variously published. Alexander Eckstein, Walter Galenson, and Ta-chung Liu, eds., *Economic Trends in Communist China* (Chicago: Aldine, 1968), present a dozen papers on major aspects, developed from a 1965 conference sponsored by the Social Science Research Council, Committee on the Economy of China. Other volumes sponsored by this committee include Nai-Ruenn Chen, *Chinese Economic Statistics* (Chicago: Aldine, 1967); Nai-Ruenn Chen, *The Economy of Mainland China, 1949–1963: A Bibliography of Materials in English* (Berkeley: SSRC Committee on the Economy of China, 1963); and Nai-Ruenn Chen and Walter Galenson, *The Chinese Economy under Communism* (Chicago: Aldine, 1969). For the most recent, and neat, survey see Christopher Howe, *China's Economy: A Basic Guide* (Basic Books, 1978).

The most recent bibliographies are by Patricia Blair, with an

5. The People's Republic

essay by A. Doak Barnett, *Development in the People's Republic of China: A Selected Bibliography* (Washington, D.C.: Overseas Development Council, December, 1976); and John Philip Emerson, Robert Michael Field, Michel Oksenberg, and Florence L. Yuan, comps., *The Provinces of the People's Republic of China: A Political and Economic Bibliography* (Washington, D.C.: U.S. Department of Commerce, Bureau of Economic Analysis, 1976).

Two pioneer studies of national income, made in the 1950s when a modicum of statistics was available, are William W. Hollister, *China's Gross National Product and Social Accounts, 1950–1957* (Glencoe: The Free Press, 1958); and Alexander Eckstein, *The National Income of Communist China* (Glencoe: The Free Press, 1961). A later study by Ta-chung Liu and Kung-chia Yeh, *The Economy of the Chinese Mainland: National Income and Economic Development, 1933–1959* (Princeton UP, 1965), made for the Rand Corporation, compares 1952–57 with 1933 and finds a lowering of per capita consumption.

Other general works include Audrey Donnithorne, *China's Economic System* (Praeger, 1967); Yuan-li Wu, *The Economy of Communist China: An Introduction* (Praeger, 1965); Chao Kuo-chun, *Agrarian Policy of the Chinese Communist Party, 1921–1959* (Asia Publishing House, 1960), a well-documented survey of land reform policies from the 1920s to 1959; Choh-ming Li, *Economic Development of Communist China: An Appraisal of the First Five Years of Industrialization* (U. of Calif. Press, 1959); T. J. Hughes and D. E. T. Luard, *The Economic Development of Communist China, 1949–1958* (Oxford UP, 1959; 2nd ed. of 1961 adds 8 pp.); and United States Congress, Joint Economic Committee, *An Economic Profile of Mainland China* (Washington, D.C.: U.S. Government Printing Office, 1967), 2 vols. Leo Goodstadt, *China's Search for Plenty: The Economics of Mao Tse-tung* (Weatherhill, 1973, Longman ed., 1972), is a popular account by an editor of the *Far Eastern Economic Review*. John R. Gurley, *China's Economy and the Maoist Strategy* (Monthly Review Press, 1976), is a rather bland survey. Jan S. Prybyla, *The Chinese Economy: Problems and Policies* (Columbia: U. of S.

Carolina Press, 1978), is somewhat more informative. The latest study of PRC planning and decentralized management is Nicholas Lardy, *Economic Growth and Distribution in China* (Cambridge UP, 1978), an important work.

5.12 *Science and Professional Manpower.* Several factual appraisals have been prepared in Washington: Leo A. Orleans, *Professional Manpower and Education in Communist China* (Washington, D.C.: National Science Foundation, 1961); Sidney H. Gould, ed., *Sciences in Communist China* (Washington, D.C.: American Association for the Advancement of Science, 1961), appraisals by some 30 contributors to a symposium of 1960; Chuyuan Cheng, *Scientific and Engineering Manpower in Communist China, 1949–1963* (Washington, D.C.: U.S. Government Printing Office for the National Science Foundation, 1965); Yuanli Wu and Robert B. Sheeks, *The Organization and Support of Scientific Research and Development in Mainland China* (Praeger, for the National Science Foundation, 1970); and John Philip Emerson, *Administrative and Technical Manpower in the People's Republic of China* (Washington, D.C.: U.S. Department of Commerce, Bureau of Economic Analysis, 1973).

Organization for Economic Cooperation and Development, *Science and Technology in the People's Republic of China* (Paris: Director of Information, OECD, 1977), consists of papers from a conference of January 1976. Richard P. Suttmeier, *Research and Revolution: Science Policy and Societal Change in China* (Lexington, Mass.: D. C. Heath, 1974), discusses the Chinese approach historically and organizationally as well as theoretically. Anne Fitzgerald and Charles P. Slichter (chairman of delegation), eds., *Solid State Physics in the People's Republic of China: A Trip Report of the American Solid State Physics Delegation* (Washington, D.C.: National Academy of Sciences, Committee on Scholarly Communication with the People's Republic of China, 1976), is representative of a series of reports produced by American scientific delegations to the PRC. Robert Chin and Ai-li S. Chin, *Psychological Research in Communist China, 1949–1966* (M.I.T. Press, 1969), surveys mainland work in this field, with glossary and bibliography. Mikhail A. Klochko, *Soviet*

Scientist in Red China (Praeger, 1964), offers first-hand observations on scientific work by a specialist who was in China in 1958 and 1960, and defected in 1961.

5.13 *Industrialization.* This of course includes several aspects. Dwight H. Perkins, *Market Control and Planning in Communist China* (Harvard UP, 1966), analyzes CCP efforts to guide the economy and maintain its stability down to 1963. On the financing of development, Kang Chao, *Capital Formation in Mainland China, 1952–1965* (U. of Calif. Press, 1974), now provides an authoritative history. See also Katharine Huang Hsiao, *Money and Monetary Policy in Communist China* (Columbia UP, 1971); and George N. Ecklund, *Financing the Chinese Government Budget: Mainland China, 1950–1959* (Chicago: Aldine, 1966), another study sponsored by the SSRC Committee on the Economy of China. On aspects of industry, see Chao Kang, *The Rate and Pattern of Industrial Production in Communist China* (Ann Arbor: U. of Mich. Press, 1965); Kang Chao, *The Construction Industry in Communist China* (Chicago: Aldine, 1968); Yuan-li Wu, *The Spatial Economy of Communist China: A Study on Industrial Location and Transportation* (Praeger, for the Hoover Institution on War, Revolution and Peace, 1967); and Choh-ming Li, ed., *Industrial Development in Communist China* (Praeger, 1964), a dozen articles that formed a special issue of *The China Quarterly*, 1964.

On the large subject of industrial management, see Stephen Andors, *China's Industrial Revolution: Politics, Planning, and Management, 1949 to the Present* (Pantheon Books, 1977). Also Stephen Andors, ed. and intro., *Workers and Workplaces in Revolutionary China* (White Plains: M. E. Sharpe, 1977), a documentary collection; Charles Bettelheim, *Cultural Revolution and Industrial Organization in China: Changes in Management and the Division of Labor* (Monthly Review Press, 1974), trans. from French ed., based on four trips to the PRC; William Brugger, *Democracy and organization in the Chinese industrial enterprise, 1948–1953* (Cambridge UP, 1976); and Barry M. Richman, *Industrial Society in Communist China* (Random House, 1969), by a

Canadian specialist in management technology who saw his opposite numbers during two months in 1966.

On work incentives, see Charles Hoffman, *The Chinese Worker* (State U. of New York Press, 1974); Christopher Howe, *Employment and Economic Growth in Urban China, 1949–1957* (Cambridge UP, 1971); and especially Christopher Howe, *Wage Patterns and Wage Policy in Modern China, 1919–1972* (Cambridge UP, 1973).

Among studies of particular industries, note Ronald Hsia, *Steel in China: Its Output, Behavior, Productivity and Growth Pattern* (Wiesbaden: Otto Harrassowitz, 1971), by a professor of economics then at Hong Kong University. M. Gardner Clark, *Development of China's Steel Industry and Soviet Technical Aid* (Ithaca: Committee on the Economy of China of the Social Science Research Council, 1973), reports on plants, coal, coke, ore, technology, etc., with an account also of the backyard iron smelters of 1958. On the newly developing oil supply: Chu-yuan Cheng, *China's Petroleum Industry: Output Growth and Export Potential* (Praeger, 1976); and Selig S. Harrison, *China, Oil, and Asia: Conflict Ahead?* (Columbia UP, 1977).

5.14 *Agriculture and Rural Industry.* René Dumont, *Révolution dans les campagnes chinoises* (Paris: Editions du Seuil, 1957), is by a broadly experienced agronomist who investigated Chinese farm conditions at first-hand in the early 1950s. Réne Dumont, *Chine surpeuplé: Tiers-monde affamé* (Paris: Editions du Seuil, 1965), is both well informed and alarming on China's struggle to feed her growing population. On agriculture see also Owen L. Dawson, *Communist China's Agriculture: Its Development and Future Potential* (Praeger, 1970), well-informed estimates by the former U.S. agricultural attaché in China; Kenneth R. Walker, *Planning in Chinese Agriculture, Socialisation and the Private Sector, 1956–1962* (London: Frank Cass and Co., 1965); and Kang Chao, *Agricultural Production in Communist China, 1949–1965* (U. of Wisc. Press, 1970). Note also John Wong, *Land Reform in the People's Republic of China: Institutional Transformation in Agriculture* (Praeger, 1973), a historical survey; Benedict Stavis, *Making Green Revolution—The Politics of Agricultural Development in China* (Cornell UP, 1974), a description of agricultural modernization; and Leslie T. C. Kuo, *Agriculture in the People's Republic of China: Structural Changes and Technical Transformation* (Praeger, 1976). S. D. Richardson, *Forestry in Communist China* (Johns Hopkins Press, 1966), is a comprehensive technical look-see by an experienced forester, from New Zealand by way of the University of Wisconsin. Of the many, many reports on communes, one of the most graphic is Peggy Printz and Paul Steinle, *Commune: Life in Rural China* (Dodd Mead, 1973). Gordon Bennett, *Huadong: The Story of a Chinese People's Commune* (Boulder: Westview Press, 1978), is an all-around account of a large suburban commune 30 miles north of Canton, visited in the 1970s by a great many observers, whose reports are synthesized.

The important topic of rural industry has been appraised by a team of American specialists: Dwight Perkins, ed., for the American Rural Small-scale Industry Delegation (of the Committee on Scholarly Communication with the People's Republic of China), *Rural Small-scale Industry in the People's Republic of China* (U. of Calif. Press, 1977). Another study is by Jon Sigurdson, *Rural Industrialization in China* (Harvard UP, 1977).

5.15 *Medicine and Public Health.* American interest in health has skyrocketed since 1972. Shadid Akhtar, *Health Care in the People's Republic of China: A Bibliography with Abstracts* (Ottawa: International Development Research Center, 1975), annotates 560 articles, books, and pamphlets dealing with history of medicine, disease control, medical education, health care, family planning, dental, nutritional, and other aspects. Most books are products of conferences: Arthur Kleinman, et al., eds., *Medicine in Chinese Cultures: Comparative Studies of Health Care in Chinese and Other Societies* (Washington, D.C.: Superintendent of Documents, U.S. Government Printing Office, 1975), papers from 33 contributors at a 1974 conference, mainly on Chinese areas outside of the PRC; Joseph R. Quinn, ed., *Medicine and Public Health in the People's Republic of China* (Washington, D.C.: National Institutes of Health, Public Health Service, U.S. Dept. of Health, Education and Welfare, 1973), 16 contributions

5. The People's Republic

from a symposium on medicine, health care, and health problems; John Z. Bowers and Elizabeth F. Purcell, eds., *Medicine and Society in China* (Josiah Macy, Jr., Foundation, 1974), from a conference that fruitfully brought together a number of China specialists; Myron E. Wegman, Tsungyi Lin, and Elizabeth F. Purcell, *Public Health in the People's Republic of China* (Josiah Macy, Jr., Foundation, 1973), report of a conference held by the School of Public Health and Center for Chinese Studies at Michigan and the Macy Foundation, with a dozen contributors.

Reports of individuals include Victor W. Sidel and Ruth Sidel, *Serve the People: Observations on Medicine in the People's Republic of China* (Josiah Macy, Jr., Foundation, 1973), a wide-ranging survey with tables and charts by a community physician and psychiatric social worker who visited the PRC in 1971 and 1972; Joshua S. Horn, M.D., *Away with All Pests: An English Surgeon in People's China, 1954–1969,* intro. by Edgar Snow (Monthly Review Press, 1969), by an experienced British teacher and army surgeon who volunteered; and E. Grey Dimond, M.D., *More than Herbs and Acupuncture* (W. W. Norton, 1975), by a well-informed observer who went first with Dr. Paul Dudley White. David M. Lampton, *The Politics of Medicine in China: The Policy Process, 1949–1977* (Boulder: Westview Press, 1977) is a systematic, historical-institutional study of policy making, originally a Stanford thesis. Now available in translation, *A Barefoot Doctor's Manual* (Philadelphia: Running Press, 1977), deals with acupuncture in addition to everything else.

5.16 *Population including Minorities.* Leo A. Orleans, *China's Experience in Population Control: The Elusive Model* (Washington, D.C.: U.S. Government Printing Office, 1974), in a report written for the House Committee on Foreign Affairs, concludes China may be the first large developing country to reduce growth to below 1 percent a year. See also Leo A. Orleans, *Every Fifth Child: The Population of China* (Stanford UP, 1972), which deals with major aspects, beginning with the census of 1953. H. Yuan Tien, *China's Population Struggle: Demographic Decisions of the People's Republic 1949–1969* (Ohio State UP, 1973), considers distribution and stabilization, transfers and land reclamation, and control of numbers by various methods, based on research in Hong Kong in 1961–62 and again in 1972. John S. Aird, *The Size, Composition and Growth of the Population of Mainland China* (Washington, D.C.: Bureau of the Census, U.S. Department of Commerce, 1961; reprint by AMS Press, New York, 1973), is a major early research study.

Minority problems and policies are canvassed in an important work by June Teufel Dreyer, *China's Forty Millions: Minority Nationalites and National Integration in the People's Republic of China* (Harvard UP, 1976). George V. H. Moseley III, *The Consolidation of the South China Frontier* (U. of Calif. Press, 1973), studies the decade 1950–60 using Chinese provincial papers.

5.17 *Women in Society.* The long-neglected story of Chinese women's modern emancipation has now begun to receive attention. Delia Davin, *Woman-Work: Women and the Party in Revolutionary China* (Oxford: Clarendon, 1976), is a broad historical account with extensive bibliography. Margery Wolf and Roxane Witke, eds., *Women in Chinese Society* (Stanford UP, 1975), presents ten articles from a 1973 conference sponsored by the Joint Committee on Contemporary China subcommittee on Chinese society. Margery Wolf, *Women and the Family in Rural Taiwan* (Stanford UP, 1972), is a fascinating analysis of how women live mainly in their uterine family, centered around motherhood. Marilyn B. Young, ed., *Women in China: Studies in Social Change and Feminism* (Ann Arbor: Center for Chinese Studies, U. of Mich., 1973), has articles by 10 contributors. Ruth Sidel, *Women and Child Care in China: A First-hand Report* (Hill and Wang, 1972), deals with women's liberation, child care, multiple mothering, etc., including comparisons with Israel and the USSR. Claudie Broyelle, preface by Han Suyin, *Women's Liberation in China,* trans. from French (Atlantic Highlands, N.J.: Humanities Press, 1977), is very upbeat. Kenneth Rexroth and Ling Chung, *The Orchid Bear* (McGraw Hill, 1972), selects women's poetry in translation from the earliest court poetry to contemporary Chinese women living East and West. Note also Elisabeth Croll, *The Women's Movement in China: A Selection of Readings, 1949–1973* (London: Anglo-Chinese Educational

Institute, 1974); and *Signs: Journal of Women in Culture and Society* 2.1 (Autumn 1976), a special issue on women in China.

5.18 *Education.* In China this is a broad area extending from child training to mass persuasion. Study of it is still largely at the documentary stage. Stewart Fraser and Hsu Kuang-liang, *Chinese Education and Society: A Bibliographic Guide, the Cultural Revolution and Its Aftermath* (White Plains: International Arts and Sciences Press, 1972), indicates the very extensive literature available. Stewart Fraser, ed., *Chinese Communist Education: Records of the First Decade* (Vanderbilt UP, 1965), offers 340 pages of documents and 85 of bibliography. Stewart E. Fraser, *Education and Communism in China: An Anthology of Commentary and Documents* (Hong Kong: International Studies Group, 1969), reprints articles by a number of observers. Peter J. Seybolt, *Revolutionary Education in China: Documents and Commentary* (White Plains: International Arts and Sciences Press, 1973), presents 32 key documents with comments touching on all aspects. Shi Ming Hu and Eli Seifman, eds., *Toward a New World Outlook: A Documentary History of Education in the People's Republic of China 1949–1976* (AMS Press, Inc., 1976), is divided into seven periods, each with a commentary and documents. Theodore H. E. Chen, *The Maoist Educational Revolution* (Praeger, 1974), traces policies and programs through a succession of periods, with a hundred-page documentary appendix. R. F. Price, *Education in Communist China* (Praeger, 1970), is another systematic appraisal; the author taught in Peking 1965–67. John N. Hawkins, *Mao Tse-tung and Education: His Thoughts and Teachings* (Hamden, Conn.: Linnet Books, 1974), quotes the Chairman on various goals and aims, educational administration, curriculum, relations of teachers and students, etc. On one continuing but unfinished topic, see Peter J. Seybolt and Gregory Kuei-ko Chiang, eds., and intro., *Language Reform in China: Documents and Commentary* (White Plains: M. E. Sharpe, 1978).

One outstanding work is by Jane L. Price, *Cadres, Commanders and Commissars: The Training of the Chinese Communist Leadership, 1920–1945* (Boulder: Westview Press, 1976), dealing with party schools in the USSR and China, the Whampoa Academy, the Peasant Institute at Canton, Sun Yat-sen University in Moscow, and schools at Yenan—how the educators were educated. William Kessen, ed., *Childhood in China* (Yale UP, 1975), is the influential report of an American delegation on early childhood development in the PRC, stressing the importance of stable expectations as to how Chinese children should behave. Charles Price Ridley, Paul H. B. Gowin, Dennis J. Doolin, *The Making of a Model Citizen in Communist China* (Stanford: The Hoover Institution Press, 1971), is a content analysis of 10 school readers, discussing such topics as elementary education, the technique of language teaching, and the model child. Richard W. Wilson, *The Moral State: A Study of the Political Socialization of Chinese and American Children* (The Free Press, 1974), is a technical study of socialization and learning, based on research in Taiwan, Hong Kong and Chinatown, New York. Frank Swetz, *Mathematics Education in China: Its Growth and Development* (MIT Press, 1974), provides a history of Chinese mathematical thought in the modern school system 1903–49 and in socialist education including a century of continuous reform from 1870 to 1970; appendices of texts and examinations. Frederick T. C. Yu, *Mass Persuasion in Communist China* (Praeger, 1964), is a survey by media.

5.19 *Law.* For surveys of this area, see Jerome Alan Cohen, ed., *Contemporary Chinese Law: Research Problems and Perspectives* (Harvard UP, 1970); and Shao-chuan Leng, *Justice in Communist China: A Survey of the Judicial System of the Chinese People's Republic* (Dobbs Ferry, N.Y.: Oceana Publications, 1967). For documents and bibliography, see Albert P. Blaustein, ed., *Fundamental Legal Documents of Communist China* (South Hackensack, N.J.: Rothman, 1962); and Tao-Tai Hsia, *Guide to Selected Legal Sources of Mainland China* (Washington, D.C.: Library of Congress, 1967). For exemplary monographs see Jerome Alan Cohen, *The Criminal Process in the People's Republic of China, 1949–1963: An Introduction* (Harvard UP, 1968); and M. J. Meijer, *Marriage Law and Policy in the Chinese People's Republic* (Hong Kong UP, 1971).

5. The People's Republic

A number of legal studies stress foreign relations: Jerome Alan Cohen, ed., *China's Practice of International Law: Some Case Studies* (Harvard UP, 1972), with 12 contributors; Hungdah Chiu, *The People's Republic of China and the Law of Treaties* (Harvard UP, 1972); Shao-chuan Leng and Hungdah Chiu, eds., *Law in Chinese Foreign Policy: Communist China and Selected Problems of International Law* (Dobbs Ferry, N.Y.: Oceana Publications, 1972); Gene T. Hsiao, *The Foreign Trade of China: Policy, Law, and Practice* (U. of Calif. Press, 1977); Victor H. Li, ed., *Law and Politics in China's Foreign Trade* (U. of Wash. Press, 1976); and James Chieh Hsiung, *Law and Policy in China's Foreign Relations: A Study of Attitudes and Practices* (Columbia UP, 1972). Douglas M. Johnston and Hungdah Chiu, *Agreements of the People's Republic of China, 1949–1967: A Calendar* (Harvard UP, 1968), lists some 2000 international agreements of all kinds.

Comparisons of law and values between China and America are attempted in Victor H. Li, *Law without Lawyers: A Comparative View of Law in the United States and China* (Boulder: Westview Press, 1978); and in Ross Terrill, ed., *The China Difference* (Harper and Row, 1979).

5.20 *Thought Reform*. Since thought reform concerned mainly the intellectuals in the 1950s, this section interpenetrates the following section on *Literature and the Arts*. For an analysis of the reform process in psychological terms, see Robert Jay Lifton, *Thought Reform and the Psychology of Totalism: A Study of "Brainwashing" in China* (W. W. Norton, 1961). Also Theodore H. E. Chen, *Thought Reform of the Chinese Intellectuals* (Hong Kong UP, 1960); Roderick MacFarquhar, *The Hundred Flowers Campaign and the Chinese Intellectuals* (Praeger, 1960); and Franklin W. Houn, *To Change a Nation: Propaganda and Indoctrination in Communist China* (The Free Press of Glencoe, 1961). On the particular fate of creative writers, see Merle Goldman, *Literary Dissent in Communist China* (Harvard UP, 1967); and D. W. Fokkema, *Literary Doctrine in China and Soviet Influence, 1956–1960* (The Hague: Mouton, 1965).

On the handling of opposition, Peter R. Moody, *Opposition and Dissent in Contemporary China* (Stanford: The Hoover Institution Press, 1977). As to life in detention, Patricia E. Griffin, *The Chinese Communist Treatment of Counter-revolutionaries, 1924–1949* (Princeton UP, 1976), is a carefully researched history of prison management, noting an oscillation between guerrillaism and regularization and concluding that environment influenced prison policy, while rejecting legal codes and using vague terminology allowed flexible interpretation by cadres. The Chinese experience of reform through labor is described with unique detail and insight by a Franco-Chinese who survived six years and after release as a French citizen in 1964 described it to a journalist, Bao Ruo-Wang (Jean Pasqualini) and Rudolph Chelminski, *Prisoner of Mao* (Coward, McCann and Geoghegan, Inc., 1973). For fictionized examples of experiences by a Taiwan-born American-educated resident of China 1966–73, see Chen Jo-hsi, *The Execution of Mayor Yin and Other Stories from the Great Proletarian Cultural Revolution* (Indiana UP, 1978), advertised as "dissent literature."

5.21 *Literature and the Arts.* Much of the great PRC activity in these fields is classed, from the outside, as political and so, in outsiders' terms, as stereotyped and uncreative (perhaps our problem, not theirs?). Of the few academic studies that have appeared, several have been cited in section 4.16. Note Meishi Tsai, *Contemporary Chinese Novels and Short Stories, 1949–1974: An Annotated Bibliography* (Harvard UP, 1979). Kai-yu Hsu, *The Chinese Literary Scene: A Writer's Visit to the People's Republic* (Vintage, 1975), offers notes on writers and numerous translations from 6 months' visiting in 1973 after 30 years' absence. Ralph C. Croizier, ed., *China's Cultural Legacy and Communism* (Praeger, 1970), compiles Chinese and Western writings on the arts, literature, thought, etc., arranged topically. One pioneer work, by an author who grew up on the mainland, Joe C. Huang, *Heroes and Villains in Communist China: The Contemporary Chinese Novel as a Reflection of Life* (Pica Press, 1973), tries to reconstruct the operation of the Communist system in successive periods: first, formative years in city and village, then underground struggle in white areas among intellectuals and in prisons, then guerrilla warfare, the civil war, land reform, agricultural collectivization, and the army in peacetime, condensing many bits of novels and stories in vivid form. A Hong Kong writer, Humphrey Evans, *The Adventures of Li Chi: A Modern Chinese Legend* (E. P. Dutton, 1967), records the antibureaucratic exploits of a folk-legend hero who beats the system by knowing its rules. Cyril Birch, ed., *Chinese Communist Literature* (Praeger, 1963), has a dozen articles from a 1962 *China Quarterly* conference. Lois Wheeler Snow, *China on Stage: An American Actress in the People's Republic* (Random House, 1972), includes texts of some of Chiang Ch'ing's Cultural Revolution operas. Martin Ebon, ed., *Five Chinese Communist Plays* (John Day, 1975), has scripts of the main repertoire of the early 1970s. John D. Mitchell, ed., *The Red Pear Garden: Three Great Dramas of Revolutionary China* (Boston: David R. Godine, 1973), includes "Taking Tiger Mountain."

5.22 *Religion*. Among many writings on Christianity under the Communists, Francis Price Jones, *The Church in Communist China: A Protestant Appraisal* (Friendship Press, 1962), with bibliography, is by the editor of the newsletter *China Bulletin* (subsequently *China Notes*). Richard C. Bush, Jr., *Religion in Communist China* (Abingdon Press, 1970), is a careful study of CCP policy and actions and the repercussions on Christianity, both Protestant and Catholic, also on Islam and Buddhism. Donald E. MacInnis, *Religious Policy and Practice in Communist China: A Documentary History* (Macmillan, 1972), has 117 documents, rather widely selected. George Urban, ed. and intro., *The Miracles of Chairman Mao: A Compendium of Devotional Literature, 1966–1970* (Los Angeles: Nash Publishing, 1971), deals with faith; abnegation of self; class love; socialist sacrifice; guilt and confession; etc. Holmes Welch, *Buddhism under Mao* (Harvard UP, 1972), completes a remarkable trilogy on Buddhism in modern China.

5.23 *Foreign Relations*. This is a large area but broad patterns seem still lacking. For wide-ranging surveys see John Gittings, *The World and China, 1922–1972* (Harper & Row, 1974); and

Harold C. Hinton, *China's Turbulent Quest* (Macmillan, 1970), on the phases in China's foreign relations since 1950. Harold C. Hinton, *Communist China in World Politics* (Boston: Houghton Mifflin, 1966), is a systematic account by areas and aspects. A. Doak Barnett, ed., *Communist Strategies in Asia: A Comparative Analysis of Governments and Parties* (Praeger, 1963), presents papers by eight area specialists. Alastair Buchan, ed., *China and the Peace of Asia* (Praeger, 1965), includes several papers on China, from a 1964 conference of the Institute for Strategic Studies. J. D. Armstrong, *Revolutionary Diplomacy: Chinese Foreign Policy and the United Front Doctrine* (U. of Calif. Press, 1977), traces the use of the United Front abroad, in the cases of Indonesia, Pakistan, Cambodia, Tanzania. Note also Ian Wilson, ed., *China and the World Community* (Angus and Robertson, in association with the Australian Institute of International Affairs, 1973), with 10 contributors; Samuel S. Kim, *China, the United Nations, and World Order* (Princeton UP, 1978); and Byron S. J. Weng, *Peking's UN Policy: Continuity and Change* (Praeger, 1972), with a foreword by Jerome Alan Cohen. Another systematic overview is Peter Van Ness, *Revolution and Chinese Foreign Policy: Peking's Support for Wars of National Liberation* (U. of Calif. Press, 1970).

Specialized studies of the PRC's relations on its frontiers include Allen S. Whiting, *China Crosses the Yalu: The Decision to Enter the Korean War* (Macmillan, 1960); George Ginsburgs and Michael Mathos, *Communist China and Tibet: The First Dozen Years* (The Hague: Martinus Nijhoff, 1964); Alastair Lamb, *The China-India Border: The Origins of the Disputed Boundaries* (Oxford UP, 1964), on the McMahon Line; Neville Maxwell, *India's China War* (London: Jonathan Cape, 1970); and an important study by Allen S. Whiting, *The Chinese Calculus of Deterrence: India and Indochina* (Ann Arbor: U. of Mich. Press, 1975), on Chinese foreign policy behavior concerning these two areas, including the warfare of October 1962. King C. Chen, *Vietnam and China, 1938–1954* (Princeton UP, 1969), concerns Chinese influence on Ho Chi-minh and after World War II. On the recent decade, Robert G. Sutter, *Chinese Foreign*

5. The People's Republic

Policy after the Cultural Revolution, 1966–1977 (Boulder: West-view Press, 1978), deals with both phases and issues. On relations with major powers, see Peter G. Mueller and Douglas A. Ross, *China and Japan: Emerging Global Powers* (Praeger, 1975), a rather broad Canadian study; Donald C. Hellmann, ed., *China and Japan: A New Balance of Power,* vol. XII in the series Critical Choices for Americans (Lexington, Mass.: D. C. Heath, 1976), with articles on China by D. Perkins, Thomas Robinson and M. Oksenberg; Robert Boardman, *Britain and the People's Republic of China, 1949–74* (Barnes and Noble, 1976), a chrono-logical account; Anwar Hussain Syed, *China and Pakistan: Diplomacy of an Entente Cordiale* (U. of Mass. Press, 1974), also a chronological account; and David Mozingo, *Chinese Policy toward Indonesia, 1949–1967* (Cornell UP, 1976), by the leading specialist on the subject. Among sociological studies of Chinese abroad and/or PRC policy are Stephen Fitzgerald, *China and the Overseas Chinese: A Study of Peking's Changing Policy, 1949–1970* (Cambridge UP, 1973); Richard J. Coughlin, *Double Identity: The Chinese in Modern Thailand* (Hong Kong UP, 1960), a sociological survey from fieldwork in 1951–52 and later; and J. A. C. Mackie, ed., *The Chinese in Indonesia: Five Essays* (U. of Hawaii, in association with the Australian Institute of International Affairs, 1976), on patterns of Chinese political activity in Indonesia and anti-Chinese outbreaks.

On Hong Kong, note the volumes by I. C. Jarvie, ed., with Joseph Agassi, *Hong Kong, A Society in Transition: Contributions to the Study of Hong Kong Society* (London: Routledge and Kegan Paul, 1969), papers on a variety of topics; Richard Hughes, *Hong Kong: Borrowed Place—Borrowed Time* (Praeger, 1968), comments and vignettes by an oldtimer; and David Fu-keung Ip, Chi-keung Leung, Chung-tong Wu, *Hong Kong: A Social Sciences Bibliography* (U. of Hong Kong, Centre of Asian Studies, 1974), preface by Frank King, director.

On Chinese activities in Africa, the first historical survey is Bruce D. Larkin, *China and Africa, 1949–1970: The Foreign Policy of the People's Republic of China* (U. of Calif. Press, 1971); more recent, Alan Hutchison, *China's African Revolution*

(Boulder: Westview Press, 1976); Alaba Agunsanwo, *China's Policy in Africa, 1958–71* (Cambridge UP, 1974), a London thesis by a Nigerian scholar; George T. Yu, *China's African Policy: A Study of Tanzania* (Praeger, 1975), on the Chinese-Tanzanian alliance and the railway; and Warren Weinstein, ed., *Chinese and Soviet Aid to Africa* (Praeger, 1975), papers developed in a seminar at the City University of New York in 1973.

Foreign aid from the PRC is analyzed by John Franklin Copper, *China's Foreign Aid: An Instrument of Peking's Foreign Policy* (Lexington: D. C. Heath, 1976), giving data by regions and countries; Kurt Müller, *The Foreign Aid Programs of the Soviet Bloc and Communist China* (Walker & Co., 1967), updating a German book of 1964, a comparison of data as well as conceptual approaches; and Alvin Z. Rubinstein, *Soviet and Chinese Influences in the Third World* (Praeger, 1975), which tries to assess "influence" country by country in eight cases.

On PRC nuclear policy see Alice Langley Hsieh, *Communist China's Strategy in the Nuclear Era* (Prentice Hall, 1962); Morton H. Halperin, *China and the Bomb* (Praeger, 1965); and Morton H. Halperin and Dwight H. Perkins, *Communist China and Arms Control* (Praeger, 1965).

Two studies appraise the arms race: Morton H. Halperin, ed., *Sino-Soviet Relations and Arms Control* (MIT Press, 1967), papers developed from a 1965 conference; and Walter C. Clemens, Jr., *The Arms Race and Sino-Soviet Relations* (Stanford: Hoover Institution on War, Revolution and Peace, 1968), concerning 1950–64.

On the history of Chinese-Russian relations the major, and impressive, conspectus is O. Edmund Clubb, *China and Russia: The "Great Game"* (Columbia UP, 1971), which supersedes earlier works. The Sino-Soviet split has been viewed usually without this historical insight: Donald S. Zagoria, *The Sino-Soviet Conflict, 1956–1961* (Princeton UP, 1962); Donald W. Treadgold, ed., *Soviet and Chinese Communism: Similarities and Differences* (Seattle: U. of Wash. Press, 1967), papers by a score of specialists on China or the USSR from a conference of 1965; William E. Griffith, *The Sino-Soviet Rift* (MIT Press, 1964), narrative and documents to late 1963; Dennis J. Doolin, *Territorial Claims in the Sino-Soviet Conflict: Documents and Analysis* (Stanford: Hoover Institution, 1965); and John Gittings, *Survey of the Sino-Soviet Dispute: A Commentary and Extracts from the Recent Polemics, 1963–1967* (Oxford UP, 1968).

6. CHINESE-AMERICAN RELATIONS

6.1 *Surveys.* This badly neglected subject is beginning to receive attention. The best general guides to research topics and materials are Kwang-Ching Liu, *Americans and Chinese: A Historical Essay and a Bibliography* (Harvard UP, 1963), which lists manuscript collections; and James C. Thomson, Jr., and Ernest R. May, eds., *American-East Asian Relations: A Survey* (Harvard UP, 1971), which looks at themes and publications period by period. As stimulating introductions to this field, see Warren I. Cohen, *America's Response to China: An Interpretative History of Sino-American Relations* (John Wiley & Sons, 1971), which wraps up 185 years in 225 pages; and Akira Iriye, *Across the Pacific: An Inner History of American-East Asian Relations* (Harcourt, Brace & World, 1967), which keeps China in context with Japan. Both are full of ideas.

6.2 *The Old China Trade.* Leading studies on this date from half a century ago: Samuel Eliot Morison, *The Maritime History of Massachusetts, 1783–1860* (Boston: Houghton Mifflin, 1921); Kenneth Wiggins Porter, *John Jacob Astor* (Harvard UP, 1931; reprinted by Russell), an exhaustive monograph. On the investment of Russell and Company's China trade funds in mid-western railways, see Arthur M. Johnson and Barry E. Supple, *Boston Capitalists and Western Railroads: A Study in the Nineteenth-Century Railroad Investment Process* (Harvard UP, 1967). Americans of course figure in the general literature; see section 4.4 *et seq.* There are voluminous materials awaiting attention.

6.3 *Chinese in America and American Images of China.* Important new studies are by Stuart Creighton Miller, *The Unwelcome Immigrant: The American Image of the Chinese, 1785–1882* (U. of Calif. Press, 1969), on Chinese exclusion policy in the Eastern United States as well as the West Coast; Delber

McKee, *Chinese Exclusion versus the Open Door Policy, 1900–1906* (Detroit: Wayne State UP, 1977), including the effort of Chinese in the United States to promote the 1905–06 boycott in desperation at American attitudes generally; and Victor G. and Brett deBary Nee, *Longtime Californ': A Documentary Study of an American Chinatown* (Pantheon, 1972, 1973), in San Francisco. Also on the Chinese community in California, see Gunther Barth, *Bitter Strength: A History of the Chinese in the United States, 1850–1870* (Harvard UP, 1964). Data on the Chinese community and legislation affecting it is given by S. W. Kung, *Chinese in American Life: Some Aspects of Their History, Status, Problems, and Contributions* (U. of Wash. Press, 1962). Gladys C. Hansen and William F. Heintz, comps., *The Chinese in California: A Brief Bibliographic History* (Portland, Ore.: Richard Abel & Co., 1970), annotates several hundred items from 1850 to 1968 at the San Francisco Public Library. The chief study of the Chinese Educational Mission to Hartford in the 1870s is still Thomas E. La Fargue, *China's First Hundred* (Pullman: State College of Wash., 1942).

There is of course a large literature on the westward expansion of the American people, in which "China" often figures but in purely rhetorical terms. A path-breaking investigation of present-day images by a scholar-journalist is Harold R. Isaacs, *Scratches on Our Minds: American Images of China and India* (John Day, 1958; paperback ed. entitled *Images of Asia: American Views of China and India,* Capricorn, 1962). See also Dorothy B. Jones, *The Portrayal of China and India on the American Screen, 1896–1955* (MIT Center for International Affairs, 1955); Robert McClellan, *Heathen Chinee: The American Image of China* (Ohio State UP, 1971); and Francis L. K. Hsu, *Americans and Chinese: Purpose and Fulfillment in Great Civilizations* (Natural History Press, 1970), which offers insights of a social anthropologist from China teaching at Northwestern University.

6.4 *The Missionary Movement.* On one principal organization, Clifton Jackson Phillips, *Protestant America and the Pagan World: The First Half Century of the American Board of Commissioners for Foreign Missions, 1810–1860* (Harvard

UP, 1969). For comparative purposes, note that two recent studies of America in the Near East take account of missionaries there: James A. Field, Jr., *America and the Mediterranean World, 1776–1882* (Princeton UP, 1969); and David H. Finnie, *Pioneers East: The Early American Experience in the Middle East* (Harvard UP, 1967). China is included in general histories of church expansion: for example, Wade Crawford Barclay, *History of Methodist Missions* (Board of Missions of the Methodist Church), 6 vols.; see especially vol. III, *Widening Horizons, 1845–95* (1957), pp. 365-448. On the American side of China missions, see Valentin Rabe, *The Home Base of American China Missions, 1880–1920* (Harvard UP, 1978).

6.5 *United States Policy toward China to 1941.* This is a very spotty field. The two chief surveys of "Far Eastern policy" are long since out of date: Tyler Dennett, *Americans in Eastern Asia: A Critical Study of the Policy of the United States with Reference to China, Japan and Korea in the 19th Century* (Macmillan, 1922; reprinted, Gloucester, Mass.: Peter Smith, 1959); and A. Whitney Griswold, *The Far Eastern Policy of the United States* (Harcourt, Brace, 1938). For a recent critique of our "traditional" historiography in this area, see Dorothy Borg, comp., *Historians and American Far Eastern Policy* (Columbia U., East Asian Institute Occasional Papers, 1966).

China figures in a great number of general works dealing with American foreign policy and expansion. Recent examples are Ernest R. May, *Imperial Democracy: The Emergence of America as a Great Power* (Harcourt, Brace and World, 1961); Walter LaFeber, *The New Empire: An Interpretation of American Expansion, 1860–1898* (Cornell UP, 1963); and Howard K. Beale, *Theodore Roosevelt and the Rise of America to World Power* (Collier, 1956). This list could be greatly extended.

On the reappraisal of the Open Door the principal study is Michael H. Hunt, *Frontier Defense and the Open Door: Manchuria in Chinese-American Relations, 1895–1911* (Yale UP, 1973), which brings the Chinese side into existence, debunking Willard Straight in the process. See also the substantial monographs by Paul A. Varg, *Open Door Diplomat: The Life of*

W. W. Rockhill (U. of Illinois Press, 1952); Charles S. Campbell, *Special Business Interests and the Open Door Policy* (Yale UP, 1951); Thomas McCormick, *China Market: America's Quest for Informal Empire, 1893–1901* (Chicago: Quadrangle, 1967); and Marilyn B. Young, *The Rhetoric of Empire: American China Policy, 1895–1901* (Harvard UP, 1968). On the era of dollar diplomacy, Charles Vevier, *The United States and China, 1906–1913: A Study of Finance and Diplomacy* (Rutgers UP, 1955); and Paul A. Varg, *The Making of a Myth: The United States and China, 1897–1912* (East Lansing: Mich. State UP, 1968). On the Wilsonian era see Tien-yi Li, *Woodrow Wilson's China Policy, 1913–1917* (Twayne, 1952); Russell H. Fifield, *Woodrow Wilson and the Far East: The Diplomacy of the Shantung Question* (Crowell, 1952); and Roy W. Curry, *Woodrow Wilson and Far Eastern Policy, 1913–1921* (Bookman Associates, 1957). On the Twenty-one Demands, see in Arthur S. Link, *Wilson: The Struggle for Neutrality, 1914–1915* (Princeton UP, 1960). Warren I. Cohen, *The Chinese Connection: Roger S. Greene, Thomas W. Lamont, George E. Sokolsky and American-East Asian Relations* (Columbia UP, 1978), explores the influence of leading individuals.

On the Nationalist era, Dorothy Borg, *American Policy and the Chinese Revolution, 1925–1928* (American Institute of Pacific Relations and Macmillan, 1947); Robert H. Ferrell, *American Diplomacy in the Great Depression: Hoover-Stimson Foreign Policy, 1929–1933* (Yale UP, 1957); Christopher Thorne, *The Limits of Foreign Policy: The West, the League, and the Far Eastern Crisis of 1931–1933* (G. P. Putnam's Sons, 1972), the most recent appraisal of the diplomatic record; and Dorothy Borg, *The United States and the Far Eastern Crisis of 1933–1938* (Harvard UP, 1964), the principal study of Sino-American relations in the 1930s. On the contemporary policy of our closest friends, Nicholas Clifford, *Retreat from China: British Policy in the Far East, 1937–1941* (Seattle: U. of Wash. Press, 1967). On the era of World War II, W. L. Langer, and S. E. Gleason, *The World Crisis and American Foreign Policy,* vol. I, *The Challenge to Isolation 1937–1940,* vol. II, *The Undeclared War, 1940–41*

(Harper, 1952, 1953); and W. R. Fishel, *The End of Extraterritoriality in China* (U. of Calif. Press, 1952).

On the large question of American participation in domestic reform and social change under the Kuomintang, James C. Thomson, Jr., *While China Faced West: American Reformers in Nationalist China, 1928–1937* (Harvard UP, 1969). The solid achievements of a Rockefeller Foundation program in medicine are recorded by Mary E. Ferguson, *China Medical Board and Peking Union Medical College: A Chronicle of Fruitful Collaboration, 1914–1951* (China Medical Board of New York, 1970), an administrative-institutional history; and John Z. Bowers, M.D., *Western Medicine in a Chinese Palace: Peking Union Medical College, 1917–1951* (Josiah Macy, Jr., Foundation, 1972), with main attention to medical achivements and personnel.

One of the few studies of business history is Irvine H. Anderson, Jr., *The Standard-Vacuum Oil Company and United States East Asian Policy, 1933–1941* (Princeton UP, 1975).

6.6 *The United States and China in the 1940s.* An enthralling introduction is Barbara Tuchman, *Stilwell and the American Experience in China, 1911–1945* (Macmillan, 1971), a well-researched best-seller. On early American impressions of the Communist movement, Kenneth E. Shewmaker, *Americans and Chinese Communists, 1927–1945: A Persuading Encounter* (Cornell UP, 1971). The diplomatic policy record is traced out by several historians, most recently Christopher Thorne, *Allies of a Kind: The United States, Britain and the War against Japan, 1941–1945* (Oxford UP, 1978), which puts China policy in the broader context; and Paul A. Varg, *The Closing of the Door: Sino-American Relations, 1936–1946* (East Lansing: Mich. State UP, 1973), based on extensive American documentation: also Herbert Feis, *The China Tangle: The American Effort in China from Pearl Harbor to the Marshall Mission* (Princeton UP, 1953); and Tang Tsou, *America's Failure in China, 1941–1950* (U. of Chicago Press, 1963). On the military record and the Stilwell saga, see the exemplary military theater history by Charles F. Romanus and Riley Sunderland, *United States Army in World War II: China-Burma-India Theater* (Washington, D.C.: Office of the Chief of Military History, Department of the Army), 3 vols., vol. I, *Stilwell's Mission to China* (1953); vol. II, *Stilwell's Command Problems* (1956); vol. III, *Time Runs Out in CBI* (1959). For one vivid, mud-slogging aspect, see Leslie Anders, *The Ledo Road: General Joseph W. Stilwell's Highway to China* (U. of Oklahoma Press, 1965). David D. Barrett, *Dixie Mission: The United States Army Observer Group in Yenan, 1944* (U. of Calif. Center for Chinese Studies, 1970), is by our wartime military attaché who headed the mission. Oliver J. Caldwell, *A Secret War: Americans in China, 1944–1945* (Southern UP, 1972), is the memoir of a China-born OSS man who found himself working with the Chinese secret service in Happy Valley. On the air force, see W. F. Craven, and J. L. Cate, *The Army Air Forces in World War II*, vol. V, *Pacific: Matterhorn to Nagasaki* (U. of Chicago Press, 1953). For documentation, see U. S. Department of State, *United States Relations with China with Special Reference to the Period 1944–1949* (Washington, D.C.: Government Printing Office, 1949; reprinted, Stanford UP, 1967), the famous China White Paper of recently confidential documents, published in advance of the usual volumes in *Foreign Relations of the United States.* Further documents, labeled "Top Secret" until 1974, have now appeared: Lyman Van Slyke, intro., *Marshall's Mission to China, December 1945–January 1947: The Report and Appended Documents* (Arlington, Va.: University Publications of America, 1976), 2 vols., the report written by George C. Marshall about his year-long mediation effort. For a quick appraisal of the policy problems, see Ernest R. May, *The Truman Administration and China, 1945–49* (Philadelphia: J. B. Lippincott, 1975), 50 pages on alternatives with 50 pages of documents. On the United States aid program, Arthur N. Young, *China and the Helping Hand, 1937–1945* (Harvard UP, 1963). For personal notes by a principal officer of the American Embassy during and after the Marshall mediation, see John F. Melby, *The Mandate of Heaven: Record of a Civil War. China, 1945–49* (U. of Toronto Press, 1968).

As examples of vivid, eye-witness reporting of the Chinese scene in wartime, see Theodore H. White and Annalee Jacoby,

6. Chinese-American Relations

Thunder Out of China (Sloan Associates, 1946), now viewed in perspective in a fascinating memoir—Theodore H. White, *In Search of History* (Harper & Row, 1978); Jack Belden, *China Shakes the World* (Harper, 1949; reprinted, Monthly Review Press, 1970), already cited in section 4.19; and Graham Peck, *Two Kinds of Time* (Boston: Houghton Mifflin, 1950; first half reprinted, 1968).

On the who-lost-China controversy in American politics, a straightforward study by Ross Y. Koen, *The China Lobby* (Macmillan, 1960), was printed, distributed for publication, and then withdrawn by the publishers, who destroyed 4000 copies. It has now been republished by the Committee of Concerned Asian Scholars: Ross Y. Koen, *The China Lobby in American Politics,* ed. and intro. by Richard C. Kagan (Harper & Row, 1974). The Joseph McCarthy view is well represented by Dr. Anthony Kubek, *How the Far East was Lost: American Policy and the Creation of Communist China, 1941–1949* (Chicago: Regnery, 1963). For an analysis of the McCarthy era, see Earl Latham, *The Communist Controversy in Washington: From the New Deal to McCarthy* (Harvard UP, 1966); and Lewis McCarroll Purifoy, *Harry Truman's China Policy: McCarthyism and the Diplomacy of Hysteria, 1947–1951* (New Viewpoints, 1976), a journalistic account. For a useful summary of the IPR investigation in particular, see John N. Thomas, *The Institute of Pacific Relations: Asian Scholars and American Politics* (Seattle: U. of Wash. Press, 1974).

There is now a substantial series of memoirs by Foreign Service officers involved in the so-called "loss of China": O. Edmund Clubb, *The Witness and I* (Columbia UP, 1975); John Paton Davies, Jr., *Dragon by the Tail: American, British, Japanese and Russian Encounters with China and One Another* (Norton, 1972); John K. Emmerson, *The Japanese Thread: A Life in the U.S. Foreign Service* (Holt, Rinehart and Winston, 1978); and John S. Service, *The Amerasia Papers: Some Problems in the History of US-China Relations* (U. of Calif. Center for Chinese Studies, 1971). Note also Joseph W. Esherick, ed., *Lost Chance in China: The World War II Despatches of John S. Service* (Random

House, 1974), a useful compendium. E. J. Kahn, Jr., *The China Hands* (Random House, 1975), puts the human story together, *New Yorker*-style. To keep the "loss of China" furor in perspective, note that David Caute, *The Great Fear: The Anti-Communist Purge under Truman and Eisenhower* (Simon and Schuster, 1978), in 542 pages devotes only a dozen pages or at most a score to China.

6.7 *Taiwan*. As a province of China, Taiwan is included in this section because of its special role in Chinese-American relations. It is also increasingly a field of modern research. Among studies of industrialization, most recent and comprehensive is Samuel P. S. Ho, *Economic Development of Taiwan, 1860–1970* (Yale UP, 1978). For background see E. Patricia Tsurumi, *Japanese Colonial Education in Taiwan, 1895–1945* (Harvard UP, 1977), an able study of the Japanese program and its results; and Leonard H. Gordon, *Taiwan: Studies in Chinese Local History* (Columbia UP, 1970), mainly on the 1895 resistance. George H. Kerr, *Formosa: Licensed Revolution and the Home Rule Movement, 1895–1945* (U. of Hawaii, 1974), concerns Formosan reactions to Japanese colonial rule during fifty years. Paul K. T. Sih (Hsueh Kuang-ch'ien), ed. and intro., *Taiwan in Modern Times* (St. John's U., 1973), is a symposium of twelve authors on a historical framework. A special study is by George W. Barclay, *Colonial Development and Population in Taiwan* (Princeton UP, 1954). On the Nationalist massacres of 1947, George H. Kerr, *Formosa Betrayed* (Boston: Houghton Mifflin, 1965), researched by an eyewitness.

On the substantial achievements in rural reconstruction, the authoritative work is by T. H. Shen (Tsung-han), *The Sino-American Joint Commission on Rural Reconstruction: Twenty Years of Cooperation for Agricultural Development* (Cornell UP, 1970). For a general survey, Neil H. Jacoby, *U. S. Aid to Taiwan: A Study of Foreign Aid, Self-Help, and Development* (Praeger, 1966). On the birth control program, see Ronald Freedman and John Y. Takeshita, *Family Planning in Taiwan: An Experiment in Social Change* (Princeton UP, 1969). A number of social science research studies concerning Taiwan have been listed in earlier sections. Note also Bernard Gallin, *Hsin Hsing, Taiwan: A Chinese Village in Change* (U. of Calif. Press, 1966), based on a 16 months' stay in 1957–58; and Myron L. Cohen, *House United, House Divided: The Chinese Family in Taiwan* (Columbia UP, 1976), in the series of the East Asian Institute; Richard W. Wilson, *Learning to be Chinese: The Political Socialization of Children in Taiwan* (MIT Press, 1970), with chapters on group orientation, leadership and political style, and hostility. On attitudes affecting Taiwan independence, Douglas Mendel, *The Politics of Formosan Nationalism* (U. of Calif. Press, 1970), based on extensive interviews in Taiwan and elsewhere by a public opinion specialist. Lung-chu Chen and Harold Lasswell, *Formosa, China, and the United Nations: Formosa in the World Community* (St. Martin's Press, 1967), gives an analysis of factors affecting the independence of Taiwan. Peng Ming-min, *A Taste of Freedom: Memoirs of a Formosan Independence Leader* (Holt, Rinehart and Winston, 1972), is a personal account of his own life, the 1947 uprising, and his later escape. Among many works on Taiwan's future status, note Chiu Hungdah, ed., *China and the Question of Taiwan: Documents and Analysis* (Praeger, 1973); and Ralph Clough, *Island China* (Harvard UP, 1978), by one of the most experienced American observers. Taiwan has of course figured in several preceding sections on religion, literature, etc.

6.8 *United States Policy toward the People's Republic.* This topic is treated, explicitly or implicitly, in much of the American writing on China. Among systematic studies in the era before the Nixon trip to Peking of February 1972, A. Doak Barnett, *Communist China and Asia: Challenge to American Policy* (Harper and Brothers, for the Council on Foreign Relations, 1960), surveyed China's evolving international role in the 1950s. Subsequently, Robert Blum organized a series and wrote a volume (edited after his untimely death by A. Doak Barnett) on *The United States and China in World Affairs* (McGraw-Hill for the Council on Foreign Relations, 1966). Among the other volumes in this series are Archibald T. Steele, *The American People and China* (McGraw-Hill, 1966), a field survey of public opinion; Alexander Eckstein, *Communist China's Economic Growth and Foreign Trade: Implications for U.S. Policy* (McGraw-Hill, 1966); A. M. Halpern, *Policies toward China: Views from Six Continents* (McGraw-Hill, 1965), on attitudes of other nations; and Fred Greene, *U.S. Policy and the Security of Asia* (McGraw-Hill, 1968), treating security interests, treaties, Communist threats, the nuclear factor. Historical perspectives were attempted in a collection of articles, John K. Fairbank, *China: The People's Middle Kingdom and the U.S.A.* (Harvard UP, 1967). For a useful chronology of events and documentation, see Congressional Quarterly Service, *China and U.S. Far East Policy, 1945–1966* (Washington, D.C.: Congressional Quarterly, April, 1967); also Congressional Quarterly, ed., *China and U.S. Foreign Policy,* 2nd ed. (Washington, D.C.: Congressional Quarterly, 1973), with data on Congressional hearings, lobbies, documents published. Akira Iriye, ed., *U.S. Policy toward China: Testimony Taken from the Senate Foreign Relations Committee Hearings, 1966* (Boston: Little, Brown, 1968) is a convenient topical rearrangement of statements by 14 persons. A symposium edited by Tang Tsou was on *China's Policies in Asia and America's Alternatives* (U. of Chicago Press, 1968). Alexander Eckstein, ed., *China Trade Prospects and U.S. Policy* (Praeger, for the National Committee on United States–China Relations, 1971), offered a useful appraisal by experts. Finally, for vigorous, even strident criticism of most previous work see Edward Friedman and Mark Selden, eds., *America's Asia: Dissenting Essays on Asian-American Relations* (Pantheon, 1971), with contributions by a dozen scholars.

Since 1972 there has been a bit more historical appraisal of Chinese-American relations: Akira Iriye, *The Cold War in Asia: A Historical Introduction* (Englewood Cliffs: Prentice Hall, 1974); John K. Fairbank, *China Perceived: Images and Policies in Chinese-American Relations* (Knopf, 1974; Vintage, 1976); Foster Rhea Dulles, *American Policy toward Communist China, 1949–1969* (Thomas Y. Crowell, 1972), tracing especially Congressional opinion; Roderick MacFarquhar, *Sino-American Relations, 1949–71* (Praeger, under the auspices of the Royal

Institute of International Affairs, 1972), narrative and analytic sections by the editor, with documents showing evolution of American policy; J. H. Kalicki, *The Pattern of Sino-American Crises: Political-Military Interactions in the 1950s* (Cambridge UP, 1975), a study of diplomatic developments: Korea, Indochina, the two Taiwan Straits crises of 1954–55 and 1958. See also Melvin Gurtov, *The First Vietnam Crisis: Chinese Communist Strategy and United States Involvement, 1953–1954* (Columbia UP, 1967). Stanley D. Bachrack, *The Committee of One Million: "China Lobby" Politics, 1953–1971* (Columbia UP, 1976), traces the long-continued lobby "against the admission of Communist China to the United Nations." Robert G. Sutter, *China-Watch: Towards Sino-American Reconciliation* (Johns Hopkins UP, 1978), recounts the phases of rapprochement to 1972.

The search for new policies for the future is represented in several able discussions: Ralph N. Clough, A Doak Barnett, Morton H. Halperin, Jerome H. Kohan, *The United States, China, and Arms Control* (Washington, D.C.: Brookings Institution, 1975); William J. Barnds, ed., *China and America: The Search for a New Relationship* (New York UP, 1977, for the Council on Foreign Relations), a symposium from a study group; Michel Oksenberg and Robert B. Oxnam, *Dragon and Eagle: United States–China Relations: Past and Future* (Basic Books, 1978), a well-informed masterly survey of the problems involved; and Selig S. Harrison, *The Widening Gulf: Asian Nationalism and American Policy* (The Free Press, 1978)—can America deal adequately with Asian nationalism?

John M. H. Lindbeck, *Understanding China: An Assessment of American Scholarly Resources: A Report to the Ford Foundation* (Praeger, 1971), is based on a worldwide survey of Chinese studies and especially the facilities and procedures in the United States, with recommendations, now out of date but an important record.

Index to Suggested Reading

Publishers have taken their revenge on the Wade-Giles system for spelling Chinese names by sometimes printing its abominable apostrophes and sometimes not. Since we follow what is on the title pages, some authors named Ch'en, for example, are under Chen below and some under Ch'en.

General Index

Abbassid caliphate (750-1258), 88

Academia Sinica, national research academy, 330-331, 334

"Action by inaction" (*wu-wei*), Taoist concepts, 125, 130

Aden, 150

Administration: of Confucian government under Han, 60-62; Ming and Ch'ing, 107-112; Nationalist, 267-270; in People's Republic, 426. *See also* Bureaucracy

Africa, 64, 151, 476; reached by Chinese explorers, 149; Mao's encouragement of wars of liberation in, 425

Afro-Asian conference, 425

Agrarian reform: early CCP program, 295; Chiang Kai-shek's attitude toward, 470. *See also* Land reform; Rural reconstruction

"Agrarian reformers, mere," 295

Agricultural Credit Administration, 265

Agricultural producers' cooperatives, 375, 394, 413

Agriculture: intensive, 12-13; control of, in "Oriental society," 31; new crops, 174; poverty as social institution in, 271; under National Government, 271-275; CCP collectivization of, 374-375, 393-399; and the Great Leap Forward, 408; mechanization of, 447-448; modern

problems of, 475. *See also* Collectivization; Land reform; Peasant

Aksai-Chin region, 407

Alaska, purchase of (1867), 316

Alchemy, Taoist interest in, 125-126

Alexander the Great, 101

Alien rule, 82

Alitto, Guy, 275

All-China Association of Industry and Commerce, 367

All-China Federation of Trade Unions, 367

All-China Federations: of Democratic Women, 367; of Democratic Youth, 367; of Cooperative Workers, 367; of Literature and Art, 367; Students', 367; Young Pioneer corps, 367

All Men Are Brothers (Shui-hu chuan), 284

"All under heaven" (*t'ien-hsia*), 461

Ambivalence, American, toward China, 314-320

Amitabha (O-mi-to'fo), 128

Amoy: as treaty port, 167; international settlement at, 249; Communist-Nationalist confrontation near, 406

Amur, Russian penetration of, 154; Sino-Soviet clashes along, 424

Analects of Confucius *(Lun-yü)*: quoted on ruler's right conduct, 59; one of the Four Books, 62; quoted by Taipings, 185

General Index

Credits for Illustrations and Figures

This illustration program is much indebted to Wilma Fairbank.

302 Teaching public health. *Woodcuts of War-Time China, 1937-1945,* Chinese Woodcut Association, 1946.

310-311 Missionaries and mandarins. Mandarins, Peabody Museum of Salem. Missionaries, Drew Collection, Harvard Chinese/Japanese Library.

332 Liberals in Shanghai. Eastfoto.

338-339 Americans in China in World War II. From *All in Line* (Duell, Sloane and Pierce), © 1944, 1972, Saul Steinberg, originally in *The New Yorker.*

349 The problem of distribution in the 1940s. George Silk, Time/Life.

396-397 Manpower agriculture. Transplanting, *P'ei-wen-chai kung-chi-t'u.* Harvesting, *China Pictorial,* no. 2 (1963).

428-429 A revolution of youth. Chou and his wife, Centre de recherches asiatiques, European. Chou, Mao, and others, Eastfoto.

442 Chou En-lai in Peking in 1973. Audrey Topping.

445 The archaeological revolution. Audrey Topping.

471 Liberation and industry. *China Reconstructs,* 23.8, (August 1974).

108-109 Administrative areas under the Ch'ing dynasty. From *East Asia: The Modern Transformation* by John K. Fairbank, Edwin O. Reischauer, and Albert M. Craig (Boston: Houghton, Mifflin, 1965).

166 Foreign encroachment on China. From *East Asia: The Modern Transformation.*

259 Railways of China. From *The Outsiders: The Western Experience in India and China* by Rhoads Murphey (Ann Arbor: U. of Mich. Press, 1977).

The American Foreign Policy Library

THE PEOPLE'S REPUBLIC
OF CHINA

Lake Balkhash

Ili River

OUTER

• Urumchi

SINKIANG- UIGHUR

Tarim River

• Kashgar

Autonomous Region

Lop Nor

KANSU

Inner

Great

AKSAI-CHIN

Koko Nor

TSINGHAI

Sining La

H

TIBETAN

Autonomous

Region

NEPAL

Brahmaputra River

• Lhasa

Yangtze River

SZECHW

Chen

BHUTAN

Ganges River

INDIA

BANGLADESH

Salween River

Mekong River

Kunming

BURMA

YUNNAN

VIET

Bay of Bengal

85°

THAILAND

LAOS